BARRON'S
STUDENTS' #1 CHOICE

PASS KEY

TO THE

SAT I *

MW01048454

Fourth Edition

Sharon Weiner Green
Former Instructor in English
Merritt College, Oakland, California

Ira K. Wolf, Ph.D.
President, PowerPrep, Inc.
Former High School Teacher, College Professor,
and University Director of Teacher Preparation

BARRON'S EDUCATIONAL SERIES, INC.

All inquiries should be addressed to:
Barron's Educational Series, Inc.
250 Wireless Boulevard
Hauppauge, New York 11788
http://www.barronseduc.com

Library of Congress Catalog Card No. 00-068015

International Standard Book No. 0-7641-1663-0

Library of Congress Cataloging-in-Publication Data

Green, Sharon.
     Pass key to the SAT I / Sharon Weiner Green, Ira K. Wolf.
—4th ed.
        p.   cm.
     At head of title: Barron's
     "Adapted from How to prepare for the SAT I"—T.p. verso.
     ISBN 0-7641-1663-0
     1. Scholastic Assessment Test—Study guides.   2. Universities
and colleges—United States—Entrance examinations—Study guides.
I. Title: Barron's pass key to the SAT I. II. Wolf, Ira K.
III. How to prepare for SAT I. IV. Title.
LB2353.57.G74   2001
378.1'662—dc21   00-068015

PRINTED IN THE UNITED STATES OF AMERICA
987654321

Contents

Preface

You have in your hands *Barron's Pass Key to the SAT I*, the compact version of Barron's classic *How to Prepare for the SAT I*. Small enough to toss in your backpack, portable enough to read on the bus, this short course in SAT I preparation provides you with the basic tips and strategies you need to cope with the SAT I.

If you feel unready for the SAT I, if you don't quite know what to expect on it, *Pass Key* may be just the eye-opener you need.

It offers you dozens of specific tips that will help you attack every type of SAT I question, and provides you with practice exercises.

It offers you the newly-revised-for-the-millennium, exclusive SAT I High Frequency Word List, your best chance to acquaint yourself with the actual words that computer analysis shows occur again and again on recently published SATs.

It not only gives you all of the math facts and formulas you need to know, it provides over twenty special tactics (all illustrated with sample problems) to show you how to answer every type of SAT I math question.

Best of all, it offers you the chance to take not one, not two, but three complete practice SAT I exams that correspond to actual SAT I tests in content, format, and level of difficulty. Each test has an answer key and complete solutions and explanations.

Read the tips. Go over the strategies. Do the practice exercises. *Then* take the practice SATs and see how you score. Study the answer explanations, especially those for questions you were unsure of or answered incorrectly. You'll come out feeling far more secure about what it will be like to take the SAT I.

SAT I Format   Total Time: 3 Hours

Section 1: Verbal—   9 Sentence Completion
            30 Questions   6 Analogy
                                  15 Reading Comprehension

Time—30 minutes

Section 2: Mathematics—   25 Standard Multiple-Choice
            25 Questions
Time—30 minutes

Section 3: Verbal—   10 Sentence Completion
            35 Questions   13 Analogy
                                  12 Reading Comprehension

Time—30 minutes

Section 4: Mathematics—   15 Quantitative Comparison
            25 Questions   10 Student-Produced
                                     Response Questions
                                     (Grid-in)

Time—30 minutes

Section 5: Verbal—   13 Reading Comprehension
            13 Questions
Time—15 minutes

Section 6: Mathematics—   10 Standard Multiple-Choice
            10 Questions
Time—15 minutes

There will also be a seventh 30-minute section in either Verbal
Reasoning or Mathematical Reasoning. It is experimental and the
score will not be part of your record. Because there is no way to
know which of the sections is experimental, you must do your
best on every section.

SAT I Test Dates

Test Dates	Registration Deadlines	
	Regular	**Late**
2001 October 13 November 3 December 1	September 11 September 28 October 26	September 15 October 10 November 7
2002 January 26 March 16 May 4 June 1	December 21 February 8 March 29 April 26	January 2 February 20 April 10 May 8

Acknowledgments

The authors gratefully acknowledge the following copyright holders for permission to reprint material used in reading passages:

Pages 55–57: From "Renaissance to Modern Tapestries in the Metropolitan Museum of Art" in the *Metropolitan Museum Bulletin*, Spring 1987 by Edith Appleton Standen, ©1987. Reprinted with permission of the Metropolitan Museum of Art.

Pages 58–60: From "I Love Paul Revere Whether He Rode or Not" by Richard Shenkman. Copyright ©1991 by Richard Shenkman. Reprinted by permission of HarperCollins Publishers, Inc.

Pages 66–68: From *The Greenpeace Book of Dolphins*, John May, editor ©1990. Reprinted with permission of Greenpeace.

Pages 189–190: From *Black Boy* by Richard Wright. Copyright ©1937, 1942, 1944, 1945 by Richard Wright. Copyright renewed 1973 by Ellen Wright. Reprinted by permission of HarperCollins Publishers, Inc.

Pages 192–193: From *King Solomon's Ring* by Konrad Z. Lorenz, ©1952 by Harper & Row, Publishers, Inc. Reprinted by permission of HarperCollins Publishers, Inc.

Pages 208–210: From *Bury My Heart at Wounded Knee* by Dee Brown ©1970 by Dee Brown. Reprinted by permission of Henry Holt and Co., LLC.

Pages 224–225: From "Let's Say You Wrote Badly This Morning" in *The Writing Habit* by David Huddle, ©1989, 1994. Reprinted with permission of the University Press of New England.

Pages 225–226: From "My Two One-Eyed Coaches" by George Garrett, ©1988. Reprinted with permission of *The Virginia Quarterly Review*.

Pages 306–307: From *Take Time for Paradise*, ©1989 by the Estate of A. Bartlett Giamatti. Reprinted with permission of the Estate of A. Bartlett Giamatti.

Page 308: From *City* by William H. Whyte, ©1989 by William Whyte. Used by permission of Doubleday, a division of Random House, Inc.

Pages 353–354: From *The Overworked American: The Unexpected Decline of Leisure* by Juliet B. Schor, ©1991. Reprinted by permission of Basic Books, a division of HarperCollins Publishers, Inc.

Pages 373–375: From *The Soul of the Night* by Chet Raymo, ©1985. Reprinted by permission of Chet Raymo.

1 About the SAT I

COMMONLY ASKED QUESTIONS ABOUT THE SAT I

What Is the SAT I?

Many colleges and universities require their applicants to take a three-hour standardized examination called the SAT I. Consequently, most of you as high school juniors or seniors will take this test as part of the college admissions process. The SAT I, which is written and administered by the Educational Testing Service (ETS), purports to evaluate students' verbal and quantitative reasoning abilities. As a result, you will actually get two scores: a verbal score and a math score, each of which lies between 200 and 800. For both the verbal and the math tests, the median score is 500, meaning that about 50 percent of all students score below 500 and about 50 percent above 500. In discussing their results, students often add the two scores (the sums range from 400 to 1600, with a median of about 1000) and say, "John got a 950," or "Mary got a 1300."

What Types of Questions Are on the Verbal Sections?

There are three types of questions on the verbal sections: sentence completions, analogies, and reading comprehension questions. All are multiple-choice questions, with five answer choices. The sentence completion questions ask you to fill in the blanks. You have to find the word or phrase that best completes the sentence's meaning. The analogy questions ask you to determine the relationship in a pair of words and then recognize a similar or parallel relationship in a different pair of words. You are given one pair of words, and from the five pairs given as answer choices, you must choose another pair that is related in the same way. The reading comprehension questions test your ability to understand what you read—both content and technique. Each verbal section will include one or two reading passages followed by from six to thirteen reading comprehension questions. The questions ask about the passage's main idea or specific details, the author's attitude to the subject, the author's logic and techniques, the implications of the discussion, or the meaning of specific words.

For strategies, tips, and practice on verbal questions, turn to Chapter 3.

What Types of Questions Are on the Math Sections?

There are three types of questions on the math sections: the five-choice multiple-choice type, quantitative comparisons, and student-produced response questions, also known as grid-ins. The standard multiple-choice questions are like the questions you're used to seeing in your math textbooks and on math tests in school. For the quantitative comparison questions you will be given two quantities. You must decide whether one of the quantities is greater than the other, whether they are equal, or whether there is not enough information for you to make a decision. The student-produced response questions are similar in content to the standard multiple-choice questions. They differ only in the fact that you must arrive at your answer and enter it on a grid.

For strategies, tips, and practice for the math questions, as well as information about the use of calculators on the test, turn to Chapter 5.

How Is the SAT I Scored?

When the SAT I you take is graded, a raw score will be calculated for each part (verbal and mathematics). For each of the 78 verbal questions, you will receive 1 point for a correct answer; for each incorrect answer, $\frac{1}{4}$ of a point is deducted. For example, if you were to answer 68 of the verbal questions, getting 60 right and

8 wrong, your raw score would be calculated as follows: $60 - 8(\frac{1}{4})$ $= 60 - 2 = 58$. Notice that points were neither added nor deducted for the 10 questions you omitted. This raw score is then converted to a scaled score between 200 (the lowest possible grade) and 800 (the highest possible grade). The exact same procedure is followed on the mathematics part, except that the deduction for incorrect answers on quantitative comparison questions is $\frac{1}{3}$ of a point and no deduction is made for incorrect grid-ins. Because a deduction is made for incorrect answers, you may think that you should only answer a question if you are sure of the answer. That is a very poor strategy. On average, you will break even by guessing wildly on questions that you don't know how to do or haven't even read, and will come out ahead by guessing anytime that you can eliminate one or more of the choices.

When you receive your score report in the mail, you will get only your scaled scores—one for the verbal part of the exam and one for the mathematics part. On each part, the median grade is about 500, meaning that about 50 percent of the students taking the test score below 500, and 50 percent score above 500. On each part, earning only half of the number of points possible (39 out of 78 on the verbal; 30 out of 60 on the math) will result in a grade above 500. You certainly don't have to answer all, or even most, of the questions to earn a good score. In fact, unless you are in the top 5 percent of all students, and think that you might score over 700 on one of the parts, you shouldn't even attempt to finish the test. Working slowly and carefully will undoubtedly earn you higher scores.

How Important Is the SAT I?

In addition to your application form, the essays you write, and the letters of recommendation that your teachers and guidance counselor write, colleges receive two important pieces of numerical data. One is your high school transcript, which shows the grades you have earned in all your courses during a three-*year* period. The other is your SAT I scores, which show how well you did during a three-*hour* period one Saturday morning. Which is more important? Your transcript, by far. However, your scores on the SAT I definitely do count, and it is precisely because you want your SAT I scores to be as high as possible that you purchased this book. If you use this book wisely, you will not be disappointed.

How Can This Book Help You Score High on the SAT I?

This book is packed full with review materials, practice exercises, and test-taking strategies. Use them: They'll prepare you to do well on the SAT I. The vocabulary list will help boost your word power. Chapter 5 will pinpoint the important math facts and formulas you need to know and show you how to handle each of the three types of math questions. The dozens of testing tips and strategies will teach you how to make the most of what you learn.

After going through this review and taking the practice tests at the end of the book, you will know exactly what to expect on the SAT I. You will be ready to face the test with confidence, knowing you have done your best to prepare yourself.

2 Tips and Strategies for the SAT I

The easiest way to answer a question correctly is to know the answer. If you know what all the words mean in an analogy question and you understand the relationship between the words, you won't have any trouble choosing the right answer. If you know exactly how to solve a mathematics question and you don't make any mistakes in arithmetic, you won't have any trouble choosing the right answer. But you won't always be absolutely sure of the right answer. Here are some suggestions that may help you. (You'll find specific strategies and tips for each type of question in later chapters of the book.)

GUESSING

More controversy surrounds the issue of guessing than any other aspect of the SAT I. If you run out of time and still have 10 questions to go, should you guess? If you do, on average you will get two right and miss the other eight. Is that good or bad? Neither. For the two that you get right, your raw score will increase by two points; for the eight that you miss, your raw score will decrease by $8 \times \frac{1}{4} = 2$ points. The most likely scenario is that your raw score (and hence your scaled score) will not change. So whether or not you guess randomly is a personal decision.

There is no decision to make, however, if you can eliminate some of the choices—now *you must guess*. Suppose that the five answer choices to a particular math question are

(A) –2 (B) –1 (C) 0 (D) 1 (E) 2

and that although you have no idea how to solve it, you know that the answer must be positive. Eliminate (A), (B), and (C) and guess. Similarly, if you can eliminate three of the choices in a verbal analogy, but you have no idea which of the other two choices is correct because they contain words that you never heard of, you must guess.

The reason for this is simple. When you guess between two choices, you have a 50-50 chance of being right. If you had 10 such questions on the test, on average you would get half right and half wrong. For the five correct answers your raw score would increase by five points; for the five incorrect answers your raw score would decrease by $5 \times \frac{1}{4} = 1\frac{1}{4}$ points. This would result in a raw score gain of $3\frac{3}{4}$ points, which would raise your scaled score by about 30 points. You simply cannot afford not to guess.

If you can only eliminate one or two choices, the results are not as dramatic, but *it still pays to guess*.

TIMING

You have only a limited amount of time in which to complete each section of the test, and you don't want to waste any of it. So here are three suggestions.

1. Memorize the directions for each type of question. They appear in the practice tests, later in this book. They present the same information that you will find on the SAT I. However, the time you spend reading directions at the actual test is test time. If you don't have to read the directions, you have that much more time to answer the questions.

2. By the time you get to the actual test, you should have a fair idea of how much time to spend on each question. If a question is taking too long, leave it and go on to the next question. This is no time to try to show the world that you can stick to a job no matter how long it takes. All the machine that grades the test will notice is that you didn't have any correct answers after question 17.

3. In every section (except critical reading), the questions proceed from easy to medium to difficult. It makes no sense to miss a few easy questions by

going too fast, just so you have time to work on some difficult questions at the end, which you may miss anyway. Almost all students taking the SAT I make the mistake of trying to answer too many questions. It is better to go slower and not finish a section than to go faster, get to the end, but make some careless mistakes on some easy questions along the way. Unless you can score over 700 on the math or the verbal part, if you are answering all the questions in that part, you are probably going too fast. *You will increase your score by slowing down and answering fewer questions.*

HOW TO USE THIS BOOK

To help you make the best use of your time before the SAT I, we have created two possible study plans to follow. Select the plan that best reflects your situation, and feel free to modify it as necessary.

7-Day Study Plan

With only seven days to go before the Sat I, your best bet is to concentrate on working through our practice tests. Use the following pattern:

Day 1

Get a general overview of what to expect by reading the general test-taking strategies in Chapter 2 and the pointers on verbal questions in Chapter 3. Look over the mathematics tips in Chapter 5, in particular the list of mathematical formulas. Pay particular attention to the formulas you already know: This is not the time to try to master something new.

Day 2

Take Practice Exam 1 under simulated test conditions. Complete the exam in one sitting. Use a clock or timer. Allow precisely 30 minutes each for sections 1 through 4, and 15 minutes each for sections 5 and 6. After each section, give yourself a five-minute break. When you have finished the exam, check your answers against the answer key.

Day 3

Go through the answer explanations for Practice Exam 1, concentrating on the explanations to any questions you answered incorrectly. Refer to the tips in Chapters 3 and 5 as necessary.

Day 4

Take Practice Exam 2 under simulated test conditions, following the directions given for Day 2. Again, when you have finished the exam, check your answers against the answer key.

Day 5

Go through the answer explanations for Practice Exam 2, concentrating on the explanations to any questions you answered incorrectly. Refer to the tips in Chapters 3 and 5 as necessary.

Day 6

Take Practice Exam 3 under simulated test conditions, following the directions given for Day 2. Once again, when you have finished the exam, check your answers against the answer key.

Day 7

Go through the answer explanations for Practice Exam 3, concentrating on the explanations to any questions you answered incorrectly.

30-Day Study Plan

With a full month to go before the SAT I, you have plenty of time to review the tips on verbal and mathematical reasoning in Chapters 3 and 5, to increase your familiarity with frequently tested vocabulary terms, and to work your way through our practice tests. Use the following pattern:

Day 1

Get a general overview of what to expect by reading the general test-taking strategies in Chapter 2. Pay particular attention to the tips on guessing and timing.

Day 2

Take Practice Exam 1 under simulated test conditions. Complete the exam in one sitting. Use a clock or timer. Allow precisely 30 minutes each for sections 1 through 4, and 15 minutes each for sections 5 and 6. After each section, give yourself a five-minute break. When you have finished the exam, check your answers against the answer key.

Day 3

Go through the answer explanations for Practice Exam 1, concentrating on the explanations to any questions you answered incorrectly.

Day 4

Study the first 30 words on the High-Frequency Word List in Chapter 4. Pay special attention to the words that are unfamiliar to you.

Day 5

Read the introduction to the mathematical reasoning sections in Chapter 5, including the guidelines for using a calculator. Review the list of important formulas and key facts, refreshing your memory of concepts you have covered in school.

Day 6

Study the second group of 30 words on the High-Frequency Word List in Chapter 4. Again, pay special attention to the words that are unfamiliar to you.

Day 7

Read the general introduction to the verbal reasoning sections in Chapter 3. Then study the specific tips on answering sentence completion questions and do Practice Exercise A. Check your answers.

Day 8

Study the third group of 30 words on the High-Frequency Word List in Chapter 4.

Day 9

In Chapter 5, read Mathematical Reasoning Tips 1–5 on working with diagrams. Then review Tips 6–9 on how to improve your speed and accuracy in answering these questions.

Day 10

In Chapter 5, do the Practice Exercises following Tip 9 and review your answers.

Day 11

Study the fourth group of 30 words on the High-Frequency Word List in Chapter 4.

Day 12

In Chapter 3, do Sentence Completion Practice Exercises B and C. Check your answers.

Day 13

Study the fifth group of 30 words on the High-Frequency Word List in Chapter 4.

Day 14

Take Practice Exam 2 under simulated test conditions. Complete the exam in one sitting. Use a clock or timer. Allow precisely 30 minutes each for sections 1 through 4, and 15 minutes each for sections 5 and 6. After each section, give yourself a five-minute break. When you have finished the exam, check your answers against the answer key.

Day 15

Go through the answer explanations for Practice Exam 2, concentrating on the explanations to any questions you answered incorrectly.

Day 16

In Chapter 5, read Mathematical Reasoning Tips 10–14 on answering general multiple-choice questions. Then do the Practice Exercises following Tip 14 and review your answers.

Day 17

Study the sixth group of 30 words on the High-Frequency Word List in Chapter 4.

Day 18

In Chapter 3, study the specific tips on answering analogy questions and do Practice Exercise A. Check your answers.

Day 19

Study the seventh group of 30 words on the High-Frequency Word List in Chapter 4.

Day 20

In Chapter 5, study Mathematical Reasoning Tips 15–19 on handling quantitative comparison questions. Then do the Practice Exercises following Tip 19 and review your answers.

Day 21

Study the eighth group of 30 words on the High-Frequency List in Chapter 4.

Day 22

In Chapter 3, do Analogy Practice Exercises B and C. Check your answers.

Day 23

In Chapter 5, study Mathematical Reasoning Tips 20–21 on handling grid-in questions. Then do the Practice Exercises following Tip 21 and review your answers.

Day 24

In Chapter 3, study the specific tips on handling critical reading questions and do Practice Exercise A. Check your answers.

Day 25

Study the ninth group of 30 words on the High-Frequency List in Chapter 4.

Day 26

In Chapter 3, do Critical Reading Practice Exercises B and C. Check your answers.

Day 27

Study the tenth and final group of words on the High-Frequency List in Chapter 4.

Day 28

Take Practice Exam 3 under simulated test conditions. Complete the exam in one sitting. Use a clock or timer. Allow precisely 30 minutes each for sections 1 through 4, and 15 minutes each for sections 5 and 6. After each section, give yourself a five-minute break. When you have finished the exam, check your answers against the answer key.

Day 29

Go through the answer explanations for Practice Exam 3, concentrating on the explanations to any questions you answered incorrectly. Refer to the tips in Chapters 3 and 5 as necessary. In Chapter 5, once again review the list of important formulas and key facts, this time concentrating on those concepts that gave you difficulty when you took your practice exams.

Day 30

Follow the instructions in Chapter 2, Before the Test. Do not study. Just relax, knowing you have done a good job preparing yourself to take the SAT I.

BEFORE THE TEST

1. Set out your test kit the night before. You will need your admission ticket, a photo ID (a driver's license or a non-driver picture ID, a passport, or a school ID), your calculator, four or five sharp No. 2 pencils (with erasers), plus a map or directions showing how to get to the test center.

2. Get a good night's sleep so you are well rested and alert.

3. Wear comfortable clothes. Dress in layers. Bring a sweater in case the room is cold.

4. Bring an accurate watch—not one that beeps—in case the room has no clock.

5. Don't be late. Allow plenty of time for getting to the test site. You want to be in your seat, relaxed, before the test begins.

DURING THE TEST

1. Do not waste any time reading the directions or looking at the sample problems at the beginning of every section. You already know all of the rules for answering each question type that appears on the SAT I. They will not change.

2. First answer all the easy questions; then tackle the hard ones if you have time.

3. Pace yourself. Don't work so fast that you start making careless errors. On the other hand, don't get bogged down on any one question.

4. Play the percentages: Guess whenever you can eliminate one or more of the answers.

5. Make educated guesses, not random ones. Don't mark down answers when you haven't even looked at the questions.

6. Watch out for eye-catchers, answer choices that are designed to tempt you into guessing wrong.

7. Change answers only if you have a reason for doing so; don't change them on a last-minute hunch or whim.

8. Check your assumptions. Make sure you are answering the question asked and not the one you *thought* was going to be asked.

9. Remember that you are allowed to write in the test booklet. Use it to do your math computations and to draw diagrams. Underline key words in sentence

completion questions and reading passages. Cross out any answer choices you are *sure* are wrong. Circle questions you want to return to.

10. Be careful not to make any stray marks on your answer sheet. The test is graded by a machine, and a machine cannot tell the difference between an accidental mark and a filled-in answer.

11. Check frequently to make sure you are answering the questions in the right spots.

12. Remember that you don't have to answer every question to do well.

3 The Verbal Sections: Strategies, Tips, and Practice

In this chapter you'll learn how best to handle the three types of verbal questions on the SAT I—sentence completions, analogies, and reading comprehension—using strategies and tips that have helped thousands of SAT-takers before you. You'll also find practice exercises for each question type. After doing the exercises, you'll feel confident taking the exam because you'll be familiar with the types of questions on it.

General Tips for Answering Verbal Questions

1. An important point to remember when you are answering the verbal questions is that the test is looking for the best answer, the most likely answer. This is not the time to try to show how clever you can be by imagining exotic situations that would justify different answers. If you can imagine a weird situation that would make one of the sentence completions correct—Forget it! This test is scored by a machine, which has absolutely no imagination or sense of humor; an imaginative answer is a wrong answer. Stick to the most likely answer.

2. Remember also that the sentence completion and analogy sections begin with easy questions and get harder as they go along. If you get bogged down early and forget about the time, you may never get to the easy questions up ahead.

3. Consider secondary meanings of words. If none of the answer choices seem right to you, take another look. A word may have more than one meaning.

THE SENTENCE COMPLETION QUESTION

The sentence completion questions ask you to choose the best way to complete a sentence from which one or two words have been omitted. These questions test a combination of reading comprehension skills and vocabulary. You must be able to recognize the logic, style, and tone of the sentence, so that you will be able to choose the answer that makes sense in this context. You must also be able to recognize the way words are normally used. Once you understand the implications of the sentence, you should be able to choose the answer that will make the sentence clear, logical, and stylistically consistent. The sentences cover a wide variety of topics, but this is not a test of your general knowledge. You may feel more comfortable if you are familiar with the topic the sentence is discussing, but you should be able to handle any of the sentences using your understanding of the English language.

Tips to Help You Cope

1. Before you look at the choices, read the sentence and think of a word that makes sense. The word you think of may not be the exact word that appears in the answer choices, but it will probably be similar in meaning to the right answer.

2. Look at all the possible answers before you make your final choice. You are looking for the word that *best* fits the meaning of the sentence as a whole. In order to be sure you have not been hasty in making your decision, substitute all the answer choices for the missing word. That way you can satisfy yourself that you have come up with the answer that best fits.

3. In double-blank sentences, go through the answers, testing the *first* word in each choice (and eliminating those that don't fit). Read through the entire sentence. Then insert the first word of each answer pair in the sentence's first blank. Ask yourself whether this particular word makes sense in this blank. If the initial word of an answer pair makes no sense in the sentence, you can eliminate that answer pair.

4. Use your knowledge of word parts and context clues to get at the meanings of unfamiliar words. If a word used by the author is unfamiliar, or if an answer choice is unknown to you, look at its context in the sentence to see whether the context provides a clue to the meaning of the word. Often authors will use an unfamiliar word and then immediately define it within the same sentence. Similarly, look for familiar word parts—prefixes, suffixes, and roots—in unfamiliar words.

5. Watch out for negative words and words signaling frequency or duration. Only a small change makes these two sentences very different in meaning:

> They were not lovers.
> They were not often lovers.

6. Look for words or phrases that indicate a contrast between one idea and another—words like *although, however, despite,* or *but.* In such cases an antonym or near-antonym for another word in the sentence should provide the correct answer.

7. Look for words or phrases that indicate similarities—words like *in the same way, in addition,* and *also.* In such cases, a synonym or near-synonym for another word in the sentence may provide the correct answer.

8. Look for words or phrases that indicate that one thing causes another—words like *because, since, therefore,* or *thus.*

9. In eliminating answer choices, check words for positive or negative connotations. Ask yourself whether the sentence calls for a positive or negative word.

Examples to Get You Started

EXAMPLE 1

See how the first tip works with the following sentence.

The psychologist set up the experiment to test the rat's ----; he wished to see how well the rat adjusted to the changing conditions it had to face.

Even before you look at the answer choices, you can figure out what the answer *should* be.

A psychologist is trying to test some particular quality or characteristic of a rat. What quality? How do you get the answer?

Look at the sentence's second clause, the part following the semicolon. This clause is being used to define or clarify what the psychologist is trying to test. He is trying to see how well the rat *adjusts*. What words does this suggest to you? *Flexibility*, possibly, or *adaptability*. Either of these words could complete the sentence's thought.

Here are the five answer choices given.

(A) reflexes   (B) communicability   (C) stamina
(D) sociability   (E) adaptability

The best answer clearly is (E) adaptability.

EXAMPLE 2

When you're racing the clock, you feel like marking down the first correct-sounding answer you come across. *Don't.* You may be going too fast.

Because the enemy had a reputation for engaging in sneak attacks, we were ---- on the alert.

(A) frequently   (B) furtively   (C) evidently   (D) constantly
(E) occasionally.

A hasty reader might be content with choice (A), *frequently*, but *frequently* is not the best fit. The best answer is choice (D), *constantly*, because "frequent" periods of alertness would not be enough to provide the necessary protection against sneak attacks that could occur at any time. "Constant" vigilance is called for: the troops would have to be always on the alert.

EXAMPLE 3

Dealing with double-blank sentences can be tricky. Testing the first word of each answer pair helps you narrow things down.

The opossum is ---- the venom of snakes in the rattlesnake subfamily and thus views the reptiles not as ---- enemies but as a food source.

(A) vulnerable to..natural   (B) indicative of..mortal
(C) impervious to..lethal   (D) injurious to..deadly
(E) defenseless against..potential

Your first job is to eliminate any answer choices you can on the basis of their first word. While opossums might be *vulnerable* or *impervious* to snake poison, and might even be *defenseless* against it, they're unlikely to be *indicative* or suggestive of it. They're even less likely to be *injurious* or harmful to the poison. The words make no sense; you can eliminate choices (B) and (D).

Now examine the second half of the sentence. Opossums look on rattlesnakes as a food source. They can eat rattlers *because* they're *impervious* to the poison (that is, unharmed by it). That's the reason they can treat the rattlesnake as a potential source of food and not as a *lethal* or deadly enemy. The correct answer is choice (C).

Note the cause-and-effect signal *thus.* The nature of the opossum's response to the venom explains *why* it can look on a dangerous snake as a possible prey.

EXAMPLE 4

After a tragedy, many people claim to have had a ---- of disaster.

(A) taste   (B) dislike   (C) presentiment   (D) context
(E) verdict

Take the unfamiliar word *presentiment.* Break it down into parts. A *sentiment* is a *feeling* (the root *sens* means *feel*). *Pre-* means *before.* A *presentiment* is something you *feel before* it happens, a foreboding. Your best answer is choice (C).

EXAMPLE 5

Watch out for *not:* it's easy to overlook, but it's a key word.

Madison was not ---- person and thus made few public addresses; but those he made were memorable, filled with noble phrases.

(A) a reticent   (B) a stately   (C) an inspiring
(D) an introspective   (E) a communicative

What would happen if you overlooked *not* in this question? Probably you'd wind up choosing (A):

Madison was a *reticent* (quiet; reserved) man. *For this reason* he made few public addresses.

Unfortunately, you'd have gotten things backwards. The sentence isn't telling you what Madison was like. It's telling you what he was *not* like. And he was not a *communicative* person; he didn't express himself freely. However, when he did get around to expressing himself, he had valuable things to say.

EXAMPLE 6

We expected him to be jubilant over his victory, but he was ---- instead.

(A) triumphant   (B) adult   (C) morose   (D) talkative
(E) culpable

But suggests that the winner's expected reaction contrasts with his actual one. Instead of being "jubilant" (extremely joyful), he is sad. The correct answer is choice (C), *morose.*

EXAMPLE 7

The simplest animals are those whose bodies are simplest in structure and which do the things done by all animals, such as eating, breathing, moving, and feeling, in the most ---- way.

(A) haphazard   (B) bizarre   (C) advantageous   (D) primitive
(E) unique

The transition *and* signals you that the writer intends to develop the concept of simplicity introduced in the sentence. You should know from your knowledge of biology that *primitive* life forms were simple in structure and that the more complex forms evolved later. Choice (C) may seem possible. However, to secure the most *advantageous* way of conducting the activities of life, the animal would have to become specialized and complex. Thus, choice (D), *primitive,* is best, because it is the only choice that develops the idea of simplicity.

EXAMPLE 8

Because his delivery was ----, the effect of his speech on the voters was nonexistent.

(A) halting   (B) plausible   (C) moving   (D) respectable
(E) audible

What sort of delivery would cause a speech to have no effect? Obviously, you would not expect a moving or eloquent delivery to have such a sorry result. A *halting* or stumbling speech, however, would normally have little or no effect. Thus, choice (A) is best.

EXAMPLE 9

Although she enjoyed great renown as a movie star in the 1940s, Gloria Stuart experienced her greatest ---- when she was featured in *Titanic* in 1997.

(A) reprieve   (B) disclosure   (C) celebrity   (D) setback
(E) incentive

The phrase "experienced her greatest ----" indicates that something highly positive happened to Stuart when she returned to the motion picture industry. Therefore, you know that only positive words (such as *success, triumph,* or *renown*) make sense in the blank, and you can eliminate any answers with negative words. Thus, you can immediately eliminate choice (D), *setback*. In addition, you can eliminate any words that make *no* sense whatsoever. Specifically, you can eliminate choice (B), *disclosure*. It makes no sense to talk about experiencing a disclosure.

Look at the first part of the sentence. Though Stuart won fame in the 1940s, she enjoyed even more fame in the 1990s. In other words, she enjoyed her greatest *celebrity*. The correct answer is choice (C).

Practice Exercises   **Answers given on page 29.**

Each of the following sentences contains one or two blanks; these blanks indicate that a word or set of words has been left out. Below the sentence are five words or phrases, lettered A through E. Select the word or set of words that best completes the sentence.

Example:

Fame is ----; today's rising star is all too soon tomorrow's washed-up has-been.

(A) rewarding   (B) gradual   (C) essential
   (D) spontaneous   (E) transitory

Exercise A

1. Although the play was not praised by the critics, it did not ---- thanks
    to favorable word-of-mouth comments.
    (A) succeed   (B) translate   (C) function   (D) close
    (E) continue

2. Perhaps because something in us instinctively distrusts such displays
    of natural fluency, some readers approach John Updike's fiction with
    ---- .
    (A) indifference   (B) suspicion   (C) veneration   (D) recklessness
    (E) bewilderment

3. We lost confidence in him because he never ---- the grandiose
    promises he had made.
    (A) forgot about   (B) reneged on   (C) tired of   (D) delivered on
    (E) retreated from

4. Because the hawk is ---- bird, farmers try to keep it away from their
    chickens.
    (A) a migratory   (B) an ugly   (C) a predatory   (D) a reclusive
    (E) a huge

5. We were amazed that a woman who had been heretofore the most
    ---- of public speakers could, in a single speech, electrify an audience
    and bring them cheering to their feet.
    (A) enthralling   (B) accomplished   (C) pedestrian   (D) auspicious
    (E) masterful

6. Despite the mixture's ---- nature, we found that by lowering its
    temperature in the laboratory we could dramatically reduce its
    tendency to vaporize.
    (A) resilient   (B) volatile   (C) homogeneous   (D) insipid
    (E) acerbic

7. New concerns about growing religious tension in northern India were
    ---- this week after at least fifty people were killed and hundreds were
    injured or arrested in rioting between Hindus and Moslems.
    (A) lessened   (B) invalidated   (C) restrained   (D) dispersed
    (E) fueled

8. In a revolutionary development in technology, several manufacturers
    now make biodegradable forms of plastic: some plastic six-pack
    rings, for example, gradually ---- when exposed to sunlight.
    (A) harden   (B) stagnate   (C) inflate   (D) propagate
    (E) decompose

9. To alleviate the problem of contaminated chicken, the study panel recommends that the federal government shift its inspection emphasis from cursory bird-by-bird visual checks to a more ---- random sampling for bacterial and chemical contamination.

   (A) rigorous   (B) perfunctory   (C) symbolic   (D) discreet
   (E) dubious

10. Shy and hypochondriacal, Madison was uncomfortable at public gatherings; his character made him a most ---- lawmaker and practicing politician.

    (A) conscientious   (B) unlikely   (C) fervent   (D) gregarious
    (E) effective

11. The tapeworm is an example of ---- organism, one that lives within or on another creature, deriving some or all of its nutriment from its host.

    (A) a hospitable   (B) an exemplary   (C) a parasitic
    (D) an autonomous   (E) a protozoan

12. Truculent in defending their rights of sovereignty under the Articles of Confederation, the newly-formed states ---- constantly.

    (A) apologized   (B) digressed   (C) conferred   (D) acquiesced
    (E) squabbled

13. Written in an amiable style, the book provides a comprehensive overview of European wines that should prove inviting to both the virtual ---- and the experienced connoisseur.

    (A) prodigal   (B) novice   (C) zealot   (D) miser
    (E) glutton

14. Traffic speed limits are set at a level that achieves some balance between the danger of ---- speed and the desire of most people to travel as quickly as possible.

    (A) marginal   (B) normal   (C) prudent   (D) inadvertent
    (E) excessive

15. Although the economy suffers downturns, it also has strong ---- and self-correcting tendencies.

    (A) unstable   (B) recidivist   (C) inauspicious   (D) recuperative
    (E) self-destructive

Exercise B

1. More than one friendly whale has nudged a boat with such ---- that passengers have been knocked overboard.

(A) enthusiasm   (B) lethargy   (C) hostility   (D) serenity
(E) animosity

2. Chaotic in conception but not in ----, Kelly's canvases are as neat as the proverbial pin.

(A) conceit   (B) theory   (C) execution   (D) origin   (E) intent

3. Some students are ---- and want to take only courses that have an immediate practical application.

(A) theoretical   (B) impartial   (C) pragmatic   (D) idealistic
(E) opinionated

4. Although Josephine Tey is arguably as good a mystery writer as Agatha Christie, she is clearly far less ---- than Christie, having written only six books in comparison to Christie's sixty.

(A) coherent   (B) prolific   (C) equivocal   (D) pretentious
(E) gripping

5. Fitness experts claim that jogging is ----; once you begin to jog regularly, you may be unable to stop, because you are sure to love it more and more all the time.

(A) exhausting   (B) illusive   (C) addictive   (D) exotic
(E) overrated

6. The ---- of such utopian notions is reflected by the quick disintegration of the idealistic community of Brooke Farm.

(A) timeliness   (B) creativity   (C) impracticability
(D) effervescence   (E) vindication

7. Although newscasters often use the terms Chicano and Latino ----, students of Hispanic-American culture are profoundly aware of the ---- the two.

(A) interchangeably . . . dissimilarities between
(B) indifferently . . . equivalence of
(C) deprecatingly . . . controversies about
(D) unerringly . . . significance of
(E) confidently . . . origins of

8. I was so bored with the verbose and redundant style of Victorian novelists that I welcomed the change to the ---- style of Hemingway.

(A) prolix   (B) consistent   (C) terse   (D) logistical
(E) florid

9. His listeners enjoyed his ---- wit but his victims often ---- at its satire.

   (A) lugubrious . . . suffered   (B) caustic . . . laughed
   (C) kindly . . . smarted   (D) subtle . . . smiled
   (E) trenchant . . . winced

10. Given Marian Diamond's obvious scientific ---- , her college advisor encouraged her to major in the biological sciences.

   (A) doctrine   (B) bent   (C) ambiguity   (D) proximity
   (E) hypothesis

11. Breaking with established artistic and social conventions, Dali was ---- genius whose heterodox works infuriated the traditionalists of his day.

   (A) a derivative   (B) an iconoclastic   (C) an uncontroversial
   (D) a venerated   (E) a trite

12. Dr. Smith cautioned that the data so far are not sufficiently ---- to warrant dogmatic assertions by either side in the debate.

   (A) hypothetical   (B) tentative   (C) controversial
   (D) unequivocal   (E) imponderable

13. She is an interesting ----, an infinitely shy person who, in apparent contradiction, possesses an enormously intuitive ---- for understanding people.

   (A) aberration . . . disdain   (B) caricature . . . talent
   (C) specimen . . . loathing   (D) phenomenon . . . disinclination
   (E) paradox . . . gift

14. There is nothing ---- or provisional about Moore's early critical pronouncements; she deals ---- with what were then radical new developments in poetry.

   (A) tentative . . . confidently   (B) positive . . . expertly
   (C) dogmatic . . . arbitrarily   (D) shallow . . . superficially
   (E) imprecise . . . inconclusively

15. So intense was his ambition to attain the pinnacle of worldly success that not even the opulence and lavishness of his material possessions seemed ---- the ---- of that ambition.

   (A) necessary for . . . fulfillment   (B) adequate to . . . fervor
   (C) appropriate to . . . ebullience   (D) relevant to . . . languor
   (E) consonant with . . . insignificance

Exercise C

1. John Gielgud crowns a distinguished career of playing Shakespearean roles by giving a performance that is ----.
   (A) mediocre   (B) outmoded   (C) superficial   (D) unsurpassable
   (E) insipid

2. Like many other reformers, Alice Paul, author of the Equal Rights Amendment introduced in Congress in 1923, received little honor in her lifetime but has gained considerable fame ----.
   (A) posthumously   (B) anonymously   (C) privately
   (D) prematurely   (E) previously

3. This well-documented history is of importance because it carefully -----the ----accomplishments of Indian artists who are all too little known to the public at large.
   (A) recognizes . . . negligible   (B) overlooks . . . purported
     (C) scrutinizes . . . illusory   (D) distorts . . . noteworthy
       (E) substantiates . . . considerable

4. Fossils may be set in stone, but their interpretation is not; a new find may necessitate the ---- of a traditional theory.
   (A) ambiguity   (B) revision   (C) formulation   (D) validation
   (E) assertion

5. The linguistic ---- of refugee children is reflected in their readiness to adopt the language of their new homeland.
   (A) conservatism   (B) inadequacy   (C) adaptability
   (D) philosophy   (E) structure

6. It is remarkable that a man so in the public eye, so highly praised and imitated, can retain his ----.
   (A) magniloquence   (B) dogmas   (C) bravado
   (D) idiosyncracies   (E) humility

7. As a sportscaster, Cosell was apparently never ----; he made ---- comments about every boxing match he covered.
   (A) excited . . . hysterical   (B) relevant . . . pertinent
     (C) satisfied . . . disparaging   (D) amazed . . . awe-struck
       (E) impressed . . . laudatory

8. Despite the growing ---- of Hispanic actors in the American theater, many Hispanic experts feel that the Spanish-speaking population is ---- on the stage.
   (A) decrease . . . inappropriate   (B) emergence . . . visible
     (C) prominence . . . underrepresented   (D) skill . . . alienated
       (E) number . . . misdirected

9. The incidence of smoking among women, formerly ----, has grown to such a degree that lung cancer, once a minor problem, has become the chief ---- of cancer-related deaths among women.

   (A) negligible . . . cause   (B) minor . . . antidote
     (C) pre-eminent . . . cure   (D) relevant . . . modifier
       (E) pervasive . . . opponent

10. Despite the numerous films he had to his credit and his reputation for technical ----, the moviemaker lacked originality; all his films were sadly ---- of the work of others.

    (A) skill . . . independent   (B) ability . . . unconscious
      (C) expertise . . . derivative   (D) competence . . . contradictory
        (E) blunders . . . enamored

11. He is much too ---- in his writings: he writes a page when a sentence should suffice.

    (A) devious   (B) lucid   (C) verbose   (D) efficient
      (E) pleasant

12. An experienced politician who knew better than to launch a campaign in troubled political waters, she intended to wait for a more ---- occasion before she announced her plans.

    (A) propitious   (B) provocative   (C) unseemly   (D) questionable
      (E) theoretical

13. No real life hero of ancient or modern days can surpass James Bond with his nonchalant ---- of death and the ---- with which he bears torture.

    (A) contempt . . . distress   (B) disregard . . . fortitude
      (C) veneration . . . guile   (D) concept . . . terror
        (E) impatience . . . fickleness

14. Surrounded by sycophants who invariably ---- her singing, Callas wearied of the constant adulation and longed for honest criticism.

    (A) orchestrated   (B) thwarted   (C) assailed   (D) extolled
      (E) reciprocated

15. Unlike the highly ---- Romantic poets of the previous century, Arnold and his fellow Victorian poets were ---- and interested in moralizing.

    (A) rhapsodic . . . lyrical   (B) frenetic . . . distraught
      (C) emotional . . . didactic   (D) sensitive . . . strange
        (E) dramatic . . . warped

Answer Key

Exercise A

1. D	5. C	9. A	13. B
2. B	6. B	10. B	14. E
3. D	7. E	11. C	15. D
4. C	8. E	12. E	

Exercise B

1. A	5. C	9. E	13. E
2. C	6. C	10. B	14. A
3. C	7. A	11. B	15. B
4. B	8. C	12. D	

Exercise C

1. D	5. C	9. A	13. B
2. A	6. E	10. C	14. D
3. E	7. C	11. C	15. C
4. B	8. C	12. A	

THE ANALOGY QUESTION

Analogy questions ask you to determine the relationship in a pair of words and then recognize a similar or parallel relationship in a different pair of words. You are given one pair of words. You must choose from the five pairs given as answer choices another pair that is related in the same way. The relationship between the words in the original pair will always be specific and precise; the same is true for the relationship between the words in the correct answer pair.

Note these common types of relationships that may exist between words:

1. Definition
   REFUGE : SHELTER
   A *refuge* (place of asylum) by definition *shelters*.

2. Defining Characteristic
   TIGER : CARNIVOROUS
   A *tiger* is defined as a *carnivorous* or meat-eating animal.

3. Class and Member
   AMPHIBIAN : SALAMANDER
   A *salamander* is a kind of *amphibian*.

4. Group and Member
   HOUND : PACK
   A *hound* is a member of a *pack*.

5. Antonyms
   WAX : WANE
   Wax, to grow larger, and *wane*, to dwindle, are opposites.

6. Antonym Variants
   NERVOUS : POISE
   Nervous means lacking in *poise*.

7. Synonyms
   MAGNIFICENT : GRANDIOSE
   Magnificent and *grandiose* are synonyms; they have the same meaning.

8. Synonym Variants
   VERBOSE : WORDINESS
   Someone *verbose* is wordy; he or she exhibits *wordiness*.

9. Degree of Intensity
   FLURRY : BLIZZARD
   A *flurry* or shower of snow is less extreme than a *blizzard*.

10. Part to Whole
    ISLAND : ARCHIPELAGO
    Many *islands* make up an *archipelago*.

THE VERBAL SECTIONS   31

11. Function
    BALLAST : STABILITY
    Ballast provides *stability*.

12. Manner
    STRUT : WALK
    To *strut* is to *walk* in a proud manner.

13. Action and Its Significance
    WINCE : PAIN
    A *wince* is a sign that one feels *pain*.

14. Worker and Article Created
    POET : SONNET
    A *poet* creates a *sonnet*.

15. Worker and Tool
    PAINTER : BRUSH
    A *painter* uses a *brush*.

16. Worker and Action
    ACROBAT : CARTWHEEL
    An *acrobat* performs a *cartwheel*.

17. Worker and Workplace
    MINER : QUARRY
    A *miner* works in a *quarry* or pit.

18. Tool and Its Action
    CROWBAR : PRY
    A *crowbar* is a tool used to *pry* things apart.

19. Cause and Effect
    SEDATIVE : SLEEPINESS
    A *sedative* causes *sleepiness*.

20. Sex
    DOE : STAG
    A *doe* is a female deer; a *stag*, a male deer.

---

21. Age
COLT : STALLION
A *colt* is a young *stallion*.

---

22. Time Sequence
CORONATION : REIGN
The *coronation* precedes the *reign*.

---

23. Spatial Sequence
ROOF : FOUNDATION
The *roof* is the highest point of a house; the *foundation*, the lowest point.

---

24. Symbol and Quality It Represents
DOVE : PEACE
A *dove* is the symbol of *peace*.

Tips to Help You Cope

1. Before you look at the choices, try to state the relationship between the capitalized words in a good sentence. Then use the word pairs from the answer choices in the same sentence. Frequently, only one will make sense, and you will have the correct answer.

2. Do not be misled if the choices are from different fields or areas, or seem to deal with different items, from the given pair. Study the capitalized words until you see the connection between them; then search for the same relationship among the choices. BOTANIST : MICROSCOPE :: CARPENTER : HAMMER, even though the two workers may have little else in common besides their use of tools.

3. If more than one answer fits the relationship in your sentence, look for a narrower approach. For example:

MITTEN : HAND :: (A) bracelet : wrist
(B) belt : waist   (C) muffler : neck
(D) ring : finger   (E) sandal : foot

You make up the sentence, "You wear a mitten on your hand." Unfortunately, *all* the answer choices will fit that sentence. So you say to yourself, "Why do you wear a mitten? You wear a mitten to keep your hand warm." Now when you try to substitute, only choice (C) works, so you have your answer.

4. Watch out for errors stemming from grammatical reversals. Ask yourself who is doing what to whom. BEGGAR : PLEAD is not the same as LAUGHING-STOCK : MOCK. A beggar is the person who pleads; a laughingstock is the person who *is* mocked.

5. Again, don't confuse "contract" the verb with "contract" the noun. Use the answer choices as a source of information about the original pair of words. If your answer choices are a noun and a verb, your original pair are a noun and a verb also. If they are an adjective and a noun, your original pair are an adjective and a noun.

6. Watch out for eye-catchers among your answer choices. Remember, these distracting answer choices are set up to remind you in some way of the original capitalized pair. Try spotting the eye-catcher in the following model analogy:

   FUGITIVE : FLEE :: (A) witness : summon
   (B) refugee : harbor   (C) lawyer : retain
   (D) bodyguard : protect   (E) captor : release

   The eye-catcher here is choice (B), *refugee : harbor.* It's there to tempt readers who mentally associate the words *fugitive* and *refugee.* Although both words share a common root, they function differently in the two analogies. A fugitive is a person who flees. A refugee is a person who seeks to be harbored or given refuge. The correct answer is (D).

7. Eliminate answer choices whose terms are only casually linked. One of your basic SAT I strategies is to eliminate as many wrong answer choices as you

can. In the case of analogy questions, look for answer pairs whose terms lack a clear, defined relationship. In your capitalized pairs, the words are always clearly linked:

An island *is part of* an archipelago.

Something perfunctory *is lacking in* enthusiasm.

To gibe or sneer *is to exhibit* scorn.

In the answer pairs, the relationship between the words may sometimes seem casual at best. Take for example, choice (E) in the previous analogy. A *captor* may or may not *release* a captive. There is no necessary, dictionary-defined relationship between these words. Discard such choices.

Examples to Get You Started

EXAMPLE 1

CONSTELLATION : STARS :: (A) prison : bars
(B) assembly : speaker   (C) troupe : actors
(D) mountain : peak   (E) flock : shepherds

A *constellation* is made up of *stars.* A *troupe* (not *troop* but *troupe*) is made up of *actors* (and actresses, of course). Choice (C) is correct.

EXAMPLE 2

MOSAIC : PIECE :: (A) forest : tree (B) canvas : frame
(C) chain : link (D) dune : sand (E) puzzle : clue

Suppose you phrase your sentence as follows: "A mosaic is made up of pieces." Although you have stated a relationship between the capitalized words, you have not stated a relationship that is precise enough. After all, forests are made up of trees, chains are made up of links, and dunes are made of sand.

Go back to the original pair of words for more details. A mosaic is made up of pieces that have been *assembled* together into an arrangement. A forest is a tract of land covered with densely growing trees. A dune is a mass of sand driven together by the wind. A chain, however, is made up of links that have been *assembled* together. Choice (C) is correct.

EXAMPLE 3

PARIAH : SHUNNED :: (A) heckler : jeered (B) suitor : rejected (C) athlete : applauded (D) exile : banished (E) patron : supported

In solving this analogy, eliminate answer choices whose terms are only vaguely linked. *By definition*, a pariah or outcast is someone who is *shunned*; being shunned is a pariah's *defining characteristic*. However, a *suitor* is not necessarily *rejected*; an *athlete* is not necessarily *applauded*. You can eliminate choices (B) and (C). Likewise, you can eliminate choices (A) and (E): a *heckler* is defined as one who jeers others, not as one who is *jeered* himself; a *patron* is defined as one who supports others, not as one who is *supported* himself. (Note the grammatical reversal here.)

Only choice (D) works. By definition, an *exile* is someone who is *banished* or cast out from his own country by others.

EXAMPLE 4

HUSBAND : STRENGTH :: (A) conserve : resources (B) expend : energy (C) minimize : weight (D) inspect : building (E) amend : text

At first glance, *husband* and *strength* seem only vaguely related. After all, by definition a husband is simply a married man; he may have strength, or he may not. However, take a look at the answer pairs. *Conserve, expend* and *minimize* are verbs, not nouns. *Husband* must be a verb as well.

You now know you're dealing with an unfamiliar meaning of *husband*. However, you also know that husbanding is an action that has something to do with *strength* or force. What actions are likely? You can increase your strength, building it up. You can deplete your strength, expending it. Or you can conserve your strength, using it judiciously. You've just narrowed your decision to choice (A), *conserve : resources*, and choice (B), *expend : energy*. Choice (B), however, is an eye-catcher; it catches your attention because *strength* reminds you of *energy*. The correct answer is choice (A). To husband one's strength is to use it wisely and economically, conserving it to meet later needs. This is directly comparable to conserving one's resources.

EXAMPLE 5

ADDITION : BUILDING :: (A) sentence : paragraph
(B) lease : property (C) tenure : position (D) story : skyscraper
(E) rider : bill

At first glance, this analogy seems simple. An addition is an extension of a building, something attached to the main structure. The relationship between the capitalized words is clear: part to whole. However, the simplicity of this question is deceptive: This is a very easy question *to get wrong*. The problem lies not in the original analogy but in the answer pairs.

Consider the answer choices closely. Choices (A), (B), (C), and (D) seem clear enough. A *sentence* is a unit of words that forms part of a *paragraph*. A *lease* is a contract for renting a piece of *property*. *Tenure* is the manner in which one holds a responsible *position*. A *story* is a complete horizontal section of a *skyscraper*. Choice (E), on the other hand, seems odd. How does a *rider* relate to a *bill* or piece of legislation? Certainly not the way a rider relates to a horse! When faced with such a strange pairing, most people just shrug their shoulders and skip to a less unusual seeming answer choice. In this case, they'd be making a big mistake. Choice (E) is the answer: A *rider*, as used here, is an addition or amendment to a document, like an endorsement added to an insurance policy or a codicil attached to a will. Just as an addition is added to a building, a rider is added to a bill.

Practice Exercises   **Answers given on page 41.**

Each of the following examples introduces a capitalized pair of words or phrases linked by a colon (:); this colon indicates that these words are related in some way. Following the capitalized pair are five pairs of words or phrases lettered A through E. Select the pair whose relationship is most similar to the relationship illustrated by the capitalized pair.

Example:

CLOCK : TIME :: (A) watch : wrist   (B) pedometer : speed
(C) thermometer : temperature   (D) hourglass : sand
  (E) radio : sound

Exercise A

1. CUB : LION :: (A) kit : fox   (B) dam : beaver   (C) tigress : tiger
   (D) pack : wolf   (E) beak : eagle
2. DIET : WEIGHT :: (A) alter : shape   (B) measure : length
   (C) copy : pattern   (D) bleach : color   (E) calculate : odds
3. SIGNATURE : ILLUSTRATION :: (A) byline : column
   (B) alias : charge   (C) credit : purchase   (D) note : scale
     (E) reference : recommendation
4. CHAINS : CLANK :: (A) glasses : shatter   (B) flowers : sway
   (C) bells : chime   (D) birds : flutter   (E) boards : warp
5. ENROLL : STUDENT :: (A) interview : applicant
   (B) dismiss : employee   (C) enact : lawyer   (D) enlist : soldier
     (E) evaluate : counselor
6. MASTHEAD : NEWSPAPER :: (A) footnote : essay   (B) credits : film
   (C) spine : book   (D) ream : paper   (E) advertisement : magazine
7. REPOSE : WEARY :: (A) clothing : meek   (B) shelter : thirsty
   (C) protection : poor   (D) refreshment : spirited
     (E) nourishment : hungry
8. PARCHED : MOISTURE :: (A) listless : energy   (B) feverish : warmth
   (C) frail : delicacy   (D) unruffled : poise   (E) erect : posture
9. FRAYED : FABRIC :: (A) thawed : ice   (B) renovated : building
   (C) frazzled : nerves   (D) watered : lawn   (E) cultivated : manner

10. INDOLENT : WORK :: (A) decisive : act   (B) gullible : cheat
    (C) perceptive : observe   (D) theatrical : perform
    (E) taciturn : speak
11. SURPRISE : EXCLAMATION :: (A) insolence : bow
    (B) dismay : groan   (C) happiness : grimace   (D) deference : nod
    (E) contentment : mutter
12. PERFORATE : HOLES :: (A) speckle : spots   (B) evaporate : perfume
    (C) decorate : rooms   (D) filter : water   (E) repent : sins
13. MAP : CARTOGRAPHER :: (A) blueprint : draftsman
    (B) building : inspector   (C) photograph : topographer
    (D) scheme : surveyor   (E) chart : optician
14. EXCESSIVE : MODERATION :: (A) extensive : duration
    (B) arbitrary : courage   (C) impulsive : reflection
    (D) distinguished : reverence   (E) expensive : cost
15. IRREFUTABLE : DISPROVED :: (A) intolerable : biased
    (B) insoluble : eradicated   (C) interminable : remembered
    (D) incomparable : applauded   (E) irreparable : mended
16. DEADBEAT : PAY :: (A) killjoy : lament   (B) spoilsport : refrain
    (C) daredevil : risk   (D) diehard : quit   (E) turncoat : betray
17. LACHRYMOSE : TEARS :: (A) effusive : requests   (B) ironic : jests
    (C) morose : speeches   (D) profound : sighs   (E) verbose : words
18. DRUDGERY : IRKSOME :: (A) encumbrance : burdensome
    (B) journey : wearisome   (C) ambivalence : suspicious
    (D) compliance : forced   (E) dissonance : harmonious
19. CANONIZE : SAINT :: (A) train : athlete   (B) guard : dignitary
    (C) deify : sinner   (D) lionize : celebrity   (E) humanize : scholar
20. TIRADE : ABUSIVE :: (A) monologue : lengthy
    (B) aphorism : boring   (C) prologue : conclusive
    (D) encomium : laudatory   (E) critique : insolent

Exercise B

1. SNOW : DRIFT :: (A) mountain : boulder   (B) sand : dune
   (C) pane : glass   (D) desert : oasis   (E) mud : rain
2. HEART : PUMP :: (A) lungs : collapse   (B) appendix : burst
   (C) stomach : digest   (D) intestine : twist   (E) teeth : ache
3. STANZA : POEM :: (A) flag : anthem   (B) story : building
   (C) mural : painting   (D) program : recital   (E) rhyme : prose
4. SPARK : BLAZE :: (A) nick : gash   (B) ember : coal
   (C) flag : badge   (D) wind : banner   (E) flood : shower
5. MURAL : WALL :: (A) statue : courtyard   (B) painting : portrait
   (C) quarry : stone   (D) etching : paper   (E) water color : tempera

6. FOLLOW : STALK :: (A) regret : rejoice   (B) look : spy
   (C) execute : condemn   (D) lurk : hide   (E) beckon : gesture
7. DAMPEN : DRENCH :: (A) glide : drift   (B) gambol : play
   (C) simmer : boil   (D) stagnate : flow   (E) ignite : quench
8. SHRUG : INDIFFERENCE :: (A) grin : deference   (B) wave : fatigue
   (C) nod : assent   (D) blink : scorn   (E) scowl : desire
9. TETHER : HORSE :: (A) safari : tiger   (B) specimen : animal
   (C) brand : calf   (D) bone : dog   (E) handcuff : prisoner
10. FRIVOLOUS : SERIOUSNESS :: (A) acute : perception
    (B) meticulous : organization   (C) outspoken : reticence
       (D) lavish : money   (E) industrious : perseverance
11. ALLAY : PAIN :: (A) mollify : fright   (B) cancel : order
    (C) arbitrate : dispute   (D) mitigate : offense   (E) testify : court
12. HECKLER : JEER :: (A) snob : flatter   (B) grumbler : complain
    (C) mentor : repent   (D) laughingstock : mock   (E) miser : weep
13. SLINK : STEALTH :: (A) whine : querulousness
    (B) snarl : mockery   (C) disguise : alias   (D) praise : friendship
       (E) invest : capital
14. AMUSING : UPROARIOUS :: (A) puzzling : dumbfounding
    (B) quiet : noisy   (C) intractable : stubborn
       (D) petty : narrow-minded   (E) exhausted : weary
15. ANGER : CHOLERIC :: (A) wrath : ironic   (B) love : idyllic
    (C) island : volcanic   (D) greed : avaricious   (E) pride : malicious
16. OLFACTORY : NOSE :: (A) peripheral : eyes   (B) gustatory : tongue
    (C) ambulatory : patient   (D) tactile : ears   (E) perfunctory : skin
17. CARAPACE : TURTLE :: (A) speed : hare   (B) chameleon : lizard
    (C) amphibian : frog   (D) shell : snail   (E) kennel : dog
18. BACTERIUM : COLONY :: (A) microbe : disease   (B) fish : shoal
    (C) stockade : settlement   (D) virus : immunization
       (E) sovereign: kingdom
19. TURNCOAT : TREACHEROUS :: (A) seamstress : generous
    (B) firebrand : mysterious   (C) mountebank : serious
       (D) spoilsport : notorious   (E) killjoy : lugubrious
20. SHUN : PARIAH :: (A) hunt : predator   (B) transmute : alchemist
    (C) beg : mendicant   (D) flatter : sycophant   (E) ridicule : butt

Exercise C

1. PEA : POD :: (A) orange : section   (B) bean : crock
   (C) pumpkin : stem   (D) nut : shell   (E) potato : stew
2. CANDLE : TALLOW :: (A) banana : peel   (B) temple : altar
   (C) statue : bronze   (D) fireplace : hearth   (E) furniture : polish

3. THERMOMETER : HEAT :: (A) filament : light
   (B) chronometer : color   (C) odometer : waves
      (D) Geiger counter : radiation   (E) barometer : electricity

4. AIRPLANE : HANGAR :: (A) ship : channel   (B) jet : runway
   (C) helicopter : pad   (D) motorcycle : sidecar
      (E) automobile : garage

5. SIP : GULP :: (A) giggle : guffaw   (B) eat : dine
   (C) marry : divorce   (D) fret : worry   (E) hunt : fish

6. SPINE : CACTUS :: (A) backbone : man   (B) quill : porcupine
   (C) root : oak   (D) pit : olive   (E) binding : book

7. TRUNK : BOUGH :: (A) hook : eye   (B) leaf : branch
   (C) detour : highway   (D) torso : arm   (E) keg : flask

8. COBBLER : SHOES : (A) mechanic : automobile
   (B) carpenter : saw   (C) painter : easel   (D) spy : plans
      (E) interrogator : questions

9. FROWN : DISPLEASURE :: (A) blush : pallor
   (B) smile : commiseration   (C) sneer : contempt   (D) snore : relief
      (E) smirk : regret

10. PRIDE : LION :: (A) bevy : quail   (B) lair : bear
    (C) fish : minnow   (D) flag : banner   (E) anger : symbol

11. MENTOR : COUNSEL :: (A) poet : criticism   (B) plea : mercy
    (C) bodyguard : protection   (D) sermon : conscience
       (E) judge : lawyer

12. CREST : WAVE :: (A) basin : water   (B) crown : tree
    (C) sand : dune   (D) mountain : range   (E) dregs : wine

13. INVENTORY : MERCHANDISE :: (A) repertory : theater
    (B) roster : members   (C) gadget : profits   (D) bankruptcy : debts
       (E) dormitory : college

14. UNATTRACTIVE : HIDEOUS :: (A) complex : confused
    (B) dormant : sleeping   (C) marred : spoiled
       (D) thrifty : parsimonious   (E) profane : sacred

15. ENTREPRENEUR : PROFITS :: (A) philanthropist : charity
    (B) organizer : union   (C) charlatan : converts
       (D) hermit : companionship   (E) scholar : knowledge

16. INDIGENT : WEALTHY :: (A) irate : sober   (B) taciturn : silent
    (C) meticulous : painstaking   (D) frivolous : serious
       (E) scholarly : witty

17. POET : ECLOGUE :: (A) philosopher : nature   (B) dramatist : scenery
    (C) sculptor : marble   (D) seamstress : gown
       (E) astronomer : planet

18. VIRTUOSO : EXPERIENCED :: (A) rogue : knavish
    (B) democrat : dictatorial   (C) saint : dissolute
       (D) leader : deferential   (E) evildoer : repentant

19. ASCETIC : INTEMPERANCE :: (A) hypocrite : brevity
(B) fanatic : zeal   (C) bigot : idolatry   (D) altruist : fidelity
 (E) miser : extravagance
20. DIATRIBE : INVECTIVE :: (A) elegy : mirth   (B) encomium : praise
(C) statute : limitation   (D) circumlocution : clarity
 (E) parody : performance

Answer Key

Exercise A

1. **A**	5. **D**	9. **C**	13. **A**	17. **E**
2. **D**	6. **B**	10. **E**	14. **C**	18. **A**
3. **A**	7. **E**	11. **B**	15. **E**	19. **D**
4. **C**	8. **A**	12. **A**	16. **D**	20. **D**

Exercise B

1. **B**	5. **D**	9. **E**	13. **A**	17. **D**
2. **C**	6. **B**	10. **C**	14. **A**	18. **B**
3. **B**	7. **C**	11. **D**	15. **D**	19. **E**
4. **A**	8. **C**	12. **B**	16. **B**	20. **E**

Exercise C

1. **D**	5. **A**	9. **C**	13. **B**	17. **D**
2. **C**	6. **B**	10. **A**	14. **D**	18. **A**
3. **D**	7. **D**	11. **C**	15. **E**	19. **E**
4. **E**	8. **A**	12. **B**	16. **D**	20. **B**

THE READING COMPREHENSION QUESTION

SAT I reading comprehension questions test your ability to understand what you read—both content and technique. Each verbal section will include one or two reading passages of different length, followed by six to thirteen questions. The third verbal section on SAT I will consist of a pair of passages with some questions on one passage, some on the other, and some comparing the two. One passage on the test will be **narrative**: a passage from a novel, a short story, an autobiography, or a personal essay. One will deal with the **sciences** (including medicine, botany, zoology, chemistry, physics, geology, astronomy); another with the **humanities** (including art, iterature, music, philosophy, folklore); a third, with the **social sciences** (including history, economics, sociology, government). Some passages may be what the College Board calls **argumentative**; these passages present a definite point of view on a subject.

One passage will most likely be **ethnic** in content: whether it is a history passage, a personal narrative, or a passage on music, art, or literature, it will deal with concerns of a particular minority group.

The questions that come after each passage are not arranged in order of difficulty. They are arranged to suit the way the passage's content is organized. (A question based on information found at the beginning of the passage will come before a question based on information at the passage's end.) If you are stumped by a tough reading question, do not skip the other questions on that passage. A tough question may be just one question away from an easy one.

Tips to Help You Cope

1. Save the reading comprehension questions for last. On the SAT I, you get the same points for answering a "quick and easy" question correctly as you do for answering a time-consuming one. Reading questions take time. Answer the less time-consuming questions first.

2. When you have a choice, tackle a passage with a familiar subject before one with an unfamiliar one. It is hard to concentrate when you read about something wholly unfamiliar to you. Give yourself a break. When there are two passages in a section, first tackle the one that interests you or that deals with the topics in which you are well-grounded.

3. First read the passage; then read the questions. Reading the questions before you read the passage will not save you time. It will cost you time. If you read the questions first, when you turn to the passage you will have a number of question words and phrases dancing around in your head. You will be so involved in trying to spot the places they occur in the passage that you'll be unable to concentrate on comprehending the passage as a whole.

4. Read as rapidly as you can with understanding, but do not force yourself. Do not worry about the time element. If you worry about not finishing the test, you will begin to take short cuts and miss the correct answer in your haste.

5. Make use of the italicized introductions to acquaint yourself with the text. As you read the italicized introductory material and tackle the passage's opening sentences, try to anticipate what the passage will be about. You'll be in a better position to understand what you read.

6. As you continue reading, try to remember in which part of the passage the author makes major points. In that way, when you start looking for the phrase or sentence which will justify your choice of answer, you will be able to save time by going to that section of the passage immediately rather than having to reread the entire section.

7. When you tackle the questions, go back to the passage to verify your choice of answer. Do not rely on your memory alone.

8. Watch out for words or phrases in the question that can alert you to the kind of question being asked. Questions asking for information stated in the passage:

> *the author asserts*
> *the author mentions all of the following EXCEPT*
> *according to the passage*
> *according to the author*

Questions asking you to draw a conclusion:

> *it can be inferred*
> *would most likely*
> *is best described*
> *it can be argued*
> *suggests that*
> *the author implies*
> *the author probably considers*
> *would probably*

Questions asking about the main idea of the passage:

> *which of the following titles*
> *main/central/primary purpose*
> *main point of the passage*
> *chiefly concerned with*
> *passage as a whole*
> *primary emphasis*

Questions asking about contextual meaning:

> *as used in the passage*
> *what the author means in saying*
> *in context, the word/phrase*
> *in the context of the passage*

9. When asked to find the main idea, be sure to check the opening and summary sentences of each paragraph. Authors typically provide readers with a sentence that expresses a paragraph's main idea succinctly. Although such topic sentences may appear anywhere in the paragraph, readers customarily look for them in the opening or closing sentences.

10. When asked to choose a title, watch out for choices that are too specific or too broad. A paragraph is a group of sentences revolving around a central theme. An appropriate title for a paragraph, therefore, must include this central theme. It should be neither too broad nor too narrow in its scope; it should be specific and yet comprehensive enough to include all the essential ideas presented by the sentences. A good title for a passage of two or more paragraphs should include the thoughts of ALL the paragraphs.

11. When asked to make inferences, take as your answer what the passage logically suggests, not what it states directly. Look for clues in the passage; then choose as your answer a statement which is a logical development of the information the author has provided.

12. When asked to determine the questions of attitude, mood, or tone, look for words that convey emotion, express values, or paint pictures. These images and descriptive phrases get the author's feelings across.

13. Use the line numbers in the questions to be sure you've gone back to the correct spot in the passage. Fortunately, the lines are numbered in the passages, and the questions often refer you to specific lines in the passage by number. It takes less time to locate a line number than to spot a word or phrase.

14. Try to answer all the questions on a particular passage. Don't let yourself get bogged down on any one question. Skip the one that's got you stumped, but make a point of coming back to it later, after you've answered one or two more questions on the passage. Often, working through other questions on the same passage will provide you with information you can use to answer questions that stumped you the first time around.

15. When asked to give the meaning of an unfamiliar word, look for nearby context clues. Words in the immediate vicinity of the word you are trying to

define will often give you a sense of the meaning of the unfamiliar word.

16. When dealing with double passages, tackle them one at a time. After reading the lines in italics introducing both passages, read Passage 1; then jump straight to the questions, and answer all those based on Passage 1. Next read Passage 2; then answer all the questions based on Passage 2. Finally, tackle the two or three questions that refer to both passages. Go back to both passages as needed.

Practice Exercises   Answers given on page 72.

> Each passage below precedes questions based on its content.
> Answer all questions following a passage based on what that
> passage <u>states</u> directly or <u>implies</u>.

Exercise A

Each of the following passages comes from a novel or short story collection that has provided reading passages on prior SATs. Use this exercise to acquaint yourself with the sort of fiction you will confront on the test and to practice answering critical reading questions based on literature.

The following passage is taken from Great Expectations *by Charles Dickens. In it, the hero, Pip, recollects a dismal period in his youth during which he for a time lost hope of ever bettering his fortunes.*

It is a most miserable thing to feel ashamed of home.
There may be black ingratitude in the thing, and the punishment may be retributive and well deserved; but, that it is a
Line miserable thing, I can testify. Home had never been a very
(5) pleasant place to me, because of my sister's temper. But Joe
had sanctified it and I believed in it. I had believed in the best
parlor as a most elegant salon; I had believed in the front
door as a mysterious portal of the Temple of State whose
solemn opening was attended with a sacrifice of roast fowls;
(10) I had believed in the kitchen as a chaste though not magnificent
apartment; I had believed in the forge as the glowing road to
manhood. Now, it was all coarse and common, and I would not
have had Miss Havisham and Estella see it on any account.
Once, it had seemed to me that when I should at last roll

(15) up my shirt sleeves and go into the forge, Joe's 'prentice, I
should be distinguished and happy. Now the reality was in
my hold, I only felt that I was dusty with the dust of small
coal, and that I had a weight upon my daily remembrance to
which the anvil was a feather. There have been occasions in
(20) my later life (I suppose as in most lives) when I have felt for
a time as if a thick curtain had fallen on all its interest and
romance, to shut me out from any thing save dull endurance
any more. Never has that curtain dropped so heavy and
blank, as when my way in life lay stretched out straight
(25) before me through the newly-entered road of apprenticeship
to Joe.

I remember that at a later period of my "time," I used to
stand about the churchyard on Sunday evenings, when night
was falling, comparing my own perspective with the windy
(30) marsh view, and making out some likeness between them by
thinking how flat and low both were, and how on both there
came an unknown way and a dark mist and then the sea. I
was quite as dejected on the first working-day of my apprenticeship as in that after time; but I am glad to know that I
(35) never breathed a murmur to Joe while my indentures lasted.
It is about the only thing I *am* glad to know of myself in that
connection.

For, though it includes what I proceed to add, all the
merit of what I proceed to add was Joe's. It was not because
(40) I was faithful, but because Joe was faithful, that I never ran
away and went for a soldier or a sailor. It was not because I
had a strong sense of the virtue of industry, but because Joe
had a strong sense of the virtue of industry, that I worked
with tolerable zeal against the grain. It is not possible to know
(45) how far the influence of any amiable honesthearted duty-
going man flies out into the world; but it is very possible to
know how it has touched one's self in going by, and I know
right well that any good that intermixed itself with my apprenticeship came of plain contented Joe, and not of restless
(50) aspiring discontented me.

THE VERBAL SECTIONS 49

1. The passage as a whole is best described as

   (A) an analysis of the reasons behind a change in attitude
   (B) an account of a young man's reflections on his emotional state
   (C) a description of a young man's awakening to the harsh conditions
       of working class life
   (D) a defense of a young man's longings for romance and glamour
   (E) a criticism of young people's ingratitude to their elders

2. It may be inferred from the passage that the young man has been
   apprenticed to a

   (A) cook
   (B) forger
   (C) coal miner
   (D) blacksmith
   (E) grave digger

3. In the passage, Joe is portrayed most specifically as

   (A) distinguished
   (B) virtuous
   (C) independent
   (D) homely
   (E) coarse

4. The passage suggests that the narrator's increasing discontent with
   his home during his apprenticeship was caused by

   (A) a new awareness on his part of how his home would appear to
       others
   (B) the increasing heaviness of the labor involved
   (C) the unwillingness of Joe to curb his sister's temper
   (D) the narrator's lack of an industrious character
   (E) a combination of simple ingratitude and sinfulness

5. According to the passage, the narrator gives himself a measure of
   credit for

   (A) working diligently despite his unhappiness
   (B) abandoning his hope of a military career
   (C) keeping his menial position secret from Miss Havisham
   (D) concealing his despondency from Joe
   (E) surrendering his childish beliefs

The following passage is excerpted from the short story "Clay" in Dubliners *by James Joyce. In this passage, tiny, unmarried Maria oversees tea for the washerwomen, all the while thinking of the treat in store for her: a night off.*

The matron had given her leave to go out as soon as the women's tea was over and Maria looked forward to her evening out. The kitchen was spick and span: the cook said *Line* you could see yourself in the big copper boilers. The fire was
(5) nice and bright and on one of the side-tables were four very big barmbracks. These barmbracks seemed uncut; but if you went closer you would see that they had been cut into long thick even slices and were ready to be handed round at tea. Maria had cut them herself.
(10)   Maria was a very, very small person indeed but she had a very long nose and a very long chin. She talked a little through her nose, always soothingly: "Yes, my dear," and "No, my dear." She was always sent for when the women quarrelled over their tubs and always succeeded in making
(15) peace. One day the matron had said to her:
     "Maria, you are a veritable peace-maker!"
     And the sub-matron and two of the Board ladies had heard the compliment. And Ginger Mooney was always saying what she wouldn't do to the dummy who had charge
(20) of the irons if it wasn't for Maria. Everyone was so fond of Maria.
     When the cook told her everything was ready, she went into the women's room and began to pull the big bell. In a few minutes the women began to come in by twos and
(25) threes, wiping their steaming hands in their petticoats and pulling down the sleeves of their blouses over their red steaming arms. They settled down before their huge mugs which the cook and the dummy filled up with hot tea, already mixed with milk and sugar in huge tin cans. Maria super-
(30) intended the distribution of the barmbrack and saw that every woman got her four slices. There was a great deal of laughing

and joking during the meal. Lizzie Fleming said Maria was
sure to get the ring and, though Fleming had said that for so
many Hallow Eves, Maria had to laugh and say she didn't
(35) want any ring or man either; and when she laughed her grey-
green eyes sparkled with disappointed shyness and the tip of
her nose nearly met the tip of her chin. Then Ginger Mooney
lifted her mug of tea and proposed Maria's health while all
the other women clattered with their mugs on the table, and
(40) said she was sorry she hadn't a sup of porter to drink it in.
And Maria laughed again till the tip of her nose nearly met
the tip of her chin and till her minute body nearly shook itself
asunder because she knew that Mooney meant well though,
of course, she had the notions of a common woman.

6. The author's primary purpose in the second paragraph is to

(A) introduce the character of a spinster
(B) describe working conditions in a public institution
(C) compare two women of different social classes
(D) illustrate the value of peace-makers in society
(E) create suspense about Maria's fate

7. The language of the passage most resembles the language of

(A) a mystery novel
(B) an epic
(C) a fairy tale
(D) institutional board reports
(E) a sermon

8. It can be inferred from the passage that Maria would most likely view
the matron as which of the following?

(A) A political figurehead
(B) An inept administrator
(C) A demanding taskmaster
(D) An intimate friend
(E) A benevolent superior

9. We may infer from the care with which Maria has cut the barmbracks (lines 6–8) that

   (A) she fears the matron
   (B) she is in a hurry to leave
   (C) she expects the Board members for tea
   (D) it is a dangerous task
   (E) she takes pride in her work

10. It can be inferred from the passage that all the following are characteristic of Maria EXCEPT

   (A) a deferential nature
   (B) eagerness for compliments
   (C) respect for authority
   (D) dreams of matrimony
   (E) reluctance to compromise

The following passage is taken from Jane Austen's novel Mansfield Park. *This excerpt presents Sir Thomas Bertram, owner of Mansfield Park, who has just joined the members of his family.*

Sir Thomas was indeed the life of the party, who at his suggestion now seated themselves round the fire. He had the best right to be the talker; and the delight of his sensations in
Line being again in his own house, in the center of his family,
(5) after such a separation, made him communicative and chatty in a very unusual degree; and he was ready to answer every question of his two sons almost before it was put. All the little particulars of his proceedings and events, his arrivals and departures, were most promptly delivered, as he sat by Lady
(10) Bertram and looked with heartfelt satisfaction at the faces around him—interrupting himself more than once, however, to remark on his good fortune in finding them all at home—coming unexpectedly as he did—all collected together exactly as he could have wished, but dared not depend on.
(15)   By not one of the circle was he listened to with such unbroken unalloyed enjoyment as by his wife, whose feelings

were so warmed by his sudden arrival, as to place her nearer
agitation than she had been for the last twenty years. She
had been almost fluttered for a few minutes, and still
(20) remained so sensibly animated as to put away her work,
move Pug from her side, and give all her attention and all the
rest of her sofa to her husband. She had no anxieties for anybody to cloud *her* pleasure; her own time had been irre-
proachably spent during his absence; she had done a great
(25) deal of carpet work and made many yards of fringe; and she
would have answered as freely for the good conduct and
useful pursuits of all the young people as for her own. It was
so agreeable to her to see him again, and hear him talk, to
have her ear amused and her whole comprehension filled by
(30) his narratives, that she began particularly to feel how dread-
fully she must have missed him, and how impossible it
would have been for her to bear a lengthened absence.
　　　Mrs. Norris was by no means to be compared in happi-
ness to her sister. Not that she was incommoded by many
(35) fears of Sir Thomas's disapprobation when the present state
of his house should be known, for her judgment had been so
blinded, that she could hardly be said to show any sign of
alarm; but she was vexed by the manner of his return. It had
left her nothing to do. Instead of being sent for out of the
(40) room, and seeing him first, and having to spread the happy
news through the house, Sir Thomas, with a very reasonable
dependence perhaps on the nerves of his wife and children,
had sought no confidant but the butler, and had been following him almost instantaneously into the drawing-room. Mrs.
(45) Norris felt herself defrauded of an office on which she had
always depended, whether his arrival or his death were to be
the thing unfolded; and was now trying to be in a bustle without having any thing to bustle about. Would Sir Thomas have
consented to eat, she might have gone to the housekeeper
(50) with troublesome directions; but Sir Thomas resolutely
declined all dinner; he would take nothing, nothing till tea
came—he would rather wait for tea. Still Mrs. Norris was at

intervals urging something different; and in the most interesting moment of his passage to England, when the alarm of a
(55) French privateer was at the height, she burst through his
recital with the proposal of soup. "Sure, my dear Sir Thomas,
a basin of soup would be a much better thing for you than
tea. Do have a basin of soup."

  Sir Thomas could not be provoked. "Still the same anxi-
(60) ety for everybody's comfort, my dear Mrs. Norris," was his
answer. "But indeed I would rather have nothing but tea."

11. We can infer from the opening paragraph that Sir Thomas is
customarily

  (A) unwelcome at home
  (B) tardy in business affairs
  (C) dissatisfied with life
  (D) more restrained in speech
  (E) lacking in family feeling

12. The passage suggests that Sir Thomas's sudden arrival

  (A) was motivated by concern for his wife
  (B) came as no surprise to Lady Bertram
  (C) was timed by him to coincide with a family reunion
  (D) was expected by the servants
  (E) was received with mixed emotions

13. Which of the following titles best describes the passage?

  (A) An Unexpected Return
  (B) The Conversation of the Upper Class
  (C) Mrs. Norris's Grievance
  (D) A Romantic Reunion
  (E) An Account of a Voyage Abroad

14. The author's tone in her description of Lady Bertram's sensations
(lines 15–32) is

  (A) markedly scornful
  (B) mildly bitter
  (C) gently ironic
  (D) manifestly indifferent
  (E) warmly sympathetic

THE VERBAL SECTIONS 55

15. By stressing that Lady Bertram "had no anxieties for anybody to cloud *her* pleasure" (lines 22–23), the author primarily intends to imply that

(A) Lady Bertram was hardhearted in ignoring the sufferings of others
(B) it was unusual for Lady Bertram to be so unconcerned
(C) others in the company had reason to be anxious
(D) Sir Thomas expected his wife to be pleased to see him
(E) Lady Bertram lived only for pleasure

16. Sir Thomas's attitude toward Mrs. Norris can best be described as one of

(A) sharp irritation
(B) patient forbearance
(C) solemn disapproval
(D) unreasoned alarm
(E) unmixed delight

17. The office of which Mrs. Norris feels herself defrauded is most likely that of

(A) butler
(B) housekeeper
(C) wife
(D) world traveler
(E) message-bearer

Exercise B

The following passage is taken from the introduction to the catalog of a major exhibition of Flemish tapestries.

Tapestries are made on looms. Their distinctive weave is basically simple: the colored weft threads interface regularly with the monochrome warps, as in darning or plain cloth, but
Line as they do so, they form a design by reversing their direction
(5) when a change of color is needed. The wefts are beaten down to cover the warps completely. The result is a design or picture that is the fabric itself, not one laid upon a ground like an embroidery, a print, or brocading. The back and front of a tapestry show the same design. The weaver always

(10) follows a preexisting model, generally a drawing or painting, known as the cartoon, which in most cases he reproduces as exactly as he can. Long training is needed to become a professional tapestry weaver. It can take as much as a year to produce a yard of very finely woven tapestry.

(15) Tapestry-woven fabrics have been made from China to Peru and from very early times to the present day, but large wall hangings in this technique, mainly of wool, are typically Northern European. Few examples predating the late fourteenth century have survived, but from about 1400 tapestries

(20) were an essential part of aristocratic life. The prince or great nobleman sent his plate and his tapestries ahead of him to furnish his castles before his arrival as he traveled through his domains; both had the same function, to display his wealth and social position. It has frequently been suggested

(25) that tapestries helped to heat stone-walled rooms, but this is a modern idea; comfort was of minor importance in the Middle Ages. Tapestries were portable grandeur, instant splendor, taking the place, north of the Alps, of painted frescoes further south. They were hung without gaps between

(30) them, covering entire walls and often doors as well. Only very occasionally were they made as individual works of art such as altar frontals. They were usually commissioned or bought as sets, or "chambers," and constituted the most important furnishings of any grand room, except for the dis-

(35) play of plate, throughout the Middle Ages and the sixteenth century. Later, woven silks, ornamental wood carving, stucco decoration, and painted leather gradually replaced tapestry as expensive wall coverings, until at last wallpaper was introduced in the late eighteenth century and eventually swept

(40) away almost everything else.

By the end of the eighteenth century, the "tapestry-room" [a room with every available wall surface covered with wall hangings] was no longer fashionable: paper had replaced wall coverings of wool and silk. Tapestries, of

(45) course, were still made, but in the nineteenth century they

often seem to have been produced mainly as individual
works of art that astonish by their resemblance to oil
paintings, tours de force woven with a remarkably large
number of wefts per inch. In England during the second half
(50) of the century, William Morris attempted to reverse this trend
and to bring tapestry weaving back to its true principles,
those he considered to have governed it in the Middle Ages.
He imitated medieval tapestries in both style and technique,
using few warps to the inch, but he did not make sets; the
(55) original function for which tapestry is so admirably suited—
completely covering the walls of a room and providing sumptu-
ous surroundings for a life of pomp and splendor—could not
be revived. Morris's example has been followed, though with
less imitation of medieval style, by many weavers of the pre-
(60) sent century, whose coarsely woven cloths hang like single
pictures and can be admired as examples of contemporary art.

1. Tapestry weaving may be characterized as which of the following?
  I. Time-consuming
  II. Spontaneous in concept
  III. Faithful to an original

  (A) I only
  (B) III only
  (C) I and II only
  (D) I and III only
  (E) II and III only

2. The word "distinctive" in line 1 means

  (A) characteristic
  (B) stylish
  (C) discriminatory
  (D) eminent
  (E) articulate

3. Renaissance nobles carried tapestries with them to demonstrate their

(A) piety
(B) consequence
(C) aesthetic judgment
(D) need for privacy
(E) dislike for cold

4. The word "ground" in line 7 means

(A) terrain
(B) dust
(C) thread
(D) base
(E) pigment

5. In contrast to nineteenth-century tapestries, contemporary tapestries

(A) are displayed in sets of panels
(B) echo medieval themes
(C) faithfully copy oil paintings
(D) have a less fine weave
(E) indicate the owner's social position

6. The primary purpose of the passage is to

(A) explain the process of tapestry making
(B) contrast Eastern and Western schools of tapestry
(C) analyze the reasons for the decline in popularity of tapestries
(D) provide a historical perspective on tapestry making
(E) advocate a return to a more colorful way of life

The following passage is taken from a book of popular history written in 1991.

　　The advantage of associating the birth of democracy with the Mayflower Compact is that it is easy to do so. The public loves a simple explanation, and none is simpler than
Line the belief that on November 11, 1620—the day the compact
(5) was approved—a cornerstone of American democracy was laid. Certainly it makes it easier on schoolchildren. Marking

the start of democracy in 1620 relieves students of the
responsibility of knowing what happened in the hundred
some years before, from the arrival of the *Santa Maria* to the
(10) landing of the *Mayflower.*

The compact, to be sure, demonstrated the Englishman's
striking capacity for self-government. And in affirming the
principle of majority rule, the Pilgrims showed how far they
had come from the days when the king's whim was law and
(15) nobody dared say otherwise.

But the emphasis on the compact is misplaced.
Scholarly research in the last half century indicates that the
compact had nothing to do with the development of self-
government in America. In truth, the Mayflower Compact was
(20) no more a cornerstone of American democracy than the
Pilgrim hut was the foundation of American architecture. As
Samuel Eliot Morison so emphatically put it, American
democracy "was not born in the cabin of the *Mayflower.*"

The Pilgrims indeed are miscast as the heroes of
(25) American democracy. They spurned democracy and
would have been shocked to see themselves held up as its
defenders. George Willison, regarded as one of the most
careful students of the Pilgrims, states that "the merest
glance at the history of Plymouth" shows that they were not
(30) democrats.

The mythmakers would have us believe that even if the
Pilgrims themselves weren't democratic, the Mayflower
Compact itself was. But in fact the compact was expressly
designed to curb freedom, not promote it. The Pilgrim
(35) governor and historian, William Bradford, from whom we
have gotten nearly all of the information there is about the
Pilgrims, frankly conceded as much. Bradford wrote that the
purpose of the compact was to control renegades aboard the
Mayflower who were threatening to go their own way when
(40) the ship reached land. Because the Pilgrims had decided to
settle in an area outside the jurisdiction of their royal patent,
some aboard the *Mayflower* had hinted that upon landing

they would "use their owne libertie, for none had power to command them." Under the terms of the compact, they
(45) couldn't; the compact required all who lived in the colony to "promise all due submission and obedience" to it.

Furthermore, despite the compact's mention of majority rule, the Pilgrim fathers had no intention of turning over the colony's government to the people. Plymouth was to be ruled
(50) by the elite. And the elite wasn't bashful in the least about advancing its claims to superiority. When the Mayflower Compact was signed, the elite signed first. The second rank consisted of the "goodmen." At the bottom of the list came four servants' names. No women or children signed. Whether
(55) the compact was or was not actually hostile to the demo-cratic spirit, it was deemed sufficiently hostile that during the Revolution the Tories put it to use as "propaganda for the crown." The monarchists made much of the fact that the Pilgrims had chosen to establish an English-style govern-
(60) ment that placed power in the hands of a governor, not a cleric, and a governor who owed his allegiance not to the people or to a church but to "our dread Sovereign Lord King James." No one thought it significant that the Tories had adopted the principle of majority rule. Tory historian George
(65) Chalmers, in a work published in 1780, claimed the central meaning of the compact was the Pilgrims' recognition of the necessity of royal authority. This may have been not only a convenient argument but a true one. It is at least as plausible as the belief that the compact stood for democracy.

7. The author's attitude toward the general public (lines 2–6) can best be described as

(A) egalitarian
(B) grateful
(C) sympathetic
(D) envious
(E) superior

8. The phrase "held up" in line 26 means

(A) delayed
(B) cited
(C) accommodated
(D) carried
(E) waylaid

9. According to the passage (lines 33–34), the compact's primary purpose was to

(A) establish legal authority within the colony
(B) outlaw non-Pilgrims among the settlers
(C) preach against heretical thinking
(D) protect each individual's civil rights
(E) countermand the original royal patent

10. The author of the passage can best be described as

(A) an iconoclast
(B) an atheist
(C) a mythmaker
(D) an elitist
(E) an authoritarian

11. In lines 52–55, the details about the signers of the Mayflower Compact are used to emphasize

(A) the Pilgrims' respect for the social hierarchy
(B) the inclusion of servants among those signing
(C) their importance to American history
(D) the variety of social classes aboard
(E) the lack of any provision for minority rule

Rock musicians often affect the role of social revolutionaries. The following passage is taken from an unpublished thesis on the potential of rock and roll music to contribute to political and social change.

It should be clear from the previous arguments that rock and roll cannot escape its role as a part of popular culture. One important part of that role is its commercial nature. Rock and roll is "big corporation business in America and around the globe. As David De Voss has noted: 'Over fifty US rock artists annually earn from $2 million to $6 million. At last count, thirty-five artists and fifteen additional groups make from three to seven times more than America's highest paid business executive.'"

(10)   Perhaps the most damning argument against rock and roll as a political catalyst is suggested by John Berger in an essay on advertising. Berger argues that "publicity turns consumption into a substitute for democracy. The choice of what one eats (or wears or drives) takes the place of signifi-

(15) cant political choice." To the extent that rock and roll is big business, and that it is marketed like other consumer goods, rock and roll also serves this role. Our freedom to choose the music we are sold may be distracting us from more important concerns. It is this tendency of rock and roll,

(20) fought against but also fulfilled by punk, that Julie Burchill and Tony Parsons describe in *The Boy Looked at Johnny: The Obituary of Rock and Roll.*

Never mind, kid, there'll soon be another washing-machine/spot-cream/rock-band on the market to solve

(25)   all your problems and keep you quiet/off the street/distracted from the real enemy/content till the next pay-day.
Anyhow, God Save Rock and Roll . . . it made you a consumer, a potential Moron . . .

(30)   IT'S ONLY ROCK AND ROLL AND IT'S PLASTIC, PLASTIC, YES IT IS!!!!!!

This is a frustrating conclusion to reach, and it is especially frustrating for rock and roll artists who are dissatisfied with the political systems in which they live. If rock and roll's

(35) ability to promote political change is hampered by its popularity, the factor that gives it the potential to reach significant numbers of people, to what extent can rock and roll artists act politically? Apart from charitable endeavors, with which rock and roll artists have been quite successful at raising

(40) money for various causes, the potential for significant political activity promoting change appears quite limited.
The history of rock and roll is filled with rock artists

who abandoned, at least on vinyl, their political commitment.
Bob Dylan, who, by introducing the explicit politics of folk
(45) music to rock and roll, can be credited with introducing the
political rock and roll of the sixties, quickly abandoned politics for more personal issues. John Lennon, who was perhaps more successful than any other rock and roll artist at
getting political material to the popular audience, still had a
(50) hard time walking the line between being overtly political but
unpopular and being apolitical and extremely popular. In
1969 "Give Peace a Chance" reached number fourteen on the
Billboard singles charts. 1971 saw "Power to the People" at
number eleven. But the apolitical "Instant Karma" reached
(55) number three on the charts one year earlier. "Imagine,"
which mixed personal and political concerns, also reached
number three one year later. Lennon's most political album,
Some Time in New York City, produced no hits. His biggest
hits, "Whatever Gets You Through the Night" and "Starting
(60) Over," which both reached number one on the charts, are
apolitical. Jon Wiener, in his biography of Lennon, argues
that on "Whatever Gets You Through the Night," "it seemed
like John was turning himself into Paul, the person without
political values, who put out Number One songs and who
(65) managed to sleep soundly. Maybe that's why John (Lennon)
told Elton John that 'Whatever Gets You Through the Night'
was 'one of my least favorites.'" When, after leaving music
for five years, Lennon returned in 1980 with the best-selling
Double Fantasy album, the subject of his writing was "caring,
(70) sharing, and being a whole person."

The politically motivated rock and roll artist's other
option is to maintain his political commitment without fool-
ing himself as to the ultimate impact his work will have. If
his music is not doomed to obscurity by the challenge it pre-
(75) sents to its listeners the artist is lucky. But even such luck
can do nothing to protect his work from the misinterpreta-
tion it will be subjected to once it is popular. Tom Greene of
the Mekons expresses the frustration such artists feel when
he says, "You just throw your hands up in horror and try and

(80)   . . . I don't know. I mean, what can you do? How can you
possibly avoid being a part of the power relations that
exist?" The artist's challenge is to *try* to communicate with
his audience. But he can only take responsibility for his own
intentions. Ultimately, it is the popular audience that must

(85)   take responsibility for what it does with the artist's work. The
rock and roll artist cannot cause political change. But, if he is
very lucky, the popular audience might let him contribute to
the change it makes.

12. De Voss's comparison of the salaries of rock stars and corporate
executives (lines 5–9) is cited primarily in order to

(A) indicate the author's familiarity with current pay scales
(B) argue in favor of higher pay for musical artists
(C) support the thesis that rock and roll is a major industry
(D) refute the assertion that rock stars are underpaid
(E) demonstrate the lack of limits on the wages of popular stars

13. The word "consumption" in line 13 means

(A) supposition
(B) beginning a task
(C) advertising a product
(D) using up goods
(E) culmination

14. In the quotation cited in lines 23–31, Burchill and Parsons most likely
run the words "washing-machine/spot-cream/rock-band" together to
indicate that

(A) they are products with universal appeal
(B) to the consumer they are all commodities
(C) advertisers need to market them differently
(D) rock music eliminates conventional distinctions
(E) they are equally necessary parts of modern society

15. The word "plastic" in the Burchill and Parsons quotation (line 30) is
being used

(A) lyrically
(B) spontaneously
(C) metaphorically
(D) affirmatively
(E) skeptically

16. Their comments in lines 28–29 suggest that Burchill and Parsons primarily regard consumers as

(A) invariably dimwitted
(B) markedly ambivalent
(C) compulsively spendthrift
(D) unfamiliar with commerce
(E) vulnerable to manipulation

17. The author's comments about Bob Dylan (lines 44–47) chiefly suggest that

(A) Dylan readily abandoned political rock and roll for folk music
(B) Dylan lacked the necessary skills to convey his political message musically
(C) rock and roll swiftly replaced folk music in the public's affections
(D) folk music gave voice to political concerns long before rock and roll music did
(E) Dylan betrayed his fans' faith in him by turning away from political commentary

18. In lines 59–70, "Starting Over" and the *Double Fantasy* album are presented as examples of

(A) profitable successes lacking political content
(B) overtly political recordings without general appeal
(C) bold applications of John's radical philosophy
(D) uninspired and unpopular rock and roll records
(E) atypical recordings that effected widespread change

19. In the last paragraph, the author concludes that the rock and roll artist's contribution to political change is

(A) immediate
(B) decisive
(C) irresponsible
(D) flagrant
(E) indirect

Exercise C

The questions that follow the two passages in this section relate to the content of both, and to their relationship. The correct response may be stated outright in the passages or merely suggested.

Questions 1–13 are based on the following passages.

The following passages are excerpted from popular articles on dolphins, the first dating from the 1960s, the second written in 1990.

Passage 1

Most of the intelligent land animals have prehensile, grasping organs for exploring their environment—hands in human beings and their anthropoid relatives, the sensitive
Line inquiring trunk in the elephant. One of the surprising things
(5) about the dolphin is that his superior brain is unaccompanied by any type of manipulative organ. He has, however, a remarkable range-finding ability involving some sort of echo-sounding. Perhaps this acute sense—far more accurate than any that human ingenuity has been able to devise artificially
(10) —brings him greater knowledge of his watery surroundings than might at first seem possible. Human beings think of intelligence as geared to things. The hand and the tool are to us the unconscious symbols of our intellectual attainment. It is difficult for us to visualize another kind of lonely, almost
(15) disembodied intelligence floating in the wavering green fairy-land of the sea—an intelligence possibly near or comparable to our own but without hands to build, to transmit knowledge by writing, or to alter by one hairsbreadth the planet's surface. Yet at the same time there are indications that this is a
(20) warm, friendly, and eager intelligence quite capable of coming to the assistance of injured companions and striving to rescue them from drowning. Dolphins left the land when mammalian brains were still small and primitive. Without the stimulus provided by agile exploring fingers, these great sea
(25) mammals have yet taken a divergent road toward intelligence of a high order. Hidden in their sleek bodies is an impressively elaborated instrument, the reason for whose appearance is a complete enigma. It is as though both the human being and the dolphin were each part of some great eye

(30) which yearned to look both outward on eternity and inward
to the sea's heart—that fertile entity like the mind in its
swarming and grotesque life.

Passage 2

Nothing about dolphins has been more widely or pas-
sionately discussed over the centuries than their supposed
(35) intelligence and communicative abilities. In fact, a persistent
dogma holds that dolphins are among the most intelligent of
animals and that they communicate with one another in complex ways. Implicit in this argument is the belief that dolphin
cultures are at least as ancient and rich as our own. To sup-
(40) port the claim of high intelligence amongst dolphins, propo-
nents note that they have large brains, live in societies
marked as much by co-operative as by competitive interactions and rapidly learn the artificial tasks given to them in
captivity. Indeed, dolphins are clearly capable of learning
(45) through observation and have good memories. People who
spend time with captive dolphins are invariably impressed by
their sense of humor, playfulness, quick comprehension of
body language, command of situations, mental agility, and
emotional resilience. Individual dolphins have distinctive per-
(50) sonalities and trainers often speak of being trained by their
subjects, rather than the other way round.

The extremely varied repertoires of sounds made by
dolphins are often invoked as *prima facie* evidence of
advanced communication abilities. In addition, some "scien-
(55) tific" experiments done by John Lilly and his associates
during the 1950s and 1960s were claimed to show that dolphins communicate not only with one another but also with
humans, mimicking human speech and reaching out across
the boundaries that divide us.
(60) These conclusions about dolphin intelligence and communication have not withstood critical scrutiny. While they
have fueled romantic speculation, their net impact has been

to mislead. Rather than allowing dolphins to be discovered
and appreciated for what they are, Lilly's vision has forced us
(65) to measure these animals' value according to how close they
come to equalling or exceeding our own intelligence, virtue,
and spiritual development.

The issues of dolphin intelligence and communication
have been inseparable in most people's minds, and the pre-
(70) sumed existence of one has been taken as proof of the other,
a classic case of begging the question. Not surprisingly then,
most experiments to evaluate dolphin intelligence have
measured the animals' capacity for cognitive processing as
exhibited in their understanding of the rudiments of
(75) language.

From the early work of researchers like Dwight Batteau
and Jarvis Bastian through the more recent work of Louis
Herman and associates, dolphins have been asked to accept
simple information, in the form of acoustic or visual symbols
(80) representing verbs and nouns, and then to act on the information following a set of commands from the experimenter.

The widely publicized results have been somewhat dis-
appointing. Although they have demonstrated that dolphins
do have the primary skills necessary to support understand-
(85) ing and use of a language, they have not distinguished the
dolphins from other animals in this respect. For example,
some seals, animals we do not normally cite as members of
the intellectual or communicative elite, have been found to
have the same basic capabilities.

(90)   What, then, do the results of experiments to date mean?
Either we have not devised adequate tests to permit us to
detect, measure, and rank intelligence as a measure of a
given species' ability to communicate, or we must acknowledge that the characteristics that we regard as rudimentary
(95) evidence of intelligence are held more commonly by many
"lower" animals than we previously thought.

1. According to Passage 1, which of the following statements about dolphins is true?

(A) They have always been water-dwelling creatures.
(B) They at one time possessed prehensile organs.
(C) They lived on land in prehistoric times.
(D) Their brains are no longer mammalian in nature.
(E) They developed brains to compensate for the lack of a prehensile organ.

2. The author of Passage 1 suggests that human failure to understand the intelligence of the dolphin is due to

(A) the inadequacy of human range-finding equipment
(B) a lack of knowledge about the sea
(C) the want of a common language
(D) the primitive origins of the human brain
(E) the human inclination to judge other life by our own

3. In Passage 1, the author's primary purpose is apparently to

(A) examine the dolphin's potential for surpassing humankind
(B) question the need for prehensile organs in human development
(C) refute the theory that dolphins are unable to alter their physical environment
(D) reassess the nature and extent of dolphin intelligence
(E) indicate the superiority of human intelligence over that of the dolphin

4. The word "acute" in line 8 means

(A) excruciating
(B) severe
(C) keen
(D) sudden and intense
(E) brief in duration

5. The "impressively elaborated instrument" referred to in lines 26–27 is best interpreted to mean which of the following?

(A) A concealed manipulative organ
(B) An artificial range-finding device
(C) A complex, intelligent brain
(D) The dolphin's hidden eye
(E) An apparatus for producing musical sounds

6. According to the author's simile in line 31, the human mind and the heart of the sea are alike in that both

(A) teem with exotic forms of life
(B) argue in support of intelligence
(C) are necessary to the evolution of dolphins
(D) are directed outward
(E) share a penchant for the grotesque

7. Which of the following best characterizes the tone of Passage 1?

(A) Restrained skepticism
(B) Pedantic assertion
(C) Wondering admiration
(D) Amused condescension
(E) Ironic speculation

8. The author of Passage 2 puts quotation marks around the word *scientific* in lines 54–55 to indicate he

(A) is faithfully reproducing Lilly's own words
(B) intends to define the word later in the passage
(C) believes the reader is unfamiliar with the word as used by Lilly
(D) advocates adhering to the scientific method in all experiments
(E) has some doubts as to how scientific those experiments were

9. The author of Passage 2 maintains that the writings of Lilly and his associates have

(A) overstated the extent of dolphin intelligence
(B) been inadequately scrutinized by critics
(C) measured the worth of the dolphin family
(D) underrated dolphins as intelligent beings
(E) established criteria for evaluating dolphin intelligence

10. By calling the argument summarized in lines 68–70 a classic case of begging the question, the author of Passage 2 indicates he views it with

(A) trepidation
(B) optimism
(C) detachment
(D) skepticism
(E) credulity

11. Which of the following would most undercut the studies on which the author bases his conclusion in lines 90–96?

   (A) Evidence proving dolphin linguistic abilities to be far superior to those of other mammals
   (B) An article recording attempts by seals and walruses to communicate with human beings
   (C) The reorganization of current intelligence tests by species and level of difficulty
   (D) A reassessment of the definition of the term "lower animals"
   (E) The establishment of a project to develop new tests to detect intelligence in animals

12. The author of Passage 2 would find Passage 1

   (A) typical of the attitudes of Lilly and his associates
   (B) remarkable for the perspective it offers
   (C) indicative of the richness of dolphin culture
   (D) supportive of his fundamental point of view
   (E) intriguing for its far-reaching conclusions

13. Compared to Passage 2, Passage 1 is

   (A) more figurative
   (B) less obscure
   (C) more objective
   (D) more current
   (E) less speculative

Answer Key

Exercise A

1. **B**	6. **A**	11. **D**	16. **B**
2. **D**	7. **C**	12. **E**	17. **E**
3. **B**	8. **E**	13. **A**	
4. **A**	9. **E**	14. **C**	
5. **D**	10. **E**	15. **C**	

Exercise B

1. **D**	6. **D**	11. **A**	16. **E**
2. **A**	7. **E**	12. **C**	17. **D**
3. **B**	8. **B**	13. **D**	18. **A**
4. **D**	9. **A**	14. **B**	19. **E**
5. **D**	10. **A**	15. **C**	

Exercise C

1. **C**	5. **C**	9. **A**	13. **A**
2. **E**	6. **A**	10. **D**	
3. **D**	7. **C**	11. **A**	
4. **C**	8. **E**	12. **A**	

4 Building Your Vocabulary

      Recognizing the meaning of words is essential to comprehending what you read. The more you stumble over unfamiliar words in a text, the more you have to take time out to look up words in your dictionary, the more likely you are to wind up losing track of what the author has to say.

      To succeed in college, you must develop a college-level vocabulary. The time you put in now learning vocabulary-building techniques for the SAT I will pay off later, and not just on the day of the test. In this chapter you will find a fundamental tool that will help you build your vocabulary: Barron's SAT I High-Frequency Word List.

      No matter how little time you have before you take the SAT I, you can familiarize yourself with the sort of vocabulary you will be facing on the test. Look over the words on our SAT I High-Frequency Word List: each of these words, ranging from everyday words such as *abstract* and *relevant* to less commonly known ones such as *abstruse* and *surreptitious*, has appeared (as answer choices or as question words) from five to twenty times on SATs published in the past two decades.

      Not only will looking over the SAT I High-Frequency Word List reassure you that you *do* know some SAT-type words, but also it may well help you on the actual day of the test. These words have turned up on recent tests; some of them may turn up on the test you take.

For those of you who intend to work your way through the *entire* SAT I High-Frequency Word List and feel the need for a plan, we recommend that you follow the procedures described below in order to use the list most profitably:

1. Divide the list into groups of twenty words.
2. Allot a definite time each day for the study of a group.
3. Devote at least one hour to each group.
4. First go through the group looking at the short, simple-looking words (6 letters at most). Mark those you don't know. In studying, pay particular attention to them.
5. Go through the group again looking at the longer words. Pay particular attention to words with more than one meaning and familiar-looking words which have unusual definitions that come as a surprise to you. Study these secondary definitions.
6. List unusual words on index cards that you can shuffle and review from time to time. (Study no more than 5 cards at a time.)
7. Use the illustrative sentences as models and make up new sentences of your own.
8. In making up new sentences, use familiar examples and be concrete: the junior high school band tuning up sounds *discordant*, the wicked queen in "Snow White" is *malicious.*

For each word, the following is provided:

1. The word (printed in heavy type).
2. Its part of speech (abbreviated).
3. A brief definition.
4. A sentence illustrating the word's use.
5. Whenever appropriate, related words are provided, together with their parts of speech.

The word list is arranged in strict alphabetical order.

SAT I HIGH-FREQUENCY WORD LIST

abridge V. condense or shorten. Because the publishers felt the public wanted a shorter version of *War and Peace*, they proceeded to *abridge* the novel.

abstemious ADJ. sparing in eating and drinking; temperate. Concerned whether her vegetarian son's *abstemious* diet provided him with sufficient protein, the worried mother begged him to eat more.

abstract ADJ. theoretical; not concrete; nonrepresentational. To him, hunger was an *abstract* concept; he had never missed a meal.

abstruse ADJ. obscure; profound; difficult to understand. She read *abstruse* works in philosophy.

accessible ADJ. easy to approach; obtainable. We asked our guide whether the ruins were *accessible* on foot.

acclaim V. applaud; announce with great approval. The NBC sportscasters *acclaimed* every American victory in the Olympics and decried every American defeat. also N.

acknowledge V. recognize; admit. Although I *acknowledge* that the Beatles' tunes sound pretty dated today, I still prefer them to the "gangsta rap" songs my brothers play.

adulation N. flattery; admiration. The rock star thrived on the *adulation* of his groupies and yes men. adulate, V.

adversary N. opponent. The young wrestler struggled to defeat his *adversary*.

adversity N. misfortune; distress. In *Up from Slavery*, young Booker T. Washington shows courage and perseverance in his struggles with *adversity*.

advocate V. urge; plead for. The abolitionists *advocated* freedom for the slaves. also N.

aesthetic ADJ. artistic; dealing with or capable of appreciation of the beautiful. The beauty of Tiffany's stained glass appealed to Alice's *aesthetic* sense. aesthete, N.

affable ADJ. easily approachable; warmly friendly. Accustomed to cold, aloof supervisors, Nicholas was amazed at how *affable* his new employer was.

affirmation N. positive assertion; confirmation; solemn pledge by one who refuses to take an oath. Despite Tom's *affirmations* of innocence, Aunt Polly still suspected he had eaten the pie.

alleviate V. relieve. This should *alleviate* the pain; if it does not, we shall have to use stronger drugs.

aloof ADJ. apart; reserved. Shy by nature, she remained *aloof* while all the rest conversed.

altruistic ADJ. unselfishly generous; concerned for others. In providing tutorial assistance and college scholarships for hundreds of economically disadvantaged youths, Eugene Lang performed a truly *altruistic* deed. altruism, N.

ambiguous ADJ. unclear or doubtful in meaning. His *ambiguous* instructions misled us; we did not know which road to take. ambiguity, N.

ambivalence N. the state of having contradictory or conflicting emotional attitudes. Torn between loving her parents one minute and hating them the next, she was confused by the *ambivalence* of her feelings. ambivalent, ADJ.

analogous ADJ. comparable. Some feminists contend that a woman's need for a man is *analogous* to a fish's need for a bicycle. analogy, N.

anarchist N. person who rebels against the established order. Only the total overthrow of all governmental regulations would satisfy the *anarchist.*

anecdote N. short account of an amusing or interesting event. Rather than make concrete proposals for welfare reform, President Reagan told *anecdotes* about poor people who became wealthy despite their impoverished backgrounds.

animosity N. active enmity; ill will. The recent killings on the West Bank have sharpened the longstanding *animosity* between the Palestinians and the Israelis.

antagonism N. hostility; active resistance. Barry showed *antagonism* toward his new stepmother by ignoring her whenever she tried talking to him. antagonistic, ADJ.

antidote N. medicine to counteract a poison or disease. When Marge's child accidentally swallowed some cleaning fluid, the poison control hotline instructed Marge how to administer the *antidote*.

antiquated ADJ. old-fashioned; obsolete. Philip had grown so accustomed to editing his papers on word processors that he thought typewriters were too *antiquated* for him to use.

apathy N. lack of caring; indifference. A firm believer in democratic government, she could not understand the *apathy* of people who never bothered to vote. apathetic, ADJ.

appease V. pacify; soothe. We have discovered that, when we try to *appease* our enemies, we encourage them to make additional demands.

apprehension N. fear. His nervous glances at the passersby on the deserted street revealed his *apprehension*.

arbitrary ADJ. unreasonable or capricious; randomly selected without any reason; based solely on one's unrestricted will or judgment. The coach claimed the team lost because the umpire made some *arbitrary* calls.

archaic ADJ. antiquated. "Methinks," "thee," and "thou" are *archaic* words that are no longer part of our normal vocabulary.

arid ADJ. dry; barren. The cactus has adapted to survive in an *arid* environment.

arrogance N. pride; haughtiness. Convinced that Emma thought she was better than anyone else in the class, Ed rebuked her for her *arrogance*.

articulate ADJ. effective; distinct. Her *articulate* presentation of the advertising campaign impressed her employers. also V.

artifact N. object made by human beings, either handmade or mass-produced. Archaeologists debated the significance of the *artifacts* discovered in the ruins of Asia Minor but came to no conclusion about the culture they represented.

artisan N. a manually skilled worker. Elderly *artisans* from Italy trained Harlem teenagers to carve the stone figures that would decorate the new wing of the cathedral.

ascendancy N. controlling influence. Leaders of religious cults maintain *ascendancy* over their followers by methods that can verge on brainwashing.

ascetic ADJ. practicing self-denial; austere. The wealthy, self-indulgent young man felt oddly drawn to the strict, *ascetic* life led by members of some monastic orders. also N.

aspire V. seek to attain; long for. Because he *aspired* to a career in professional sports, Philip enrolled in a graduate program in sports management. aspiration, N.

astute ADJ. wise; shrewd; keen. The painter was an *astute* observer, noticing every tiny detail of her model's appearance and knowing the exact importance of each one.

attribute V. ascribe; explain. I *attribute* her success in science to the encouragement she received from her parents.

augment V. increase; add to. Armies *augment* their forces by calling up reinforcements; teachers *augment* their salaries by taking odd jobs.

austere ADJ. forbiddingly stern; severely simple and unornamented. The headmaster's *austere* demeanor tended to scare off the more timid students who never visited his study willingly. The room reflected the man, *austere* and bare, like a monk's cell, with no touches of luxury to moderate its *austerity*.

authoritarian ADJ. favoring or exercising total control; nondemocratic. The people had no control over their own destiny; they were forced to obey the dictates of the *authoritarian* regime. also N.

autonomous ADJ. self-governing. This island is a colony; however, in most matters, it is *autonomous* and receives no orders from the mother country. autonomy, N.

aversion N. firm dislike. Bert had an *aversion* to yuppies; Alex had an *aversion* to punks. Their mutual *aversion* was so great that they refused to speak to one another.

belie V. contradict; give a false impression. His coarse, hard-bitten exterior *belied* his inner sensitivity.

benevolent ADJ. generous; charitable. His *benevolent* nature prevented him from refusing any beggar who accosted him. benevolence, N.

bolster V. support; reinforce. The debaters amassed file boxes full of evidence to *bolster* their arguments.

braggart N. boaster. Modest by nature, she was no *braggart*, preferring to let her accomplishments speak for themselves.

brevity N. conciseness. *Brevity* is essential when you send a telegram or cablegram; you are charged for every word.

cajole V. coax; wheedle. Diane tried to *cajole* her father into letting her drive the family car. cajolery, N.

calculated ADJ. deliberately planned; likely. Lexy's choice of clothes to wear to the debate tournament was carefully *calculated*. Her conventional suit was *calculated* to appeal to the conservative judges.

candor N. frankness; open honesty. Jack can carry *candor* too far: when he told Jill his honest opinion of her, she nearly slapped his face. candid, ADJ.

capricious ADJ. fickle; incalculable. The storm was *capricious* and changed course constantly.

censorious ADJ. critical. *Censorious* people delight in casting blame.

censure V. blame; criticize. The senator was *censured* for behavior inappropriate to a member of Congress. also N.

coercion N. use of force to get someone to obey. The inquisitors used both physical and psychological *coercion* to force Joan of Arc to deny that her visions were sent by God. coerce, V.

commemorate V. honor the memory of. The statue of the Minute Man *commemorates* the valiant soldiers who fought in the Revolutionary War.

compile V. assemble; gather; accumulate. We planned to *compile* a list of the words most frequently used on SAT I examinations.

complacency N. self-satisfaction; smugness. Full of *complacency* about his latest victories, he looked smugly at the row of trophies on his mantelpiece. complacent, ADJ.

compliance N. readiness to yield; conformity in fulfilling requirements. When I give an order, I expect *compliance*, not defiance. The design for the new school had to be in *compliance* with the local building code. comply, V.

composure N. mental calmness. Even the latest work crisis failed to shake her *composure*.

comprehensive ADJ. thorough; inclusive. This book provides a *comprehensive* review of verbal and math skills for the SAT I.

concede V. admit; yield. Despite all the evidence Monica had assembled, Mark refused to *concede* that she was right.

conciliatory ADJ. reconciling; soothing. She was still angry despite his *conciliatory* words. conciliate, V.

concise ADJ. brief and compact. When you define a new word, be *concise*; the shorter the definition, the easier it is to remember.

concur V. agree. Did you *concur* with the decision of the court or did you find it unfair?

condone V. overlook voluntarily; forgive. We cannot *condone* your recent criminal cooperation with the gamblers.

conflagration N. great fire. In the *conflagration* that followed the 1906 earthquake, much of San Francisco was destroyed.

confound v. confuse; puzzle. No mystery could *confound* Sherlock Holmes for long.

consensus N. general agreement. After hours of debate, the *consensus* of the group was that we should approve the executive director's proposal.

constraint N. compulsion; repression of feelings. Because he trusted his therapist completely, he discussed his feelings openly with her without feeling the least *constraint*. constrain, v.

contend v. assert earnestly; struggle; compete. Sociologist Harry Edwards *contends* that young black athletes are exploited by some college recruiters.

contentious ADJ. quarrelsome. Disagreeing violently with the referees' ruling, the coach became so *contentious* that they threw him out of the game.

contract v. compress or shrink; make a pledge; catch a disease. Warm metal expands; cold metal *contracts*.

conviction N. strongly held belief. Nothing could shake his *conviction* that she was innocent. (secondary meaning)

cordial ADJ. gracious; heartfelt. Our hosts greeted us at the airport with a *cordial* welcome and a hearty hug.

corroborate v. confirm. Unless we find a witness to *corroborate* your evidence, it will not stand up in court.

credulity N. belief on slight evidence. The witch doctor took advantage of the *credulity* of the superstitious natives. credulous, ADJ.

criterion N. standard used in judging. What *criterion* did you use when you selected this essay as the prizewinner? criteria, PL.

cryptic ADJ. mysterious; hidden; secret. Thoroughly baffled by Holmes's *cryptic* remarks, Watson wondered whether Holmes was intentionally concealing his thoughts about the crime.

cursory ADJ. casual; hastily done. Because a *cursory* examination of the ruins indicates the possibility of arson, we believe the insurance agency should undertake a more extensive investigation of the fire's cause.

curtail V. shorten; reduce. Diane told Herb that she couldn't go out with him because her dad had ordered her to *curtail* her social life.

decorum N. propriety; orderliness and good taste in manners. Even the best-mannered students have trouble behaving with *decorum* on the last day of school. decorous, ADJ.

deference N. courteous regard for another's wish. In *deference* to his desires, the employers granted him a holiday. defer, V.

degradation N. humiliation; debasement; degeneration. Some secretaries object to fetching the boss a cup of coffee because they resent the *degradation* of being made to do such lowly tasks. degrade, V.

delineate N. portray. He is a powerful storyteller, but he is weakest when he attempts to *delineate* character. delineation, N.

denounce V. condemn; criticize. The reform candidate *denounced* the corrupt city officers for having betrayed the public's trust. denunciation, N.

deplore V. regret; disapprove of. Although I *deplore* the vulgarity of your language, I defend your right to express yourself freely.

depravity N. corruption; wickedness. The *depravity* of the tyrant's behavior shocked all. deprave, V.

deprecate V. express disapproval of; protest against; belittle. A firm believer in old-fashioned courtesy, Miss Post *deprecated* the modern tendency to address new acquaintances by their first names. deprecatory, ADJ.

deride V. ridicule; make fun of. The critics *derided* his pretentious dialogue and refused to take his play seriously. derision, N.

derivative ADJ. unoriginal; derived from another source. Although her early poetry was clearly *derivative* in nature, the critics thought she had promise and eventually would find her own voice.

despondent ADJ. depressed; gloomy. To the dismay of his parents, William became seriously *despondent* after he broke up with Jan; they despaired of finding a cure for his gloom. despondency, N.

detached ADJ. emotionally removed; calm and objective; indifferent. A psychoanalyst must maintain a *detached* point of view and stay uninvolved with her patients' personal lives. detachment, N. (secondary meaning)

deterrent N. something that discourages; hindrance. Does the threat of capital punishment serve as a *deterrent* to potential killers? deter, V.

detrimental ADJ. harmful; damaging. The candidate's acceptance of major financial contributions from a well-known racist ultimately proved *detrimental* to his campaign, for he lost the backing of many of his early grassroots supporters. detriment, N.

devious ADJ. roundabout; erratic; not straightforward. The Joker's plan was so *devious* that it was only with great difficulty we could follow its shifts and dodges.

devise V. think up; invent; plan. How clever he must be to have *devised* such a devious plan! What ingenious inventions might he have *devised* if he had turned his mind to science and not to crime.

diffuse ADJ. wordy; rambling; spread out (like a gas). If you pay authors by the word, you tempt them to produce *diffuse* manuscripts rather than brief ones. diffusion, N.

digression N. wandering away from the subject. Nobody minded when Professor Renoir's lectures wandered away from their official theme; his *digressions* were always more fascinating than the topic of the day. digress, V.

diligence N. steadiness of effort; persistent hard work. Her employers were greatly impressed by her *diligence* and offered her a partnership in the firm. diligent, ADJ.

diminution N. lessening; reduction in size. Old Jack was as sharp at eighty as he had been at fifty; increasing age led to no *diminution* of his mental acuity.

discerning ADJ. mentally quick and observant; having insight. Because he was considered the most *discerning* member of the firm, he was assigned the most difficult cases. discern, V. discernment, N.

disclose V. reveal. Although competitors offered him bribes, he refused to *disclose* any information about his company's forthcoming product. disclosure, N.

discordant ADJ. not harmonious; conflicting. Nothing is quite so *discordant* as the sound of a junior high school orchestra tuning up.

discount V. disregard. Be prepared to *discount* what he has to say about his ex-wife.

discrepancy N. lack of consistency; difference. The police noticed some *discrepancies* in his description of the crime and did not believe him.

discriminating ADJ. able to see differences; prejudiced. They feared he was not sufficiently *discriminating* to judge complex works of modern art. (secondary meaning) discrimination, N.

disdain V. view with scorn or contempt. In the film *Funny Face*, the bookish heroine *disdained* fashion models for their lack of intellectual interests. also N.

disinclination N. unwillingness. Some mornings I feel a great *disinclination* to get out of bed.

dismiss V. put away from consideration; reject. Believing in John's love for her, she *dismissed* the notion that he might be unfaithful. (secondary meaning)

disparage V. belittle. Do not *disparage* anyone's contribution; these little gifts add up to large sums. disparaging, ADJ.

disparity N. difference; condition of inequality. Their *disparity* in rank made no difference at all to the prince and Cinderella.

disperse V. scatter. The police fired tear gas into the crowd to *disperse* the protesters.

disputatious ADJ. argumentative; fond of argument. People avoided οⱼ cussing contemporary problems with him because of his *disputatious* manner.

disseminate V. distribute; spread; scatter (like seeds). By their use of the Internet, propagandists have been able to *disseminate* their pet doctrines to new audiences around the globe.

dissent V. disagree. In the recent Supreme Court decision, Justice O'Connor *dissented* from the majority opinion. also N.

divergent ADJ. differing; deviating. The two witnesses presented the jury with remarkably *divergent* accounts of the same episode. divergence, N.

doctrine N. teachings, in general; particular principle (religious, legal, etc.) taught. He was so committed to the *doctrines* of his faith that he was unable to evaluate them impartially.

document V. provide written evidence. She kept all the receipts from her business trip in order to *document* her expenses for the firm. also N.

dogmatic ADJ. opinionated; arbitrary; doctrinal. We tried to discourage Doug from being so *dogmatic*, but never could convince him that his opinions might be wrong.

dubious ADJ. questionable; filled with doubt. Many critics of the SAT I contend the test is of *dubious* worth. Jay claimed he could get a perfect 1600 on the SAT I, but Ellen was *dubious*: she knew he hadn't cracked a book in three years.

duplicity N. double-dealing; hypocrisy. When Tanya learned that Mark had been two-timing her, she was furious at his *duplicity*.

eclectic ADJ. composed of elements drawn from disparate sources. His style of interior decoration was *eclectic*: bits and pieces of furnishings from widely divergent periods, strikingly juxtaposed to create a unique decor. eclecticism, N.

egotism N. excessive self-centeredness; sense of self-importance; conceit. Pure *egotism:* "But enough of this chit-chat about you and your little problems. Let's talk about what's really important: *Me!*"

elated ADJ. overjoyed; in high spirits. Grinning from ear to ear, Bonnie Blair was clearly *elated* by her Olympic victory. elation, N.

eloquence N. expressiveness; persuasive speech. The crowds were stirred by Martin Luther King's *eloquence.* eloquent, ADJ.

elusive ADJ. evasive; baffling; hard to grasp. Trying to pin down exactly when the contractors would be done remodeling the house, Nancy was frustrated by their *elusive* replies. elude, V.

embellish V. adorn; ornament. The costume designer *embellished* the leading lady's ball gown with yards and yards of ribbon and lace.

emulate V. imitate; rival. In a brief essay, describe a person you admire, someone whose virtues you would like to *emulate.*

endorse V. approve; support. Everyone waited to see which one of the rival candidates for the city council the mayor would *endorse.* (secondary meaning) endorsement, N.

enhance V. increase; improve. You can *enhance* your chances of being admitted to the college of your choice by learning to write well; an excellent essay can *enhance* any application.

enigma N. puzzle. Despite all attempts to decipher the code, it remained an *enigma.*

enmity N. ill will; hatred. At Camp David, President Carter labored to bring an end to the *enmity* that prevented the peaceful coexistence of Egypt and Israel.

ephemeral ADJ. short-lived; fleeting. The mayfly is an *ephemeral* creature.

equivocal ADJ. ambiguous; intentionally misleading. Rejecting the candidate's *equivocal* comments on tax reform, the reporters pressed him to state clearly where he stood on the issue. equivocate, V.

erroneous ADJ. mistaken; wrong. I thought my answer was correct, but it was *erroneous*.

erudite ADJ. learned; scholarly. Though his fellow students thought him *erudite*, Paul knew he would have to study many years before he could consider himself a scholar.

esoteric ADJ. hard to understand; known only to the chosen few. *New Yorker* short stories often include *esoteric* allusions to obscure people and events: the implication is, if you are in the in-crowd, you'll get the reference; if you come from Cleveland, you won't.

eulogy N. expression of praise, often on the occasion of someone's death. Instead of delivering a spoken *eulogy* at Genny's memorial service, Jeff sang a song he had written in her honor.

euphemism N. mild expression in place of an unpleasant one. The expression "he passed away" is a *euphemism* for "he died."

exacerbate V. worsen; embitter. The latest bombing *exacerbated* England's already existing bitterness against the IRA, causing the prime minister to break off the peace talks abruptly.

exalt V. raise in rank or dignity; praise. The actor Alec Guinness was *exalted* to the rank of knighthood by the queen.

execute V. put into effect; carry out. The choreographer wanted to see how well she could *execute* a pirouette. (secondary meaning) execution, N.

exemplary ADJ. serving as a model; outstanding. At commencement the dean praised Ellen for her *exemplary* behavior as class president.

exemplify V. serve as an example of; embody. For a generation of ballet goers, Rudolf Nureyev *exemplified* the ideal of masculine grace.

exhaustive ADJ. thorough; comprehensive. We have made an *exhaustive* study of all published SAT tests and are happy to share our research with you.

exhilarating ADJ. invigorating and refreshing; cheering. Though some of the hikers found tramping through the snow tiring, Jeffrey found the walk on the cold, crisp day *exhilarating*.

exonerate V. acquit; exculpate. I am sure this letter naming the actual culprit will *exonerate* you.

expedient ADJ. suitable; practical, politic. A pragmatic politician, he was guided by what was *expedient* rather than by what was ethical. expediency, N.

expedite V. hasten. Because we are on a tight schedule, we hope you will be able to *expedite* the delivery of our order.

explicit ADJ. totally clear; definite; outspoken. Don't just hint around that you're dissatisfied; be *explicit* about what's bugging you.

exploit V. make use of, sometimes unjustly. Cesar Chavez fought attempts to *exploit* migrant farmworkers in California. exploitation, N.

extol V. praise; glorify. The president *extolled* the astronauts, calling them the pioneers of the Space Age.

extraneous ADJ. not essential; superfluous. No wonder Ted can't think straight! His mind is so cluttered up with *extraneous* trivia, he can't concentrate on the essentials.

extricate V. free; disentangle. He found that he could not *extricate* himself from the trap.

exuberance N. overflowing abundance; joyful enthusiasm; flamboyance; lavishness. I was bowled over by the *exuberance* of Annie's welcome. What an enthusiastic greeting!

facilitate V. help bring about; make less difficult. Rest and proper nourishment should *facilitate* the patient's recovery.

fallacious ADJ. false; misleading. Paradoxically, *fallacious* reasoning does not always yield erroneous results: even though your logic may be faulty, the answer you get may nevertheless be correct. fallacy, N.

fanaticism N. excessive zeal; extreme devotion to a belief or cause. When Islamic fundamentalists demanded the death of Salman Rushdie because his novel questioned their faith, world opinion condemned them for their *fanaticism.*

fastidious ADJ. difficult to please; squeamish. Bobby was such a *fastidious* eater that he would eat a sandwich only if his mother first cut off every scrap of crust.

feasible ADJ. practical. Is it *feasible* to build a new stadium for the Yankees on New York's west side? Without additional funding, the project is clearly unrealistic.

fervor N. glowing ardor. Their kiss was full of the *fervor* of first love.

flagrant ADJ. conspicuously wicked. We cannot condone such *flagrant* violations of the rules.

frivolous ADJ. lacking in seriousness; self-indulgently carefree; relatively unimportant. Though Nancy enjoyed Bill's *frivolous,* lighthearted companionship, she sometimes wondered whether he could ever be serious. frivolity, N.

frugality N. thrift; economy. In economically hard times, anyone who doesn't practice *frugality* risks bankruptcy. frugal, ADJ.

furtive ADJ. stealthy; sneaky. The boy gave a *furtive* look at his classmate's test paper.

garrulous ADJ. loquacious; wordy; talkative. My Uncle Henry can out-talk any three people I know; he is the most *garrulous* person in Cayuga County. garrulity, N.

glutton N. someone who eats too much. When Mother saw that Bobby had eaten all the cookies, she called him a little *glutton.* gluttonous, ADJ.

gratify V. please. Lori's parents were *gratified* by her outstanding performance on the SAT.

gratuitous ADJ. given freely; unwarranted; uncalled for. Quit making *gratuitous* comments about my driving; no one asked you for your opinion.

gravity N. seriousness. We could tell we were in serious trouble from the *gravity* of her expression. (secondary meaning) grave, ADJ.

gregarious ADJ. sociable. Typically, party-throwers are *gregarious;* hermits are not.

guile N. deceit; duplicity; wiliness; cunning. Iago uses considerable *guile* to trick Othello into believing that Desdemona has been unfaithful.

gullible ADJ. easily deceived. He preyed upon *gullible* people, who believed his stories of easy wealth.

hamper V. obstruct. The minority party agreed not to *hamper* the efforts of the leaders to secure a lasting peace.

hardy ADJ. sturdy; robust; able to stand inclement weather. We asked the gardening expert to recommend particularly *hardy* plants that could withstand our harsh New England winters.

haughtiness N. pride; arrogance. When she realized that Darcy believed himself too good to dance with his inferiors, Elizabeth took great offense at his *haughtiness*.

hedonist N. one who believes that pleasure is the sole aim in life. A thoroughgoing *hedonist*, he considered only his own pleasure and ignored any claims others had on his money or time.

heresy N. opinion contrary to popular belief; opinion contrary to accepted religion. Galileo's assertion that the earth moved around the sun directly contradicted the religious teachings of his day; as a result, he was tried for *heresy*. heretic, N.

hierarchy N. arrangement by rank or standing; authoritarian body divided into ranks. To be low man on the totem pole is to have an inferior place in the *hierarchy*.

homogeneous ADJ. of the same kind. Educators try to put pupils of similar abilities into the same classes because they believe that this *homogeneous* grouping is advisable. homogeneity, N.

hypocritical ADJ. pretending to be virtuous; deceiving. I res____ *cal* posing as a friend for I know he is interested o. advancement. hypocrisy, N.

hypothetical ADJ. based on assumptions or hypotheses. Why do we ____ consider *hypothetical* cases when we have actual case histories we can examine? hypothesis, N.

idiosyncrasy N. individual trait, usually odd in nature; eccentricity. One of Richard Nixon's little *idiosyncrasies* was his liking for ketchup on cottage cheese. One of Hannibal Lecter's little *idiosyncrasies* was his liking for human flesh.

illusory ADJ. deceptive; not real. Unfortunately, the costs of running a concession stand were so high that Tom's profits proved *illusory*.

immutable ADJ. unchangeable. All things change over time; nothing is *immutable*.

impair V. injure; hurt. Drinking alcohol can *impair* your ability to drive safely; if you're going to drink, don't drive.

impeccable ADJ. faultless. The uncrowned queen of the fashion industry, Diana was acclaimed for her *impeccable* taste.

impede V. hinder; block; delay. A series of accidents *impeded* the launching of the space shuttle.

implausible ADJ. unlikely; unbelievable. Though her alibi seemed *implausible*, it turned out to be true.

implement V. put into effect; supply with tools. The mayor was unwilling to *implement* the plan until she was sure it had the governor's backing. also N.

impudence N. impertinence; insolence. Kissed on the cheek by a perfect stranger, Lady Catherine exclaimed, "Of all the nerve! Young man, I should have you horse-whipped for your *impudence*."

inadvertent ADJ. unintentional; careless or heedless. Elizabeth, I am sure your omission from the guest list was *inadvertent:* Darcy would never intentionally slight you so.

ADJ. silly; senseless. There's no point in what you're saying. Why are you bothering to make such *inane* remarks?

incisive ADJ. cutting; sharp. His *incisive* remarks made us see the fallacy in our plans.

incite V. arouse to action. The demagogue *incited* the mob to take action into its own hands.

inclusive ADJ. tending to include all. The comedian turned down the invitation to join the Players' Club, saying any club that would let him in was too *inclusive* for him.

incongruous ADJ. not fitting; absurd. Dave saw nothing *incongruous* about wearing sneakers with his tuxedo; he couldn't understand why his date took one look at him and started to laugh. incongruity, N.

inconsequential ADJ. insignificant; unimportant. Brushing off Ali's apologies for having broken the wine glass, Tamara said, "Don't worry about it; it's *inconsequential.*"

incorrigible ADJ. uncorrectable. Though Widow Douglass hoped to reform Huck, Miss Watson pronounced him *incorrigible* and said he would come to no good end.

indict V. charge. If the grand jury *indicts* the suspect, he will go to trial. indictment, N.

indifferent ADJ. unmoved; lacking concern. Because she felt no desire to marry, she was *indifferent* to his constant proposals.

indiscriminate ADJ. choosing at random; confused. She disapproved of her son's *indiscriminate* television viewing and decided to restrict him to educational programs.

induce V. persuade; bring about. After the quarrel, Tina said nothing could *induce* her to talk to Tony again. inducement, N.

inert ADJ. inactive; lacking power to move. "Get up, you lazybones," she cried to her husband, who lay in bed *inert.* inertia, N.

ingenious ADJ. clever; resourceful. Kit admired the *ingenious* way that her computer keyboard opened up to reveal the built-in CD-ROM. ingenuity, N.

inherent ADJ. firmly established by nature or habit. Katya's *inherent* love of justice caused her to champion anyone she considered treated unfairly by society.

innate ADJ. inborn. Mozart's parents soon recognized young Wolfgang's *innate* talent for music.

innocuous ADJ. harmless. An occasional glass of wine with dinner is relatively *innocuous* and should have no ill effect on you.

innovation N. change; introduction of something new. She loved *innovations* just because they were new. innovate, V.

insipid ADJ. lacking in flavor; dull. Flat prose and flat ginger ale are equally *insipid;* both lack sparkle.

instigate V. urge; start; provoke. Rumors of police corruption led the mayor to *instigate* an investigation into the department's activities.

insularity N. narrow-mindedness; isolation. The *insularity* of the islanders manifested itself in their suspicion of anything foreign. insular, ADJ.

integrity N. uprightness; wholeness. Lincoln, whose personal *integrity* has inspired millions, fought a civil war to maintain the *integrity* of the Republic, that these United States might remain undivided for all time.

intervene V. come between. When close friends get into a fight, be careful if you try to *intervene;* they may join forces to gang up on you.

intimidate V. frighten. I'll learn karate and then those big bullies won't be able to *intimidate* me any more.

intrepid ADJ. fearless. For her *intrepid* conduct nursing the wounded during the war, Florence Nightingale was honored by Queen Victoria.

inundate v. overwhelm; flood; submerge. This semester I am *inundated* with work: you should see the piles of paperwork flooding my desk. Until the great dam was built, the waters of the Nile used to *inundate* the river valley like clockwork every year.

invert v. turn upside down or inside out. When he *inverted* his body in a hand stand, he felt the blood rush to his head.

ironic ADJ. resulting in an unexpected and contrary manner. It is *ironic* that his success came when he least wanted it.

lament v. grieve; express sorrow. Even advocates of the war *lamented* the loss of so many lives in combat. lamentation, N.

laud v. praise. The Soviet premier *lauded* the heroic efforts of the rescue workers after the Armenian earthquake. laudable, laudatory, ADJ.

lavish ADJ. liberal; wasteful. The actor's *lavish* gifts pleased her. also v.

lethargic ADJ. drowsy; dull. The stuffy room made her *lethargic:* she felt as if she was about to nod off.

levity N. lack of seriousness; lightness. Stop giggling and wriggling around in your seats; such *levity* is improper in church.

linger v. loiter or dawdle; continue or persist. Hoping to see Juliet pass by, Romeo *lingered* outside the Capulet house for hours. Though Mother made stuffed cabbage on Monday, the smell *lingered* around the house for days.

listless ADJ. lacking in spirit or energy. We had expected him to be full of enthusiasm and were surprised by his *listless* attitude.

lofty ADJ. very high. Though Barbara Jordan's fellow students used to tease her about her *lofty* ambitions, she rose to hold one of the highest positions in the land.

malicious ADJ. hateful; spiteful. Jealous of Cinderella's beauty, her *malicious* stepsisters expressed their spite by forcing her to do menial tasks. malice, N.

marred ADJ. damaged; disfigured. She had to refinish the *marred* surface of the table. mar, v.

materialism N. preoccupation with physical comforts and things. By its nature, *materialism* is opposed to idealism, for where the *materialist* emphasizes the needs of the body, the idealist emphasizes the needs of the soul.

methodical ADJ. systematic. An accountant must be *methodical* and maintain order among his financial records.

meticulous ADJ. excessively careful; painstaking; scrupulous. Martha Stewart was a *meticulous* housekeeper, fussing about each and every detail that went into making up her perfect home.

miserly ADJ. stingy; mean. The *miserly* old man hoarded his coins not out of prudence but out of greed. miser, N.

mitigate v. appease. Nothing he did could *mitigate* her wrath; she was unforgiving.

morose ADJ. ill-humored; sullen; melancholy. Forced to take early retirement, Bill acted *morose* for months until he shook off his sullen mood and reverted to his usual cheerful self.

mundane ADJ. worldly as opposed to spiritual; everyday. Uninterested in philosophical questions, Tom talked only of *mundane* matters such as the latest basketball results.

negate v. cancel out; nullify; deny. A sudden surge of adrenalin can *negate* the effects of fatigue: there's nothing like a good shock to wake you up.

nonchalance N. indifference; lack of concern; composure. Cool, calm, and collected under fire, James Bond shows remarkable *nonchalance* in the face of danger.

notoriety N. disrepute; ill fame. To the starlet, any publicity was good publicity: if she couldn't have a good reputation, she'd settle for *notoriety*. notorious, ADJ.

novelty N. something new; newness. The computer is no longer a *novelty* around the office. novel, ADJ.

nurture V. nourish; educate; foster. The Head Start program attempts to *nurture* pre-kindergarten children so that they will do well when they enter public school. also N.

obliterate V. destroy completely. The tidal wave *obliterated* several island villages.

oblivion N. forgetfulness. Her works had fallen into a state of *oblivion;* no one bothered to read them. oblivious, ADJ.

obscure V. darken; make unclear. At times he seemed purposely to *obscure* his meaning, preferring mystery to clarity.

obstinate ADJ. stubborn. We tried to persuade him to give up smoking, but he was *obstinate* and refused to change.

ominous ADJ. threatening. These clouds are *ominous;* they suggest a severe storm is on the way.

opaque ADJ. dark; not transparent. The *opaque* window shade kept the sunlight out of the room. opacity, N.

opportunist N. individual who sacrifices principles for expediency by taking advantage of circumstances. Forget ethics! He's such an *opportunist* that he'll vote in favor of any deal that will give him a break.

optimist N. person who looks on the good side. The pessimist says the glass is half-empty; the *optimist* says it is half-full.

opulence N. extreme wealth; luxuriousness; abundance. The glitter and *opulence* of the ballroom took Cinderella's breath away. opulent, ADJ.

orator N. public speaker. The abolitionist Frederick Douglass was a brilliant *orator* whose speeches centered on the evils of slavery.

ostentatious ADJ. showy; pretentious; trying to attract attention. Trump's latest casino in Atlantic City is the most *ostentatious* gambling palace in the East; it easily outglitters its competitors. ostentation, N.

pacifist N. one opposed to force; antimilitarist. The *pacifists* urged that we reduce our military budget and recall our troops stationed overseas.

partisan ADJ. one-sided; prejudiced; committed to a party. On certain issues of conscience, she refused to take a *partisan* stand. also N.

peripheral ADJ. marginal; outer. We lived, not in central London, but in one of those *peripheral* suburbs that spring up on the outskirts of a great city.

perpetuate V. make something last; preserve from extinction. Some critics attack *The Adventures of Huckleberry Finn* because they believe Twain's book *perpetuates* a false image of Blacks in this country.

pervasive ADJ. permeating; spread throughout every part. Despite airing them for several hours, she could not rid her clothes of the *pervasive* odor of mothballs that clung to them. pervade, v.

pessimism N. belief that life is basically bad or evil; gloominess. The good news we have been receiving lately indicates that there is little reason for your *pessimism.*

phenomena N. observable facts; subjects of scientific investigation. We kept careful records of the *phenomena* we noted in the course of these experiments.

philanthropist N. lover of mankind; doer of good. As he grew older, he became famous as a *philanthropist* and benefactor of the needy.

piety N. religious devotion; godliness. The nuns in the convent were noted for their *piety;* they spent their days in worship and prayer. pious, ADJ.

placate V. pacify; conciliate. The store manager tried to *placate* the angry customer.

ponderous ADJ. weighty; unwieldy. His humor lacked the light touch; his jokes were always *ponderous.*

pragmatic ADJ. practical (as opposed to idealistic); concerned with the practical worth or impact of something. This coming trip to France should provide me with a *pragmatic* test of the value of my conversational French class.

preclude v. make impossible; eliminate. The fact that the band was already booked to play in Hollywood on New Year's Eve *precluded* their accepting the New Year's Eve gig in London they were offered.

precocious ADJ. advanced in development. Listening to the grown-up way the child discussed serious topics, we couldn't help remarking how *precocious* she was. precocity, N.

predator N. creature that seizes and devours another animal; person who robs or exploits others. A wide variety of *predators*—cats, owls, hawks— catch mice for dinner. A carnivore is by definition *predatory*, for he *preys* on weaker creatures.

predecessor N. former occupant of a post. I hope I can live up to the fine example set by my late *predecessor* in this office.

presumptuous ADJ. arrogant; taking liberties. It seems *presumptuous* for one so relatively new to the field to challenge the conclusions of its leading experts. presumption, N.

pretentious ADJ. ostentatious; pompous; making unjustified claims; overly ambitious. None of the other prize winners are wearing their medals; isn't it a bit *pretentious* of you to wear yours?

prevalent ADJ. widespread; generally accepted. A radical committed to social change, Reed had no patience with the conservative views *prevalent* in the America of his day.

prodigal ADJ. wasteful; reckless with money. The *prodigal* son squandered his inheritance. also N.

profane v. violate; desecrate. Tourists are urged not to *profane* the sanctity of holy places by wearing improper garb. also ADJ.

profound ADJ. deep; not superficial; complete. Freud's remarkable insights into human behavior caused his fellow scientists to honor him as a *profound* thinker. profundity, N.

profusion N. lavish expenditure; overabundant condition. Seldom have I seen food and drink served in such *profusion* as at the wedding feast.

proliferation N. rapid growth; spread; multiplication. Times of economic hardship inevitably encourage the *proliferation* of countless get-rich-quick schemes. proliferate, V.

prolific ADJ. abundantly fruitful. She was a *prolific* writer and wrote as many as three books a year.

provincial ADJ. pertaining to a province; limited in outlook; unsophisticated. As *provincial* governor, Sir Henry administered the Queen's law in his remote corner of Canada. Caught up in local problems, out of touch with London news, he became sadly *provincial*.

proximity N. nearness. The deer sensed the hunter's *proximity* and bounded away.

prudent ADJ. cautious; careful. A miser hoards money not because he is *prudent* but because he is greedy. prudence, N.

qualified ADJ. limited; restricted. Unable to give the candidate full support, the mayor gave him only a *qualified* endorsement. (secondary meaning)

quandary N. dilemma. When both Harvard and Stanford accepted Laura, she was in a *quandary* as to which school she should attend.

ramble V. wander aimlessly (physically or mentally). Listening to the teacher *ramble*, Judy wondered whether he'd ever get to his point.

rancor N. bitterness; hatred. Thirty years after the war, she could not let go of the past but was still consumed with *rancor* against the foe.

ratify V. approve formally; verify. Before the treaty could go into effect, it had to be *ratified* by the president.

rebuttal N. refutation; response with contrary evidence. The defense lawyer confidently listened to the prosecutor sum up his case, sure that she could answer his arguments in her *rebuttal*.

recluse N. hermit; loner. Disappointed in love, Miss Emily became a *recluse*; she shut herself away in her empty mansion and refused to see another living soul. reclusive, ADJ.

recount v. narrate or tell; count over again. A born storyteller, my father loved to *recount* anecdotes about his early years in New York.

rectify v. set right; correct. You had better send a check to *rectify* your account before American Express cancels your credit card.

redundant ADJ. superfluous; excessively wordy; repetitious. Your composition is *redundant;* you can easily reduce its length. redundancy, N.

refute v. disprove. The defense called several respectable witnesses who were able to *refute* the false testimony of the prosecution's only witness.

relegate v. banish to an inferior position; delegate; assign. After Ralph dropped his second tray of drinks that week, the manager swiftly *relegated* him to a minor post cleaning up behind the bar.

remorse N. guilt; self-reproach. The murderer felt no *remorse* for his crime.

renounce v. abandon; discontinue; disown; repudiate. Joan of Arc refused to *renounce* her statements even though she knew she would be burned at the stake as a witch.

repel v. drive away; disgust. At first, the Beast's ferocious appearance *repelled* Beauty, but she came to love the tender heart hidden behind that beastly exterior.

reprehensible ADJ. deserving blame. Shocked by the viciousness of the bombing, politicians of every party uniformly condemned the terrorists' *reprehensible* deed.

reprimand v. reprove severely; rebuke. Every time Ermengarde made a mistake in class, she was afraid that Miss Minchin would *reprimand* her and tell her father how badly she was doing in school. also N.

reprove v. censure; rebuke. The principal *reproved* the students when they became unruly in the auditorium. reproof, N.

repudiate v. disown; disavow. He announced that he would *repudiate* all debts incurred by his wife.

reserve N. self-control; formal but distant manner. Although some girls were attracted by Mark's air of *reserve,* Judy was put off by it, for she felt his aloofness indicated a lack of openness. reserved, ADJ.

resigned ADJ. unresisting; patiently submissive. Bob Cratchit was too *resigned* to his downtrodden existence to protest Scrooge's bullying. resignation, N.

resolution N. determination; resolve. Nothing could shake his *resolution* that his children would get the best education possible. resolute, ADJ.

resolve N. determination; firmness of purpose. How dare you question my *resolve* to take up skydiving! Of course I haven't changed my mind!

restraint N. moderation or self-control; controlling force; restriction. Control yourself, young lady! Show some *restraint!*

reticence N. reserve; uncommunicativeness; inclination to silence. Fearing his competitors might get advance word about his plans from talkative staff members, Hughes preferred *reticence* from his employees to loquacity.

retract v. withdraw; take back. He dropped his libel suit after the newspaper finally *retracted* its statement. retraction, N.

reverent ADJ. respectful; worshipful. Though I bow my head in church and recite the prayers, sometimes I don't feel properly *reverent.* revere, v.

rhetorical ADJ. pertaining to effective communication; insincere in language. To win his audience, the speaker used every *rhetorical* trick in the book.

rigor N. severity. Many settlers could not stand the *rigors* of the harsh New England winters.

robust ADJ. vigorous; strong. After pumping iron and taking karate for six months, the little old lady was far more *robust* in health and could break a plank with her fist.

sage N. person celebrated for wisdom. Hearing tales of a mysterious Master of All Knowledge who lived in the hills of Tibet, Sandy was possessed with a burning desire to consult the legendary *sage.* also ADJ.

sanction v. approve; ratify. Nothing will convince me to *sanction* the engagement of my daughter to such a worthless young man.

satirical ADJ. mocking. The humor of cartoonist Gary Trudeau often is *satirical;* through the comments of the Doonesbury characters, Trudeau ridicules political corruption and folly.

saturate v. soak thoroughly. *Saturate* your sponge with water until it can't hold any more.

scanty ADJ. meager; insufficient. Thinking his helping of food was *scanty,* Oliver Twist asked for more.

scrupulous ADJ. conscientious; extremely thorough. Though Alfred is *scrupulous* in fulfilling his duties at work, he is less conscientious about his obligations to his family and friends.

scrutinize v. examine closely and critically. Searching for flaws, the sergeant *scrutinized* every detail of the private's uniform.

seclusion N. isolation; solitude. One moment she loved crowds; the next, she sought *seclusion.*

servile ADJ. slavishly submissive; fawning; cringing. Constantly fawning on his employer, Uriah Heep was a *servile* creature.

skeptic N. doubter; person who suspends judgment until the evidence supporting a point of view has been examined. I am a *skeptic* about the new health plan; I want some proof that it can work. skepticism, N.

sluggish ADJ. slow; lazy; lethargic. After two nights without sleep, she felt *sluggish* and incapable of exertion.

somber ADJ. gloomy; depressing. From the doctor's grim expression, I could tell he had *somber* news.

sporadic ADJ. occurring irregularly. Although you can still hear *sporadic* outbursts of laughter and singing outside, the big Halloween parade has passed; the party's over till next year.

squander v. waste. The prodigal son *squandered* the family estate.

stagnant ADJ. motionless; stale; dull. The *stagnant* water was a breeding ground for disease. stagnate, V.

static ADJ. unchanging; lacking development. Nothing had changed at home; things were *static*. stasis, N.

submissive ADJ. yielding; timid. Crushed by his authoritarian father, Will had no defiance left in him; he was totally *submissive* in the face of authority.

subordinate ADJ. occupying a lower rank; inferior; submissive. Bishop Proudie's wife expected the *subordinate* clergy to behave with great deference to her.

subside V. settle down; descend; grow quiet. The doctor assured us that the fever would eventually *subside*.

substantiate V. establish by evidence; verify; support. These endorsements from satisfied customers *substantiate* our claim that Barron's *How to Prepare for SAT I* is the best SAT-prep book on the market.

succinct ADJ. brief; terse; compact. Don't bore your audience with excess verbiage: be *succinct*.

superficial ADJ. trivial; shallow. Since your report gave only a *superficial* analysis of the problem, I cannot give you more than a passing grade.

superfluous ADJ. excessive; overabundant; unnecessary. Please try not to include so many *superfluous* details in your report; just give me the bare facts. superfluity, N.

surpass V. exceed. Her SAT I scores *surpassed* our expectations.

surreptitious ADJ. secret; furtive; sneaky; hidden. Hoping to discover where his mom had hidden the Christmas presents, Timmy took a *surreptitious* peek into the master bedroom closet.

susceptible ADJ. impressionable; easily influenced; having little resistance, as to a disease; receptive to. Said the patent medicine man to his very *susceptible* customer: "Buy this new miracle drug, and you will no longer be *susceptible* to the common cold."

sustain v. experience; support; nourish. He *sustained* such a severe injury that the doctors feared he would be unable to work to *sustain* his growing family.

sycophant N. servile flatterer; bootlicker; yes man. Fed up with the toadies and flunkies who made up his entourage, the star cried, "Get out, all of you! I'm sick of *sycophants*!" sycophancy, N.

taciturn ADJ. habitually silent; talking iittle. The stereotypical cowboy is a *taciturn* soul, answering lengthy questions with a "Yep" or "Nope."

temper v. moderate; restrain; tone down or toughen (steel). Not even her supervisor's grumpiness could *temper* Nancy's enthusiasm for her new job.

tentative ADJ. provisional; experimental. Your *tentative* plans sound plausible; let me know when the final details are worked out.

terse ADJ. concise; abrupt; pithy. There is a fine line between speech that is *terse* and to the point and speech that is too abrupt.

thrive v. prosper; flourish. Despite the impact of the recession on the restaurant trade, Philip's cafe *thrived*.

tranquillity N. calmness; peace. After the commotion and excitement of the city, I appreciate the *tranquillity* of these fields and forests.

transient ADJ. momentary; temporary; staying for a short time. Ann's joy at finding the perfect Christmas gift for Phil was *transient*; she still had to find presents for her cousins. Located near the airport, this hotel caters to a largely *transient* trade.

trite ADJ. hackneyed; commonplace. The *trite* and predictable situations in many television programs turn off many viewers, who, in turn, turn off their sets.

turbulence N. state of violent agitation. We were frightened by the *turbulence* of the ocean during the storm.

turmoil N. great commotion and confusion. Lydia running off with a soldier! Mother fainting at the news! The Bennet household was in *turmoil.*

undermine V. weaken; sap. The recent corruption scandals have *undermined* many people's faith in the city government. The recent torrential rains have washed away much of the cliffside; the deluge threatens to *undermine* the pillars supporting several houses at the edge of the cliff.

uniformity N. sameness; monotony. After a while, the *uniformity* of TV situation comedies becomes boring.

unwarranted ADJ. unjustified; groundless; undeserved. We could not understand Martin's *unwarranted* rudeness to his mother's guests.

usurp V. seize another's power or rank. The revolution ended when the victorious rebel general succeeded in his attempt to *usurp* the throne.

vacillate V. waver; fluctuate. Uncertain which suitor she ought to marry, the princess *vacillated*, saying now one, now the other. The boss likes his staff to be decisive. When he asks for your opinion, whatever you do, don't *vacillate.* vacillation, N.

venerate V. revere. In Tibet today, the common people still *venerate* their traditional spiritual leader, the Dalai Lama.

verbose ADJ. wordy. This article is too *verbose;* we must edit it.

vigor N. active strength. Although he was over seventy years old, Jack had the *vigor* of a man in his prime. vigorous, ADJ.

vilify V. slander. Refusing to wage a negative campaign, the candidate would not stoop to *vilifying* his opponent's reputation. vilification, N.

vindicate V. clear from blame; exonerate; justify or support. The lawyer's goal was to *vindicate* her client and prove him innocent on all charges. The critics' extremely favorable reviews *vindicate* my opinion that *The Full Monty* is a brilliant movie.

virtuoso N. highly skilled artist. The child prodigy Yehudi Menuhin grew into a *virtuoso* whose violin performances thrilled millions. virtuosity, N.

volatile ADJ. changeable; explosive; evaporating rapidly. The political climate today is extremely *volatile;* no one can predict what the electorate will do next. Ethyl chloride is an extremely *volatile* liquid; it evaporates instantly.

whimsical ADJ. capricious; fanciful. He dismissed his generous gift to his college as a sentimental fancy, an old man's *whimsical* gesture.

zealot N. fanatic; person who shows excessive zeal. Though Glenn was devout, he was no *zealot;* he never tried to force his beliefs on his friends.

5 The Mathematics Sections: Strategies, Tips, and Practice

The College Board considers the SAT I to be "a test of general reasoning abilities." It attempts to use basic concepts of arithmetic, algebra, and geometry as a method of testing your ability to think logically. The Board is not testing whether you know how to calculate an average, find the area of a circle, use the Pythagorean theorem, or read a bar graph. *It assumes you can*. In fact, because the Board is not even interested in testing your memory, most of the formulas you will need are listed at the beginning of each math section. In other words, the College Board's objective is to use your familiarity with numbers and geometric figures as a way of testing your *logical thinking skills*.

Most of the arithmetic that you need to know for the SAT I is taught in elementary school, and much of the other material is taught in middle school or junior high school. The only high school math that you need is some elementary algebra and a little basic geometry. To do well on the SAT I, you must know this basic material. But that's not enough. You have to be able to use these concepts in ways that may be unfamiliar to you. That's where the test-taking tactics come in.

THE USE OF CALCULATORS ON THE SAT I

There isn't a single question on any section of the SAT I for which a calculator is required. In fact, on most questions a calculator is completely useless. There are several questions, however, for which a calculator *could* be used; and since calculators are permitted, you should definitely bring one with you when you take the SAT I.

If you forget to bring a calculator to the actual test, you will not be able to use one, since none will be provided and you will not be allowed to share one with a friend. For the same reason, be sure that you have new batteries in your calculator or that you bring a spare, because if your calculator fails during the test, you will have to finish without one.

What Calculator Should You Use?

Almost any four-function, scientific, or graphic calculator is acceptable. Since you don't "need" a calculator at all, you don't "need" any particular type. There is absolutely no advantage to having a graphic calculator; but we do recommend a scientific calculator, since it is occasionally useful to have parentheses keys, ( ); a reciprocal key, $\frac{1}{x}$; and an exponent key, y^x or $\wedge$. All scientific calculators have these features. If you tend to make mistakes in working with fractions, you may want to get a calculator that can do fractional arithmetic. With such a calculator, for example, you can add $\frac{1}{3}$ and $\frac{1}{5}$ by entering 1 / 3 + 1 / 5; the readout will be 8/15, not the decimal 0.5333333. Some, but not most, scientific calculators have this capability.

When Should Calculators Be Used?

If you have strong math skills and are a good test-taker, you will probably use your calculator infrequently, if at all.

On the other hand, if you are less confident about your mathematical ability or your test-taking skills, you will probably find your calculator a useful tool.

Throughout this book, the icon will be placed next to a problem where the use of a calculator is recommended. As you will see, this judgment is very subjective. Sometimes a question can be answered in a few seconds, with no calculations whatsoever, if you see the best approach. In that case, the use of a calculator is not recommended. If you don't see the easy way, however, and have to do some arithmetic, you may prefer to use a calculator.

Let's look at a few sample questions on which some students would use calculators a lot, others a little, and still others not at all.

Example 1.

If $16 \times 25 \times 36 = (4a)^2$, what is the value of a?

(A) 6   (B) 15   (C) 30   (D) 36   (E) 60

 (i)   **Heavy calculator use:** WITH A CALCULATOR multiply: $16 \times 25 \times 36 = 14{,}400$. Observe that $(4a)^2 = 16a^2$, and so $16a^2 = 14{,}400$. WITH A CALCULATOR divide: $a^2 = 14{,}400 \div 16 = 900$. Finally, WITH A CALCULATOR take the square root: $a = \sqrt{900} = 30$. The answer is **C**.

 (ii)   **Light calculator use:** Immediately notice that you can "cancel" the 16 on the left-hand side with the 4^2 on the right-hand side. WITH A CALCULATOR multiply: $25 \times 36 = 900$, and WITH A CALCULATOR take the square root of 900: $\sqrt{900} = 30$.

(iii) **No calculator use:** "Cancel" the 16 and the 4^2. Notice that $25 = 5^2$ and $36 = 6^2$, so $a^2 = 5^2 \times 6^2 = 30^2$, and $a = 30$.

Example 2 (Grid-in).

If the length of a diagonal of a rectangle is 13, and if one of the sides is 5, what is the perimeter?

Whether you intend to use your calculator a lot, a little, or not at all, the first thing to do is to draw a diagram.

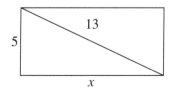

 (i)   **Heavy calculator use:** By the Pythagorean theorem, $x^2 + 5^2 = 13^2$. Observe that $5^2 = 25$, and WITH A CALCULATOR evaluate: $13^2 = 169$. Then WITH A CALCULATOR subtract:

$169 - 25 = 144$, so $x^2 = 144$. Hit the square-root key on your CALCULATOR to get $x = 12$. Finally, WITH A CALCULATOR add to find the perimeter: $5 + 12 + 5 + 12 = \mathbf{34}$.

(ii)   **Light calculator use:** The steps are the same as in (i) except that *some of the calculations* are done mentally: taking the square root of 144 and adding at the end.

(iii)   **No calculator use:** *All calculations* are done mentally. Better yet, *no calculations are done at all,* because you immediately see that each half of the rectangle is a 5-12-13 right triangle, and you add the sides mentally.

	Column A	Column B
Example 3.	$(-15)(-43)$	$(-4)(-9)(-18)$

(i)   **Using a calculator.** Do both multiplications, making sure to enter the negative signs on the CALCULATOR. Compare the answers: 645 versus –648. Column **A** is greater.

(ii)   **No calculator use:** Column A is positive since it is the product of two negative numbers, whereas Column B, which is the product of three negative numbers, is negative.

MEMORIZE IMPORTANT FACTS AND DIRECTIONS

On the first page of every mathematics section of the SAT I, you will see the following mathematical facts (see page 111), though in a slightly different arrangement:

The College Board's official guide, *Taking the SAT I Reasoning Test*, offers the following tip:

> The test doesn't require you to memorize formulas. Commonly used formulas are provided in the test booklet at the beginning of each mathematical section.

If you interpret this to mean "Don't bother memorizing the formulas provided," this is terrible advice. It may be reassuring to know that, if you should forget a basic geometry fact, you can

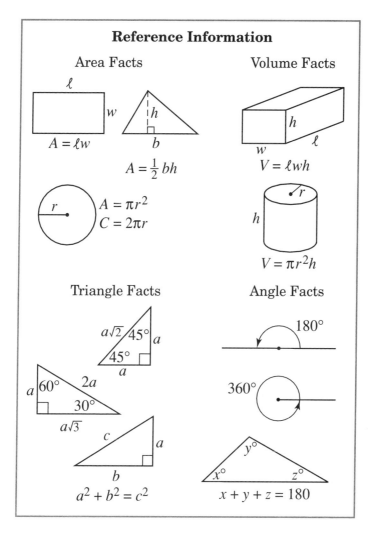

Reference Information

Area Facts

$A = \ell w$

$A = \frac{1}{2} bh$

$A = \pi r^2$
$C = 2\pi r$

Volume Facts

$V = \ell wh$

$V = \pi r^2 h$

Triangle Facts

$a^2 + b^2 = c^2$

Angle Facts

$180°$

$360°$

$x + y + z = 180$

look it up in the box headed "Reference Information," but you should decide right now that you will never have to do that. During the test, you don't want to spend any precious time looking up facts that you can learn now. All of these "commonly used formulas" and other important facts are listed in this chapter. As you learn and review these facts, you should commit them to memory. Also in this chapter you will learn the instructions for the three types of mathematics questions on the SAT I. *They will not change.* They will be exactly the same on the test you take.

Helpful Hint

As you prepare for this test, memorize the directions for each section. *When you take the SAT I, do not waste even one second reading directions.*

AN IMPORTANT SYMBOL

Throughout the book, the symbol "$\Rightarrow$" is used to indicate that one step in the solution of a problem follows *immediately* from the preceding one, and that no explanation is necessary. You should read:

$$2x = 12 \Rightarrow x = 6$$

as $2x = 12$ *implies* (or *which implies*) *that* $x = 6$, or, *since* $2x = 12$, then $x = 6$.

Here is a sample solution, using $\Rightarrow$, to the following problem:

What is the value of $3x^2 - 7$ when $x = -5$?

$$x = -5 \Rightarrow x^2 = (-5)^2 = 25 \Rightarrow 3x^2 = 3(25) = 75 \Rightarrow$$
$$3x^2 - 7 = 75 - 7 = \mathbf{68}.$$

When the reason for a step is not obvious, $\Rightarrow$ is not used: rather, an explanation is given. In many solutions, some steps are explained, while others are linked by the $\Rightarrow$ symbol, as in the following example:

In the diagram at the right, if $w = 10$, what is z?

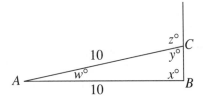

- $w + x + y = 180$.
- Since $\triangle ABC$ is isosceles, $x = y$.

- Therefore, $w + 2y = 180 \Rightarrow 10 + 2y = 180 \Rightarrow$ $2y = 170 \Rightarrow y = 85$.
- Finally, since $y + z = 180$, $85 + z = 180 \Rightarrow z = \mathbf{95}$.

IMPORTANT DEFINITIONS, FACTS, FORMULAS, AND STRATEGIES

1. **Sum:** the result of an addition: 8 is the sum of 6 and 2

2. **Difference:** the result of a subtraction: 4 is the difference of 6 and 2

3. **Product:** the result of a multiplication: 12 is the product of 6 and 2

4. **Quotient:** the result of a division: 3 is the quotient of 6 and 2

5. **Remainder:** when 15 is divided by 6, the quotient is 2 and the remainder is 3: $15 = 6 \times 2 + 3$

6. **Integers:** $\{\ldots, -3, -2, -1, 0, 1, 2, 3, \ldots\}$

7. **Factor** or **Divisor:** any integer that leaves no remainder (i.e., a remainder of 0) when it is divided into another integer: 1, 2, 5, 10 are the factors (or divisors) of 10

8. **Multiple:** the product of one integer by a second integer: 7, 14, 21, 28, ... are multiples of 7 ($7 = 1 \times 7$, $14 = 2 \times 7$, and so on)

9. **Even integers:** the multiples of 2: $\{\ldots, -4, -2, 0, 2, 4, \ldots\}$

10. **Odd integers:** the non-multiples of 2: $\{\ldots, -3, -1, 1, 3, 5, \ldots\}$

11. **Consecutive integers:** two or more integers, written in sequence, each of which is 1 more than the preceding one. For example:

    $$7, 8, 9 \qquad -2, -1, 0, 1, 2 \qquad n, n + 1, n + 2$$

12. **Prime number:** a positive integer that has exactly two divisors. The first few primes are 2, 3, 5, 7, 11, 13, 17. (*not* 1)

13. **Exponent:** a number written as a superscript: the 3 in 7^3. On the SAT I, the only exponents you need to know about are positive integers: $2^n = 2 \times 2 \times 2 \times \ldots \times 2$, where 2 appears as a factor n times.

14. **Laws of Exponents:**

    For any numbers b and c and positive integers m and n:

    (i) $b^m b^n = b^{m+n}$ (ii) $\dfrac{b^m}{b^n} = b^{m-n}$ (iii) $(b^m)^n = b^{mn}$

    (iv) $b^m c^m = (bc)^m$

15. **Square root of a positive number:** if a is positive, $\sqrt{a}$ is the only positive number whose square is a: $(\sqrt{a})^2 = \sqrt{a} \times \sqrt{a} = a$

16. The product and the quotient of two positive numbers or two negative numbers are positive; the product and the quotient of a positive number and a negative number are negative.

17. • The product of an *even* number of negative factors is positive.
    • The product of an *odd* number of negative factors is negative.

18. For any positive numbers a and b:

    $$\sqrt{ab} = \sqrt{a} \times \sqrt{b} \quad \text{and} \quad \sqrt{\dfrac{a}{b}} = \dfrac{\sqrt{a}}{\sqrt{b}}$$

19. For any real numbers a, b, and c:

    • $a(b + c) = ab + ac$ • $a(b - c) = ab - ac$

    and, if $a \neq 0$,

    • $\dfrac{b + c}{a} = \dfrac{b}{a} + \dfrac{c}{a}$ • $\dfrac{b - c}{a} = \dfrac{b}{a} - \dfrac{c}{d}$

20. To compare two fractions, use your calculator to convert them to decimals.

21. To multiply two fractions, multiply their numerators and multiply their denominators:

    $$\frac{3}{5} \times \frac{4}{7} = \frac{3 \times 4}{5 \times 7} = \frac{12}{35}$$

22. To divide any number by a fraction, multiply that number by the reciprocal of the fraction.

    $$\frac{3}{5} \div \frac{2}{3} = \frac{3}{5} \times \frac{3}{2} = \frac{9}{10}$$

23. To add or subtract fractions with the same denominator, add or subtract the numerators and keep the denominator:
$$\frac{4}{9} + \frac{1}{9} = \frac{5}{9} \quad \text{and} \quad \frac{4}{9} - \frac{1}{9} = \frac{3}{9} = \frac{1}{3}$$

24. To add or subtract fractions with different denominators, first rewrite the fractions as equivalent fractions with the same denominator:
$$\frac{1}{6} + \frac{3}{4} = \frac{2}{12} + \frac{9}{12} = \frac{11}{12}$$

25. **Percent:** a fraction whose denominator is 100:
$$15\% = \frac{15}{100} = .15$$

26. The *percent increase* of a quantity is
$$\frac{\text{actual increase}}{\text{original amount}} \times 100\%.$$
The *percent decrease* of a quantity is
$$\frac{\text{actual decrease}}{\text{original amount}} \times 100\%.$$

27. **Ratio:** a fraction that compares two quantities that are measured in the same units. The ratio *2 to 3* can be written $\frac{2}{3}$ or 2:3.

28. In any ratio problem, write the letter x after each number and use some given information to solve for x.

29. **Proportion:** an equation that states that two ratios (fractions) are equal. Solve proportions by cross-multiplying: if $\frac{a}{b} = \frac{c}{d}$, then $ad = bc$.

30. **Average of a set of n numbers:** the sum of those numbers divided by n:
$$\text{average} = \frac{\text{sum of the } n \text{ numbers}}{n} \quad \text{or simply}$$
$$A = \frac{\text{sum}}{n}$$

31. If you know the average, A, of a set of n numbers, multiply A by n to get their sum: sum = nA.

32. To multiply two binomials, use the FOIL method: multiply each term in the first parentheses by each term in the second parentheses and simplify by combining terms, if possible.

$$(2x - 7)(3x + 2) = \underbrace{(2x)(3x)}_{\text{First terms}} + \underbrace{(2x)(2)}_{\text{Outer terms}} + \underbrace{(-7)(3x)}_{\text{Inner terms}} + \underbrace{(-7)(2)}_{\text{Last terms}} =$$

$$6x^2 + 4x - 21x - 14 = 6x^2 - 17x - 14$$

33. The three most important binomial products on the SAT I are these:
    - $(x - y)(x + y) = x^2 - y^2$
    - $(x - y)^2 = (x - y)(x - y) = x^2 - 2xy + y^2$
    - $(x + y)^2 = (x + y)(x + y) = x^2 + 2xy + y^2$

34. All distance problems involve one of three variations of the same formula:

$$\text{distance} = \text{rate} \times \text{time} \qquad \text{rate} = \frac{\text{distance}}{\text{time}}$$

$$\text{time} = \frac{\text{distance}}{\text{rate}}$$

35.

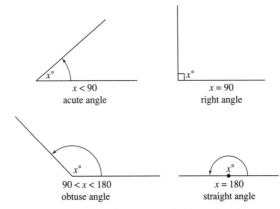

36. If two or more angles form a straight angle, the sum of their measures is 180°.

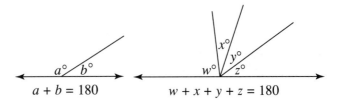

37. The sum of all the measures of all the angles around a point is 360°.

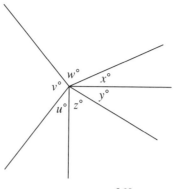

$$u + v + w + x + y + z = 360$$

38.

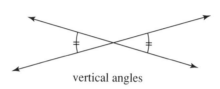

vertical angles

39. Vertical angles have equal measures.

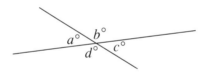

$a = c$ and $b = d$.

40. If a pair of parallel lines is cut by a transversal that is *not* perpendicular to the parallel lines:
    - Four of the angles are acute, and four are obtuse.
    - All four acute angles are equal: $a = c = e = g$.
    - All four obtuse angles are equal: $b = d = f = h$.
    - The sum of any acute angle and any obtuse angle is 180°: for example, $d + e = 180$, $c + f = 180$, $b + g = 180$, ...

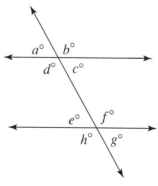

41. In any triangle, the sum of the measures of the three angles is 180°: $x + y + z = 180$.

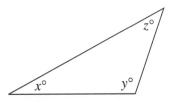

42. The measure of an exterior angle of a triangle is equal to the sum of the measures of the two opposite interior angles.

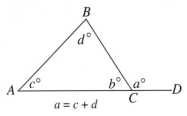

43. In any triangle:
   - the longest side is opposite the largest angle;
   - the shortest side is opposite the smallest angle;
   - sides with the same length are opposite angles with the same measure.

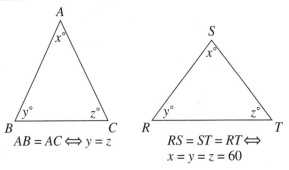

44. In any right triangle, the sum of the measures of the two acute angles is 90°.

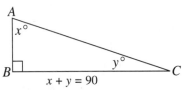

45.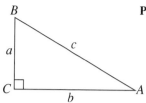

Pythagorean theorem
$$a^2 + b^2 = c^2$$

46. In a 45-45-90 right triangle, the sides are x, x, and $x\sqrt{2}$.

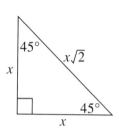

47. In a 30-60-90 right triangle the sides are x, $x\sqrt{3}$, and $2x$.

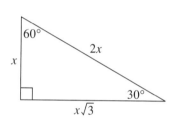

48. The sum of the lengths of any two sides of a triangle is greater than the length of the third side.

The difference between the lengths of any two sides of a triangle is less than the length of the third side.

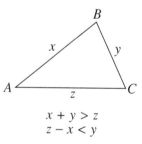

$$x + y > z$$
$$z - x < y$$

49. The area of a triangle is given by $A = \frac{1}{2}bh$, where b = base and h = height.

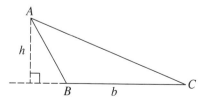

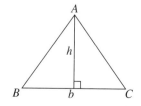

50. If A represents the area of an equilateral triangle with side s, then $A = \dfrac{s^2\sqrt{3}}{4}$.

51. In any quadrilateral, the sum of the measures of the four angles is 360°.

52. A ***parallelogram*** is a quadrilateral in which both pairs of opposite sides are parallel. A ***rectangle*** is a parallelogram in which all four angles are right angles. A ***square*** is a rectangle in which all four sides have the same length.

53. In any parallelogram:
    - Opposite sides are equal: $AB = CD$ and $AD = BC$.
    - Opposite angles are equal: $a = c$ and $b = d$.
    - Consecutive angles add up to 180°: $a + b = 180$, $b + c = 180$, and so on.
    - The two diagonals bisect each other: $AE = EC$ and $BE = ED$.

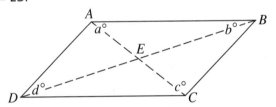

54. In any rectangle:
    - The measure of each angle in a rectangle is 90°.
    - The diagonals of a rectangle have the same length: $AC = BD$.

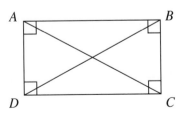

55. In any square:
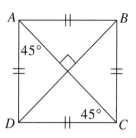

- All four sides have the same length.
- Each diagonal divides the square into two 45-45-90 right triangles.
- The diagonals are perpendicular to each other: $AC \perp BD$.

56. **Formulas for perimeter and area:**

- For a parallelogram: $A = bh$ and $P = 2(a + b)$.
- For a rectangle: $A = \ell w$ and $P = 2(\ell + w)$.
- For a square: $A = s^2$ or $A = \frac{1}{2}d^2$ and $P = 4s$.

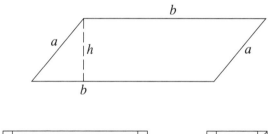

57. Let r be the radius, d the diameter, C the circumference, and A the area of a circle, then

$$d = 2r \quad C = \pi d = 2\pi r \quad A = \pi r^2$$

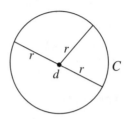

58. The formula for the volume of a rectangular solid is $V = \ell wh$.

In a cube, all the edges are equal. Therefore, if e is the edge, the formula for the volume is $V = e^3$.

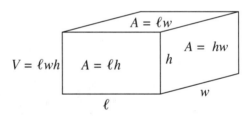

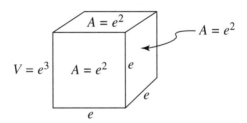

59. The formula for the surface area of a rectangular solid is $A = 2(\ell w + \ell h + wh)$. The formula for the surface area of a cube is $A = 6e^2$.

60. The formula for the volume, V, of a cylinder is $V = \pi r^2 h$. The surface area, A, of the side of the cylinder is $A = 2\pi rh$. The area of the top and bottom are each πr^2.

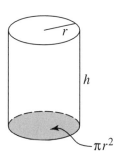

61. The distance, d, between two points, $A(x_1, y_1)$ and $B(x_2, y_2)$, can be calculated using the distance formula:
$$d = \sqrt{(x_2 - x_1)^2 + (y_2 - y_1)^2}$$

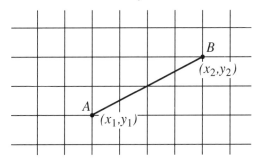

62. The slope of the line is given by:
$$\text{slope} = \frac{y_2 - y_1}{x_2 - x_1}$$

63. • The slope of any horizontal line is 0.
    • The slope of any line that goes up as you move from left to right is positive.
    • The slope of any line that goes down as you move from left to right is negative.

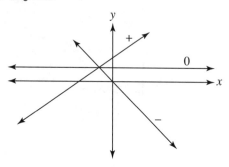

64. **The Counting Principle:** If two jobs need to be completed and there are m ways to do the first job and n ways to do the second job, then there are $m \times n$ ways to do one job followed by the other. This principle can be extended to any number of jobs.

65. If E is any event, the **probability** that E will occur is given by

$$P(E) = \frac{\text{number of favorable outcomes}}{\text{total number of possible outcomes}},$$

assuming that all of the possible outcomes are equally likely.

66.–69. Let E be an event, and let $P(E)$ be the probability that it will occur.

66. If E is *impossible,* then **$P(E) = 0$**.

67. If it is *certain* that E will occur, then **$P(E) = 1$**.

68. In all other cases, **$0 < P(E) < 1$**.

69. The probability that event E will *not* occur is **$1 - P(E)$**.

70. If an experiment is done 2 (or more) times, the probability that first one event will occur, and then a second event will occur, is the product of the probabilities.

GENERAL MATH STRATEGIES

Later in this chapter, you will learn tactics that will help you with the three specific types of math questions on the SAT I. In this section you will learn several important strategies that can be used on any of these questions. Mastering these tactics will improve your performance on all mathematics tests.

Testing Tactics

1. Draw a Diagram.

On any geometry question for which a figure is not provided, draw one (as accurately as possible) in your test booklet.

Let's consider some examples.

Example 1.

What is the area of a rectangle whose length is twice its width and whose perimeter is equal to that of a square whose area is 1?

Solution. Don't even think of answering this question until you have drawn a square and a rectangle and labeled each of them: each side of the square is 1; and if the width of the rectangle is w, its length is $2w$.

Now, write the required equation and solve it:

$$6w = 4 \Rightarrow w = \frac{4}{6} = \frac{2}{3} \Rightarrow 2w = \frac{4}{3}$$

The area of the rectangle $= lw = \left(\frac{4}{3}\right)\left(\frac{2}{3}\right) = \frac{8}{9}$.

Drawings should not be limited, however, to geometry questions; there are many other questions on which drawings will help.

Example 2.

A jar contains 10 red marbles and 30 green ones. How many red marbles must be added to the jar so that 60% of the marbles will be red?

Solution. Draw a diagram and label it. From the diagram it is clear that there are now $40 + x$ marbles in the jar, of which $10 + x$ are red. Since we want the fraction of red marbles to be

60% $\left(= \dfrac{3}{5}\right)$, we have $\dfrac{10 + x}{40 + x} = \dfrac{3}{5}$.

x	Red
30	Green
10	Red

Cross-multiplying, we get:

$$50 + 5x = 120 + 3x \Rightarrow 2x = 70 \Rightarrow x = \mathbf{35}.$$

Of course, you could have set up the equation and solved it without the diagram, but the drawing makes the solution easier and you are less likely to make a careless mistake.

2. If a Diagram Is Drawn to Scale, Trust It, and Use Your Eyes.

Remember that every diagram that appears on the SAT I has been drawn as accurately as possible *unless* you see "<u>Note</u>: Figure not drawn to scale" written below it.

For figures that are drawn to scale, the following are true: line segments that appear to be the same length *are* the same length; if an angle clearly looks obtuse, it *is* obtuse; and if one angle appears larger than another, you may assume that it *is* larger.

Example 3.

In the figure at the right, what is the sum of the measures of all of the marked angles?

(A) 360°   (B) 540°
(C) 720°   (D) 900°
(E) 1080°

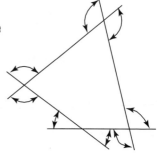

THE MATHEMATICS SECTIONS 127

Solution. Make your best estimate of each angle, and add up the values. The five choices are so far apart that, even if you're off by 15° or more on some of the angles, you'll get the right answer. The sum of the estimates shown is 690°, so the correct answer *must* be 720° **(C)**.

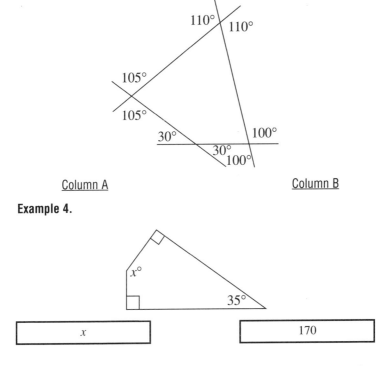

Column A   Column B

Example 4.

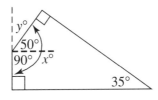

| *x* |

| 170 |

Solution. Since the diagram is drawn to scale, trust it. Look at *x*: it appears to be *about* 90 + 50 = 140; it is *definitely* less than 170.

Also, *y*, drawn above is clearly more than 10, so *x* is less than 170. Choose **B**.

3. If a Diagram Is *Not* drawn to Scale, Redraw It to Scale, and Then Use Your Eyes.

For figures that have not been drawn to scale, you can make *no* assumptions. Lines that look parallel may not be; an angle that appears to be obtuse may, in fact, be acute; two line segments may have the same length even though one looks twice as long as the other.

Example 5.

In △*ACB*, what is the value of *x*?

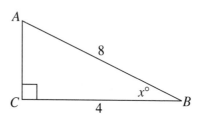

Note: Figure not drawn to scale

(A) 75   (B) 60   (C) 45   (D) 30   (E) 15

Solution. In what way is this figure not drawn to scale? *AB* = 8 and *BC* = 4, but in the figure *AB* is *not* twice as long as *BC*. Redraw the triangle so that *AB is* twice as long as *BC*. Now, just look: *x* is about **60 (B)**.

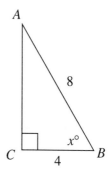

In fact, *x* is exactly 60. If the hypotenuse of a right triangle is twice the length of one of the legs, you have a 30-60-90 triangle, and the angle formed by the hypotenuse and that leg is 60°.

Example 6.

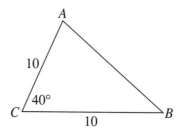

Note: Figure not drawn to scale

AB

10

Solution. In the given diagram, *AB* is longer than *AC*, which is 10, but *we cannot trust the diagram*. Actually, there are two things wrong: ∠*C* is labeled 40°, but looks much more like 60° or 70°, and *AC* and *BC* are each labeled 10, but *BC* is drawn much longer. Use TACTIC 3.
Redraw the triangle with a 40° angle and two sides of the same length. Now, it's clear that *AB* < 10. Choose **B**.

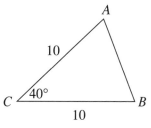

4. Add a Line to a Diagram.

Occasionally, after staring at a diagram, you still have no idea how to solve the problem to which it applies. It looks as though there isn't enough given information. When this happens, it often helps to draw another line in the diagram.

Example 7.

In the figure at the right, *Q* is a point on the circle whose center is *O* and whose radius is *r*, and *OPQR* is a rectangle. What is the length of diagonal *PR*?

(A) r (B) r^2 (C) $\dfrac{r^2}{\pi}$ (D) $\dfrac{r\sqrt{2}}{\pi}$

(E) It cannot be determined from the information given.

Solution. If, after staring at the diagram and thinking about rectangles, circles, and the Pythagorean theorem, you're still lost, don't give up. Ask yourself, "Can I add another line to this diagram?" As soon as you think to draw in *OQ*, the other diagonal, the problem becomes easy: the two diagonals are equal, and, since *OQ* is a radius, it is equal to *r* **(A)**.

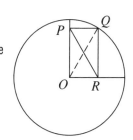

5. Subtract to Find Shaded Regions.

Whenever part of a figure is white and part is shaded, the straightforward way to find the area of the shaded portion is to find the area of the entire figure and then subtract from it the area of the white region. Of course, if you are asked for the area of the white region, you can, instead, subtract the shaded area from the total area. Occasionally, you may see an easy way to calculate the shaded area directly, but usually you should subtract.

Example 8.

In the figure below, *ABCD* is a rectangle, and *BE* and *CF* are arcs of circles centered at *A* and *D*. What is the area of the shaded region?

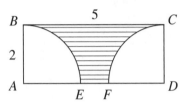

(A) $10 - \pi$ (B) $2(5 - \pi)$ (C) $2(5 - 2\pi)$
(D) $6 + 2\pi$ (E) $5(2 - \pi)$

Solution. The entire region is a 2×5 rectangle whose area is 10. Since each white region is a quarter-circle of radius 2, the combined area of these regions is that of a semicircle of radius 2:

$$\frac{1}{2}\pi(2)^2 = 2\pi.$$

Therefore, the area of the shaded region is $10 - 2\pi = \mathbf{2(5 - \pi)}$ **(B)**.

6. Don't Do More Than You Have To.

Look for shortcuts. Since a problem can often be solved in more than one way, you should always look for the easiest method. Consider the following examples.

Example 9.

If $5(3x - 7) = 20$, what is $3x - 8$?

It's not difficult to solve for *x*:

$$5(3x - 7) = 20 \Rightarrow 15x - 35 = 20 \Rightarrow 15x = 55 \Rightarrow$$
$$x = \frac{55}{15} = \frac{11}{3}$$

But it's too much work. Besides, once you find that $x = \frac{11}{3}$, you still have to multiply to get $3x$: $3\left(\frac{11}{3}\right) = 11$, and then subtract to get $3x - 8$: $11 - 8 = \mathbf{3}$.

Solution. The key is to recognize that you don't need *x*. Finding $3x - 7$ is easy (just divide the original equation by 5), and $3x - 8$ is just 1 less:

$$5(3x - 7) = 20 \Rightarrow 3x - 7 = 4 \Rightarrow 3x - 8 = \mathbf{3}.$$

Column A	Column B

Example 10.

Zach worked from 9:47 A.M. until 12:11 P.M.
Sam worked from 9:11 A.M. until 12:47 P.M.

The number of minutes Zach worked	The number of minutes Sam worked

Solution. Don't spend any time calculating how many minutes either boy worked. You need to know only which column is greater; and since Sam started earlier and finished later, he clearly worked longer. The answer is **B**.

7. Pay Attention to Units.

Often the answer to a question must be in units different from those used in the given data. As you read the question, <u>underline</u> exactly what you are being asked. Do the examiners want hours or minutes or seconds, dollars or cents, feet or inches, meters or centimeters? On multiple-choice questions an answer with the wrong units is almost always one of the choices.

Example 11.

At a speed of 48 miles per hour, how many minutes will be required to drive 32 miles?

(A) $\frac{2}{3}$ (B) $\frac{3}{2}$ (C) 40   (D) 45   (E) 2400

 Solution. This is a relatively easy question. Just be attentive. Since $\frac{32}{48} = \frac{2}{3}$, it will take $\frac{2}{3}$ of an *hour* to drive 32 miles. Choice A is $\frac{2}{3}$; but that is *not* the correct answer because you are asked how many *minutes* will be required. (Did you underline the word "minutes" in the question?) The correct answer is $\frac{2}{3}(60) = $ **40 (C)**.

8. Systematically Make Lists.

When a question asks "how many," often the best strategy is to make a list of all the possibilities. It is important that you make the list in a *systematic* fashion so that you don't inadvertently leave something out. Often, shortly after starting the list, you can see a pattern developing and can figure out how many more entries there will be without writing them all down.

Example 12.

The product of three positive integers is 300. If one of them is 5, what is the least possible value of the sum of the other two?

Solution. Since one of the integers is 5, the product of the other two is 60 ($5 \times 60 = 300$). Systematically, list all possible pairs, (a, b), of positive integers whose product is 60, and check their sums. First, let $a = 1$, then 2, and so on.

a	b	$a + b$
1	60	61
2	30	32
3	20	23
4	15	19
5	12	17
6	10	16

The answer is **16**.

Example 13.

A palindrome is a number, such as 93539, that reads the same forward and backward. How many palindromes are there between 100 and 1000?

Solution. First, write down the numbers in the 100's that end in 1: 101, 111, 121, 131, 141, 151, 161, 171, 181, 191

Now write the numbers beginning and ending in 2: 202, 212, 222, 232, 242, 252, 262, 272, 282, 292

By now you should see the pattern: there are 10 numbers beginning with 1, and 10 beginning with 2, and there will be 10 beginning with 3, 4, ..., 9 for a total of $9 \times 10 =$ **90** palindromes.

9. Handle Strange Symbols Properly.

On almost all SAT I's a few questions use symbols, such as: ⊕, □, ☺, ✠, and ✜, that you have never before seen in a mathematics problem. How can you answer such a question? Don't panic! It's easy; you are always told exactly what the symbol means! All you have to do is follow the directions carefully.

Example 14.

If a ☺ $b = \dfrac{a + b}{a - b}$, what is the value of 25 ☺ 15?

Solution. The definition of "☺" tells us that, whenever two numbers surround a "happy face," we are to form a fraction in which the numerator is the sum of the numbers and the denominator is their difference. Here, 25 ☺ 15 is the fraction whose numerator is 25 + 15 = 40 and whose denominator is 25 − 15 = 10: $\frac{40}{10} = $ **4**.

Sometimes the same symbol is used in two (or even three) questions. In these cases, the first question is easy and involves only numbers; the second is a bit harder and usually contains variables.

Column A	Column B

Examples 15–16 refer to the following definition.

For any real numbers x and y: $x \updownarrow y = x + y^2$

Example 15.

1 $\updownarrow$ 3	6 $\updownarrow$ 2

Example 16.

The number of pairs, (x, y), of positive integers that are solutions of $x \updownarrow y = 10$	2

Solution 15. Column A: $1 + 3^2 = 1 + 9 = 10$
Column B: $6 + 2^2 = 6 + 4 = 10$
The answer is **C**.

Solution 16. Use TACTIC 8: *systematically* list the solutions of $x \updownarrow y = 10$. Start with $y = 1$ and continue:

$$9 + 1^2 = 10; \quad 6 + 2^2 = 10; \quad \text{and} \quad 1 + 3^2 = 10.$$

There are three solutions, so Column **A** is greater.

Example 17.

For any real numbers c and d, $c \boxplus d = c^d + d^c$. What is the value of $1 \boxplus (2 \boxplus 3)$?

Solution. Remember the correct order of operations: always do first what's in the parentheses.

$$2 \boxplus 3 = 2^3 + 3^2 = 8 + 9 = 17$$
$$\text{and}$$
$$1 \boxplus 17 = 1^{17} + 17^1 = 1 + 17 = 18.$$

Grid-in **18**.

Practice Exercises   Answers given on pages 137–140.

Multiple-Choice Questions

1. In the figure at the right, if the radius of circle O is 10, what is the length of diagonal AC of rectangle $OABC$?

(A) $\sqrt{2}$ (B) $\sqrt{10}$ (C) $5\sqrt{2}$

(D) 10   (E) $10\sqrt{2}$

2. In the figure below, $ABCD$ is a square and AED is an equilateral triangle. If $AB = 2$, what is the area of the shaded region?

(A) $\sqrt{3}$ (B) 2   (C) 3   (D) $4 - 2\sqrt{3}$ (E) $4 - \sqrt{3}$

3. If $5x + 13 = 31$, what is the value of $\sqrt{5x + 31}$?

(A) $\sqrt{13}$ (B) $\sqrt{\dfrac{173}{5}}$ (C) 7   (D) 13   (E) 169

4. At Nat's Nuts a $2\frac{1}{4}$-pound bag of pistachio nuts costs $6.00.

At this rate, what is the cost, in cents, of a bag weighing 9 ounces?

(A) 1.5   (B) 24   (C) 150   (D) 1350   (E) 2400

5. In the figure at the right, three circles of radius 1 are tangent to one another. What is the area of the shaded region between the circles?

(A) $\dfrac{\pi}{2} - \sqrt{3}$ (B) 1.5   (C) $\pi - \sqrt{3}$

(D) $\sqrt{3} - \dfrac{\pi}{2}$ (E) $2 - \dfrac{\pi}{2}$

Quantitative Comparison Questions

	Column A	Column B
6.	The number of odd positive factors of 30	The number of even positive factors of 30

Questions 7–8 refer to the following definition.

{a, b} represents the remainder when a is divided by b.

7.	{10^3, 3}	{10^5, 5}

c and d are integers with $c < d$.

8.	{c, d}	{d, c}

Grid-in Questions

9. In writing all of the integers from 1 to 300, how many times is the digit 1 used?

10. If $a + 2b = 14$ and $5a + 4b = 16$, what is the average (arithmetic mean) of a and b?

11. A bag contains 4 marbles, 1 of each color: red, blue, yellow, and green. The marbles are removed at random, 1 at a time. If the first marble is red, what is the probability that the yellow marble is removed before the blue marble?

12. The area of circle O in the figure below is 12. What is the area of the shaded sector?

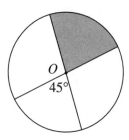

Note: Figure not drawn to scale

Answer Key

| 1. **D** | 3. **C** | 5. **D** | 7. **A** |
| 2. **E** | 4. **C** | 6. **C** | 8. **A** |

9.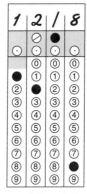

10.

or 2.5

11.

or 1/2 *or* .5

12.

or 3/2 *or* 1.5

Answer Explanations

1. D. Even if you can't solve this problem, don't omit it. Use TACTIC 2: trust the diagram. *AC* is clearly longer than *OC*, and very close to radius *OE*.

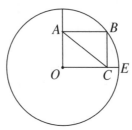

Therefore, *AC* must be about 10. Either by inspection or with your calculator, check the choices. They are approximately as follows:

(A) $\sqrt{2} = 1.4$;   (B) $\sqrt{10} = 3.1$;   (C) $5\sqrt{2} = 7$;

(D) 10;   (E) $10\sqrt{2} = 14$. The answer must be **10**.

The answer *is* **10. The two diagonals are equal, and diagonal *OB* is a radius.

2. E. Use TACTIC 5: subtract to find the shaded area. The area of square *ABCD* is 4. By Fact 50, the area of $\triangle AED$ is

$\dfrac{2^2\sqrt{3}}{4} = \dfrac{4\sqrt{3}}{4} = \sqrt{3}$. Then the area of the shaded region is $4 - \sqrt{3}$.

3. C. Use TACTIC 6: don't do more than you have to. In particular, don't solve for *x*. Here

$5x + 13 = 31 \Rightarrow 5x = 18 \Rightarrow 5x + 31 =$
$18 + 31 = 49 \Rightarrow \sqrt{5x + 31} = \sqrt{49} = 7$.

4. C. This is a relatively simple ratio, but use TACTIC 7 and make sure you get the units right. You need to know that there are 100 cents in a dollar and 16 ounces in a pound.

$\dfrac{\text{price}}{\text{weight}} : \dfrac{6 \text{ dollars}}{2.25 \text{ pounds}} = \dfrac{600 \text{ cents}}{36 \text{ ounces}} = \dfrac{x \text{ cents}}{9 \text{ ounces}}$

Now cross-multiply and solve: $36x = 5400 \Rightarrow x = \textbf{150}$.

5. D.   Use TACTIC 4 and add some
lines: connect the centers of the
three circles to form an equilateral triangle whose sides are 2.
Now use TACTIC 5 and find the
shaded area by subtracting the
area of the three sectors from
the area of the triangle,

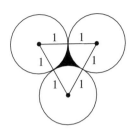

which is $\dfrac{2^2\sqrt{3}}{4} = \sqrt{3}$ (Fact 50). Each sector is $\dfrac{1}{6}$ of a

circle of radius 1. Together the three sectors form $\dfrac{1}{2}$ of such

a circle, so their total area is $\dfrac{1}{2}\pi(1)^2 = \dfrac{\pi}{2}$. Finally, subtract: the

area of the shaded region is $\sqrt{3} - \dfrac{\pi}{2}$.

6. C.   Use TACTIC 8. Systematically list all the factors of 30, either
individually or in pairs: 1, 30, 2, 15, 3, 10, 5, 6. Of the 8 factors,
4 are even and 4 are odd. The columns are equal (C).

7. A.   Use TACTIC 9: Follow the directons carefully! Column A: when
10^3 (1000) is divided by 3, the quotient is 333 and the remainder
is 1. Column B: 10^5 is divisible by 5, so the remainder is 0.
Column A is greater.

8. A.   Column A: since $c < d$, the quotient when c is divided by d is 0,
and the remainder is c. Column B: when d is divided by c, the
remainder must be less than c. Column A is greater.

9. (160)   Use TACTIC 8. Systematically list the numbers that contain
the digit 1, writing as many as you need to see the pattern.
Between 1 and 99 the digit 1 is used 10 times as the units digit
(1, 11, 21, ..., 91) and 10 times as the tens digit (10, 11, 12, ...,
19) for a total of 20 times. From 200 to 299, there are 20 more
times (the same 20 but preceded by 2). Finally, from 100 to 199
there are 20 more plus 100 numbers where the digit 1 is used in
the hundreds place. The total is 20 + 20 + 20 + 100 = **160**.

10. $\left(\frac{5}{2} \text{ or } 2.5\right)$ Use TACTIC 6: don't do more than is necessary. You don't need to solve this system of equations; you don't need to know the values of a and b, only their average. Adding the two equations gives

$$6a + 6b = 30 \Rightarrow a + b = 5 \Rightarrow \frac{a+b}{2} = $$

$$\frac{5}{2} \text{ or } 2.5.$$

11. $\left(\frac{3}{6} \text{ or } \frac{1}{2} \text{ or } .5\right)$ Use TACTIC 8. Systematically list all of the orders in which the marbles could be drawn. With 4 colors, there would ordinarily have been 24 orders, but since the first marble drawn was red, there are only 6 arrangements for the other 3 colors: BYG, BGY, YGB, YBG, GYB, GBY. In 3 of these 6 the yellow comes before the blue, and in the other 3 the blue comes before the yellow. Therefore, the probability that the yellow marble will be removed before the blue marble is $\frac{3}{6}$ or $\frac{1}{2}$ or .5.

12. $\left(\frac{12}{8} \text{ or } \frac{3}{2} \text{ or } 1.5\right)$ The shaded sector is $\frac{45}{360} = \frac{1}{8}$ of the circle, so its area is $\frac{1}{8}$ of 12: $\frac{12}{8}$ or $\frac{3}{2}$ or **1.5**.

If you didn't see that, use TACTIC 8-3 and redraw the figure to scale by making the angle as close as possible to 45°. It is now clear that the sector is $\frac{1}{8}$ of the circle (or very close to it).

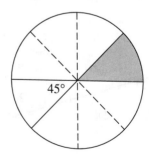

THE MULTIPLE-CHOICE QUESTION

Two of the three mathematics sections on the SAT I contain only multiple-choice questions. One of the 30-minute sections has 25 multiple-choice questions, and the 15-minute section has 10. Since in each of these sections the questions proceed from easy to difficult, you should refer to Chapter 2 for advice on how to pace yourself.

On the first page of each of these sections, you will see the following directions:

In this section *solve each problem,* using any available space on the page for scratchwork. *Then* decide which is the best of the choices given and fill in the corresponding oval on the answer sheet. (Emphasis added.)

The directions are very simple. Basically, they tell you to ignore, at first, the fact that these are multiple-choice questions. Just *solve each problem,* and *then* look at the five choices to see which one is best. As you will learn in this section, however, that is not always the best strategy.

In this section you will learn important strategies you need to help you answer multiple-choice questions on the SAT I. However, as invaluable as these tactics are, use them only when you need them. *If you know how to solve a problem and are confident that you can do so accurately and reasonably quickly, JUST DO IT!*

10. Test the Choices, Starting with C.

TACTIC 10, often called *backsolving*, is useful when you are asked to solve for an unknown and you understand what needs to be done to answer the question, but you want to avoid doing the algebra. The idea is simple: test the various choices to see which one is correct.

NOTE: On the SAT I the answers to virtually all numerical multiple-choice questions are listed in either increasing or decreasing order. Consequently, C is the middle value; and in applying TACTIC 10, *you should always start with C.* For example, assume that choices A, B, C, D, and E are given in increasing order. Try C. If it works, you've found the answer. If C doesn't work, you should now know whether you need to test a larger number or a smaller one, and that information permits you to eliminate two more choices. If C is too small, you need a larger number, so A and B are out; if C is too large, you can eliminate D and E, which are even larger.

Examples 18 and 19 illustrate the proper use of TACTIC 10.

Example 18.

> If the average (arithmetic mean) of 2, 7, and x is 12, what is the value of x?
>
> (A) 9   (B) 12   (C) 21   (D) 27   (E) 36

Solution. Use TACTIC 10. Test choice C: $x = 21$.

- Is the average of 2, 7, and 21 equal to 12?

- No: $\dfrac{2 + 7 + 21}{3} = \dfrac{30}{3} = 10$, which is *too small.*

- Eliminate C; also, since, for the average to be 12, x must be *greater* than 21, eliminate A and B.

- Try choice D: $x = \mathbf{27}$. Is the average of 2, 7, and 27 equal to 12?

- Yes: $\dfrac{2 + 7 + 27}{3} = \dfrac{36}{3} = 12$. The answer is **D**.

Every problem that can be solved using TACTIC 10 can be solved directly, usually in less time. Therefore, we stress: *if you are confident that you can solve a problem quickly and accurately, just do so.*

Example 19.

> If the sum of five consecutive odd integers is 735, what is the largest of these integers?
>
> (A) 155   (B) 151   (C) 145   (D) 143   (E) 141

Solution. Use TACTIC 10. Test choice C: 145.

- If 145 is the largest of the five integers, the integers are 145, 143, 141, 139, and 137. Quickly add them on your calculator. The sum is 705.
- Since 705 is too small, eliminate C, D, and E.
- If you noticed that the amount by which 705 is too small is 30, you should realize that each of the five numbers needs to be increased by 6; therefore, the largest is **151 (B)**.
- If you didn't notice, just try 151, and see that it works.

This solution is easy, and it avoids having to set up and solve the required equation:

$$n + (n + 2) + (n + 4) + (n + 6) + (n + 8) = 735.$$

11. Replace Variables with Numbers.

Mastery of TACTIC 11 is critical for anyone developing good test-taking skills. This tactic can be used whenever the five choices involve the variables in the question. There are three steps:

1. Replace each letter with an easy-to-use number.

2. Solve the problem using those numbers.

3. Evaluate each of the five choices with the numbers you picked to see which choice is equal to the answer you obtained.

Examples 20 and 21 illustrate the proper use of TACTIC 11.

Example 20.

If a is equal to b multiplied by c, which of the following is equal to b divided by c?

(A) $\dfrac{a}{bc}$ (B) $\dfrac{ab}{c}$ (C) $\dfrac{a}{c}$ (D) $\dfrac{a}{c^2}$ (E) $\dfrac{a}{bc^2}$

Solution.

• Pick three easy-to-use numbers that satisfy $a = bc$: for example, $a = 6$, $b = 2$, $c = 3$.
• Solve the problem with these numbers: $b \div c = \dfrac{b}{c} = \dfrac{2}{3}$.

• Check each of the five choices to see which one is equal to $\dfrac{2}{3}$:

• (A) $\dfrac{a}{bc} = \dfrac{6}{(2)(3)} = 1$: NO.   (B) $\dfrac{ab}{c} = \dfrac{(6)(2)}{3} = 6$: NO.

(C) $\dfrac{a}{c} = \dfrac{6}{3} = 2$: NO.   (D) $\dfrac{a}{c^2} = \dfrac{6}{3^2} = \dfrac{6}{9} = \dfrac{2}{3}$: YES!

Still check (E): $\dfrac{a}{bc^2} = \dfrac{6}{2(3^2)} = \dfrac{6}{18} = \dfrac{1}{3}$: NO.
• The answer is **D**.

Example 21.

If the sum of four consecutive odd integers is s, then, in terms of s, what is the greatest of these integers?

(A) $\dfrac{s-12}{4}$ (B) $\dfrac{s-6}{4}$ (C) $\dfrac{s+6}{4}$ (D) $\dfrac{s+12}{4}$

(E) $\dfrac{s+16}{4}$

Solution.

- Pick four easy-to-use consecutive odd integers: say, 1, 3, 5, 7. Then s, their sum, is 16.
- Solve the problem with these numbers: the greatest of these integers is 7.
- When $s = 10$, the five choices are $\dfrac{s-12}{4} = \dfrac{4}{4}$,

  $$\dfrac{s-6}{4} = \dfrac{10}{4}, \dfrac{s+6}{4} = \dfrac{22}{4}, \mathbf{\dfrac{s+12}{4}} = \dfrac{28}{4}, \dfrac{s+16}{4} = \dfrac{32}{4}.$$

- Only $\dfrac{28}{4}$, choice **D**, is equal to 7.

Of course, Examples 20 and 21 can be solved without using TACTIC 11 *if your algebra skills are good.*

The important point is that, if you are uncomfortable with the correct algebraic solution, you don't have to omit these questions. You can use TACTIC 11 and *always* get the right answer.

Example 22 is somewhat different. You are asked to reason through a word problem involving only variables. Most students find problems like these mind-boggling. Here, the use of TACTIC 11 is essential.

Helpful Hint

Replace the letters with numbers that are easy to use, not necessarily ones that make sense. *It is perfectly OK to ignore reality.* A school can have five students, apples can cost $10 each, trains can go 5 miles per hour or 1000 miles per hour—it doesn't matter.

Example 22.

If a school cafeteria needs c cans of soup each week for each student, and if there are s students in the school, for how many weeks will x cans of soup last?

(A) $\dfrac{cx}{s}$ (B) $\dfrac{xs}{c}$ (C) $\dfrac{s}{cx}$ (D) $\dfrac{x}{cs}$ (E) csx

Solution.

- Replace c, s, and x with three easy-to-use numbers. If a school cafeteria needs 2 cans of soup each week for each student, and if there are 5 students in the school, how many weeks will 20 cans of soup last?
- Since the cafeteria needs $2 \times 5 = 10$ cans of soup per week, 20 cans will last for 2 weeks.
- Which of the choices equals 2 when $c = 2$, $s = 5$, and $x = 20$?
- The five choices become: $\frac{cx}{x} = 8, \frac{xs}{c} = 50, \frac{x}{cs} = \frac{1}{8}$,

$\frac{x}{cs} = 2$, $csx = 200$. The answer is **D**.

12. Choose an Appropriate Number.

TACTIC 12 is similar to TACTIC 11 in that we pick convenient numbers. However, here no variable is given in the problem. TACTIC 12 is especially useful in problems involving fractions, ratios, and percents.

Helpful Hint
In problems involving fractions, the best number to use is the least common denominator of all the fractions. In problems involving percents, the easiest number to use is 100.

Example 23.

At Central High School each student studies exactly one foreign language. Three-fifths of the students take Spanish, and one-fourth of the remaining students take Italian. If all of the others take French, what <u>percent</u> of the students take French?

(A) 10   (B) 15   (C) 20   (D) 25   (E) 30

Solution. The least common denominator of $\frac{3}{5}$ and $\frac{1}{4}$ is 20, so assume that there are 20 students at Central High. (Remember that the numbers you choose don't have to be realistic.) Then the number of students taking Spanish is 12 $\left(\frac{3}{5} \text{ of } 20\right)$. Of the remaining 8 students, 2 $\left(\frac{1}{4} \text{ of } 8\right)$ take Italian. The other 6 take French. Finally, 6 is **30%** of 20. The answer is **E**.

Example 24.

From 1994 to 1995 the sales of a book decreased by 80%. If the sales in 1996 were the same as in 1994, by what percent did they increase from 1995 to 1996?

(A) 80%   (B) 100%   (C) 120%   (D) 400%   (E) 500%

Solution. Use TACTIC 12, and assume that 100 copies were sold in 1994 (and 1996). Sales dropped by 80 (80% of 100) to 20 in 1995 and then increased by 80, from 20 back to 100, in 1996. The percent increase was

$$\frac{\text{actual increase}}{\text{original amount}} \times 100\% = \frac{80}{20} \times 100\% = \textbf{400\% (D)}.$$

13. Add Equations.

When a question involves two equations, either add them or subtract them. If there are three or more equations, add them.

Helpful Hint

Very often, answering a question does *not* require you to solve the equations. Remember TACTIC 6: *Do not do any more than is necessary.*

Example 25.

If $3x + 5y = 14$ and $x - y = 6$, what is the average of x and y?

(A) 0   (B) 2.5   (C) 3   (D) 3.5   (E) 5

Solution. Add the equations:

$$
\begin{array}{r}
3x + 5y = 14 \\
+ \quad x - y = 6 \\
\hline
4x + 4y = 20
\end{array}
$$

Divide each side by 4:

$$x + y = 5$$

The average of x and y is their sum divided by 2:

$$\frac{x+y}{2} = \frac{5}{2} = \textbf{2.5}$$

The answer is **B.**

Example 26.

If $a - b = 1$, $b - c = 2$, and $c - a = d$, what is the value of d?

(A) −3   (B) −1   (C) 1   (D) 3
(E) It cannot be determined from the information given.

Solution. Add the three equations:

$$a - b = 1$$
$$b - c = 2$$
$$\underline{+\ c - a = d}$$
$$0 = 3 + d \Rightarrow d = -3$$

The answer is **A**.

14. Eliminate Absurd Choices, and Guess.

When you have no idea how to solve a problem, eliminate all the absurd choices and *guess* from among the remaining ones.

Example 27.

The average of 5, 10, 15, and x is 20. What is x?

(A) 0   (B) 20   (C) 25   (D) 45   (E) 50

Solution. If the average of four numbers is 20, and three of them are less than 20, the other one must be greater than 20. Eliminate A and B and guess. If you further realize that, since 5 and 10 are *a lot* less than 20, x will probably be *a lot* more than 20, you can eliminate C, as well. Then guess either D or E.

Example 28.

If 25% of 220 equals 5.5% of w, what is w?

(A) 10   (B) 55   (C) 100   (D) 110   (E) 1000

Solution. Since 5.5% of w equals 25% of 220, which is surely greater than 5.5% of 220, w must be *greater* than 220. Eliminate A, B, C, and D. The answer *must* be **E**!

Practice Exercises   Answers given on pages 149–151.

1. Judy is now twice as old as Adam but 6 years ago she was 5 times as old as he was. How old is Judy now?

   (A) 10   (B) 16   (C) 20   (D) 24   (E) 32

2. If $a < b$ and c is the sum of a and b, which of the following is the positive difference between a and b?

   (A) $2a - c$ (B) $2b - c$ (C) $c - 2b$
   (D) $c - a + b$ (E) $c - a - b$

3. If w widgets cost c cents, how many widgets can you get for d dollars?

(A) $\dfrac{100dw}{c}$ (B) $\dfrac{dw}{100c}$ (C) $100cdw$

(D) $\dfrac{dw}{c}$ (E) cdw

4. If 120% of a is equal to 80% of b, which of the following is equal to $a + b$?

(A) $1.5a$ (B) $2a$ (C) $2.5a$ (D) $3a$ (E) $5a$

5. In the figure at the right, $WXYZ$ is a square whose sides are 12. AB, CD, EF, and GH are each 8, and are the diameters of the four semicircles. What is the area of the shaded region?

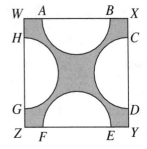

(A) $144 - 128\pi$ (B) $144 - 64\pi$
(C) $144 - 32\pi$ (D) $144 - 16\pi$
(E) 16π

6. What is a divided by $a\%$ of a?

(A) $\dfrac{a}{100}$ (B) $\dfrac{100}{a}$ (C) $\dfrac{a^2}{100}$ (D) $\dfrac{100}{a^2}$

(E) $100a$

7. On a certain Russian-American committee, $\dfrac{2}{3}$ of the members are men, and $\dfrac{3}{8}$ of the men are Americans. If $\dfrac{3}{5}$ of the committee members are Russian, what fraction of the members are American women?

(A) $\dfrac{3}{20}$ (B) $\dfrac{11}{60}$ (C) $\dfrac{1}{4}$ (D) $\dfrac{2}{5}$ (E) $\dfrac{5}{12}$

8. Nadia will be x years old y years from now. How old was she z years ago?

(A) $x + y + z$ (B) $x + y - z$ (C) $x - y - z$
(D) $y - x - z$ (E) $z - y - x$

9. If $12a + 3b = 1$ and $7b - 2a = 9$, what is the average (arithmetic mean) of a and b?

(A) 0.1   (B) 0.5   (C) 1   (D) 2.5   (E) 5

10. If $x\%$ of y is 10, what is y?

(A) $\frac{10}{x}$ (B) $\frac{100}{x}$ (C) $\frac{1000}{x}$ (D) $\frac{x}{100}$ (E) $\frac{x}{10}$

Answer Key

1. **B**	3. **A**	5. **C**	7. **A**	9. **B**
2. **B**	4. **C**	6. **B**	8. **C**	10. **C**

1. B. Use TACTIC 10: backsolve, starting with C. If Judy is now 20, Adam is 10; 6 years ago, they would have been 14 and 4, which is less than 5 times as much. Eliminate C, D, and E, and try a smaller value. If Judy is now **16**, Adam is 8; 6 years ago, they would have been 10 and 2. That's it; 10 is 5 times 2.

2. B. Use TACTIC 11. Pick simple values for a, b, and c. Let $a = 1$, $b = 2$, and $c = 3$. Then $b - a = 1$. Only $2b - c$ is equal to 1.

3. A. Use TACTIC 11: replaces variables with numbers. If 2 widgets cost 10 cents, then widgets cost 5 cents each; and for 3 dollars, you can get 60 widgets. Which of the choices equals 60 when $w = 2$, $c = 10$, and $d = 3$?

Only $\frac{100dw}{c}$.

4. C. Use Tactic 12: choose appropriate numbers. Since 120% of $80 = 80\%$ of 120, let $a = 80$ and $b = 120$. Then $a + b = 200$, and $200 \div 80 = \mathbf{2.5}$.

5. C. If you don't know how to solve this, you must use TACTIC 14: eliminate the absurd choices and guess. Which choices are absurd? Certainly, A and B, both of which are negative. Also, since choice D is about 94, which is much more than half the area of the square, it is much too large. Guess between C (about 43) and E (about 50). If you remember that the way to find shaded areas is to subtract, guess C: $\mathbf{144 - 32\pi}$.

6. B. Use TACTICS 11 and 12: replace a by a number, and use 100 since the problem involves percents.

$$100 \div (100\% \text{ of } 100) = 100 \div 100 = 1.$$

Test each choice; which one equals 1 when

$a = 100$? A and B: $\frac{100}{100} = 1$. Eliminate C, D,

and E; and test A and B with another value, 50, for a:

$$50 \div (50\% \text{ of } 50) = 50 \div (25) = 2.$$

Now, only $\dfrac{\mathbf{100}}{\mathbf{a}}$, works: $\dfrac{100}{50} = 2$.

7. A. Use TACTIC 12: choose appropriate numbers. The LCM of all the denominators is 120, so assume that the committee has 120 members. Then there are $\frac{2}{3} \times 120 = 80$ men and 40 women.

Of the 80 men, 30 $\left(\frac{3}{8} \times 80 \right)$ are American. Since there are

72 $\left(\frac{3}{5} \times 120 \right)$ Russians, there are $120 - 72 = 48$ Americans,

of whom 30 are men, so the other 18 are women. Finally, the

fraction of American women is $\dfrac{18}{120} = \dfrac{\mathbf{3}}{\mathbf{20}}$.

8. C. Use TACTIC 11: replace x, y, and z with easy-to-use numbers.

Assume Nadia will be 10 in 2 years. How old was she 3 years ago? If she will be 10 in 2 years, she is 8 now and 3 years ago was 5. Which of the choices equals 5 when $x = 10$, $y = 2$, and $z = 3$? Only $\boldsymbol{x - y - z}$.

9. B. Use TACTIC 13, and add the two equations:

$$10a + 10b = 10 \Rightarrow a + b = 1 \Rightarrow \frac{a+b}{2} = \frac{1}{2} \text{ or } \mathbf{0.5}.$$

10. C. Use TACTICS 11 and 12. Since 100% of 10 is 10, let $x = 100$ and $y = 10$. When $x = 100$, choices C and E are each 10. Eliminate A, B, and D, and try some other numbers: 50% of 20 is 10. Of C and E, only $\dfrac{1000}{x} = 20$ when $x = 50$.

THE QUANTITATIVE COMPARISON QUESTION

In one of the two 30-minute mathematics sections on the SAT I, the first 15 questions are quantitative comparisons, which, like the multiple-choice questions, proceed from easy to difficult. Since, until you started preparing for the PSAT or SAT I, you probably had never seen questions of this type, you are not likely to be familiar with the various strategies for answering them. In this section you will learn the most important tactics. After you master them, you will see that quantitative comparisons are the easiest of the three types of mathematics questions, and you will wish that there were more than just 15 of them.

On the first page of the SAT I section containing the quantitative comparison questions, you will find directions for answering quantitative comparisons and three examples, similar to those shown on the facing page.

Before learning the different strategies for answering this type of question, let's clarify the directions. In quantitative comparison questions there are two quantities, one in Column A and one in Column B, and it is your job to compare them. For these questions there are **only four possible answers:** A, B, C, and D. E is **never** the answer to a quantitative comparison question.

The correct answer to a quantitative comparison question is

A if the quantity in Column A is greater **all the time, no matter what**;
B if the quantity in Column B is greater **all the time, no matter what**;
C if the two quantities are equal **all the time, no matter what**;
D if the relationship cannot be determined from the information given; that is, **if the answer is not A, B, or C.**

Directions for Quantitative Comparison Questions

In each of questions 1–15, two quantities appear in boxes: one in Column A and one in Column B. You must compare them. The correct answer to a question is

A   if the quantity in Column A is greater;
B   if the quantity in Column B is greater;
C   if the two quantities are equal;
D   if it is impossible to determine which quantity is greater.

<u>Notes:</u>
- *The correct answer is <u>never</u> E.*
- Sometimes information about one or both of the quantities is centered above the two boxes.
- If the same symbol appears in both columns, it represents the same thing each time.
- All variables represent real numbers.

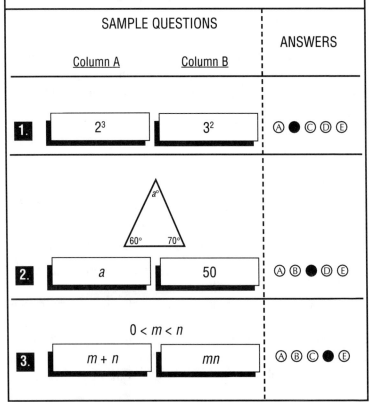

SAMPLE QUESTIONS

ANSWERS

<u>Column A</u>   <u>Column B</u>

1. 2^3 3^2 Ⓐ ● Ⓒ Ⓓ Ⓔ

2. a 50 Ⓐ Ⓑ ● Ⓓ Ⓔ

$0 < m < n$

3. $m + n$ mn Ⓐ Ⓑ Ⓒ ● Ⓔ

Therefore, *if you can find a single instance* in which the quantity in Column A is greater than the quantity in Column B, you can immediately eliminate two choices: B and C. The answer could be B only if the quantity in Column B were greater **all the time**; but you know of one instance when it isn't. Similarly, the quantities are not equal **all the time**, so the answer can't be C. The correct answer, therefore, *must be* A or D. Even if this is the hardest quantitative comparison on the test, and you have no idea of what to do next, you've narrowed down the correct answer to one of two choices, and you *must* guess. If it turns out that the quantity in Column A *is* greater all the time, then A is the answer; if it isn't, then the answer is D.

Helpful Hint

Right now, memorize the instructions given above for answering quantitative comparison questions. *When you take the SAT I, do not spend even one second reading the directions or looking at the sample problems.*

Testing Tactics

15. Replace Variables with Numbers.

Many problems that are hard to analyze because they contain variables become easy to solve when the variables are replaced by simple numbers.

TACTIC 15 is the most important tactic for quantitative comparison questions. *Be sure to master it!*

Most quantitative comparison questions contain variables. When those variables are replaced by simple numbers such as 0 and 1, the quantities in the two columns become much easier to compare.

<u>Column A</u>   <u>Column B</u>

Example 29.

$$a < b < c < d$$

ab	cd

Solution.

- Replace a, b, c, and d with easy-to-use numbers that satisfy the condition $a < b < c < d$: for example, $a = 1$, $b = 2$, $c = 5$, $d = 10$.
- Evaluate the two columns: $ab = (1)(2) = 2$, and $cd = (5)(10) = 50$.
- Therefore, *in this case*, the quantity in Column B is greater.
- Does that mean that B is the correct answer? Not necessarily. The quantity in Column B is greater this time, but will it be greater **every single time, no matter what?**
- What it does mean is that neither A nor C could possibly be the answer: Column A can't be greater **every single time, no matter what,** because it isn't greater *this* time; and the columns aren't equal **every single time, no matter what,** because they aren't equal *this* time.

The correct answer, therefore, is either B or D; and in the few seconds that it took you to plug in 1, 2, 5, and 10 for a, b, c, and d, you were able to eliminate two of the four choices. If you could do nothing else, you should now guess.

But, of course, *you can and will do something else.* You will try some other numbers. But *which* numbers? Since the first numbers you chose were positive, try some negative numbers this time.

Let $a = -5$, $b = -3$, $c = -2$, and $d = -1$.

- Evaluate: $ab = (-5)(-3) = 15$ and $cd = (-2)(-1) = 2$.
- Therefore, *in this case*, the quantity in Column A is greater.
- Column B is *not* greater all the time. B is *not* the correct answer.
- The answer is **D**.

Here are some guidelines for deciding which numbers to use when applying TACTIC 15.

1. **The very best numbers to use first are 1, 0, and −1.**

2. **Often, fractions between 0 and 1 are useful.**

3. **Occasionally, "large" numbers such as 10 or 100 can be used.**

4. **If there is more than one variable, it is permissible to replace each with the same number.**

5. **If a variable appears more than once in a problem, it must be replaced by the same number each time.**

6. **Do not impose any conditions not specifically stated.** In particular, do not assume that variables must represent integers. For example, 3 is not the only number that satisfies $2 < x < 4$ (2.1, 3.95, and π all work). The expression $a < b < c < d$ does not mean that a, b, c, d are

integers, let alone *consecutive* integers (which is why we didn't choose 1, 2, 3, and 4 in Example 29), nor does it mean that any or all of these variables are *positive*.

When you replace the variables in a quantitative comparison question with numbers, remember:

If the value in Column A is ever greater:
   eliminate B and C—the answer must be A or D.
If the value in Column B is ever greater:
   eliminate A and C—the answer must be B or D.
If the two columns are ever equal:
   eliminate A and B—the answer must be C or D.

Practice applying TACTIC 15 to these examples.

Column A	Column B

Example 30.

$$m > 0 \text{ and } m \neq 1$$

m^2	m^3

Example 31.

$w + 10$	$w - 11$

Solution 30. Use TACTIC 15. Replace m with numbers satisfying $m > 0$ and $m \neq 1$.

	Column A	Column B	Compare	Eliminate
Let $m = 2$.	$2^2 = 4$	$2^3 = 8$	B is greater.	A and C
Let $m = \frac{1}{2}$.	$\left(\frac{1}{2}\right)^2 = \frac{1}{4}$	$\left(\frac{1}{2}\right)^3 = \frac{1}{8}$	A is greater.	B

The answer is **D**.

Solution 31. Use TACTIC 15. There are no restrictions on w, so use the best numbers: 1, 0, –1.

	Column A	Column B	Compare	Eliminate
Let $w = 1$.	$1 + 10 = 11$	$1 - 11 = -10$	A is greater.	B and C
Let $w = 0$.	$0 + 10 = 10$	$0 - 11 = -11$	A is greater.	
Let $w = -1$.	$-1 + 10 = 9$	$-1 - 11 = -12$	A is greater.	

Guess **A**. We let w be a positive number, a negative number, and 0. Each time Column A was greater. That's not proof, but it justifies an educated guess.

16. Choose an Appropriate Number.

This is just like TACTIC 15. We are replacing a variable with a number, but the variable isn't mentioned in the problem.

          Column A   Column B

Example 32.

Every band member is either 15, 16, or 17 years old.
One-third of the band members are 16, and
twice as many band members are 16 as 15.

The number of 17-year-old band members	The total number of 15- and 16-year-old band members

Solution: If the first sentence of Example 32 had been "There are n students in the school band, all of whom are 15, 16, or 17 years old," the problem would have been identical to this one. Using TACTIC 15, you could have replaced n with an easy-to-use number, such as 6, and solved: $\frac{1}{3}(6) = 2$ are 16 years old; then 1 is 15, and the remaining 3 are 17. The answer is **C**.

Example 33.

Abe, Ben, and Cal divided a cash prize.

Abe took 50% of the money and spent $\frac{3}{5}$ of what he took.

Ben took 40% of the money and spent $\frac{3}{4}$ of what he took.

The amount that Abe spent	The amount that Ben spent

Solution. Use TACTIC 16. Assume the prize was $100. Then Abe took

$50 and spent $\frac{3}{\cancel{5}_1}(\cancel{\$50}^{10})$ = $30. Ben took $40 and spent $\frac{3}{\cancel{4}_1}(\cancel{\$40}^{10})$ = $30.

The answer is **C.**

17. Make the Problem Easier: Do the Same Thing to Each Column.

In solving a quantitative comparison problem, you can always add the same quantity to each column or subtract the same quantity from each column. You can multiply or divide each side of an equation or inequality by the same quantity, *but in the case of <u>inequalities</u> you can do this only if the quantity is positive.* Since you don't know whether the columns are equal or unequal, you cannot multiply or divide by a variable *unless you know that it is positive.* If the quantities in each column are positive, you may square them or take their square roots.

Here are three examples on which to practice TACTIC 17.

Column A	Column B

Example 34.

$\frac{1}{3} + \frac{1}{4} + \frac{1}{9}$	$\frac{1}{9} + \frac{1}{3} + \frac{1}{5}$

Example 35.

a is a negative number

a^2	$-a^2$

Column A   Column B

Example 36.

| $\dfrac{\sqrt{20}}{2}$ | $\dfrac{5}{\sqrt{5}}$ |

Column A   Column B

Solution 34.
Cancel (subtract)
$\frac{1}{3}$ and $\frac{1}{9}$ from

each column: $\cancel{\frac{1}{3}} + \frac{1}{4} + \cancel{\frac{1}{9}}$ $\cancel{\frac{1}{9}} + \cancel{\frac{1}{3}} + \frac{1}{5}$

Since $\frac{1}{4} > \frac{1}{5}$, the answer is **A**.

Solution 35.
Add a^2 to
each column: $a^2 + a^2 = 2a^2$ $-a^2 + a^2 = 0$

Since a is negative, $2a^2$ is positive. The answer is **A**.

Solution 36.
Square each
column: $\left(\dfrac{\sqrt{20}}{2}\right)^2 = \dfrac{20}{4} = 5$ $\left(\dfrac{5}{\sqrt{5}}\right)^2 = \dfrac{25}{5} = 5$

The answer is **C**.

18. Ask "Could They Be Equal?" and "Must They Be Equal?"

TACTIC 18 is most useful when one column contains a variable and the other contains a number. In this situation ask yourself, "Could they be equal?" If the answer is "yes," eliminate A and B, and then ask, "Must they be equal?" If the second answer is "yes," then C is correct; if the second answer is "no," then choose D. When the answer to "Could they be equal?" is "no," we usually know right away what the correct answer is.

Let's look at a few examples:

Column A   Column B

Example 37.

The sides of a triangle are 3, 4, and x.

| x | 5 |

Example 38.

Bank A has 10 tellers and bank B has 20 tellers.
Each bank has more female tellers than male tellers.

| The number of female tellers at bank A | The number of female tellers at bank B |

Example 39.

| The perimeter of a rectangle whose area is 21 | 20 |

Solution 37. Could they be equal? Could $x = 5$? Of course. That's the all-important 3-4-5 right triangle. Eliminate A and B. Must they be equal? Must $x = 5$? The answer is "no." Actually, x can be any number satisfying the inequality $1 < x < 7$.

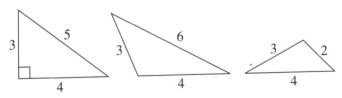

Solution 38. Could they be equal? Could the number of female tellers be the same in both banks? No. More than half (i.e., more than 10) of bank B's 20 tellers are female, but bank A has only 10 tellers in all. The answer is **B**.

Solution 39. Could they be equal? Could a rectangle whose area is 21 have a perimeter of 20? Yes, if its length is 7 and its width is 3: $7 + 3 + 7 + 3 = 20$. Eliminate A and B. Must they be equal? If you're *not* sure, guess between C and D.

There are other possibilities—lots of them; here are a 7 × 3 rectangle and a few others:

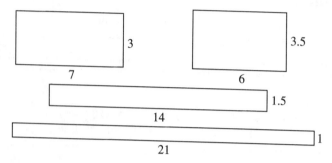

19. Don't Calculate: Compare.

Avoid unnecessary calculations. You don't have to determine the exact values of the quantities in Columns A and B; you just have to compare them.

These are problems on which poor test-takers use their calculators and good test-takers think! Practicing TACTIC 19 will help you become a good test-taker.

Now, test your understanding of TACTIC 19 by solving these problems.

Column A	Column B

Example 40.

| The number of years from 1492 to 1929 | The number of years from 1429 to 1992 |

Example 41.

| $43^2 + 27^2$ | $(43 + 27)^2$ |

Example 42.

Howie earned a 75 on each of his first three math tests and an 80 on the fourth and fifth tests.

| Howie's average after four tests. | Howie's average after five tests. |

Solution 40. The subtraction is easy enough, but why do it? The dates in Column **B** start earlier and end later. Clearly, they span more years. You don't need to know how many years.
The answer is **B**.

Solution 41. For *any* positive numbers a and b, $(a + b)^2 > a^2 + b^2$. You should do the calculations only if you don't know this fact.
The answer is **B**.

Solution 42. Remember that you want to know which average is higher, *not* what the averages are. After four tests Howie's average is clearly less than 80, so an 80 on the fifth test had to *raise* his average.
The answer is **B**.

Practice Exercises   Answers given on pages 162–164.

	Column A	Column B
	$a < 0$	
1.	$4a$	a^4
	$x > 0$	
2.	$10x$	$\dfrac{10}{x}$
	$ab < 0$	
3.	$(a + b)^2$	$a^2 + b^2$
4.	$99 + 299 + 499$	$103 + 305 + 507$
5.	The area of a circle whose radius is 17	The area of a circle whose diameter is 35

Line ℓ goes through (1,1) and (5,2).
Line m is perpendicular to ℓ.

6.	The slope of line ℓ	The slope of line m

<u>Column A</u>	<u>Column B</u>

x, y, and z are three consecutive integers
between 300 and 400.

7.

The average (arithmetic mean) of x and z	The average (arithmetic mean) of x, y, and z

$$x + y = 5$$
$$y - x = -5$$

8.

y	0

Stores A and B sell the same television set.
The regular price at store A is 10% less
than the regular price at store B.

9.

The price of the television set when store A has a 10% off sale	The price of the television set when store B has a 20% off sale

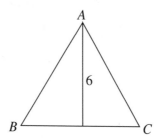

$$AB = AC$$
<u>Note:</u> Figure not drawn to scale

10.

The area of $\triangle ABC$	3

Answer Key

1. **B**	3. **B**	5. **B**	7. **C**	9. **A**
2. **D**	4. **B**	6. **A**	8. **C**	10. **D**

Answer Explanations

1. B. Use TACTIC 15. Replace a with numbers satisfying $a < 0$.

	Column A	Column B	Compare	Eliminate
Let $a = -1$.	$4(-1) = -4$	$(-1)^4 = 1$	B is greater.	A and C
Let $a = -2$.	$4(-2) = -8$	$(-2)^4 = 16$	B is greater.	

Both times, Column B was greater: choose B.

2. D. Use TACTIC 15. When $x = 1$, the columns are equal; when $x = 2$, they aren't.

3. B. Use TACTIC 17.

	Column A	Column B
Expand Column A:	$(a + b)^2 =$	
	$a^2 + 2ab + b^2$	$a^2 + b^2$
Subtract $a^2 + b^2$		
from each column:	$2ab$	0

Since it is given that $ab < 0$, then $2ab < 0$.

4. B. This can be solved in less than 30 seconds with a calculator, but in only 5 seconds without one! Use TACTIC 19: don't calculate; compare. Each of the three numbers in Column B is greater than the corresponding number in Column A. Column B is greater.

5. B. Again, use TACTIC 19: don't calculate the two areas; compare them. The circle in Column A has a radius of 17, and so its diameter is 34. Since the circle in Column B has a larger diameter, its area is greater.

6. A. Again, use TACTIC 19: don't calculate either slope. Quickly, make a rough sketch of line ℓ, going through (1,1) and (5,2), and draw line m perpendicular to it. Line ℓ has a positive slope (it slopes upward), whereas line m has a negative slope. Column A is greater.

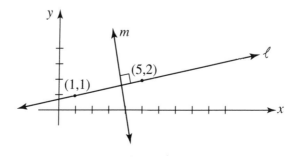

7. **C.** Use TACTIC 15: replace x, y, and z with three consecutive integers between 300 and 400—say, 318, 319, and 320, and use your calculator to find the averages.

Column A: $\dfrac{318 + 320}{2} = \dfrac{638}{2} = 319$.

Column B: $\dfrac{318 + 319 + 320}{3} = \dfrac{957}{3} = 319$.

8. **C.** Use TACTIC 18. Could $y = 0$? In each equation, if $y = 0$, then $x = 5$, so y *can* equal 0. Eliminate A and B, and either guess between C and D or try to continue. Must $y = 0$? Yes; when you have two equations in two variables, there is only one solution, so nothing else is possible.

9. **A.** Use TACTIC 16: choose an appropriate number. *The best number to use in percent problems is 100*, so assume that the regular price of the television in store B is 100 (the units don't matter). Since 10% of 100 is 10, the regular price in store A is $100 - 10 = 90$.
Column A: 10% of 90 is 9, so the sale price in store A is $90 - 9 = 81$.
Column B: 20% of 100 is 20, so the sale price in store B is $100 - 20 = 80$.

10. **D.** Use TACTIC 18. Could the area of $\triangle ABC = 3$? Since the height is 6, the area would be 3 only if the base were 1:
$\dfrac{1}{2}(1)(6) = 3$. Could $BC = 1$? Sure (see the figure). Must the base be 1? Of course not. Neither column is *always* greater, and the columns are not *always* equal (D).

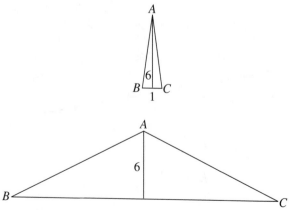

THE GRID-IN QUESTION

On the SAT I, the 30-minute section that contains the 15 quantitative comparisons has 10 additional questions for which no choices are given. These are the grid-in problems, which represent the type of question with which you are most familiar—you solve a problem and then write the answer on your answer sheet. The only difference is that, on the SAT I, you must enter the answer on a special grid that can be read by a computer.

Your answer sheet will have 10 grids, one for each question. Each one will look like the grid below. After solving a problem, the first step is to write the answer in the four boxes at the top of the grid. You then blacken the appropriate oval under each box. For example, if your answer to a question is 2450, you write 2450 at the top of the grid, one digit in each box, and then in each column blacken the oval that contains the number you wrote at the top of the column. This is not difficult; but there are some special rules concerning grid-in questions, so let's go over them before you practice gridding in some numbers.

1. The only symbols that appear in the grid are the digits 0 to 9, a decimal point, and a slash (/), used to write fractions. Keep in mind that, since there is no negative sign, ***the answer to every grid-in question is a positive number or zero.***

2. Be aware that you will receive credit for a correct answer no matter where you grid it. For example, the answer 17 could be gridded in any of three positions:

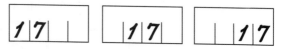

Nevertheless, we suggest that you consistently ***write all your answers*** the way numbers are usually displayed—***to the right, with blank spaces at the left.***

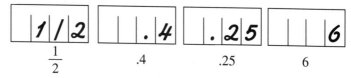

3. ***Never round off your answers.*** If a decimal answer will fit in the grid and you round it off, your answer will be marked wrong. For example, if the answer is .148 and you correctly round it off to the nearest hundredth and enter .15, you will receive *no credit.* If a decimal answer will not fit in the grid, enter a decimal point in the first column, followed by the first three digits. For example, if your answer is 0.454545..., enter it as .454. You would receive credit if you rounded it to .455, but don't. You might occasionally make a mistake in rounding, whereas you'll *never* make a mistake if you just copy the first three digits. *Note:* If the correct answer has more than two decimal digits, *you must use all four columns of the grid.* You will receive *no credit* for .4 or .5 or .45. (These answers are not accurate enough.)

4. ***Never write a 0 before the decimal point.*** The first column of the grid doesn't even have a 0 in it. If the correct answer is 0.3333..., you must grid it as .333. You can't grid 0.33, and 0.3 is not accurate enough.

5. *Never reduce fractions.*

- If your answer is a fraction that will fit in the grid, such as $\frac{2}{3}$ or $\frac{4}{18}$ or $\frac{6}{34}$, *just enter it.* Don't waste time reducing it or converting it to a decimal.

- If your answer is a fraction that won't fit in the grid, do not attempt to reduce it; use your calculator to *convert it to a decimal.* For example, $\frac{24}{65}$ won't fit in a grid—it would require five spaces: 2 4 / 6 5. Don't waste even a few seconds trying to reduce it; just divide on your calculator, and enter .369. Unlike $\frac{24}{65}$, the fraction $\frac{24}{64}$ can be reduced—to $\frac{12}{32}$, which doesn't help, or to $\frac{6}{16}$ or $\frac{3}{8}$, both of which could be entered. *Don't do it!* Reducing a fraction takes time, and you might make a mistake. You won't make a mistake if you just use your calculator: 24 ÷ 64 = .375.

6. *Be aware that you can never enter a mixed number.* If your answer is $2\frac{1}{2}$, you *cannot* leave a space and enter your answer as 2 1/2. Also, if you enter [2 1 / 2], the machine will read it as $\frac{21}{2}$ and mark it wrong. You must enter $2\frac{1}{2}$ as the improper fraction $\frac{5}{2}$ or as the decimal 2.5.

7. Since full credit is given for any equivalent answer, use these guidelines to *enter your answer in the simplest way.* If your answer is $\frac{6}{9}$, you should enter 6/9. (However, credit would be given for any of the following: 2/3, 4/6, 8/12, .666, .667.)

8. Sometimes grid-in questions have more than one correct answer. On these questions, *grid in only one of the acceptable answers.* For example, if a question asked for a positive number less than 100 that was divisible by both 5 and 7, you could enter *either* 35 *or* 70, but not both. Similarly, if a question asked for a number between $\frac{3}{7}$ and $\frac{5}{9}$, you could enter any *one* of hundreds of possibilities: fractions such as $\frac{1}{2}$ and $\frac{4}{9}$ or *any* decimal between .429 and .554—.43 or .499 or .52, for example.

9. ***Keep in mind that there is no penalty for a wrong answer to a grid-in question.*** Therefore, you might as well guess, even if you have no idea what to do. As you will see shortly, there are some strategies for making intelligent guesses.

10. Be sure to ***grid every answer very carefully.*** The computer does not read what you have written in the boxes; it reads only the answer in the grid. If the correct answer to a question is 100 and you write 100 in the boxes, but accidentally grid in 200, you get *no* credit.

11. If you know that the answer to a question is 100, can you just grid it in and not bother writing it on top? Yes, you will get full credit, and so some SAT guides recommend that you don't waste time writing the answer. This is terrible advice. Instead, **write each answer in the boxes**. It takes less than 2 seconds per answer to do this, and it definitely cuts down on careless errors in gridding. More important, if you go back to check your work, it is much easier to read what's in the boxes on top than what's in the grid.

12. Be aware that the smallest number that can be gridded is 0; the largest is 9999. No number greater than 100 can have a decimal point. The largest number less than 100 that can be gridded is 99.9; the smallest number greater than 100 that can be gridded is 101.

Testing Tactics

20. Backsolve.

If you think of a grid-in problem as a multiple-choice question in which the choices accidentally got erased, you can still use TACTIC 10: test the choices. You just have to make up the choices as you go.

Example 43.

If the average (arithmetic mean) of 2, 7, and x is 12, what is the value of x?

Solution. You could start with 10; but if you immediately realize that the average of 2, 7, and 10 is less than 10 (so it can't be 12), you'll try a bigger number, say 20. The average of 2, 7, and 20 is

$$\frac{2+7+20}{3} = \frac{29}{3} = 9\frac{2}{3},$$

which is too small. Try $x = 30$:

$$\frac{2+7+30}{3} = \frac{39}{3} = 13,$$

just a bit too big. Since 12 is closer to 13 than it is to $9\frac{2}{3}$, your next choice should be closer to 30 than 20, surely more than 25. Your third try might well be **27**, which works.

Example 44.

For every positive number $x \neq 20$: $\boxed{x} = 20 + x$ and $\widehat{x} = 20 - x$.

If $\dfrac{\boxed{x}}{\widehat{x}} = 4$, what is the value of x?

Solution. In order for $20 - x$ to be positive, x has to be less than 20.

Try $x = 15$: $\dfrac{20+15}{20-15} = \dfrac{35}{5} = 7$. That's too big.

Try $x = 10$: $\dfrac{20+10}{20-10} = \dfrac{30}{10} = 3$. That's too small.

Try $x = 12$: $\dfrac{20+12}{20-12} = \dfrac{32}{8} = $ **4**. That's it.

21. Choose an Appropriate Number.

This is exactly the same as TACTIC 12. The most appropriate numbers to choose are 100 for percent problems, the LCD (least common denominator) for fraction problems, and the LCM (least common multiple) of the coefficients for problems involving equations. Each of the problems discussed under TACTIC 12 could have been a grid-in, because we didn't even look at the choices until we had the correct answer.

Example 45.

During an Election Day sale, the price of every television set in a store was reduced by $33\frac{1}{3}$%. By what percent must these sale prices be raised so that the TVs now sell for their original prices? (Do not grid the % sign.)

Solution. Since this problem involves percents, you should think about using 100. But the fraction $\frac{1}{3}$ is also involved, so 300 is an even better choice. Assume the original price was \$300. Since $33\frac{1}{3}$% of 300 = $\frac{1}{3}$ of 300 = 100, the sale price was \$200. To restore the price to \$300, it must now be raised by \$100. The percent increase is

$$\frac{\text{actual increase}}{\text{original amount}} \times 100\% = \frac{100}{200} \times 100\% = \textbf{50\%.}$$

Practice Exercises   Answers given on pages 173–175.

> Directions: Enter your response to these problems on the grids on page 172.

1. For what number $b > 0$ is it true that b divided by b% of b equals b?

2. Patty has 150 coins, each of which is a dime or a quarter. If she has \$27.90, how many quarters does she have?

3. A fair coin is flipped repeatedly. Each time it lands "heads," Ali gets a point, and whenever it lands "tails," Jason gets a point. The game continues until someone gets 5 points. If the score is now 4 to 3 in Ali's favor, and the probability that Ali will win the game is k times the probability that Jason will win the game, what is the value of k?

4. At a certain university, $\frac{1}{4}$ of the applicants failed to meet minimum standards and were rejected immediately. Of those who met the standards, $\frac{2}{5}$ were accepted. If 1200 applicants were accepted, how many applied?

5. More than half of the members of the Key Club are girls. If $\frac{4}{7}$ of the girls and $\frac{7}{11}$ of the boys in the Key Club attended the April meeting, what is the smallest number of members the club could have?

6. Jessica copied a column of numbers and added them. The only mistake she made was that she copied one number as 5095 instead of 5.95. If the sum she got was 8545.05, what should the answer have been?

7. Jerry spent $105 for a tool kit and a box of nails. If the tool kit cost $100 more than the nails, how many boxes of nails could be purchased for the price of the tool kit?

8. Ken is now 3 times as old as his younger sister, but in 7 years he will be only twice as old as she will be then. How old is Ken now?

9. The value of an investment increased 50% in 1992 and again in 1993. In each of 1994 and 1995 the value of the investment decreased by 50%. At the end of 1995 the value of the investment was how many times the value at the beginning of 1992?

10. How many integers between 1 and 1000 are the product of two consecutive integers?

1.

2.

3.

4.

5.

6.

7.

8.

9.

10.

Answer Key

1. $1\ 0$
2. $8\ 6$
3. 3
4. $4\ 0\ 0\ 0$
5. $2\ 5$
6. $3\ 4\ 5\ 6$
7. $4\ 1$
8. $2\ 1$
9. $9\ /\ 1\ 6$ or $.\ 5\ 6\ 2$
10. $3\ 1$

Answer Explanations

1. (10) $b \div (b\% \text{ of } b) = b \div \left(\dfrac{b}{100} \times b\right) =$

$b \div \left(\dfrac{b^2}{100}\right) = b \times \dfrac{100}{b^2} = \dfrac{100}{b}.$

Since this value is to equal b, you have

$\dfrac{100}{b} = b \Rightarrow b^2 = 100 \Rightarrow b = \mathbf{10}.$

2. (86)   Use TACTIC 20: backsolve. Pick an easy starting value, say $q = 100$. If this gives a value greater than $27.90, decrease q; if it gives a value less than $27.90, increase q.

Number of Quarters	Number of Dimes	Value
100	50	$25.00 + $5.00 = $30.00
80	70	$20.00 + $7.00 = $27.00
85	65	$21.25 + $6.50 = $27.75
86	64	$21.50 + $6.40 = $27.90

3. (3)   Jason can win only if the next two flips are both tails. The probability of that happening is $\frac{1}{2} \times \frac{1}{2} = \frac{1}{4}$. Therefore, the probability that Ali wins is $1 - \frac{1}{4} = \frac{3}{4}$.

Since $\frac{3}{4} = 3\left(\frac{1}{4}\right)$, $k = $ **3**.

4. (4000)   Use TACTIC 21: choose an appropriate number. The LCD of $\frac{1}{4}$ and $\frac{2}{5}$ is 20, so *assume* that there were 20 applicants. Then $\frac{1}{4}(20) = 5$ failed to meet the minimum standards. Of the remaining 15 applicants, $\frac{2}{5}$, or 6, were accepted, so 6 of every 20 applicants were accepted. Set up a proportion:

$$\frac{6}{20} = \frac{1200}{x} \Rightarrow 6x = 24{,}000 \Rightarrow x = \textbf{4000}.$$

5. (25)   Since $\frac{4}{7}$ of the girls attended the meeting, the number of girls in the club must be a multiple of 7: 7, 14, 21, ... Similarly, the number of boys in the club must be a multiple of 11: 11, 22, ... Since there are at least 11 boys and there are more girls than boys, there must be at least 14 girls. The smallest possible total is $14 + 11 = $ **25**.

6. (3456)   To get the correct sum, subtract the number Jessica added in error and add the number she left out:
8545.05 − 5095 + 5.95 = **3456**.

7. (41)   The first thing to do is to calculate the prices of the tool kit and the nails. *Be careful*—they are *not* $100 and $5. You can get the answer algebraically or by trial and error. If you let x = cost of the nails, then 100 + x = cost of the tool kit, and

$$x + (100 + x) = 105 \Rightarrow 2x + 100 = 105 \Rightarrow$$
$$2x = 5 \Rightarrow x = 2.5.$$

Then the nails cost $2.50, and the tool kit $102.50. Finally, 102.50 ÷ 2.50 = **41**.

8. (21)   Use TACTIC 21. Pick a value for the sister's age—say, 2. Then Ken is 6. In 7 years, sister and brother will be 9 and 13, respectively. No good; 13 is less than twice 9. Try a bigger number—5. Then Ken is 15, and in 7 years the two will be 12 and 22. That's closer, but still too small. Try 7. Then Ken is **21**, and in 7 years his sister and he will be 14 and 28. That's it!

9. $\left(.562 \text{ or } \dfrac{9}{16}\right)$ Use TACTIC 21. Pick an easy-to-use starting

value—$100, say. Then the value of the investment at the end of each of the 4 years 1992, 1993, 1994, 1995 was $150, $225, $112.50, $56.25, so the final value was .5625 times the initial value. Note that some initial values would lead to an answer more easily expressed as a fraction. For example, if you start with $16, the yearly values would be $24, $36, $18, and $9,

and the answer would be $\dfrac{9}{16}$.

10. (31)   Use TACTIC 8. List the integers systematically: 1×2, 2×3, ... , 24×25, ... You don't have to multiply and list the products $(2, 6, 12, \ldots , 600, \ldots)$; you just have to know when to stop. The largest product less than 1000 is $31 \times 32 = 992$, so there are **31** numbers.

SUMMARY OF IMPORTANT TIPS AND TACTICS

1. Whenever you know how to answer a question directly, just do it. The tactics given in this chapter should be used only when you need them.

2. Memorize all the formulas you need to know. Even though some of them are printed on the first page of each math section, during the test you do not want to waste any time referring back to that reference material.

3. Be sure to bring a calculator, but use it only when you need it. Don't use it for simple arithmetic that you can easily do in your head.

4. Remember that no problem requires lengthy or difficult computations. If you find yourself doing a lot of arithmetic, stop and reread the question. You are probably not answering the question asked.

5. Answer every question you attempt. Even if you can't solve it, you can almost always eliminate two or more choices. Often you know that an answer must be negative, but two or three of the choices are positive, or an answer must be even, and some of the choices are odd.

6. Unless a diagram is labeled "<u>Note</u>: Figure not drawn to scale," it is perfectly accurate, and you can trust it in making an estimate.

7. When a diagram has not been provided, draw one, especially on any geometry problem.

8. If a diagram has been provided, feel free to label it, mark it up in any way, including adding line segments, if necessary.

9. Answer any question for which you can estimate the answer, even if you are not sure you are correct.

10. Don't panic when you see a strange symbol in a question, It will always be defined. Getting the correct answer just involves following the directions given in the definition.

11. When a question involves two equations, either add them or subtract them. If there are three or more, just add them.

12. Never make unwarranted assumptions. Do not assume numbers are positive or integers. If a question refers to two numbers, do not assume that they have to be different. If you know a figure has four sides, do not assume that it is a rectangle.

13. Be sure to work in consistent units. If the width and length of a rectangle are 8 inches and 2 feet, respectively, either convert the 2 feet to 24 inches or the 8 inches to two-thirds of a foot before calculating the area or perimeter.

Standard Multiple-Choice Questions

1. Whenever you answer a question by backsolving, start with Choice C.

2. When you replace variables with numbers, choose easy-to-use numbers, whether or not they are realistic.

3. Choose appropriate numbers. The best number to use in percent problems is 100. In problems involving fractions, the best number to use is the least common denominator.

4. When you have no idea how to solve a problem, eliminate all of the absurd choices and guess.

Quantitative Comparison Questions

1. There are only four possible answers to a quantitative comparison question: A, B, C, or D. E can *never* be the correct choice.

2. If the quantity in each column is a number (there are no variables), then the answer cannot be D.

3. Remember that you do not need to calculate the value of each column; you only have to compare them.

4. Replace variables with numbers. The best numbers to try are 1, 0, and −1. Occasionally, fractions between 0 and 1 and large numbers, such as 10 or 100, are useful.

5. Make the problem easier by doing the same thing to each column. You can always add the same number to each column or subtract the same number from each column. You can multiply or divide each column by the same number, if you know that the number is positive.

6. Ask "Could the columns be equal?" and "Must the columns be equal?"

Student-Produced Response (Grid-in) Questions

1. Write your answer in the four spaces at the top of the grid, and *carefully* grid in your answer below. No credit is given for a correct answer if it has been gridded improperly.

2. Remember that the answer to a grid-in question can never be negative.

3. You can never grid in a mixed number—you must convert it to an improper fraction or a decimal.

4. Never round off your answers and never reduce fractions. If a fraction can fit in the four spaces of the grid, enter it. If not, use your calculator to convert it to a decimal (by dividing) and enter a decimal point followed by the first three decimal digits.

5. When gridding a decimal, do not write a 0 before the decimal point.

6. If a question has more than one possible answer, only grid in one of them.

7. There is no penalty for wrong answers on grid-in questions, so you should grid in anything that seems reasonable, rather than leave out a question.

6 Practice SAT I Exams

You are now about to take a major step in preparing yourself to handle an actual SAT I. Before you are three practice tests patterned after recently released SAT I exams. Up to now, you've concentrated on specific areas and on general testing techniques. You've mastered testing tips and worked on practice exercises. Now you have a chance to test yourself before you walk in that test center door.

These practice tests resemble the actual SAT I in format, in difficulty, and in content. When you take one, take it as if it *were* the actual SAT I.

Build Your Stamina

Don't start and stop and take time out for a soda or for a phone call. To do well on the SAT I, you have to focus on the test, the test, and nothing but the test for hours at a time. Most high school students have never had to sit through a three-hour examination before they take their first SAT I. To survive such a long exam takes stamina, and, as marathon runners know, the only way to build stamina is to put in the necessary time.

Refine Your Skills

You know how to maximize your score by tackling easy questions first and by eliminating wrong answers whenever you can. Put these skills into practice. If you find yourself spending too much time on any one question, skip it and move on. Remember to check frequently to make sure you are answering the questions in the right spots. This is a great chance for you to get these skills down pat.

Take a Deep Breath—and Smile!

It's hard to stay calm when those around you are tense, and you're bound to run into some pretty tense people when you take the SAT I. So you may experience a slight case of "exam nerves" on the big day. Don't worry about it.

1. Being keyed up for an examination isn't always bad: you may outdo yourself because you are so worked up.

2. Total panic is unlikely to set in: you know too much.

3. You know you can handle a three-hour test.

4. You know you can handle the sorts of questions you'll find on the SAT I.

5. You know you can omit several questions and still score high. Answer only 50–60% of the questions correctly and you'll still get an average or better than average score (and dozens of solid, well-known colleges are out there right now, looking for serious students with just that kind of score). Answer more than that correctly and you should wind up with a superior score.

Make Your Practice Pay—Approximate the Test

1. Complete an entire Practice Exam at one sitting.

2. Use a clock or timer.

3. Allow precisely 30 minutes each for sections 1 through 4, and 15 minutes each for sections 5 and 6. (If you have time left over, review your answers or recheck the way you've marked your answer sheet.)

4. After each section, give yourself a five-minute break.

5. Allow no talking in the test room.

6. Work rapidly without wasting time.

ANSWER SHEETS—TEST 1

If a section has fewer than 35 questions, leave the extra spaces blank.

Section 1

1. Ⓐ Ⓑ Ⓒ Ⓓ Ⓔ   13. Ⓐ Ⓑ Ⓒ Ⓓ Ⓔ   25. Ⓐ Ⓑ Ⓒ Ⓓ Ⓔ
2. Ⓐ Ⓑ Ⓒ Ⓓ Ⓔ   14. Ⓐ Ⓑ Ⓒ Ⓓ Ⓔ   26. Ⓐ Ⓑ Ⓒ Ⓓ Ⓔ
3. Ⓐ Ⓑ Ⓒ Ⓓ Ⓔ   15. Ⓐ Ⓑ Ⓒ Ⓓ Ⓔ   27. Ⓐ Ⓑ Ⓒ Ⓓ Ⓔ
4. Ⓐ Ⓑ Ⓒ Ⓓ Ⓔ   16. Ⓐ Ⓑ Ⓒ Ⓓ Ⓔ   28. Ⓐ Ⓑ Ⓒ Ⓓ Ⓔ
5. Ⓐ Ⓑ Ⓒ Ⓓ Ⓔ   17. Ⓐ Ⓑ Ⓒ Ⓓ Ⓔ   29. Ⓐ Ⓑ Ⓒ Ⓓ Ⓔ
6. Ⓐ Ⓑ Ⓒ Ⓓ Ⓔ   18. Ⓐ Ⓑ Ⓒ Ⓓ Ⓔ   30. Ⓐ Ⓑ Ⓒ Ⓓ Ⓔ
7. Ⓐ Ⓑ Ⓒ Ⓓ Ⓔ   19. Ⓐ Ⓑ Ⓒ Ⓓ Ⓔ   31. Ⓐ Ⓑ Ⓒ Ⓓ Ⓔ
8. Ⓐ Ⓑ Ⓒ Ⓓ Ⓔ   20. Ⓐ Ⓑ Ⓒ Ⓓ Ⓔ   32. Ⓐ Ⓑ Ⓒ Ⓓ Ⓔ
9. Ⓐ Ⓑ Ⓒ Ⓓ Ⓔ   21. Ⓐ Ⓑ Ⓒ Ⓓ Ⓔ   33. Ⓐ Ⓑ Ⓒ Ⓓ Ⓔ
10. Ⓐ Ⓑ Ⓒ Ⓓ Ⓔ   22. Ⓐ Ⓑ Ⓒ Ⓓ Ⓔ   34. Ⓐ Ⓑ Ⓒ Ⓓ Ⓔ
11. Ⓐ Ⓑ Ⓒ Ⓓ Ⓔ   23. Ⓐ Ⓑ Ⓒ Ⓓ Ⓔ   35. Ⓐ Ⓑ Ⓒ Ⓓ Ⓔ
12. Ⓐ Ⓑ Ⓒ Ⓓ Ⓔ   24. Ⓐ Ⓑ Ⓒ Ⓓ Ⓔ

Section 2

1. Ⓐ Ⓑ Ⓒ Ⓓ Ⓔ   13. Ⓐ Ⓑ Ⓒ Ⓓ Ⓔ   25. Ⓐ Ⓑ Ⓒ Ⓓ Ⓔ
2. Ⓐ Ⓑ Ⓒ Ⓓ Ⓔ   14. Ⓐ Ⓑ Ⓒ Ⓓ Ⓔ   26. Ⓐ Ⓑ Ⓒ Ⓓ Ⓔ
3. Ⓐ Ⓑ Ⓒ Ⓓ Ⓔ   15. Ⓐ Ⓑ Ⓒ Ⓓ Ⓔ   27. Ⓐ Ⓑ Ⓒ Ⓓ Ⓔ
4. Ⓐ Ⓑ Ⓒ Ⓓ Ⓔ   16. Ⓐ Ⓑ Ⓒ Ⓓ Ⓔ   28. Ⓐ Ⓑ Ⓒ Ⓓ Ⓔ
5. Ⓐ Ⓑ Ⓒ Ⓓ Ⓔ   17. Ⓐ Ⓑ Ⓒ Ⓓ Ⓔ   29. Ⓐ Ⓑ Ⓒ Ⓓ Ⓔ
6. Ⓐ Ⓑ Ⓒ Ⓓ Ⓔ   18. Ⓐ Ⓑ Ⓒ Ⓓ Ⓔ   30. Ⓐ Ⓑ Ⓒ Ⓓ Ⓔ
7. Ⓐ Ⓑ Ⓒ Ⓓ Ⓔ   19. Ⓐ Ⓑ Ⓒ Ⓓ Ⓔ   31. Ⓐ Ⓑ Ⓒ Ⓓ Ⓔ
8. Ⓐ Ⓑ Ⓒ Ⓓ Ⓔ   20. Ⓐ Ⓑ Ⓒ Ⓓ Ⓔ   32. Ⓐ Ⓑ Ⓒ Ⓓ Ⓔ
9. Ⓐ Ⓑ Ⓒ Ⓓ Ⓔ   21. Ⓐ Ⓑ Ⓒ Ⓓ Ⓔ   33. Ⓐ Ⓑ Ⓒ Ⓓ Ⓔ
10. Ⓐ Ⓑ Ⓒ Ⓓ Ⓔ   22. Ⓐ Ⓑ Ⓒ Ⓓ Ⓔ   34. Ⓐ Ⓑ Ⓒ Ⓓ Ⓔ
11. Ⓐ Ⓑ Ⓒ Ⓓ Ⓔ   23. Ⓐ Ⓑ Ⓒ Ⓓ Ⓔ   35. Ⓐ Ⓑ Ⓒ Ⓓ Ⓔ
12. Ⓐ Ⓑ Ⓒ Ⓓ Ⓔ   24. Ⓐ Ⓑ Ⓒ Ⓓ Ⓔ

ANSWER SHEETS—TEST 1

Section 3

1. Ⓐ Ⓑ Ⓒ Ⓓ Ⓔ   13. Ⓐ Ⓑ Ⓒ Ⓓ Ⓔ   25. Ⓐ Ⓑ Ⓒ Ⓓ Ⓔ
2. Ⓐ Ⓑ Ⓒ Ⓓ Ⓔ   14. Ⓐ Ⓑ Ⓒ Ⓓ Ⓔ   26. Ⓐ Ⓑ Ⓒ Ⓓ Ⓔ
3. Ⓐ Ⓑ Ⓒ Ⓓ Ⓔ   15. Ⓐ Ⓑ Ⓒ Ⓓ Ⓔ   27. Ⓐ Ⓑ Ⓒ Ⓓ Ⓔ
4. Ⓐ Ⓑ Ⓒ Ⓓ Ⓔ   16. Ⓐ Ⓑ Ⓒ Ⓓ Ⓔ   28. Ⓐ Ⓑ Ⓒ Ⓓ Ⓔ
5. Ⓐ Ⓑ Ⓒ Ⓓ Ⓔ   17. Ⓐ Ⓑ Ⓒ Ⓓ Ⓔ   29. Ⓐ Ⓑ Ⓒ Ⓓ Ⓔ
6. Ⓐ Ⓑ Ⓒ Ⓓ Ⓔ   18. Ⓐ Ⓑ Ⓒ Ⓓ Ⓔ   30. Ⓐ Ⓑ Ⓒ Ⓓ Ⓔ
7. Ⓐ Ⓑ Ⓒ Ⓓ Ⓔ   19. Ⓐ Ⓑ Ⓒ Ⓓ Ⓔ   31. Ⓐ Ⓑ Ⓒ Ⓓ Ⓔ
8. Ⓐ Ⓑ Ⓒ Ⓓ Ⓔ   20. Ⓐ Ⓑ Ⓒ Ⓓ Ⓔ   32. Ⓐ Ⓑ Ⓒ Ⓓ Ⓔ
9. Ⓐ Ⓑ Ⓒ Ⓓ Ⓔ   21. Ⓐ Ⓑ Ⓒ Ⓓ Ⓔ   33. Ⓐ Ⓑ Ⓒ Ⓓ Ⓔ
10. Ⓐ Ⓑ Ⓒ Ⓓ Ⓔ   22. Ⓐ Ⓑ Ⓒ Ⓓ Ⓔ   34. Ⓐ Ⓑ Ⓒ Ⓓ Ⓔ
11. Ⓐ Ⓑ Ⓒ Ⓓ Ⓔ   23. Ⓐ Ⓑ Ⓒ Ⓓ Ⓔ   35. Ⓐ Ⓑ Ⓒ Ⓓ Ⓔ
12. Ⓐ Ⓑ Ⓒ Ⓓ Ⓔ   24. Ⓐ Ⓑ Ⓒ Ⓓ Ⓔ

Section 4

1. Ⓐ Ⓑ Ⓒ Ⓓ Ⓔ   9. Ⓐ Ⓑ Ⓒ Ⓓ Ⓔ
2. Ⓐ Ⓑ Ⓒ Ⓓ Ⓔ   10. Ⓐ Ⓑ Ⓒ Ⓓ Ⓔ
3. Ⓐ Ⓑ Ⓒ Ⓓ Ⓔ   11. Ⓐ Ⓑ Ⓒ Ⓓ Ⓔ
4. Ⓐ Ⓑ Ⓒ Ⓓ Ⓔ   12. Ⓐ Ⓑ Ⓒ Ⓓ Ⓔ
5. Ⓐ Ⓑ Ⓒ Ⓓ Ⓔ   13. Ⓐ Ⓑ Ⓒ Ⓓ Ⓔ
6. Ⓐ Ⓑ Ⓒ Ⓓ Ⓔ   14. Ⓐ Ⓑ Ⓒ Ⓓ Ⓔ
7. Ⓐ Ⓑ Ⓒ Ⓓ Ⓔ   15. Ⓐ Ⓑ Ⓒ Ⓓ Ⓔ
8. Ⓐ Ⓑ Ⓒ Ⓓ Ⓔ

ANSWER SHEETS—TEST 1

Section 4 (continued)

16.

17.

18.

19.

20.

21.

22.

23.

ANSWER SHEETS—TEST 1

Section 4 (continued)

24.

25.

Section 5

1. Ⓐ Ⓑ Ⓒ Ⓓ Ⓔ
2. Ⓐ Ⓑ Ⓒ Ⓓ Ⓔ
3. Ⓐ Ⓑ Ⓒ Ⓓ Ⓔ
4. Ⓐ Ⓑ Ⓒ Ⓓ Ⓔ
5. Ⓐ Ⓑ Ⓒ Ⓓ Ⓔ
6. Ⓐ Ⓑ Ⓒ Ⓓ Ⓔ
7. Ⓐ Ⓑ Ⓒ Ⓓ Ⓔ
8. Ⓐ Ⓑ Ⓒ Ⓓ Ⓔ
9. Ⓐ Ⓑ Ⓒ Ⓓ Ⓔ
10. Ⓐ Ⓑ Ⓒ Ⓓ Ⓔ
11. Ⓐ Ⓑ Ⓒ Ⓓ Ⓔ
12. Ⓐ Ⓑ Ⓒ Ⓓ Ⓔ
13. Ⓐ Ⓑ Ⓒ Ⓓ Ⓔ
14. Ⓐ Ⓑ Ⓒ Ⓓ Ⓔ
15. Ⓐ Ⓑ Ⓒ Ⓓ Ⓔ

Section 6

1. Ⓐ Ⓑ Ⓒ Ⓓ Ⓔ
2. Ⓐ Ⓑ Ⓒ Ⓓ Ⓔ
3. Ⓐ Ⓑ Ⓒ Ⓓ Ⓔ
4. Ⓐ Ⓑ Ⓒ Ⓓ Ⓔ
5. Ⓐ Ⓑ Ⓒ Ⓓ Ⓔ
6. Ⓐ Ⓑ Ⓒ Ⓓ Ⓔ
7. Ⓐ Ⓑ Ⓒ Ⓓ Ⓔ
8. Ⓐ Ⓑ Ⓒ Ⓓ Ⓔ
9. Ⓐ Ⓑ Ⓒ Ⓓ Ⓔ
10. Ⓐ Ⓑ Ⓒ Ⓓ Ⓔ
11. Ⓐ Ⓑ Ⓒ Ⓓ Ⓔ
12. Ⓐ Ⓑ Ⓒ Ⓓ Ⓔ
13. Ⓐ Ⓑ Ⓒ Ⓓ Ⓔ
14. Ⓐ Ⓑ Ⓒ Ⓓ Ⓔ
15. Ⓐ Ⓑ Ⓒ Ⓓ Ⓔ

PRACTICE TEST 1
SECTION 1

30 Questions—30 Minutes

Select the best answer to the following questions, then fill in the appropriate space on your Answer Sheet.

Each of the following sentences contains one or two blanks; these blanks indicate that a word or set of words has been left out. Below the sentence are five words or phrases, lettered A through E. Select the word or set of words that best completes the sentence.

Example:

Fame is -------- ; today's rising star is all too soon tomorrow's washed-up has-been.

(A) rewarding   (B) gradual
  (C) essential   (D) spontaneous
    (E) transitory

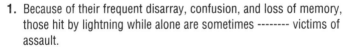

---

1. Because of their frequent disarray, confusion, and loss of memory, those hit by lightning while alone are sometimes -------- victims of assault.

    (A) mistaken for
    (B) attracted to
    (C) unaware of
    (D) avoided by
    (E) useful to

2. Having published more than three hundred books in less than fifty years, science fiction writer Isaac Asimov may well be the most ------- author of our day.

   (A) fastidious
   (B) insecure
   (C) outmoded
   (D) prolific
   (E) indigenous

3. Because his time was limited, Weng decided to read the -------- novel *War and Peace* in -------- edition.

   (A) wordy...an unedited
   (B) lengthy...an abridged
   (C) famous...a modern
   (D) romantic...an autographed
   (E) popular...a complete

4. In giving a speech, the speaker's goal is to communicate ideas clearly and -------, so that the audience will be in no ------ about the meaning of the speech.

   (A) effectively...haste
   (B) indirectly...distress
   (C) vigorously...discomfort
   (D) unambiguously...confusion
   (E) tactfully...suspense

5. Although gregarious by nature, Lisa became quiet and ------- after she was unexpectedly laid off from work.

   (A) autonomous
   (B) susceptible
   (C) assertive
   (D) withdrawn
   (E) composed

6. The increasingly popular leader of America's second largest tribe, Cherokee Chief Wilma Mankiller, has -------- the myth that only males could be leaders in American Indian government.

   (A) shattered
   (B) perpetuated
   (C) exaggerated
   (D) confirmed
   (E) venerated

7. The commission of inquiry censured the senator for his ------- expenditure of public funds, which they found to be --------.

(A) flagrant...cursory
(B) improper...vindicated
(C) lavish...unjustifiable
(D) judicious...blameworthy
(E) arbitrary...critical

8. During the Battle of Trafalgar, Admiral Nelson remained -------- and in
full command of the situation in spite of the hysteria and panic all
around him.

(A) impassable
(B) imperturbable
(C) overbearing
(D) frenetic
(E) lackadaisical

9. Although he had spent many hours at the computer trying to solve
the problem, he was the first to admit that the final solution was ------
and not the ------ of his labor.

(A) trivial...cause
(B) incomplete...intent
(C) adequate...concern
(D) schematic...fault
(E) fortuitous...result

Each of the following examples introduces a capitalized pair of
words or phrases linked by a colon (:); this colon indicates that
these words are related in some way. Following the capitalized
pair are five pairs of words or phrases lettered A through E.
Select the pair whose relationship is most similar to the relationship illustrated by the capitalized pair.

Example:

CLOCK:TIME::   (A) watch:wrist
(B) pedometer:speed   (C) thermometer:temperature
(D) hourglass:sand   (E) radio:sound

Ⓐ Ⓑ ● Ⓓ Ⓔ

10. CONSTITUTION:PREAMBLE::

(A) prelude:overture
(B) legislation:introduction
(C) opera:intermezzo
(D) book:preface
(E) play:epilogue

11. QUARRY:MARBLE::

(A) metal:silver
(B) ore:gold
(C) mine:coal
(D) prey:rabbit
(E) necklace:diamonds

12. JOY:ECSTASY::

(A) rain:drought
(B) breeze:hurricane
(C) river:creek
(D) deluge:flood
(E) jazz:opera

13. DEPTH:FISSURE::

(A) breadth:scope
(B) height:peak
(C) velocity:road
(D) weight:diet
(E) length:duration

14. BLATANT:OBTRUSIVENESS::

(A) cynical:anger
(B) weary:hopelessness
(C) erudite:ignorance
(D) lavish:extravagance
(E) arrogant:humility

15. STRIDENT:VOICE::

(A) muted:music
(B) smooth:texture
(C) acrid:taste
(D) fragrant:odor
(E) tuned:instrument

Read each of the passages below, and then answer the questions that follow each passage. The correct response may be stated outright or merely suggested in the passage.

Questions 16–21 are based on the following passage.

In this excerpt from Richard Wright's 1937 novel Black Boy, *the young African-American narrator confronts a new world in the books he illegally borrows from the "whites-only" public library.*

That night in my rented room, while letting the hot water
run over my can of pork and beans in the sink, I opened
Mencken's *A Book of Prejudices* and began to read. I was
Line jarred and shocked by the style, the clear, clean, sweeping
(5) sentences. Why did he write like that? And how did one write
like that? I pictured the man as a raging demon, slashing
with his pen, consumed with hate, denouncing everything
American, extolling everything European, laughing at the
weaknesses of people, mocking God, authority. What was
(10) this? I stood up, trying to realize what reality lay behind the
meaning of the words. Yes, this man was fighting, fighting
with words. He was using words as a weapon, using them as
one would use a club. Could words be weapons? Well, yes,
for here they were. Then, maybe, perhaps, a Negro could use
(15) them as a weapon? No. It frightened me. I read on, and what
amazed me was not what he said, but how on earth anybody
had the courage to say it.
What strange world was this? I concluded the book with
the conviction that I had somehow overlooked something
(20) terribly important in life. I had once tried to write, had once
reveled in feeling, had let my crude imagination roam, but the
impulse to dream had been slowly beaten out of me by
experience. Now it surged up again and I hungered for

books, new ways of looking and seeing. It was not a matter
(25) of believing or disbelieving what I read, but of feeling something new, of being affected by something that made the look
of the world different.

As dawn broke I ate my pork and beans, feeling dopey,
sleepy. I went to work, but the mood of the book would not
(30) die; it lingered, coloring everything I saw, heard, did. I now
felt that I knew what the white men were feeling. Merely
because I had read a book that had spoken of how they lived
and thought, I identified myself with that book. I felt vaguely
guilty. Would I, filled with bookish notions, act in a manner
(35) that would make the whites dislike me?

I forged more notes and my trips to the library became
frequent. Reading grew into a passion. My first serious novel
was Sinclair Lewis's *Main Street*. It made me see my boss,
Mr. Gerald, and identify him as an American type. I would
(40) smile when I saw him lugging his golf bags into the office. I
had always felt a vast distance separating me from the boss,
and now I felt closer to him, though still distant. I felt now
that I knew him, that I could feel the very limits of his narrow
life. This had happened because I had read a novel about a
(45) mythical man called George F. Babbitt. But I could not con-
quer my sense of guilt, my feeling that the white men around
me knew that I was changing, that I had begun to regard
them differently.

16. The narrator's initial reaction to Mencken's prose can best be
described as one of

(A) wrath
(B) disbelief
(C) remorse
(D) laughter
(E) disdain

17. To the narrator, Mencken appeared to be all of the following EXCEPT

(A) intrepid
(B) articulate
(C) satiric
(D) reverent
(E) opinionated

18. As used in line 30, "coloring" most nearly means

(A) reddening
(B) sketching
(C) blushing
(D) affecting
(E) lying

19. The narrator's attitude in lines 23–24 is best described as one of

(A) dreamy indifference
(B) sullen resentment
(C) impatient ardor
(D) wistful anxiety
(E) quiet resolve

20. The passage suggests that, when he saw Mr. Gerald carrying the golf clubs, the narrator smiled out of a sense of

(A) relief
(B) duty
(C) recognition
(D) disbelief
(E) levity

21. The passage as a whole is best characterized as

(A) an impassioned argument in favor of increased literacy for blacks
(B) a description of a youth's gradual introduction to racial prejudice
(C) a comparison of the respective merits of Mencken's and Lewis's literary styles
(D) an analysis of the impact of ordinary life on art
(E) a portrait of a youth's response to expanding intellectual horizons

Questions 22–30 are based on the following passage.

The following passage about pond-dwellers is excerpted from an essay on natural history written in 1952 by the zoologist Konrad Lorenz.

There are some terrible robbers in the pond world, and, in our aquarium, we may witness all the cruelties of an em-bittered struggle for existence enacted before our very eyes.
Line If you have introduced to your aquarium a mixed catch, you
(5) will soon see an example of such conflicts, for, amongst the new arrivals, there will probably be a larva of the water-beetle Dytiscus. Considering their relative size, the voracity and cunning with which these animals destroy their prey eclipse the methods of even such notorious robbers as tigers, lions,
(10) wolves, or killer whales. These are all as lambs compared with the Dytiscus larva.

It is a slim, streamlined insect, rather more than two inches long. Its six legs are equipped with stout fringes of bristles, which form broad oar-like blades that propel the
(15) animal quickly and surely through the water. The wide, flat head bears an enormous, pincer-shaped pair of jaws that are hollow and serve not only as syringes for injecting poison, but also as orifices of ingestion. The animal lies in ambush on some waterplant; suddenly it shoots at lightning speed
(20) towards its prey, darts underneath it, then quickly jerks up its head and grabs the victim in its jaws. "Prey," for these crea-tures, is all that moves or that smells of "animal" in any way. It has often happened to me that, while standing quietly in the water of a pond, I have been "eaten" by a Dytiscus larva.
(25) Even for man, an injection of the poisonous digestive juice of this insect is extremely painful.

These beetle larvae are among the few animals that digest "out of doors." The glandular secretion that they inject, through their hollow forceps, into their prey, dissolves the
(30) entire inside of the latter into a liquid soup, which is then

sucked in through the same channel by the attacker. Even
large victims, such as fat tadpoles or dragon-fly larvae, which
have been bitten by a Dytiscus larva, stiffen after a few defen-
sive moments, and their inside, which, as in most water
(35) animals, is more or less transparent, becomes opaque as
though fixed by formalin. The animal swells up first, then
gradually shrinks to a limp bundle of skin that hangs from
the deadly jaws, and is finally allowed to drop. In the con-
fines of an aquarium, a few large Dytiscus larvae will, within
(40) days, eat all living things over a quarter of an inch long. What
happens then? They will eat each other, if they have not
already done so; this depends less on who is bigger and
stronger than upon who succeeds in seizing the other first. I
have often seen two nearly equal sized Dytiscus larvae each
(45) seize the other simultaneously and both die a quick death by
inner dissolution. Very few animals, even when threatened
with starvation, will attack an equal sized animal of their own
species with the intention of devouring it. I only know this to
be definitely true of rats and a few related rodents; that
(50) wolves do the same thing, I am much inclined to doubt, on
the strength of some observations of which I shall speak
later. But Dytiscus larvae devour animals of their own breed
and size, even when other nourishment is at hand, and that is
done, as far as I know, by no other animal.

22. By robbers (line 1), the author refers to

(A) thieves
(B) plagiarists
(C) people who steal fish
(D) creatures that devour their prey
(E) unethical scientific observers

23. As used in line 4, a "mixed catch" most likely is

(A) a device used to shut the aquarium lid temporarily
(B) a disturbed group of water beetle larvae
(C) a partially desirable prospective denizen of the aquarium
(D) a random batch of creatures taken from a pond
(E) a theoretical drawback that may have positive results

24. The presence of Dytiscus larvae in an aquarium most likely would be of particular interest to naturalists studying

   (A) means of exterminating water-beetle larvae
   (B) predatory patterns within a closed environment
   (C) genetic characteristics of a mixed catch
   (D) the effect of captivity on aquatic life
   (E) the social behavior of dragon-fly larvae

25. The author's primary purpose in lines 12–18 is to

   (A) depict the typical victim of a Dytiscus larva
   (B) point out the threat to humans represented by Dytiscus larvae
   (C) describe the physical appearance of an aquatic predator
   (D) refute the notion of the aquarium as a peaceful habitat
   (E) clarify the method the Dytiscus larva uses to dispatch its prey

26. The passage mentions all of the following facts about Dytiscus larvae EXCEPT that they

   (A) secrete digestive juices
   (B) attack their fellow larvae
   (C) are attracted to motion
   (D) provide food for amphibians
   (E) have ravenous appetites

27. By digesting "out of doors" (line 28), the author is referring to the Dytiscus larva's

   (A) preference for open-water ponds over confined spaces
   (B) metabolic elimination of waste matter
   (C) amphibious method of locomotion
   (D) extreme voraciousness of appetite
   (E) external conversion of food into absorbable form

28. According to the author, which of the following is (are) true of the victim of a Dytiscus larva?

   I. Its interior increases in opacity.
   II. It shrivels as it is drained of nourishment.
   III. It is beheaded by the larva's jaws.
   (A) I only
   (B) II only
   (C) III only
   (D) I and II only
   (E) II and III only

29. In the final paragraph, the author mentions rats and related rodents in order to emphasize which point about Dytiscus larvae?

   (A) Unless starvation drives them, they will not resort to eating members of their own species.

   (B) They are reluctant to attack equal-sized members of their own breed.

   (C) They are capable of resisting attacks from much larger animals.

   (D) They are one of extremely few species given to devouring members of their own breed.

   (E) Although they are noted predators, Dytiscus larvae are less savage than rats.

30. The author indicates that in subsequent passages he will discuss

   (A) the likelihood of cannibalism among wolves

   (B) the metamorphosis of dragon-fly larvae into dragon-flies

   (C) antidotes to cases of Dytiscus poisoning

   (D) the digestive processes of killer whales

   (E) the elimination of Dytiscus larvae from aquariums

YOU MAY GO BACK AND REVIEW THIS
SECTION IN THE REMAINING TIME, BUT   **S T O P**
DO NOT WORK IN ANY OTHER SECTION
UNTIL TOLD TO DO SO.

SECTION 2

25 Questions—30 Minutes

For each problem in this section determine which of the five choices is correct and blacken in that choice on your answer sheet. You may use any blank space on the page for your work.

Notes:

- You may use a calculator whenever you feel it will be helpful.
- Use the diagrams provided to help you solve the problems. Unless you see the words "<u>Note</u>: Figure not drawn to scale" under a diagram, it has been drawn as accurately as possible. Unless it is stated that a figure is three-dimensional, you may assume it lies in a plane.

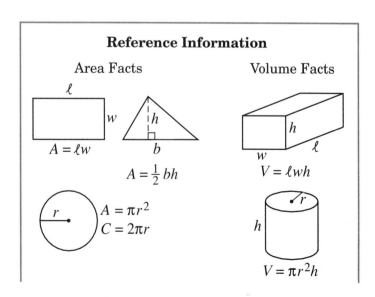

Reference Information

Area Facts

$A = \ell w$

$A = \frac{1}{2} bh$

$A = \pi r^2$

$C = 2\pi r$

Volume Facts

$V = \ell w h$

$V = \pi r^2 h$

Triangle Facts

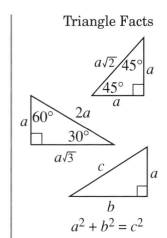

$a^2 + b^2 = c^2$

Angle Facts

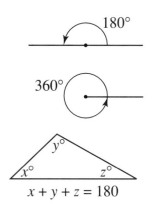

$x + y + z = 180$

1. If it is now June, what month will it be 100 months from now?

(A) January   (B) April   (C) June
(D) October   (E) December

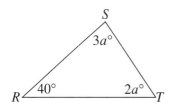

2. In the figure above, what is the value of a?

(A) 10   (B) 20   (C) 28   (D) 36   (E) 45

3. The Rivertown Little League is divided into d divisions. Each division has t teams, and each team has p players. How many players are there in the entire league?

(A) $d + t + p$ (B) dtp (C) $\dfrac{pt}{d}$ (D) $\dfrac{dt}{p}$ (E) $\dfrac{d}{pt}$

4. At the Fancy Furniture Factory, Brian bought two chairs for $299 each and a coffee table for $140. He paid $\frac{1}{6}$ of the total cost at the time of purchase and the balance in 12 equal monthly installments. What was the amount of each month's payment?

(A) $10.25   (B) $37.50   (C) $42.75
(D) $51.25   (E) $61.50

---

5. What is the value of n if $2^{n+1} = 32$?

(A) 4   (B) 5   (C) 6   (D) 7   (E) 8

---

6. In the figure at the right, what is the value of $a + b + c$?

(A) 210   (B) 220
(C) 240   (D) 270
(E) 280

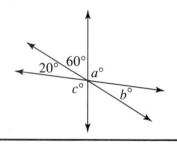

7. The operation ** is defined as follows: For any positive numbers a and b, $a**b = \sqrt{a} + \sqrt{b}$. Which of the following is an integer?

(A) 11**5   (B) 4**9   (C) 4**16   (D) 7**4   (E) 9**9

Year	1990	1991	1992	1993	1994	1995
Number of tournaments	4	5	10	6	9	12

8. The chart above shows the number of tennis tournaments that Adam entered each year from 1990 through 1995. In what year did he enter 50% more tournaments than the year before?

(A) 1991   (B) 1992   (C) 1993   (D) 1994   (E) 1995

9. If, for any number b, $b\# = b + 1$ and $\#b = b - 1$, which of the following is NOT equal to $(3\#)(\#5)$?

(A) $(1\#)(\#9)$ (B) $7\# + \#9$ (C) $(4\#)(\#4)$ (D) $(7\#)(\#3)$ (E) $\dfrac{15\#}{\#2}$

10. If a is a multiple of 5 and $b = 5a$, which of the following could be the value of $a + b$?

I. 60
II. 100
III. 150

(A) I only   (B) III only   (C) I and III only
(D) II and III only   (E) I, II, and III

11. If Scott can mow $\dfrac{2}{5}$ of a lawn each hour, how many lawns can he mow in h hours?

(A) $\dfrac{2h}{5}$ (B) $\dfrac{5h}{2}$ (C) $h - \dfrac{2}{5}$ (D) $\dfrac{2}{5h}$ (E) $\dfrac{5}{2h}$

12. If $3^a = b$ and $3^c = d$, then $bd =$

(A) 3^{ac} (B) 3^{a+c} (C) 6^{a+c} (D) 9^{ac} (E) 9^{a+c}

13. If r and s are two nonzero numbers and if $78(r + s) = (78 + r)s$, then which of the following MUST be true?

(A) $r = 78$ (B) $s = 78$ (C) $r + s = rs$
(D) $r < 1$ (E) $s < 1$

14. If the average (arithmetic mean) of three consecutive integers is A, which of the following must be true?

I. One of the numbers is equal to A.
II. The average of two of the three numbers is A.
III. A is an integer.

(A) I only (B) II only (C) III only
(D) I and II only (E) I, II, and III

---

15. A bag contains 25 slips of paper, on each of which a different integer from 1 to 25 is written. Blindfolded, Scott draws one of the slips of paper. He wins if the number on the slip he draws is a multiple of 3 or 5. What is the probability that Scott wins?

(A) $\dfrac{1}{25}$ (B) $\dfrac{8}{25}$ (C) $\dfrac{11}{25}$ (D) $\dfrac{12}{25}$ (E) $\dfrac{13}{25}$

---

16. If $m^2 = 17$, then what is the value of $(m+1)(m-1)$?

(A) $\sqrt{17} - 1$ (B) $\sqrt{17} + 1$ (C) 16 (D) 18
(E) 288

---

17. What is the value of n if $3^{10} \times 27^2 = 9^2 \times 3^n$?

(A) 6 (B) 10 (C) 12 (D) 15 (E) 30

---

18. Which of the following points lies in the interior of the circle whose radius is 10 and whose center is at the origin?

(A) $(-9,4)$ (B) $(5,-9)$ (C) $(0,-10)$
(D) $(10,-1)$ (E) $(-6,8)$

19. Assume that p, q, and r are positive integers satisfying the following conditions: (i) $p > q > r$; (ii) p, q, and r are all primes; (iii) $p - q = r$. This information is sufficient to determine the value of which integer or integers?

(A) none of them   (B) p only   (C) q only
(D) r only   (E) p, q, and r

---

20. If p pencils cost c cents, how many pencils can be bought for d dollars?

(A) cdp (B) $100cdp$ (C) $\dfrac{dp}{100c}$ (D) $\dfrac{100cd}{p}$ (E) $\dfrac{100dp}{c}$

---

21. If a is increased by 10% and b is decreased by 10%, the resulting numbers will be equal. What is the ratio of a to b?

(A) $\dfrac{9}{11}$ (B) $\dfrac{9}{10}$ (C) $\dfrac{1}{1}$ (D) $\dfrac{10}{9}$ (E) $\dfrac{11}{9}$

---

22. In the figure at the right, line segments AF and CF partition pentagon $ABCDE$ into a rectangle and two triangles. For which of the following can the value be determined?

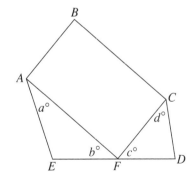

I. $a + b$
II. $b + c$
III. $a + b + c + d$

(A) II only   (B) I and II only
(C) II and III only   (D) I and III only
(E) I, II, and III

23. Which of the following CANNOT be expressed as the sum of two or more consecutive positive integers?

(A) 17   (B) 22   (C) 24   (D) 26   (E) 32

---

24. The figure at the right consists of four semicircles in a large semi-circle. If the small semicircles have radii of 1, 2, 3, and 4, what is the perimeter of the shaded region?

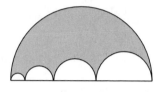

(A) 10π   (B) 20π   (C) 40π   (D) 60π   (E) 100π

---

25. In the figure at the right, the legs of right triangle *ACB* are diameters of the two semicircles. If *AB* = 4, what is the sum of the areas of the semicircles?

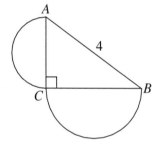

(A) π   (B) 2π   (C) 4π
(D) 8π   (E) 16π

YOU MAY GO BACK AND REVIEW THIS
SECTION IN THE REMAINING TIME, BUT **S T O P**
DO NOT WORK IN ANY OTHER SECTION
UNTIL TOLD TO DO SO.

SECTION 3

35 Questions—30 Minutes

Select the best answer to the following questions, then fill in the appropriate space on your Answer Sheet.

Each of the following sentences contains one or two blanks; these blanks indicate that a word or set of words has been left out. Below the sentence are five words or phrases, lettered A through E. Select the word or set of words that best completes the sentence.

Example:

Fame is -------- ; today's rising star is all too soon tomorrow's washed-up has-been.

(A) rewarding   (B) gradual
  (C) essential   (D) spontaneous
    (E) transitory

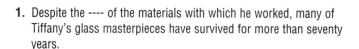

1. Despite the ---- of the materials with which he worked, many of Tiffany's glass masterpieces have survived for more than seventy years.

(A) beauty   (B) translucence   (C) abundance
(D) majesty   (E) fragility

2. Although similar to mice in many physical characteristics, voles may be ---- mice by the shortness of their tails.

(A) distinguished from
(B) classified with
(C) related to
(D) categorized as
(E) enumerated with

3. No summary of the behavior of animals toward reflected images is given, but not much else that is ---- seems missing from this comprehensive yet compact study of mirrors and mankind.

   (A) redundant (B) contemplative
    (C) relevant (D) peripheral
      (E) disputable

4. Dr. Charles Drew's technique for preserving and storing blood plasma for emergency use proved so ---- that it became the ---- for the present blood bank system used by the American Red Cross.

   (A) irrelevant...inspiration
   (B) urgent...pattern
   (C) effective...model
   (D) innocuous...excuse
   (E) complex...blueprint

5. The likenesses of language around the Mediterranean were sufficiently marked to ---- ease of movement both of men and ideas: it took relatively few alterations to make a Spanish song intelligible in Italy, and an Italian trader could, without much difficulty, make himself at home in France.

   (A) eliminate (B) facilitate (C) hinder
    (D) clarify (E) aggravate

6. Because he saw no ---- to the task assigned him, he worked at it in a very ---- way.

   (A) function...systematic
   (B) method...dutiful
   (C) purpose...diligent
   (D) end...rigid
   (E) point...perfunctory

7. Pain is the body's early warning system: loss of ---- in the extremities leaves a person ---- injuring himself unwittingly.

   (A) agony...incapable of
   (B) sensation...vulnerable to
   (C) consciousness...desirous of
   (D) feeling...habituated to
   (E) movement...prone to

8. Much of the clown's success may be attributed to the contrast between the ---- manner he adopts and the general ---- that characterizes the circus.

(A) giddy...sobriety
(B) lugubrious...hilarity
(C) gaudy...clamor
(D) joyful...hysteria
(E) frenetic...excitement

9. Fortunately, she was ---- her accomplishments, properly unwilling to ---- them before her friends.

(A) excited by...parade
(B) immodest about...discuss
(C) deprecatory about...flaunt
(D) uncertain of...concede
(E) unaware of...conceal

10. Despite their ---- of Twain's *Huckleberry Finn* for its stereotyped portrait of the slave Jim, even the novel's ---- agreed it was a masterpiece of American prose.

(A) admiration...critics
(B) denunciation...supporters
(C) criticism...detractors
(D) defense...censors
(E) praise...advocates

Each of the following examples introduces a capitalized pair of words or phrases linked by a colon (:); this colon indicates that these words are related in some way. Following the capitalized pair are five pairs of words or phrases lettered A through E. Select the pair whose relationship is most similar to the relationship illustrated by the capitalized pair.

Example:

CLOCK:TIME::   (A) watch:wrist
  (B) pedometer:speed   (C) thermometer:temperature
    (D) hourglass:sand   (E) radio:sound

11. PLAY:ACTS::

    (A) opera:arias
    (B) novel:chapters
    (C) poem:rhymes
    (D) essay:topics
    (E) game:athletes

12. GEOLOGY:SCIENCE::

    (A) biology:laboratory
    (B) astronomy:galaxy
    (C) fashion:style
    (D) fir:tree
    (E) theory:practice

13. SIGNATURE:PORTRAIT::

    (A) title:novel
    (B) negative:photograph
    (C) autograph:celebrity
    (D) postscript:letter
    (E) byline:article

14. PLANE:SMOOTH::

    (A) boat:sink
    (B) arc:circle
    (C) cheese:grate
    (D) axe:sharpen
    (E) wrench:twist

15. FUNDS:EMBEZZLED::

    (A) loot:buried
    (B) writings:plagiarized
    (C) ransom:demanded
    (D) money:deposited
    (E) truth:exaggerated

16. UNCOUTH:GRACELESSNESS::

    (A) petulant:agreement
    (B) avaricious:greed
    (C) impassive:feeling
    (D) malicious:dishonesty
    (E) reticent:shamelessness

17. ELEVATOR:SHAFT::

    (A) electricity:outlet
    (B) water:conduit
    (C) escalator:step
    (D) railroad:train
    (E) skyscraper:foundation

18. PARSIMONY:FRUGALITY::

    (A) agony:pain
    (B) steam:water
    (C) anger:wrath
    (D) warmth:flame
    (E) pleasure:gloom

19. DILETTANTE:DABBLE::

    (A) coquette:flirt
    (B) gymnast:exercise
    (C) soldier:drill
    (D) embezzler:steal
    (E) benefactor:donate

20. INDIFFERENT:CONCERN::

    (A) intrepid:bravery
    (B) arrogant:modesty
    (C) unbigoted:tolerance
    (D) unnatural:emotion
    (E) incomparable:relevance

21. TACITURNITY:LACONIC::

    (A) improvisation:unrehearsed
    (B) verbosity:pithy
    (C) silence:golden
    (D) ballet:ungainly
    (E) vacation:leisurely

22. SLANDER:DEFAMATORY::

    (A) fraud:notorious
    (B) tenet:devotional
    (C) elegy:sorrowful
    (D) edict:temporary
    (E) exhortation:cautionary

23. SLOUGH:SKIN::

(A) shed:hair
(B) polish:teeth
(C) shade:eyes
(D) tear:ligaments
(E) remove:tonsils

Read the passage below, and then answer the questions that follow the passage. The correct response may be stated outright or merely suggested in the passage.

Questions 24–35 are based on the following passage.

The passage below is excerpted from the introduction to "Bury My Heart at Wounded Knee," written in 1970 by the Native American historian Dee Brown.

Since the exploratory journey of Lewis and Clark to the Pacific Coast early in the nineteenth century, the number of published accounts describing the "opening" of the American
Line West has risen into the thousands. The greatest concentra-
(5) tion of recorded experience and observation came out of the thirty-year span between 1860 and 1890—the period covered by this book. It was an incredible era of violence, greed, audacity, sentimentality, undirected exuberance, and an almost reverential attitude toward the ideal of personal free-
(10) dom for those who already had it.
  During that time the culture and civilization of the American Indian was destroyed, and out of that time came virtually all the great myths of the American West—tales of fur traders, mountain men, steamboat pilots, goldseekers,
(15) gamblers, gunmen, cavalrymen, cowboys, harlots, mission-aries, schoolmarms, and homesteaders. Only occasionally was the voice of the Indian heard, and then more often than not it was recorded by the pen of a white man. The Indian was the dark menace of the myths, and even if he had known

(20) how to write in English, where would he have found a printer
or a publisher?

Yet they are not all lost, those Indian voices of the past. A
few authentic accounts of American western history were
recorded by Indians either in pictographs or in translated
(25) English, and some managed to get published in obscure
journals, pamphlets, or books of small circulation. In the late
nineteenth century, when the white man's curiosity about
Indian survivors of the wars reached a high point, enterpris-
ing newspaper reporters frequently interviewed warriors and
(30) chiefs and gave them an opportunity to express their
opinions on what was happening in the West. The quality of
these interviews varied greatly, depending upon the abilities
of the interpreters, or upon the inclination of the Indians to
speak freely. Some feared reprisals for telling the truth, while
(35) others delighted in hoaxing reporters with tall tales and
shaggy-dog stories. Contemporary newspaper statements by
Indians must therefore be read with skepticism, although
some of them are masterpieces of irony and others burn with
outbursts of poetic fury.
(40) Among the richest sources of first-person statements by
Indians are the records of treaty councils and other formal
meetings with civilian and military representatives of the
United States government. Isaac Pitman's new stenographic
system was coming into vogue in the second half of the
(45) nineteenth century, and when Indians spoke in council a
recording clerk sat beside the official interpreter.

Even when the meetings were in remote parts of the West,
someone usually was available to write down the speeches,
and because of the slowness of the translation process,
(50) much of what was said could be recorded in longhand.
Interpreters quite often were half-bloods who knew spoken
languages but seldom could read or write. Like most oral
peoples they and the Indians depended upon imagery to
express their thoughts, so that the English translations were
(55) filled with graphic similes and metaphors of the natural
world. If an eloquent Indian had a poor interpreter, his words

might be transformed to flat prose, but a good interpreter could make a poor speaker sound poetic.

Most Indian leaders spoke freely and candidly in councils
(60) with white officials, and as they became more sophisticated in such matters during the 1870s and 1880s, they demanded the right to choose their own interpreters and recorders. In this latter period, all members of the tribes were free to speak, and some of the older men chose such opportunities
(65) to recount events they had witnessed in the past, or sum up the histories of their peoples. Although the Indians who lived through this doom period of their civilization have vanished from the earth, millions of their words are preserved in official records. Many of the more important council proceed-
(70) ings were published in government documents and reports.

Out of all these sources of almost forgotten oral history, I have tried to fashion a narrative of the conquest of the American West as the victims experienced it, using their own words whenever possible. Americans who have always
(75) looked westward when reading about this period should read this book facing eastward.

This is not a cheerful book, but history has a way of intruding upon the present, and perhaps those who read it will have a clearer understanding of what the American
(80) Indian is, by knowing what he was. They may learn something about their own relationship to the earth from a people who were true conservationists. The Indians knew that life was equated with the earth and its resources, that America was a paradise, and they could not comprehend why the
(85) intruders from the East were determined to destroy all that was Indian as well as America itself.

24. The author finds the period of 1860–1890 noteworthy because

(A) the journals of the Lewis and Clark expedition were made public during this time
(B) in that period the bulk of original accounts of the "winning of the West" were produced
(C) during these years American Indians made great strides in regaining their lands
(D) only a very few documents dating from this period are still extant
(E) people still believed in personal freedom as an ideal

25. The author most likely uses quotation marks around the word "opening" (line 3) because

(A) the West was closed rather than opened during this period of time
(B) the American West actually was opened for settlement much earlier in the century
(C) from a Native American perspective it is an inaccurate term
(D) he is citing an authoritative source
(E) he has employed it in its figurative sense

26. A main concern of the author in this passage is to

(A) denounce the white man for his untrustworthiness and savagery
(B) evaluate the effectiveness of the military treaty councils
(C) argue for the improved treatment of Indians today
(D) suggest that Indian narratives of the conquest of the West are similar to white accounts
(E) introduce the background of the original source materials for his text

27. The word "concentration" in lines 4–5 means

(A) memory
(B) attention
(C) diligence
(D) imprisonment
(E) cluster

28. In describing the ideal of freedom revered by the pioneers as "personal freedom for those who already had it" (lines 9–10), the author is being

(A) enthusiastic
(B) ironic
(C) prosaic
(D) redundant
(E) lyrical

29. According to the passage, nineteenth-century newspaper accounts of interviews with Indians may contain inaccuracies for which of the following reasons?

   I. Lack of skill on the part of the translators
   II. The tendency of the reporters to overstate what they were told by the Indians
   III. The Indians' misgivings about possible retaliations

   (A) I only
   (B) III only
   (C) I and II only
   (D) I and III only
   (E) I, II, and III

30. The author's tone in describing the Indian survivors can best be described as

   (A) skeptical
   (B) detached
   (C) elegiac
   (D) obsequious
   (E) impatient

31. The author is most impressed by which aspect of the English translations of Indian speeches?

   (A) Their vividness of imagery
   (B) Their lack of frankness
   (C) The inefficiency of the process
   (D) Their absence of sophistication
   (E) Their brevity of expression

32. The word "flat" in line 57 means

   (A) smooth
   (B) level
   (C) pedestrian
   (D) horizontal
   (E) unequivocal

33. In treaty councils before 1870, most Indians did not ask for their own interpreters and recorders because

(A) they could not afford to hire people to take down their words
(B) the white officials provided these services as a matter of course
(C) they were unaware that they had the option to demand such services
(D) they preferred speaking for themselves without the help of translators
(E) they were reluctant to have their words recorded for posterity

34. The author most likely suggests that Americans should read this book facing eastward

(A) in an inappropriate attempt at levity
(B) out of respect for Western superstitions
(C) in order to read by natural light
(D) because the Indians came from the East
(E) to identify with the Indians' viewpoint

35. The phrase "equated with" in line 83 means

(A) reduced to an average with
(B) necessarily tied to
(C) numerically equal to
(D) fulfilled by
(E) differentiated by

YOU MAY GO BACK AND REVIEW THIS
SECTION IN THE REMAINING TIME, BUT   **S T O P**
DO NOT WORK IN ANY OTHER SECTION
UNTIL TOLD TO DO SO.

SECTION 4

25 Questions—30 Minutes

You have 30 minutes to answer the 15 Quantitative Comparison questions and 10 Student-Produced Response questions in this section. You may use any blank space on the page for your work.

Notes:

- You may use a calculator whenever you feel it will be helpful.
- Use the diagrams provided to help you solve the problems. Unless you see the words "Note: Figure not drawn to scale" under a diagram, it has been drawn as accurately as possible. Unless it is stated that a figure is three-dimensional, you may assume it lies in a plane.

Reference Information

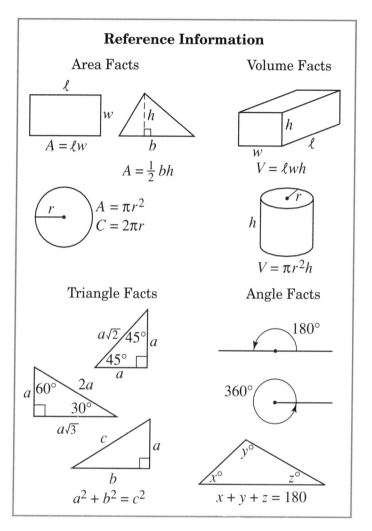

Area Facts

$A = \ell w$

$A = \frac{1}{2} bh$

$A = \pi r^2$
$C = 2\pi r$

Volume Facts

$V = \ell wh$

$V = \pi r^2 h$

Triangle Facts

$a^2 + b^2 = c^2$

Angle Facts

$180°$

$360°$

$x + y + z = 180$

Directions for the Quantitative Comparison Questions

In each of questions 1–15, two quantities appear in boxes: one in Column A and one in Column B. You must compare them. The correct answer to a question is

A   if the quantity in Column A is greater;
B   if the quantity in Column B is greater;
C   if the two quantities are equal;
D   if it is impossible to determine which quantity is greater.

Notes:
- *The correct answer is <u>never</u> E.*
- Sometimes information about one or both of the quantities is centered above the two boxes.
- If the same symbol appears in both columns, it represents the same thing each time.
- All variables represent real numbers.

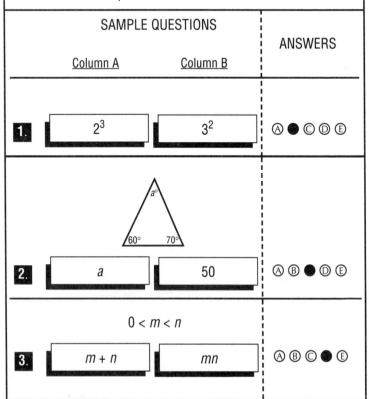

	SAMPLE QUESTIONS		ANSWERS
	Column A	Column B	
1.	2^3	3^2	Ⓐ ● Ⓒ Ⓓ Ⓔ
2.	a	50	Ⓐ Ⓑ ● Ⓓ Ⓔ
3.	$m + n$	mn	Ⓐ Ⓑ Ⓒ ● Ⓔ

For question 2, the triangle is labeled with angles $a°$ at the top, $60°$ and $70°$ at the bottom.

For question 3, the condition $0 < m < n$ is centered above the boxes.

SUMMARY DIRECTIONS FOR QUANTITATIVE COMPARISON QUESTIONS

<u>Answer:</u> A if the quantity in Column A is greater;
B if the quantity in Column B is greater;
C if the two quantities are equal;
D if it is impossible to determine which quantity is greater.

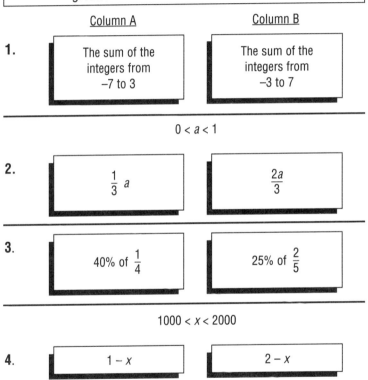

	Column A	Column B
1.	The sum of the integers from −7 to 3	The sum of the integers from −3 to 7

$$0 < a < 1$$

2.	$\frac{1}{3}\ a$	$\frac{2a}{3}$

3.	40% of $\frac{1}{4}$	25% of $\frac{2}{5}$

$$1000 < x < 2000$$

4.	$1 - x$	$2 - x$

SUMMARY DIRECTIONS FOR QUANTITATIVE COMPARISON QUESTIONS

<u>Answer:</u> A if the quantity in Column A is greater;
B if the quantity in Column B is greater;
C if the two quantities are equal;
D if it is impossible to determine which quantity is greater.

<u>Column A</u>   <u>Column B</u>

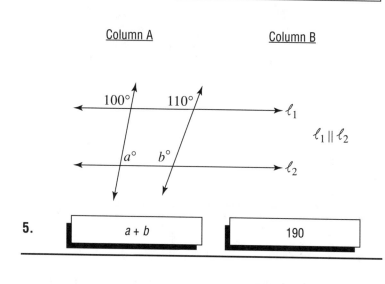

$\ell_1 \parallel \ell_2$

5. $a + b$ 190

$$x > 1$$
$$xy = 12$$
$$zx = 25$$

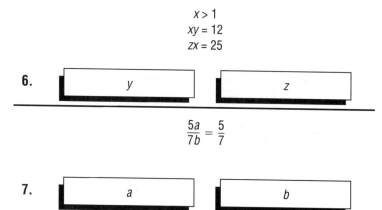

6. y z

$$\frac{5a}{7b} = \frac{5}{7}$$

7. a b

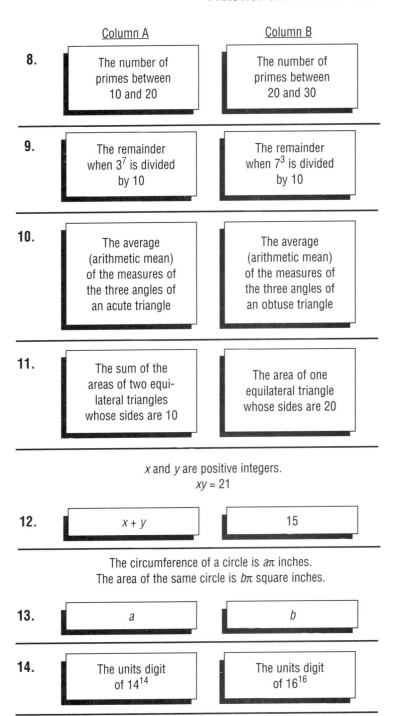

	Column A	Column B
8.	The number of primes between 10 and 20	The number of primes between 20 and 30
9.	The remainder when 3^7 is divided by 10	The remainder when 7^3 is divided by 10
10.	The average (arithmetic mean) of the measures of the three angles of an acute triangle	The average (arithmetic mean) of the measures of the three angles of an obtuse triangle
11.	The sum of the areas of two equilateral triangles whose sides are 10	The area of one equilateral triangle whose sides are 20

x and y are positive integers.
$xy = 21$

12.	$x + y$	15

The circumference of a circle is $a\pi$ inches.
The area of the same circle is $b\pi$ square inches.

13.	a	b

14.	The units digit of 14^{14}	The units digit of 16^{16}

Column A   Column B

From 1980 to 1985 the population of
Mudville decreased 20%.
From 1985 to 1990 the population of
Mudville decreased 20%.
From 1990 to 1995 the population of
Mudville decreased 20%.

15.

| The population of Mudville in 1995 | One-half the population of Mudville in 1980 |

Directions for Student-Produced Response Questions (Grid-ins)

In questions 16–25, first solve the problem, and then enter your answer on the grid provided on the answer sheet. The instructions for entering your answers are as follows:

- First, write your answer in the boxes at the top of the grid.
- Second, grid your answer in the columns below the boxes.
- Use the fraction bar in the first row or the decimal point in the second row to enter fractions and decimal answers.

Answer: $\frac{8}{15}$ Answer: 1.75

Write your answer in the boxes

Grid in your answer

Answer: 100

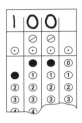

Either position is acceptable

- Grid only one space in each column.
- Entering the answer in the boxes is recommended as an aid in gridding, but is not required.
- The machine scoring your exam can read only what you grid, so you **must grid in your answers correctly to get credit.**
- If a question has more than one correct answer, grid in only one of them.
- The grid does not have a minus sign, so no answer can be negative.
- A mixed number *must* be converted to an improper

  fraction or a decimal before it is gridded. Enter $1\frac{1}{4}$ as 5/4

  or 1.25; the machine will interpret 1 1/4 as $\frac{11}{4}$ and
  mark it wrong.
- **All decimals must be entered as accurately as possible.** Here are
  the three acceptable ways of gridding

$$\frac{3}{11} = 0.272727...$$

3/11   .272   .273

- Note that rounding to .273 is acceptable, because you are using the full grid, but you would receive **no credit** for .3 or .27, because they are less accurate.

16. If a secretary types 60 words per minute, how many minutes will he take to type 330 words?

17. If $2x - 15 = 15 - 2x$, what is the value of x?

18. In the figure at the right, C is the center of the circle. What is the value of c?

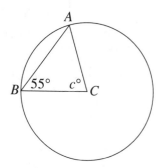

19. Maria is 6 times as old as Tina. In 20 years, Maria will be only twice as old as Tina. How old is Maria now?

20. If r, s, and t are different prime numbers less than 15, what is the greatest possible value of $\dfrac{r + s}{t}$?

21. If the average (arithmetic mean) of 10, 20, 30, 40, and x is 60, what is the value of x?

22. Line ℓ passes through the origin and point $(3,k)$, where $4 < k < 5$. What is one possible value for the slope of line ℓ?

---

23. At Central High School 50 girls play intramural basketball and 40 girls play intramural volleyball. If 10 girls play both sports, what is the ratio of the number of girls who play only basketball to the number who play only volleyball?

---

24. If A is the sum of the integers from 1 to 50 and B is the sum of the integers from 51 to 100, what is the value of $B - A$?

---

25. In the diagram at the right, O, P, and Q, which are the centers of the three circles, all lie on diameter AB. What is the ratio of the area of the entire shaded region to the area of the white region?

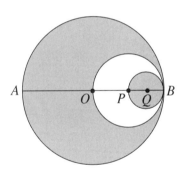

YOU MAY GO BACK AND REVIEW THIS SECTION IN THE REMAINING TIME, BUT DO NOT WORK IN ANY OTHER SECTION UNTIL TOLD TO DO SO.

S T O P

SECTION 5

13 Questions—15 Minutes

Select the best answer to the following questions, then fill in the appropriate space on your Answer Sheet.

The questions that follow the two passages in this section relate to the content of both, and to their relationship. The correct response may be stated outright in the passages or merely suggested.

Questions 1–13 are based on the following passages.

The following passages are excerpted from two recent essays that make an analogy between writing and sports. The author of Passage 1 discusses the sorts of failures experienced by writers and ballplayers. The author of Passage 2 explores how his involvement in sports affected his writing career.

Passage 1

In consigning this manuscript to a desk drawer, I am comforted by the behavior of baseball players. There are *no* pitchers who do not give up home runs, there are *no* batters
Line who do not strike out. There are *no* major league pitchers or
(5) batters who have not somehow learned to survive giving up home runs and striking out. That much is obvious.

What seems to me less obvious is how these "failures" must be digested, or put to use, in the overall experience of the player. A jogger once explained to me that the nerves of
(10) the ankle are so sensitive and complex that each time a run-

ner sets his foot down, hundreds of messages are conveyed
to the runner's brain about the nature of the terrain and the
requirements for weight distribution, balance, and muscle-
strength. I'm certain that the ninth-inning home run that Dave
(15) Henderson hit off Donny Moore registered complexly and
permanently in Moore's mind and body and that the next
time Moore faced Henderson, his pitching was informed by
his awful experience of October 1986. Moore's continuing
baseball career depended to some extent on his converting
(20) that encounter with Henderson into something useful for his
pitching. I can also imagine such an experience destroying an
athlete, registering in his mind and body in such a negative
way as to produce a debilitating fear.

Of the many ways in which athletes and artists are similar,
(25) one is that, unlike accountants or plumbers or insurance
salesmen, to succeed at all they must perform at an extraordinary level of excellence. Another is that they must be willing to extend themselves irrationally in order to achieve that
level of performance. A writer doesn't have to write all-out all
(30) the time, but he or she must be ready to write all-out any
time the story requires it. Hold back and you produce what
just about any literate citizen can produce, a "pretty good"
piece of work. Like the cautious pitcher, the timid writer can
spend a lifetime in the minor leagues.

(35) And what more than failure—the strike out, the crucial
home run given up, the manuscript criticized and rejected—
is more likely to produce caution or timidity? An instinctive
response to painful experience is to avoid the behavior that
produced the pain. To function at the level of excellence
(40) required for survival, writers, like athletes, must go against
instinct, must absorb their failures and become stronger,
must endlessly repeat the behavior that produced the pain.

Passage 2

The athletic advantages of this concentration, particularly
for an athlete who was making up for the absence of great

(45) natural skill, were considerable. Concentration gave you an edge over many of your opponents, even your betters, who could not isolate themselves to that degree. For example, in football if they were ahead (or behind) by several touchdowns, if the game itself seemed to have been settled, they
(50) tended to slack off, to ease off a little, certainly to relax their own concentration. It was then that your own unwavering concentration and your own indifference to the larger point of view paid off. At the very least you could deal out surprise and discomfort to your opponents.

(55)   But it was more than that. Do you see? The ritual of physical concentration, of acute engagement in a small space while disregarding all the clamor and demands of the larger world, was the best possible lesson in precisely the kind of selfish intensity needed to create and to finish a poem, a
(60) story, or a novel. This alone mattered while all the world going on, with and without you, did not.

    I was learning first in muscle, blood, and bone, not from literature and not from teachers of literature or the arts or the natural sciences, but from coaches, in particular this one
(65) coach who paid me enough attention to influence me to teach some things to myself. I was learning about art and life through the abstraction of athletics in much the same way that a soldier is, to an extent, prepared for war by endless parade ground drill. His body must learn to be a soldier
(70) before heart, mind, and spirit can.

    Ironically, I tend to dismiss most comparisons of athletics to art and to "the creative process." But only because, I think, so much that is claimed for both is untrue. But I have come to believe—indeed I have to believe it insofar as I believe in
(75) the validity and efficacy of art—that what comes to us first and foremost through the body, as a sensuous affective experience, is taken and transformed by mind and self into a thing of the spirit. Which is only to say what the body learns and is taught is of enormous significance—at least until the
(80) last light of the body fails.

1. Why does the author of Passage 1 consign his manuscript to a desk drawer?

   (A) To protect it from the inquisitive eyes of his family
   (B) To prevent its getting lost or disordered
   (C) Because his publisher wishes to take another look at it
   (D) Because he chooses to watch a televised baseball game
   (E) To set it aside as unmarketable in its current state

2. Why is the author of Passage 1 "comforted by the behavior of baseball players" (line 2)?

   (A) He treasures the timeless rituals of America's national pastime.
   (B) He sees he is not alone in having to confront failure and move on.
   (C) He enjoys watching the frustration of the batters who strike out.
   (D) He looks at baseball from the viewpoint of a behavioral psychologist.
   (E) He welcomes any distraction from the task of revising his novel.

3. What function in the passage is served by the discussion of the nerves in the ankle in lines 9–14?

   (A) It provides a momentary digression from the overall narrative flow.
   (B) It emphasizes how strong a mental impact Henderson's home run must have had on Moore.
   (C) It provides scientific confirmation of the neuromuscular abilities of athletes.
   (D) It illustrates that the author's interest in sports is not limited to baseball alone.
   (E) It conveys a sense of how confusing it is for the mind to deal with so many simultaneous messages.

4. The word "registered" in line 15 means

   (A) enrolled formally
   (B) expressed without words
   (C) corresponded exactly
   (D) made an impression
   (E) qualified officially

5. The attitude of the author of Passage 1 to accountants, plumbers, and insurance salesmen (lines 25–27) can best be described as

   (A) respectful   (B) cautious   (C) superior
    (D) cynical   (E) hypocritical

6. In the final two paragraphs of Passage 1, the author appears to

(A) romanticize the writer as someone heroic in his or her accomplishments
(B) deprecate athletes for their inability to react to experience instinctively
(C) minimize the travail that artists and athletes endure to do their work
(D) advocate the importance of literacy to the common citizen
(E) suggest that a cautious approach would reduce the likelihood of future failure

7. The author of Passage 2 prizes

(A) his innate athletic talent
(B) the respect of his peers
(C) his ability to focus
(D) the gift of relaxation
(E) winning at any cost

8. The word "settled" in line 49 means

(A) judged   (B) decided   (C) reconciled
(D) pacified   (E) inhabited

9. What does the author mean by "indifference to the larger point of view" (lines 52–53)?

(A) Inability to see the greater implications of the activity in which you were involved
(B) Hostility to opponents coming from larger, better trained teams
(C) Reluctance to look beyond your own immediate concerns
(D) Refusing to care how greatly you might be hurt by your opponents
(E) Being more concerned with the task at hand than with whether you win or lose

10. What is the function of the phrase "to an extent" in line 68?

(A) It denies a situation
(B) It conveys a paradox
(C) It qualifies a statement
(D) It represents a metaphor
(E) It minimizes a liability

11. The author finds it ironic that he tends to "dismiss most comparisons of athletics to art" (lines 71–72) because

(A) athletics is the basis for great art
(B) he finds comparisons generally unhelpful
(C) he is making such a comparison
(D) he typically is less cynical
(E) he rejects the so-called "creative process"

12. The authors of both passages would agree that

(A) the lot of the professional writer is more trying than that of the professional athlete
(B) athletics has little to do with the actual workings of the creative process
(C) both artists and athletes learn hard lessons in the course of mastering their art
(D) it is important to concentrate on the things that hurt us in life
(E) participating in sports provides a distraction from the isolation of a writer's life

13. How would the author of Passage 2 respond to the author of Passage 1's viewpoint that a failure such as giving up a key home run can destroy an athlete?

(A) An athlete learns through his body that failure is enormously significant and affects him both physically and spiritually.
(B) Athletes of great natural skill suffer less from the agonies of failure than less accomplished athletes do.
(C) If an athlete plays without holding back, he will surpass athletes who are more inherently adept.
(D) If the athlete focuses on the job at hand and not on past errors, he will continue to function successfully.
(E) Athletes are highly sensitive performers who need to be sheltered from the clamor and demands of the larger world.

YOU MAY GO BACK AND REVIEW THIS
SECTION IN THE REMAINING TIME, BUT   **S T O P**
DO NOT WORK IN ANY OTHER SECTION
UNTIL TOLD TO DO SO.

SECTION 6

10 Questions—15 Minutes

For each problem in this section determine which of the five choices is correct and blacken in that choice on your answer sheet. You may use any blank space on the page for your work.

Notes:

- You may use a calculator whenever you feel it will be helpful.
- Use the diagrams provided to help you solve the problems. Unless you see the words "<u>Note</u>: Figure not drawn to scale" under a diagram, it has been drawn as accurately as possible. Unless it is stated that a figure is three-dimensional, you may assume it lies in a plane.

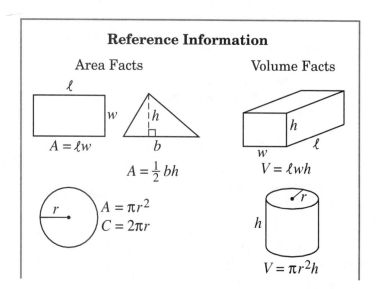

Reference Information

Area Facts

$A = \ell w$

$A = \frac{1}{2} bh$

$A = \pi r^2$
$C = 2\pi r$

Volume Facts

$V = \ell wh$

$V = \pi r^2 h$

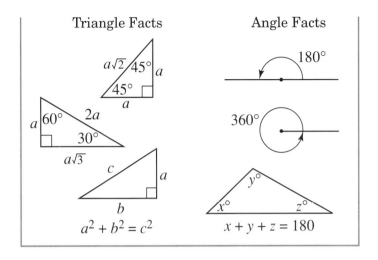

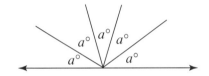

1. In the figure above, what is the value of a?

(A) 30   (B) 36   (C) 45   (D) 72
(E) It cannot be determined from the information given.

---

2. $A = \{2, 3, 4\}$, and $B = \{3, 4, 6\}$. If a is in A and b is in B, how many different values are there for the product ab?

(A) 4   (B) 6   (C) 7   (D) 8   (E) 9

Questions 3–4 are based on information in the following table.

TEAM PARTICIPATION BY CLASS AT
CENTRAL H. S. IN 1995

Class	Number of Students	Percent of Students
Freshman	180	15
Sophomore	120	x
Junior	y	40
Senior	z	w
Total	t	100

3. What is the value of t, the total number of students on teams?

(A) 450   (B) 750   (C) 1200   (D) 1800
(E) It cannot be determined from the information given.

---

4. What is the value of z, the number of seniors on teams?

(A) 360   (B) 420   (C) 630   (D) 800
(E) It cannot be determined from the information given.

---

5. Which of the following CANNOT be expressed as the sum of three consecutive integers?

(A) 18   (B) 24   (C) 28   (D) 33   (E) 36

---

6. Given that $x \neq y$ and that $(x - y)^2 = x^2 - y^2$, which of the following MUST be true?

$$\text{I. } x = 0$$
$$\text{II. } y = 0$$
$$\text{III. } x = -y$$

(A) I only   (B) II only   (C) III only   (D) I and II only
(E) I, II, and III

---

7. An international convention has a total of d delegates from c countries. If each country is represented by the same number of delegates, how many delegates does each country have?

(A) $c + d$ (B) cd (C) $\dfrac{c}{d}$ (D) $\dfrac{d}{c}$ (E) $\dfrac{c + d}{c}$

---

8. Bob and Jack share an apartment. If each month Bob pays a dollars and Jack pays b dollars, what percent of the total cost does Bob pay?

(A) $\dfrac{a}{b}\%$ (B) $\dfrac{b}{a}\%$ (C) $\dfrac{a}{a + b}\%$

(D) $\dfrac{100a}{b}\%$ (E) $\dfrac{100a}{a + b}\%$

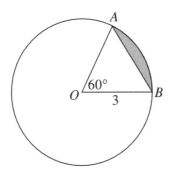

9. In the figure above, the radius of circle *O* is 3, and m∠*AOB* = 60. What is the perimeter of the shaded region?

(A) $3 + \dfrac{\pi}{2}$ (B) $\sqrt{3} + \pi$ (C) $3 + \pi$ (D) $2\sqrt{3} + \pi$

(E) It cannot be determined from the information given.

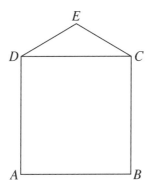

10. In the figure above, the area of square *ABCD* is 100, and the area of isosceles triangle *DEC* is 10. Find the distance from *A* to *E*.

(A) 11   (B) 12   (C) $\sqrt{146}$ (D) 13   (E) $\sqrt{244}$

YOU MAY GO BACK AND REVIEW THIS SECTION IN THE REMAINING TIME, BUT DO NOT WORK IN ANY OTHER SECTION UNTIL TOLD TO DO SO.   **S T O P**

Answer Key

Section 1   Verbal Reasoning

1. A	7. C	13. B	19. C	25. C
2. D	8. B	14. D	20. C	26. D
3. B	9. E	15. C	21. E	27. E
4. D	10. D	16. B	22. D	28. D
5. D	11. C	17. D	23. D	29. D
6. A	12. B	18. D	24. B	30. A

Section 2   Mathematical Reasoning

1. D	6. B	11. A	16. C	21. A
2. C	7. D	12. B	17. C	22. A
3. B	8. D	13. B	18. A	23. E
4. D	9. C	14. E	19. D	24. B
5. A	10. C	15. D	20. E	25. B

Section 3   Verbal Reasoning

1. E	8. B	15. B	22. C	29. D
2. A	9. C	16. B	23. A	30. C
3. C	10. C	17. B	24. B	31. A
4. C	11. B	18. A	25. C	32. C
5. B	12. D	19. A	26. E	33. C
6. E	13. E	20. B	27. E	34. E
7. B	14. E	21. A	28. B	35. B

Section 4   Mathematical Reasoning

1. B	4. B	7. C	10. C	13. D
2. B	5. C	8. A	11. B	14. C
3. C	6. B	9. A	12. D	15. A

Grid-in Questions

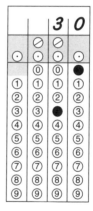

16. 5.5

or 11/2

17. 7.5

or 15/2

18. 70

19. 30

20. 12

21. 200

22.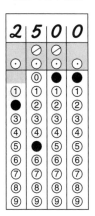

$$\frac{4}{3} < x < \frac{5}{3}$$
or
$$1.33 < x < 1.67$$

23.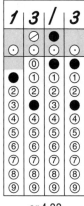

or 1.33

24.

25.

or 4.33

Section 5   Verbal Reasoning

1. **E**	4. **D**	7. **C**	10. **C**	13. **D**
2. **B**	5. **C**	8. **B**	11. **C**	
3. **B**	6. **A**	9. **E**	12. **C**	

Section 6   Mathematical Reasoning

1. **B**	3. **C**	5. **C**	7. **D**	9. **C**
2. **C**	4. **B**	6. **B**	8. **E**	10. **D**

Answer Explanations

Section 1   Verbal Reasoning

1. **(A)** Because lightning victims are so battered and confused, they seem like assault victims. Thus, they are often *mistaken* for victims of assault.   (Cause and Effect Signal)

2. **(D)** Anyone who has produced more than three hundred books in a single lifetime is an enormously productive or *prolific* writer. Writers are often described as prolific, but few, if any, have been as prolific as the late Dr. Asimov.
    Beware Eye-Catchers: Choice A is incorrect. *Fastidious* means painstakingly careful; it has nothing to do with writing fast.
    (Examples)

3. **(B)** Time limitations would cause problems for you if you were reading a *lengthy* book. To save time, you might want to read it in an *abridged* or shortened form.
    Remember to watch for signal words that link one part of the sentence to another. The use of "because" in the opening clause is a cause signal.   (Cause and Effect Signal)

4. **(D)** Speakers wish to communicate *unambiguously* in order that there may be no *confusion* about their meaning.
    Remember to watch for signal words that link one part of the sentence to another. The presence of *and* linking two items in a series indicates that the missing word may be a synonym or near-synonym for the other linked word. In this case, *unambiguously* is a synonym for *clearly*. Similarly, the use of "so that" in the second clause signals cause and effect.   (Argument Pattern)

5. **(D)** Lisa was normally *gregarious* or sociable. When she unexpectedly lost her job, she became quiet and *withdrawn* (distant; unsociable).
    Note how the signal word *Although* indicates a contrast between her normally sociable and presently unsociable states.
    (Contrast Pattern)

6. **(A)** Wilma Mankiller, a female, heads a major American Indian tribe. She performs her role successfully: she is "increasingly popular." By her success, she has *shattered* or exploded a myth of male supremacy.   (Argument Pattern)

7. **(C)** The commission censured or condemned the senator for doing something wrong. They condemned him *because* his expenditures of public funds were *lavish* or extravagant; he spent the public's money in an *unjustifiable*, unwarranted way.

   (Cause and Effect Pattern)

8. **(B)** Nelson remained calm and in control in spite of the panic of battle. In other words, he was *imperturbable*, not capable of being agitated or perturbed.

   Note how the phrase *in spite of* signals the contrast between the subject's calm and the surrounding panic. Similarly, note how other signal words link one part of the sentence to another. The presence of *and* linking two items in a series indicates that the missing word should be similar in meaning to the phrase "in full command."

   (Contrast Pattern)

9. **(E)** Despite his hard work trying to solve the problem, the solution was not the *result* or outcome of his labor. Instead, it was *fortuitous* or accidental.

   Remember to watch for signal words that link one part of the sentence to another. The use of the "was...and not..." structure sets up a contrast. The missing words must be antonyms or near-antonyms.

   (Contrast Pattern)

10. **(D)** A *constitution* is introduced by a *preamble*. A *book* is introduced by a *preface*.   (Sequence)

11. **(C)** A *quarry* is a place from which one extracts or digs *marble*. A *mine* is a place from which one extracts or digs *coal*.

    (Defining Characteristic)

12. **(B)** *Ecstasy* is an extreme form of *joy*; a *hurricane* is an extreme form of a wind or *breeze*.   (Degree of Intensity)

13. **(B)** A *fissure* (cleft) is a geographical feature measured in terms of its *depth*; a *peak* is a geographical feature measured in terms of its *height*.   (Defining Characteristic)

14. **(D)** Something *blatant* (obtrusive; brazenly obvious) is characterized by *obtrusiveness* (conspicuousness). Something *lavish* (prodigal; excessive) is characterized by *extravagance*.

    (Synonym Variant)

15. **(C)** Neither a *strident* (unpleasantly grating; shrill) *voice* nor an *acrid* (bitterly sharp) *taste* appeals to the senses.

    (Defining Characteristic)

16. **(B)** The author describes himself as "jarred and shocked" (line 4). He asks himself, "What strange world was this?" His initial reaction to Mencken's prose is one of *disbelief*. Choice A is incorrect. Mencken rages; the narrator does not. Choice C is incorrect. It is unsupported by the passage. Choices D and E are incorrect. Again, these terms apply to Mencken, not to the narrator.

17. **(D)** The narrator does *not* portray Mencken as reverent or respectful of religious belief. Instead, he says that Mencken mocks God. Choice A is incorrect. The narrator portrays Mencken as intrepid (brave); he wonders where Mencken gets his courage. Choice B is incorrect. The narrator portrays Mencken as articulate (verbally expressive); he says Mencken writes clear, clean sentences. Choice C is incorrect. The narrator portrays Mencken as satiric (mocking); he says Mencken makes fun of people's weaknesses. Choice E is incorrect. The narrator portrays Mencken as opinionated (stubborn about his opinions; prejudiced). Mencken's book, after all, is *A Book of Prejudices.*

    Remember, when asked about specific information in the passage, spot key words in the question and scan the passage to find them (or their synonyms).

18. **(D)** The mood of the book colored or *affected* the narrator's perceptions.

    Remember, when answering a vocabulary-in-context question, test each answer choice, substituting it in the sentence for the word in quotes.

19. **(C)** The narrator feels a hunger for books that surges up in him. In other words, he is filled with *impatient ardor* or eagerness. Choice A is incorrect. The narrator has his dreams, but he is involved rather than indifferent. Choices B and D are incorrect. There is nothing in the lines to suggest them. Choice E is incorrect. The narrator is determined, but his resolve is active and eager rather than quiet.

    Remember, when asked to determine the author's attitude or tone, look for words that convey emotion or paint pictures.

20. (C) The narrator is able to identify Mr. Gerald as an American type. He feels closer to Mr. Gerald, familiar with the limits of his life. This suggests that he smiles out of a sense of *recognition*. Choices A, B, D, and E are incorrect. There is nothing in the passage to suggest them.

Remember, when asked to make inferences, base your answers on what the passage implies, not what it states directly.

21. (E) Phrases like "feeling something new, being affected by something that made the look of the world different" and "filled with bookish notions" reflect the narrator's response to the new books he reads. You have here a portrait of a youth's response to his expanding intellectual horizons. Choice A is incorrect. The narrator is not arguing in favor of a cause; he is recounting an episode from his life. Choice B is incorrect. The narrator was aware of racial prejudice long before he read Mencken. Choice C is incorrect. The passage is not about Mencken's and Lewis's styles; it is about their effect in opening up the world to the narrator. Choice D is incorrect. The passage is more about the impact of art on life than about the impact of life on art.

Remember, when asked to find the main idea, be sure to check the opening and summary sentences of each paragraph.

22. (D) The terrible robbers in the pond world are the cruel creatures who, in the course of the struggle to exist, devour their fellows.

23. (D) Here, "catch" is used as in fishing: "a good catch of fish." Suppose you want to collect a sample of pond-dwellers. You lower a jar into the nearest pond and capture a random batch of creatures swimming by—fish, tadpoles, full-grown insects, larvae—in other words, a mixed catch.

24. (B) The opening paragraph states that the introduction of the Dytiscus larvae to the aquarium will result in a struggle for existence in which the larvae will destroy their prey. The larvae, thus, are predators (hunters of prey). This suggests that their presence would be of particular interest to naturalists studying predatory patterns at work within a closed environment such as an aquarium.

25. (C) The author is describing how the Dytiscus larva looks: slim body, six legs, flat head, huge jaws. Choice A is incorrect. All the details indicate the author is describing the killer, not the victim.

26. **(D)** Though the passage mentions amphibians—tadpoles—and food, it states that the tadpoles provide food for the larvae, not vice versa. The passage nowhere states that the larvae are a source of food for amphibians. Choice A is incorrect. The passage states that the larvae secrete digestive juices; it mentions secretion in line 28. Choice B is incorrect. The passage states that the larvae attack one another; they seize and devour their own breed (lines 44–52). Choice C is incorrect. The passage states that the larvae are attracted to motion; prey for them "is all that moves." Choice E is incorrect. The passage states that the larvae have ravenous appetites: their "voracity" is unique.

    Remember, when asked about specific information in the passage, spot key words in the question and scan the passage to find them (or their synonyms).

27. **(E)** Digesting "out of doors" refers to the larva's external conversion of food into absorbable form. Look at the sentence immediately following on line 28. Break down the process step by step. The larva injects a secretion into the victim. The secretion dissolves the victim's insides. That is the start of the digestive process. It takes place inside the victim's body; in other words, *outside* the larva's body—"out of doors." Only then does the larva begin to suck up the dissolved juices of his prey.

28. **(D)** Choice D is correct. You can arrive at it by the process of elimination. Statement I is true. The inside of the victim "becomes opaque" (line 35); it increases in opacity. Therefore, you can eliminate Choices B, C, and E. Statement II is also true. As it is drained, the victim's body shrivels or "shrinks to a limp bundle of skin." Therefore, you can eliminate Choice A. Statement III has to be untrue. The victim's head must stay on; otherwise, the dissolving interior would leak out. Only Choice D is left. It is the correct answer.

29. **(D)** The author mentions rats because a rat will attack and devour other rats. He is sure rodents do this; he's not sure any other animals do so. Thus, he mentions rats and related rodents to point up an uncommon characteristic also found in Dytiscus larvae.

30. **(A)** In lines 51–52 the author mentions some "observations of which I shall speak later." These observations deal with whether wolves try to devour other wolves. Thus, the author clearly intends to discuss the likelihood of cannibalism among wolves.

In answering questions about what may be discussed in sub-sequent sections of the text, pay particular attention to words that are similar in meaning to subsequent: *following, succeeding, successive, later.*

Section 2   Mathematical Reasoning

In each mathematics section, for some problems, an alternative solution, indicated by two asterisks (**), follows the first solution. When this occurs, one of the solutions is the direct mathematical one and the other is based on one of the tactics discussed in Chapter 5.

1. **(D)** Since $100 = 12 \times 8 + 4$, 100 months is 4 months more than 8 years. Therefore, 8 years from now it will again be June, and 4 months later it will be **October**.

    Look for a pattern. Since there are 12 months in a year, after every 12 months it will again be June; that is, it will be June after 12, 24, 36, 48,... months. Therefore, 96 (8×12) months from now it will again be June. Count 4 more months to **October.

2. **(C)** The sum of the measures of the three angles of a triangle is 180°, so write the equation and solve it:
    $$40 + 2a + 3a = 180 \Rightarrow 40 + 5a = 180 \Rightarrow$$
    $$5a = 140 \Rightarrow a = 28.$$
    **To answer this question, you must know that the sum of the measures of the three angles of a triangle is 180°. If you know this, but want to avoid the algebra, use TACTIC 10: backsolve. If you start with C, as you should, you get the right answer immediately.

3. **(B)** Since *d* divisions each have *t* teams, multiply to get *dt* teams; and since each team has *p* players, multiply the number of teams *(dt)* by *p* to get the total number of players: ***dtp.***
    Use TACTIC 11. Pick three numbers for *t*, *d*, and *p*; the numbers should be easy to use, not necessarily realistic. Assume that there are 2 divisions, each consisting of 4 teams, so there are $2 \times 4 = 8$ teams. Then assume that each team has 10 players, for a total of $8 \times 10 = 80$ players. Now check the choices. Which one is equal to 80 when $d = 2$, $t = 4$, and $p = 10$? Only ***dtp*.

4. **(D)** Brian's total cost was $299 + $299 + $140 = $738. At the time of purchase, he paid $123 $\left(\frac{1}{6}\text{ of }\$738\right)$ and paid the balance of $615 ($738 − $123) in 12 monthly installments: $615 ÷ 12 = **$51.25**.

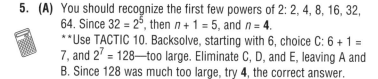

5. **(A)** You should recognize the first few powers of 2: 2, 4, 8, 16, 32, 64. Since $32 = 2^5$, then $n + 1 = 5$, and $n = $ **4**.
   Use TACTIC 10. Backsolve, starting with 6, choice C: 6 + 1 = 7, and $2^7 = 128$—too large. Eliminate C, D, and E, leaving A and B. Since 128 was much too large, try **4, the correct answer.

6. **(B)** The unmarked angle opposite the 60° angle also measures 60°, and the sum of the measures of all six angles in the diagram is 360°. Then
$$360 = a + b + c + 20 + 60 + 60 =$$
$$a + b + c + 140.$$
Subtracting 140 from each side, we get $a + b + c = $ **220**.

7. **(D)** There's nothing to do except check each choice.
   7**4 $= \sqrt{7 + \sqrt{4}} = \sqrt{7 + 2} = \sqrt{9} = 3$, which is an integer. Once you find the answer, don't waste time trying the other choices—they won't work.

8. **(D)** As in question 7, check the answers.
   In **1994** Adam entered 3 more tournaments than in 1993, an increase of $\frac{3}{6} = \frac{1}{2} = 50\%$.
   (From 1990 to 1991 the increase was 25%, from 1991 to 1992 it was 100%, from 1995 to 1996 it was $33\frac{1}{3}\%$, and from 1992 to 1993 there was a decrease.)

9. **(C)** The first step is to calculate $(3\#)(\#5) = (3 + 1)(5 − 1) = 4 \times 4 = 16$. Now check each answer until you find one that is *not* equal to 16.

   C: **(4#)(#4)** $= (4 + 1)(4 − 1) = 5 \times 3 = 15 \neq 16$.

   The other four choices are all equal to 16.

10. (C) Since a is a multiple of 5, $a = 5n$ for some integer n. Also, $b = 5a$, so $a + b = a + 5a = 6a = 6(5n) = 30n$. Then $a + b$ must be a multiple of 30. Now check I, II, and III. I: Could $a + b = 60$? Yes, $60 = 30 \times 2$ ($a = 10$ and $b = 50$). Eliminate A, B, and D. II: Could $a + b = 100$? No, 100 is not a multiple of 30. Eliminate E. The answer must be C: **I and III**. Note that we didn't have to check III, but, yes, $a + b$ could be 150 (with $n = 5$, $a = 25$, and $b = 125$).
**Use TACTIC 11: a must be a multiple of 5, so just try $a = 5$, 10, 15, ...

a	5	10	15	20	25
$b = 5a$	25	50	75	100	125
$a + b$	30	**60**	90	120	**150**

After two or three tries you can guess that $a + b$ must be a multiple of 30.

11. (A) Just multiply: $\frac{2}{5}(h) = \frac{2h}{5}$.

**Use TACTIC 11. Pick an easy-to-use number for h: 2, for example. Scott can mow $\frac{2}{5}$ of a lawn in the first hour and another $\frac{2}{5}$ of a lawn in the second hour, for a total of $\frac{4}{5}$ of a lawn. Check the choices. Only $\frac{2h}{5}$ is $\frac{4}{5}$ when $h = 2$.

12. (B) $bd = (3^a)(3^c) = 3^{a+c}$.
**Use TACTIC 11. Pick easy-to-use numbers for a and c; $a = 1$ and $c = 2$, for example. Then $b = 3^1 = 3$ and $d = 3^2 = 9$, so $bd = 27$. Check the choices. Only 3^{a+c} works.

13. (B) Use the distributive law:
$$78(r + s) = 78r + 78s \text{ and}$$
$$(78 + r)s = 78s + rs.$$
Then, $78r + 78s = 78s + rs$, which implies that $78r = rs$. Since it is given that $r \neq 0$, we can divide both sides by r to get **$s = 78$**.

14. **(E)** The average of three consecutive integers is always the middle one, which is an integer and is equal to the average of the smallest and largest of the three integers. Therefore, **I, II, and III** are all true.

   **Use TACTIC 11. Pick three consecutive integers: 2, 3, 4. Their average is $\dfrac{2+3+4}{3} = \dfrac{9}{3} = 3$, which *is* an integer (III) and which is one of the numbers (I). Also, the average of 2 and 4 is 3, so II is true.

15. **(D)** Between 1 and 25, the 8 multiples of 3 and 5 multiples of 5 would all make Scott a winner. That looks like 13 (8 + 5) winning numbers, but the number 15 has been counted twice, so we must subtract 1. There are only 12 winning numbers, and the probability is $\dfrac{12}{25}$.

   **The simplest thing to do here is to quickly list which of the 25 numbers will make Scott a winner. Just consider each number and ask, "Is it a multiple of 3 or 5?" The answers are 1 – no, 2 – no, 3 – yes, 4 – no, 5 – yes, and so on. The winning numbers are 3, 5, 6, 9, 10, 12, 15, 18, 20, 21, 24, 25. There are 12 of them. The probability is $\dfrac{12}{25}$.

16. **(C)** $(m+1)(m-1) = m^2 - 1 = 17 - 1 = \mathbf{16}$.

   Use your calculator. Since $m^2 = 17$, $m = \sqrt{17} \approx 4.123...$. Multiply $5.123 \times 3.123 = 15.999$. Choose **16. If you don't round off, your calculator will probably give you 16, exactly.

17. **(C)** $3^{10} \times 27^2 = 3^{10} \times (3^3)^2 = 3^{10} \times 3^6 = 3^{16}$. Also, $9^2 \times 3^n = (3^2)^2 \times 3^n = 3^4 \times 3^n = 3^{4+n}$ so, $3^{16} = 3^{4+n}$ and $16 = 4 + n$. Then $n = \mathbf{12}$.

   **Use your calculator. $9^2 \times 3^n = 81 \times 3^n$ and $3^{10} \times 27^2 = 43046721$, so $3^n = 43046721 \div 81 = 531441$. Now just keep taking powers of 3 until you get to $3^{12} = 531441$. (If you have a scientific calculator, use the power button; if not, just keep multiplying $3 \times 3 \times 3....$)

18. **(A)** Find the distance from each point to (0,0), the center of the circle. We're looking for a point that is *less than* 10 units from the center. The distance from (a,b) to (0,0) equals

$\sqrt{(a-0)^2 + (b-0)^2} = \sqrt{a^2 + b^2}$.

Check each point. A: **(–9,4)**

$\sqrt{(-9)^2 + 4^2} = \sqrt{81 + 16} = \sqrt{97} < 10$.

19. (D) Since 2 is the smallest prime and since p and q are each bigger than r, neither p nor q can be 2. Therefore, both p and q are odd (2 is the only even prime), which means that $p - q$ is even. But $p - q = r$, so r *must be* 2. However, there are many possibilities for p and q: $5 - 3 = 2$, $13 - 11 = 2$, $31 - 29 = 2$, etc. Therefore, the answer is **r only**.

20. (E) Use TACTIC 11. Assume that 2 pencils cost 10 cents; then pencils cost 5 cents each or 20 for a dollar. For 3 dollars, we can buy 60 pencils. Which of the choices equals 60 when $p = 2$, $c = 10$, and $d = 3$? Only $\dfrac{100dp}{c}$.

21. (A) $a + 10\%(a) = a + 0.1a = 1.1a$. Also, $b - 10\%(b) = b - 0.1b = 0.9b$. Then, $1.1a = 0.9b$, and $\dfrac{a}{b} = \dfrac{.9}{1.1} = \dfrac{9}{11}$.

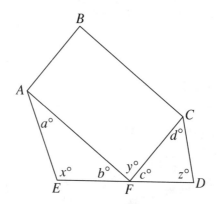

22. (A) Since DE is a line segment, $b + y + c = 180$; and since F is a corner of a rectangle, $y = 90$. Therefore, $b + 90 + c = 180$, and $b + c = 90$. (II is true.) If we knew the value of x, we could determine the value of $a + b$, but we don't. Nor do we know the value of any of the other angles, including z. Therefore, **II only** is true.

23. **(E)** Any odd number can be expressed as the sum of two consecutive integers: $8 + 9 = 17$. Eliminate A. Next try the sum of three consecutive integers: $7 + 8 + 9 = 24$. Eliminate C. Now try the sum of four consecutive integers: $4 + 5 + 6 + 7 = 22$ and $5 + 6 + 7 + 8 = 26$. Eliminate B and D. The answer must be **32**.

24. **(B)** In the given figure, the diameters of the four small semicircles are 2, 4, 6, and 8, so the diameter of the large semicircle is $2 + 4 + 6 + 8 = 20$, and its radius is 10. The perimeter of the shaded region is the sum of the circumferences of all five semicircles. Since the circumference of a semicircle is π times its radius, the perimeter is $\pi + 2\pi + 3\pi + 4\pi + 10\pi = \mathbf{20\pi}$.

25. **(B)** Let x and y be the radii of the two semicircles. Then the legs of right triangle ACB are $2x$ and $2y$, and by the Pythagorean theorem $(2x)^2 + (2y)^2 = 4^2$. Then $4x^2 + 4y^2 = 16$, and $x^2 + y^2 = 4$. Since the area of a semicircle of radius r is $\frac{1}{2}\pi r^2$, the sum of the areas of the semicircles is $\frac{1}{2}\pi x^2 + \frac{1}{2}\pi y^2 = \frac{1}{2}\pi(x^2 + y^2) = \frac{1}{2}\pi(4) = \mathbf{2\pi}$.

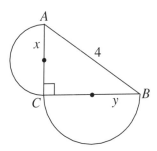

Section 3   Verbal Reasoning

1. **(E)** Tiffany's works of art have survived in spite of their *fragility* (tendency to break).
   Remember to watch for signal words that link one part of the sentence to another. The use of "despite" in the opening phrase sets up a contrast. *Despite* signals you that Tiffany's glass works were unlikely candidates to survive for several decades.
   (Contrast Signal)

2. **(A)** Voles are similar to mice; however, they are also different from them, and may be *distinguished from* them.
   Note how the use of "although" in the opening phrase sets up the basic contrast here.
   (Contrast Signal)

3. **(C)** A comprehensive or thorough study would not be missing *relevant* or important material.
   Remember to watch for signal words that link one part of the sentence to another. The use of "but" in the second clause sets up a contrast. (Contrast Signal)

4. **(C)** Because Dr. Drew's method proved *effective*, it became a *model* for other systems.
   Remember to watch for signal words that link one part of the sentence to another. The "so...that" structure signals cause and effect. (Cause and Effect Signal)

5. **(B)** The fact that the languages of the Mediterranean area were markedly (strikingly) alike eased or *facilitated* the movement of people and ideas from country to country.
   Note how the specific examples in the second part of the sentence clarify the idea stated in the first part. (Examples)

6. **(E)** Feeling that a job was *pointless* might well lead you to perform it in a *perfunctory* (indifferent or mechanical) manner.
   Remember, watch for signal words that link one part of the sentence to another. The use of "because" in the opening clause is a cause signal. (Cause and Effect Signal)

7. **(B)** Pain is a sensation. Losing the ability to feel pain would leave the body vulnerable, defenseless, lacking its usual warnings against impending bodily harm.
   Note how the second clause serves to clarify or explain what is meant by pain's being an "early warning system." (Definition)

8. **(B)** A *lugubrious* (exaggeratedly gloomy) appearance may create laughter because it is so inappropriate in the *hilarity* (noisy gaiety) of the circus. The clown's success stems from a contrast. The missing words must be antonyms or near-antonyms. You can immediately eliminate Choices C, D, and E as nonantonym pairs. In addition, you can eliminate Choice A; *sobriety* or seriousness is an inappropriate term for describing circus life. (Contrast Pattern)

9. **(C)** If she *deprecated* her accomplishments (diminished them or saw nothing praiseworthy in them), she would show her unwillingness to boast about them or *flaunt* them. Note the use of "properly" to describe her unwillingness to do something. This

suggests that the second missing word would have negative
associations. (Definition)

10. **(C)** A stereotyped or oversimplified portrait of a slave would lead sensitive readers to *criticize* it for dismissing the issue of slavery so
casually. Thus, they normally would be *detractors* of the novel.
However, *Huckleberry Finn* is such a fine work that even its
critics acknowledge its greatness. Signal words are helpful here.
Despite in the first clause implies a contrast, and *even* in the
second clause implies that the subjects somewhat reluctantly
agree that the novel is a masterpiece. (Contrast Signal)

11. **(B)** A *play* is made up of *acts*. A *novel* is made up of *chapters*.
(Part to Whole)

12. **(D)** *Geology* is an example of a *science*. A *fir* tree is an example of a
tree. (Class and Member)

13. **(E)** A *signature* on a *portrait* establishes who painted it. A *byline* on
an *article* establishes who wrote it. (Function)

14. **(E)** A *plane* is a tool used to *smooth* objects; a *wrench* is a tool used
to grip and *twist* objects. Note that *plane* here is used in a somewhat uncommon sense. Be on the alert for unfamiliar secondary
meanings of words.
Remember to watch out for errors stemming from grammatical
or logical reversals. Choice D is incorrect. An axe is sharpened. It
does not sharpen; it hews or chops. (Tool and Action)

15. **(B)** *Funds* that are *embezzled* are appropriated or taken fraudulently.
Similarly, *writings* that are *plagiarized* are appropriated
fraudulently.
Note that Choices A, C, and D are eye-catchers. Because *money*,
ransom, and *loot* all have some relationship to *funds*, these
answers may tempt you into making an incorrect choice.
(Defining Characteristic)

16. **(B)** *Uncouth* is a synonym for *graceless*. Therefore, gracelessness is
the quality of being uncouth. Similarly, *avaricious* is a
synonym for *greedy*. Therefore, greed is the quality of being
avaricious. (Synonym Variant)

17. (B) An *elevator* moves through a *shaft*. *Water* moves through a *conduit* (a pipe or channel for fluids).
Beware Eye-Catchers: Choice C is incorrect. Just because elevators and escalators have similar functions, don't expect that the relationship between *elevator* and *shaft* is similar to the relationship between *escalator* and *step*.   (Location)

18. (A) *Parsimony* (stinginess) is extreme thrift or *frugality*. *Agony* is extreme suffering or *pain*.   (Degree of Intensity)

19. (A) A *dilettante* is not serious about art; he or she merely *dabbles*. A *coquette* is not serious about her affairs of the heart; she merely *flirts*.   (Definition)

20. (B) Someone *indifferent* is uncaring or unconcerned; he or she is lacking in *concern*. Someone *arrogant* is proud and immodest; he or she is lacking in *modesty*.   (Antonym Variant)

21. (A) *Laconic* (brief, curt in speech) is similar in meaning to *taciturn* (disinclined to talk). Thus, taciturnity has the quality of being laconic. Similarly, *unrehearsed* is similar in meaning to *improvised* (composed and performed without preparation). Thus, improvisation has the quality of being unrehearsed.
                          (Synonym Variant)

22. (C) *Slander* is by its nature *defamatory* (injurious to one's reputation); an *elegy* (poem or song of mourning) is by nature *sorrowful*.
                          (Defining Characteristic)

23. (A) A snake *sloughs* or casts off its dead *skin*; people and animals *shed* their unneeded *hair*.   (Function)

24. (B) The author is writing a book about the effect of the opening of the West on the Indians living there. As a historian, he needs primary source materials—firsthand accounts of the period written by men and women living at that time. Thus, he finds the period of 1860–1890 worth mentioning because in that period the "greatest concentration of recorded experience and observation" was created.

25. (C) Only the white settlers looked on their intrusion into Indian territory as the opening of the West. To the Native Americans, it was an invasion. Thus, "opening" *from a Native American perspective is an inaccurate term*.

26. (E) Throughout the passage the author presents and comments on the nature of the original documents that form the basis for his historical narrative. Thus, it is clear that a major concern of his is to *introduce* these "sources of almost forgotten oral history" to his readers. Choice A is incorrect. The author clearly regrets the fate of the Indians. However, he does not take this occasion to denounce or condemn the white man. Choice B is incorrect. While the author discusses the various treaty councils, he does not evaluate or judge how effective they were. Choice C is incorrect. The author never touches on the current treatment of Indians. Choice D is incorrect. The author indicates no such thing.

27. (E) Of all the thousands of published descriptions of the opening of the West, the greatest concentration or *cluster* of accounts date from the period of 1860 to 1890.

28. (B) The author is describing a period in which Native Americans lost their land and much of their personal freedom to the same pioneers who supposedly revered the ideal of freedom. Thus, in describing the ideal of freedom revered by the pioneers as "personal freedom for those who already had it" (in other words, personal freedom for the pioneers, not the Indians), the author is being *ironic*.

29. (D) You can arrive at the correct choice by the process of elimination. Statement I is true. The passage states that the quality of the interviews depended on the interpreters' abilities. Inaccuracies could creep in because of the translators' lack of skill. Therefore, you can eliminate Choice B.
Statement II is untrue. The passage indicates that the Indians sometimes exaggerated, telling the reporters tall tales. It does not indicate that the reporters in turn overstated what they had been told. Therefore, you can eliminate Choices C and E.
Statement III is true. The passage indicates that the Indians sometimes were disinclined to speak the whole truth because they feared reprisals (retaliation) if they did. Therefore, you can eliminate Choice A. Only Choice D is left. It is the correct answer.

30. (C) Brown speaks of the Indians who lived through the "doom period of their civilization," the victims of the conquest of the American West. In doing so, his tone can best be described as *elegiac*, expressing sadness about their fate and lamenting their vanished civilization.

31. **(A)** In the fifth paragraph Brown comments upon the "graphic similes and metaphors of the natural world" found in the English translations of Indian speeches. Thus, he is impressed by their *vividness of imagery*.

32. **(C)** Commenting about inadequate interpreters who turned eloquent Indian speeches into "flat" prose, Brown is criticizing the translations for their *pedestrian*, unimaginative quality.

33. **(C)** Lines 60–62 state that, as the Indian leaders became more sophisticated or knowledgeable about addressing treaty councils, "they demanded the right to choose their own interpreters and recorders." Until they had become familiar with the process, *they were unaware that they had the option to demand such services*.

34. **(E)** Brown has tried to create a narrative of the winning of the West from the victims' perspective. This suggests that, in asking his readers to read the book facing eastward (the way the Indians would have been looking when they first saw the whites headed west), he is asking them metaphorically to look at things from the Indians' point of view.

35. **(B)** In the sentence immediately preceding the one in which this phrase appears, Brown calls the Indians "true conservationists." Such conservationists know that life is *necessarily tied to* the earth and to its resources, and that by destroying these resources, by imbalancing the equation, so to speak, you destroy life itself.

Section 4 Mathematical Reasoning

Quantitative Comparison Questions

1. **(B)** In each column, the sum includes the numbers from –3 to 3. All the other numbers in Column A are negative, and all those in Column B are positive, so B is greater. (Note that we didn't calculate either sum. We just used TACTIC 19 and compared the columns. Of course, we *could have* quickly calculated each sum.)

2. (B) Since $\frac{1}{3} < \frac{2}{3}$ and a is positive, $\frac{1}{3}a < \frac{2}{3}a$.
Column B is greater.

**Use TACTIC 15. Replace a with $\frac{1}{2}$, and see that Column B is greater. Eliminate A and C. Try another number between 0 and 1; Column B is again greater. Guess B.

3. (C) Just calculate. Column A: $\frac{1}{4} \times 40\% = 10\%$.

Column B: $\frac{2}{5} \times 25\% = 10\%$.

Columns A and B are equal (C).

4. (B) Use TACTIC 17. Add x to each column. Column A = 1 and Column B = 2. Column B is greater. It is irrelevant that $1000 < x < 2000$.

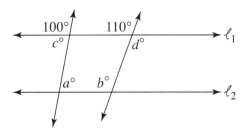

5. (C) In the figure above, $c = 80$ and $d = 110$. Since ℓ_1 and ℓ_2 are parallel, then $a = c = 80$ and $b = d = 110$. Therefore $a + b = 80 + 110 = 190$. The columns are equal (C).

6. (B) Column A: $y = \frac{12}{x}$. Column B: $z = \frac{25}{x}$. If two fractions have the same *positive* denominator, the one with the larger numerator—here, B—is greater.

**Use TACTIC 15. Let $x = 2$. Then $y = 6$ and $z = 12.5$. In this case, Column B is greater, so eliminate A and C. Try another value; Column B is again greater. Guess B.

7. (C) Since $\frac{5a}{7b} = \frac{5}{7}$ then $\frac{a}{b} = 1$. Therefore,
$a = b$; the columns are equal (C).
**Cross-multiply: $35a = 35b \Rightarrow a = b$ (C).

8. (A) There are four primes between 10 and 20: 11, 13, 17, and 19, but only two primes between 20 and 30: 23 and 29. Column A is greater.

9. (A) Column A: $3^7 = 2187$, which, when divided by 10, has a quotient of 218 and a remainder of 7 ($2187 = 10 \times 218 + 7$). Column B: $7^3 = 343$, which, when divided by 10, has a quotient of 34 and a remainder of 3 ($343 = 10 \times 34 + 3$). Column A is greater.

10. (C) The average of the measures of the three angles of *any* triangle is $180° \div 3 = 60°$. The columns are equal (C).

**Use TACTIC 15. Pick an acute triangle: say the measures of the angles are 50°, 60°, and 70°. Their average is 60°. Choose an obtuse triangle: say the measures of the angles are 100°, 40°, and 40°. Again, the average is 60°. The columns are equal (C).

11. (B) If you draw a diagram, it is immediately clear that the area of the large triangle is *more than* twice the area of the small one. In fact, it is 4 times as great. Column B is larger.

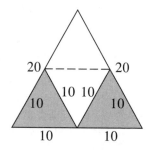

12. (D) If $x = 3$ and $y = 7$ (or vice versa), then $x + y = 10$, and Column B is greater. Eliminate A and C. If $x = 1$ and $y = 21$ (or vice versa), then $x + y = 22$. This time, Column A is greater. Eliminate B. Neither column is *always* greater, and the two columns are not *always* equal.

13. (D) Let r, C, and A represent the radius, circumference, and area of the circle:

$$C = 2\pi r = a\pi \Rightarrow a = \frac{2\pi r}{\pi} = 2r.$$

Similarly,

$$A = \pi r^2 = b\pi \Rightarrow b = \frac{\pi r^2}{\pi} = r^2.$$

The value of Column A is $2r$, and the value of Column B is r^2. Which is greater? Dividing each by r yields 2 in Column A and r

in Column B. Since there are no restrictions, r could be greater than, less than, or equal to 2. Neither column is *always* greater, and the two columns are not *always* equal (D).

**Use TACTIC 15. Let $r = 1$. Then $C = 2\pi$ and $A = \pi$; so $a = 2$ and $b = 1$. Column B is greater: eliminate A and C. Try $r = 2$. Now, $C = 4\pi$ and $A = 4\pi$; $a = b$ and the columns are equal. Eliminate B. The answer is D.

14. (C) You can't use your calculator to look at the units digits of these numbers because they're too large (14^{14} has 15 digits!). But you can use it to see that, in Column A, $14^2 = 196$, $14^3 = 2744$, $14^4 = 38416$, and that the units digits of the powers of 14 alternate 4, 6, 4, 6, 4,.... The number 14 to an even power has a units digit of 6. In Column B, *every* power of 16 ends in 6: 16, 256, 4096, 65536,.... Therefore Columns A and B are each equal to 6, and the answer is C.

15. (A) Note that, when a number is decreased by 20%, what remains is 80% of the original: 80% of 80% of 80% = $.8 \times .8 \times .8 = .512 = 51.2\%$, which is greater than 50%. Column A is larger.

**Use TACTIC 16. *Assume* that in 1980 the population of Mudville was 100. Then, in 1985 it was 80, in 1990 it was 64 (80% of 80), and in 1995 it was 51.2, which is greater than 50, one-half of the 1980 population.

Grid-in Questions

16. $\left(5.5 \text{ or } \dfrac{11}{2} \right)$ Divide. By calculator: $330 \div 60 = \mathbf{5.5}$.

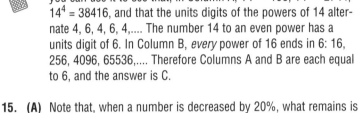

By hand: $\dfrac{330}{60} = \dfrac{33}{6} = \dfrac{\mathbf{11}}{\mathbf{2}}$.

**Set up a proportion using the ratio $\dfrac{\text{words}}{\text{minutes}}$:

$\dfrac{60}{1} = \dfrac{330}{x}$. Cross-multiply: $60x = 330$. Divide by 60: $x = \mathbf{5.5}$.

17. $\left(7.5 \text{ or } \dfrac{15}{2} \right)$ Notice that the left-hand side ($2x - 15$) of the equation is the negative of the right-hand side ($15 - 2x$), meaning that each side is equal to 0 ($a = -a \Rightarrow a = 0$). Therefore

$$2x - 15 = 0 \Rightarrow 2x = 15 \Rightarrow x = \textbf{7.5} \text{ or } \frac{15}{2}.$$

**Just solve the equation:

$$2x - 15 = 15 - 2x \Rightarrow 4x - 15 = 15 \Rightarrow$$
$$4x = 30 \Rightarrow x = \textbf{7.5}.$$

18. **(70)** Since all of the radii of a circle have the same length, $CA = CB$. Therefore, $m\angle A = m\angle B = 55°$. Therefore $c = 180 - (55 + 55) = 180 - 110 = \textbf{70}$.

19. **(30)** Let $x =$ Tina's age, and write the algebraic equation. If it helps, quickly make a table:

	Now	In 20 Years
Tina's age	x	$x + 20$
Maria's age	$6x$	$6x + 20$

$$6x + 20 = 2(x + 20)$$
$$6x + 20 = 2x + 40$$
$$4x = 20$$
$$x = 5$$

(Tina's age)

Be careful. The question asks for *Maria's* age: $6x = \textbf{30}$.

20. **(12)** To make a fraction as large as possible, make the numerator as large, and the denominator as small, as you can. Let r and s be 11 and 13, the largest primes less than 15, and let $t = 2$, the smallest prime. Then

$$\frac{r + s}{t} = \frac{11 + 13}{2} = \textbf{12}.$$

21. **(200)** If the average of five numbers is 60, their sum is $5 \times 60 = 300$. The four numbers in the question add up to 100 ($10 + 20 + 30 + 40$), so the fifth number, x, is **200** ($300 - 100$).

Use TACTIC 20. Test some numbers. Since the average, 60, is greater than each of the four given numbers, the fifth number must be substantially greater than 60. Try 100 to start. The average of 10, 20, 30, 40, and 100 is 40. That's too small. Try a larger number—150 or **200 or 300. Zoom in.

22. (1.5 or any number between $\frac{4}{3}$ or 1.33 and $\frac{5}{3}$ or 1.67) Pick a

value for k: 4.5 say, and use the slope formula. The slope of

the line through (0,0) and (3,4.5) is $\frac{4.5 - 0}{3 - 0} = \frac{4.5}{3} = 1.5$,

so grid in **1.5**.

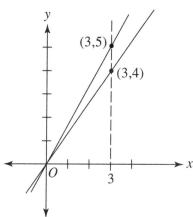

**Draw a quick sketch. The line through the origin and (3,4)

has slope $\frac{4}{3}$. Likewise, the slope of the line through the origin

and (3,5) is $\frac{5}{3}$. Therefore, the slope could be any number

greater than $\frac{4}{3}$ **(1.33) and less than** $\frac{5}{3}$ **(1.67)**, expressed as

a fraction or decimal: $\frac{3}{2}$ or 1.5 or 1.6 and so on.

23. $\left(\frac{4}{3} \text{ or } 1.33\right)$ Mentally, or by using a Venn diagram, determine

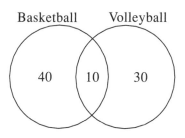

the number of girls who play only one sport. 40 play only basketball and 30 play only volleyball. The ratio is 40:30. Grid in $\frac{4}{3}$ or **1.33**.

24. **(2500)** The equation is as follows:

$$B - A = (51+52+53+...+99+100) - (1+2+3+...+49+50)$$
$$= (51-1)+(52-2)+(53-3)+...+(99-49)+(100-50)$$
$$= 50 + 50 + 50 + ... + 50 + 50 = 50 \times 50 = \textbf{2500}.$$

25. $\left(\frac{13}{3} \text{ or } 4.33 \right)$ Pick a simple number for the radius of circle Q— say, 1. Then the radius of circle P is 2, and the radius of circle O is 4. The area of the large shaded region is the area of circle O minus the area of circle P: $16\pi - 4\pi = 12\pi$. The small shaded region is just circle Q, whose area is π. Then, the total shaded area is $12\pi + \pi = 13\pi$. The white area is the area of circle P minus the area of circle Q: $4\pi - \pi = 3\pi$. Finally, the ratio of the entire shaded area to the white area is

$$\frac{13\pi}{3\pi} = \frac{13}{3} \text{ or } \textbf{4.33}.$$

Section 5   Verbal Reasoning

1. **(E)** The italicized introduction states that the author has had his manuscript rejected by his publisher. He is consigning or committing it to a desk drawer *to set it aside as unmarketable.*

2. **(B)** The rejected author identifies with these baseball players, who constantly must face "failure." *He sees he is not alone in having to confront failure and move on.*

3. **(B)** The author uses the jogger's comment to make a point about the *mental impact Henderson's home run must have had on Moore.* He reasons that, if each step a runner takes sends so many complex messages to the brain, then Henderson's ninth-inning home run must have flooded Moore's brain with messages, impressing its image indelibly in Moore's mind.

4. **(D)** The author is talking of the impact of Henderson's home run on Moore's mind. Registering in Moore's mind, the home run *made an impression* on him.

5. **(C)** The author looks on himself as someone who "to succeed at all...must perform at an extraordinary level of excellence." This level of excellence, he maintains, is not demanded of accountants, plumbers, and insurance salesmen, and he seems to pride himself on belonging to such a demanding profession. Thus, his attitude to members of less demanding professions can best be described as *superior.*

6. **(A)** The description of the writer defying his pain and extending himself irrationally to create a "masterpiece" despite the rejections of critics and publishers is a highly romantic one that elevates *the writer as someone heroic in his or her accomplishments.*

7. **(C)** The author of Passage 2 discusses the advantages of his ability to concentrate. Clearly, he prizes *his ability to focus* on the task at hand.

8. **(B)** When one football team is ahead of another by several touchdowns and there seems to be no way for the second team to catch up, the outcome of the game appears *decided* or settled.

9. **(E)** The "larger point of view" focuses on what to most people is the big question: the outcome of the game. The author is indifferent to this larger point of view. Concentrating on his own performance, he is *more concerned with the task at hand than with* winning or losing the game.

10. **(C)** Parade ground drill clearly does not entirely prepare a soldier for the reality of war. It only does so "to an extent." By using this phrase, the author is *qualifying his statement,* making it less absolute.

11. **(C)** One would expect someone who dismisses or rejects most comparisons of athletics to art to avoid making such comparisons. The author, however, *is making such a comparison.* This reversal of what would have been expected is an instance of irony.

12. **(C)** To learn to overcome failure, to learn to give one's all in performance, to learn to focus on the work of the moment, to learn to have "the selfish intensity" that can block out the rest of the world—these are hard lessons that *both athletes and artists learn.*

13. (D) Throughout Passage 2, the author stresses the advantages and the power of concentration. He believes that, if you concentrate intensely on the job at hand, you will reduce the chances of your dwelling on past failures and psyching yourself out. Thus, he is not particularly swayed by the Passage 1 author's contention that a failure such as giving up a key home run can destroy an athlete.

Section 6   Mathematical Reasoning

1. (B) Since $a + a + a + a + a = 180$, then $5a = 180 \Rightarrow a = \textbf{36}$.

2. (C) Use TACTIC 8: list systematically. Take 2, the first number in A, multiply it by each number in B, and jot down each product: 6, 8, 12. Now, take 3, the next number in A, multiply it by each number in B, and write down each *new* product: 9,   , 18. Note that, when we got to $3 \times 4 = 12$, we didn't list 12, because we already had the product 12 from 2×6. The complete list is: 6, 8, 12; 9, 18; 16, 24. There are **7** different values of ab.

3. (C) 15% of t, the total number of students, is 180. Then
$$.15t = 180 \Rightarrow t = \frac{180}{.15} = \textbf{1200}.$$

Use TACTIC 10. Try choice C, 1200. Look at the table. Is 15% of **1200 equal to 180? Yes!

4. (B) There are 480 juniors on teams (40% of 1200). Then z, the number of seniors on teams, is $1200 - (180 + 120 + 480) = 1200 - 780 = \textbf{420}$.

**Since 120 of the 1200 students are sophomores, the sophomores account for 10% of the students on teams, so the percentage, w, of seniors is
$$100 - (15 + 10 + 40) = 100 - 65 = 35.$$
Finally, 35% of 1200 is **420**.

5. (C) The sum of three consecutive integers can be expressed as
$$n + (n + 1) + (n + 2) = 3n + 3 = 3(n + 1),$$
and so must be a multiple of 3. Only **28** is *not* a multiple of 3.

**Quickly add up sets of three consecutive integers: $4 + 5 + 6 = 15$, $5 + 6 + 7 = 18$, $6 + 7 + 8 = 21$, and so on, and see the pattern (they're all multiples of 3); or cross off the choices as you come to them.

6. (B) We are given that:

$$x^2 - y^2 = (x - y)^2$$

- Expand: $x^2 - y^2 = x^2 - 2xy + y^2$
- Subtract x^2 from each side: $-y^2 = -2xy + y^2$
- Add y^2 to each side:

$$0 = 2y^2 - 2xy \Rightarrow 0 = 2y(y - x)$$

Either $y = 0$ or $y - x = 0$; but it is given that $x \ne y$, so $y - x \ne 0$. Therefore, it *must* be that $y = 0$. (II is true.) If we replace y by 0 in the original equation, we get $x^2 = x^2$, which is true for *any* value of x. Therefore, it is not true that x must equal 0. (I is false.) Also, it is not true that $x = -y$. (III is false.) Then **II only** is true.

7. (D) Divide the number of delegates, d, by the number of countries,

c: $\dfrac{d}{c}$.

**Use TACTIC 11. Pick some simple numbers. If there is a total of 10 delegates from 2 countries, then, clearly, each

country has 5 delegates. Only $\dfrac{d}{c} = 5$ when $d = 10$ and $c = 2$.

8. (E) The total rent is $a + b$, so Bob's fractional share is $\dfrac{a}{a + b}$.

To convert to a percent, simply multiply by 100%: $\dfrac{100a}{a + b}$ % .

**Use TACTIC 11. Pick two easy-to-use numbers. If Bob pays

$1 and Jack pays $2, then Bob pays $\dfrac{1}{3}$, or $33\dfrac{1}{3}$ %, of the

rent. Only $\dfrac{100a}{a + b}$ % = $33\dfrac{1}{3}$ % when $a = 1$ and $b = 2$.

9. (C) Since each radius is 3, $OA =$ OB, so m$\angle A$ = m$\angle B$. Then, $60 + x + x = 180 \Rightarrow x = 60$. Therefore $\triangle AOB$ is equilateral, and $AB = 3$. The length

of arc AB is $\dfrac{60}{360} = \dfrac{1}{6}$ of

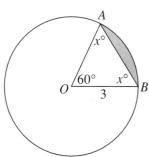

the circumference.

$C = 2\pi(3) = 6\pi$, so the length of arc $AB = \pi$. The perimeter of the region, then, is **$3 + \pi$**.

Use TACTIC 2: trust the diagram. *AB* looks about the same as *OB*, so assume it is 3, and arc *AB* is clearly slightly bigger. Hence, the perimeter is a little more than 6. Choices A and B are both less than 5 (use your calculator), which is definitely too small. Between C and D *guess*. C, **3 + π, is the better guess, because *AB might be* exactly 3.

10. (D) Draw in segment *EXY* ⊥ *AB*. Then *XY* = 10 since it is the same length as a side of the square. *EX* is the height of △ *ECD*, whose base is 10 and whose area is 10, so

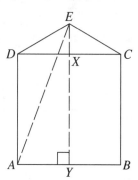

$$EX = 2\left[\frac{1}{2}\,bh = \frac{1}{2}\,(10)(2) = 10\right], \text{ and } EY = 12.$$

Since △ *ECD* is isosceles, *DX* = 5, so *AY* = 5. Finally, recognize △ *AYE* as a 5-12-13 right triangle, or use the Pythagorean theorem to find the hypotenuse, *AE*, of the triangle:

$$(AE)^2 = 5^2 + 12^2 = 25 + 144 = 169, \text{ so } AE = \mathbf{13}.$$

ANSWER SHEETS—TEST 2

If a section has fewer than 35 questions, leave the extra spaces blank.

Section 1

1. Ⓐ Ⓑ Ⓒ Ⓓ Ⓔ
2. Ⓐ Ⓑ Ⓒ Ⓓ Ⓕ
3. Ⓐ Ⓑ Ⓒ Ⓓ Ⓔ
4. Ⓐ Ⓑ Ⓒ Ⓓ Ⓔ
5. Ⓐ Ⓑ Ⓒ Ⓓ Ⓔ
6. Ⓐ Ⓑ Ⓒ Ⓓ Ⓔ
7. Ⓐ Ⓑ Ⓒ Ⓓ Ⓔ
8. Ⓐ Ⓑ Ⓒ Ⓓ Ⓔ
9. Ⓐ Ⓑ Ⓒ Ⓓ Ⓔ
10. Ⓐ Ⓑ Ⓒ Ⓓ Ⓔ
11. Ⓐ Ⓑ Ⓒ Ⓓ Ⓔ
12. Ⓐ Ⓑ Ⓒ Ⓓ Ⓔ

13. Ⓐ Ⓑ Ⓒ Ⓓ Ⓔ
14. Ⓐ Ⓑ Ⓒ Ⓓ Ⓔ
15. Ⓐ Ⓑ Ⓒ Ⓓ Ⓔ
16. Ⓐ Ⓑ Ⓒ Ⓓ Ⓔ
17. Ⓐ Ⓑ Ⓒ Ⓓ Ⓔ
18. Ⓐ Ⓑ Ⓒ Ⓓ Ⓔ
19. Ⓐ Ⓑ Ⓒ Ⓓ Ⓔ
20. Ⓐ Ⓑ Ⓒ Ⓓ Ⓔ
21. Ⓐ Ⓑ Ⓒ Ⓓ Ⓔ
22. Ⓐ Ⓑ Ⓒ Ⓓ Ⓔ
23. Ⓐ Ⓑ Ⓒ Ⓓ Ⓔ
24. Ⓐ Ⓑ Ⓒ Ⓓ Ⓔ

25. Ⓐ Ⓑ Ⓒ Ⓓ Ⓔ
26. Ⓐ Ⓑ Ⓒ Ⓓ Ⓔ
27. Ⓐ Ⓑ Ⓒ Ⓓ Ⓔ
28. Ⓐ Ⓑ Ⓒ Ⓓ Ⓔ
29. Ⓐ Ⓑ Ⓒ Ⓓ Ⓔ
30. Ⓐ Ⓑ Ⓒ Ⓓ Ⓔ
31. Ⓐ Ⓑ Ⓒ Ⓓ Ⓔ
32. Ⓐ Ⓑ Ⓒ Ⓓ Ⓔ
33. Ⓐ Ⓑ Ⓒ Ⓓ Ⓔ
34. Ⓐ Ⓑ Ⓒ Ⓓ Ⓔ
35. Ⓐ Ⓑ Ⓒ Ⓓ Ⓔ

Section 2

1. Ⓐ Ⓑ Ⓒ Ⓓ Ⓔ
2. Ⓐ Ⓑ Ⓒ Ⓓ Ⓔ
3. Ⓐ Ⓑ Ⓒ Ⓓ Ⓔ
4. Ⓐ Ⓑ Ⓒ Ⓓ Ⓔ
5. Ⓐ Ⓑ Ⓒ Ⓓ Ⓔ
6. Ⓐ Ⓑ Ⓒ Ⓓ Ⓔ
7. Ⓐ Ⓑ Ⓒ Ⓓ Ⓔ
8. Ⓐ Ⓑ Ⓒ Ⓓ Ⓔ
9. Ⓐ Ⓑ Ⓒ Ⓓ Ⓔ
10. Ⓐ Ⓑ Ⓒ Ⓓ Ⓔ
11. Ⓐ Ⓑ Ⓒ Ⓓ Ⓔ
12. Ⓐ Ⓑ Ⓒ Ⓓ Ⓔ

13. Ⓐ Ⓑ Ⓒ Ⓓ Ⓔ
14. Ⓐ Ⓑ Ⓒ Ⓓ Ⓔ
15. Ⓐ Ⓑ Ⓒ Ⓓ Ⓔ
16. Ⓐ Ⓑ Ⓒ Ⓓ Ⓔ
17. Ⓐ Ⓑ Ⓒ Ⓓ Ⓔ
18. Ⓐ Ⓑ Ⓒ Ⓓ Ⓔ
19. Ⓐ Ⓑ Ⓒ Ⓓ Ⓔ
20. Ⓐ Ⓑ Ⓒ Ⓓ Ⓔ
21. Ⓐ Ⓑ Ⓒ Ⓓ Ⓔ
22. Ⓐ Ⓑ Ⓒ Ⓓ Ⓔ
23. Ⓐ Ⓑ Ⓒ Ⓓ Ⓔ
24. Ⓐ Ⓑ Ⓒ Ⓓ Ⓔ

25. Ⓐ Ⓑ Ⓒ Ⓓ Ⓔ
26. Ⓐ Ⓑ Ⓒ Ⓓ Ⓔ
27. Ⓐ Ⓑ Ⓒ Ⓓ Ⓔ
28. Ⓐ Ⓑ Ⓒ Ⓓ Ⓔ
29. Ⓐ Ⓑ Ⓒ Ⓓ Ⓔ
30. Ⓐ Ⓑ Ⓒ Ⓓ Ⓔ
31. Ⓐ Ⓑ Ⓒ Ⓓ Ⓔ
32. Ⓐ Ⓑ Ⓒ Ⓓ Ⓔ
33. Ⓐ Ⓑ Ⓒ Ⓓ Ⓔ
34. Ⓐ Ⓑ Ⓒ Ⓓ Ⓔ
35. Ⓐ Ⓑ Ⓒ Ⓓ Ⓔ

ANSWER SHEETS—TEST 2

Section 3

1. Ⓐ Ⓑ Ⓒ Ⓓ Ⓔ
2. Ⓐ Ⓑ Ⓒ Ⓓ Ⓔ
3. Ⓐ Ⓑ Ⓒ Ⓓ Ⓔ
4. Ⓐ Ⓑ Ⓒ Ⓓ Ⓔ
5. Ⓐ Ⓑ Ⓒ Ⓓ Ⓔ
6. Ⓐ Ⓑ Ⓒ Ⓓ Ⓔ
7. Ⓐ Ⓑ Ⓒ Ⓓ Ⓔ
8. Ⓐ Ⓑ Ⓒ Ⓓ Ⓔ
9. Ⓐ Ⓑ Ⓒ Ⓓ Ⓔ
10. Ⓐ Ⓑ Ⓒ Ⓓ Ⓔ
11. Ⓐ Ⓑ Ⓒ Ⓓ Ⓔ
12. Ⓐ Ⓑ Ⓒ Ⓓ Ⓔ

13. Ⓐ Ⓑ Ⓒ Ⓓ Ⓔ
14. Ⓐ Ⓑ Ⓒ Ⓓ Ⓔ
15. Ⓐ Ⓑ Ⓒ Ⓓ Ⓔ
16. Ⓐ Ⓑ Ⓒ Ⓓ Ⓔ
17. Ⓐ Ⓑ Ⓒ Ⓓ Ⓔ
18. Ⓐ Ⓑ Ⓒ Ⓓ Ⓔ
19. Ⓐ Ⓑ Ⓒ Ⓓ Ⓔ
20. Ⓐ Ⓑ Ⓒ Ⓓ Ⓔ
21. Ⓐ Ⓑ Ⓒ Ⓓ Ⓔ
22. Ⓐ Ⓑ Ⓒ Ⓓ Ⓔ
23. Ⓐ Ⓑ Ⓒ Ⓓ Ⓔ
24. Ⓐ Ⓑ Ⓒ Ⓓ Ⓔ

25. Ⓐ Ⓑ Ⓒ Ⓓ Ⓔ
26. Ⓐ Ⓑ Ⓒ Ⓓ Ⓔ
27. Ⓐ Ⓑ Ⓒ Ⓓ Ⓔ
28. Ⓐ Ⓑ Ⓒ Ⓓ Ⓔ
29. Ⓐ Ⓑ Ⓒ Ⓓ Ⓔ
30. Ⓐ Ⓑ Ⓒ Ⓓ Ⓔ
31. Ⓐ Ⓑ Ⓒ Ⓓ Ⓔ
32. Ⓐ Ⓑ Ⓒ Ⓓ Ⓔ
33. Ⓐ Ⓑ Ⓒ Ⓓ Ⓔ
34. Ⓐ Ⓑ Ⓒ Ⓓ Ⓔ
35. Ⓐ Ⓑ Ⓒ Ⓓ Ⓔ

Section 4

1. Ⓐ Ⓑ Ⓒ Ⓓ Ⓔ
2. Ⓐ Ⓑ Ⓒ Ⓓ Ⓔ
3. Ⓐ Ⓑ Ⓒ Ⓓ Ⓔ
4. Ⓐ Ⓑ Ⓒ Ⓓ Ⓔ
5. Ⓐ Ⓑ Ⓒ Ⓓ Ⓔ
6. Ⓐ Ⓑ Ⓒ Ⓓ Ⓔ
7. Ⓐ Ⓑ Ⓒ Ⓓ Ⓔ
8. Ⓐ Ⓑ Ⓒ Ⓓ Ⓔ
9. Ⓐ Ⓑ Ⓒ Ⓓ Ⓔ
10. Ⓐ Ⓑ Ⓒ Ⓓ Ⓔ
11. Ⓐ Ⓑ Ⓒ Ⓓ Ⓔ
12. Ⓐ Ⓑ Ⓒ Ⓓ Ⓔ
13. Ⓐ Ⓑ Ⓒ Ⓓ Ⓔ
14. Ⓐ Ⓑ Ⓒ Ⓓ Ⓔ
15. Ⓐ Ⓑ Ⓒ Ⓓ Ⓔ

16.

	⊘	⊘	
⊙	⊙	⊙	⊙
	⓪	⓪	⓪
①	①	①	①
②	②	②	②
③	③	③	③
④	④	④	④
⑤	⑤	⑤	⑤
⑥	⑥	⑥	⑥
⑦	⑦	⑦	⑦
⑧	⑧	⑧	⑧
⑨	⑨	⑨	⑨

17.

	⊘	⊘	
⊙	⊙	⊙	⊙
	⓪	⓪	⓪
①	①	①	①
②	②	②	②
③	③	③	③
④	④	④	④
⑤	⑤	⑤	⑤
⑥	⑥	⑥	⑥
⑦	⑦	⑦	⑦
⑧	⑧	⑧	⑧
⑨	⑨	⑨	⑨

ANSWER SHEETS—TEST 2

Section 4 (continued)

18.

19.

20.

21.

22.

23.

24.

25.

ANSWER SHEETS—TEST 2

Section 5

1. Ⓐ Ⓑ Ⓒ Ⓓ Ⓔ
2. Ⓐ Ⓑ Ⓒ Ⓓ Ⓔ
3. Ⓐ Ⓑ Ⓒ Ⓓ Ⓔ
4. Ⓐ Ⓑ Ⓒ Ⓓ Ⓔ
5. Ⓐ Ⓑ Ⓒ Ⓓ Ⓔ
6. Ⓐ Ⓑ Ⓒ Ⓓ Ⓔ
7. Ⓐ Ⓑ Ⓒ Ⓓ Ⓔ
8. Ⓐ Ⓑ Ⓒ Ⓓ Ⓔ
9. Ⓐ Ⓑ Ⓒ Ⓓ Ⓔ
10. Ⓐ Ⓑ Ⓒ Ⓓ Ⓔ
11. Ⓐ Ⓑ Ⓒ Ⓓ Ⓔ
12. Ⓐ Ⓑ Ⓒ Ⓓ Ⓔ

13. Ⓐ Ⓑ Ⓒ Ⓓ Ⓔ
14. Ⓐ Ⓑ Ⓒ Ⓓ Ⓔ
15. Ⓐ Ⓑ Ⓒ Ⓓ Ⓔ
16. Ⓐ Ⓑ Ⓒ Ⓓ Ⓔ
17. Ⓐ Ⓑ Ⓒ Ⓓ Ⓔ
18. Ⓐ Ⓑ Ⓒ Ⓓ Ⓔ
19. Ⓐ Ⓑ Ⓒ Ⓓ Ⓔ
20. Ⓐ Ⓑ Ⓒ Ⓓ Ⓔ
21. Ⓐ Ⓑ Ⓒ Ⓓ Ⓔ
22. Ⓐ Ⓑ Ⓒ Ⓓ Ⓔ
23. Ⓐ Ⓑ Ⓒ Ⓓ Ⓔ
24. Ⓐ Ⓑ Ⓒ Ⓓ Ⓔ

25. Ⓐ Ⓑ Ⓒ Ⓓ Ⓔ
26. Ⓐ Ⓑ Ⓒ Ⓓ Ⓔ
27. Ⓐ Ⓑ Ⓒ Ⓓ Ⓔ
28. Ⓐ Ⓑ Ⓒ Ⓓ Ⓔ
29. Ⓐ Ⓑ Ⓒ Ⓓ Ⓔ
30. Ⓐ Ⓑ Ⓒ Ⓓ Ⓔ
31. Ⓐ Ⓑ Ⓒ Ⓓ Ⓔ
32. Ⓐ Ⓑ Ⓒ Ⓓ Ⓔ
33. Ⓐ Ⓑ Ⓒ Ⓓ Ⓔ
34. Ⓐ Ⓑ Ⓒ Ⓓ Ⓔ
35. Ⓐ Ⓑ Ⓒ Ⓓ Ⓔ

Section 6

1. Ⓐ Ⓑ Ⓒ Ⓓ Ⓔ
2. Ⓐ Ⓑ Ⓒ Ⓓ Ⓔ
3. Ⓐ Ⓑ Ⓒ Ⓓ Ⓔ
4. Ⓐ Ⓑ Ⓒ Ⓓ Ⓔ
5. Ⓐ Ⓑ Ⓒ Ⓓ Ⓔ
6. Ⓐ Ⓑ Ⓒ Ⓓ Ⓔ
7. Ⓐ Ⓑ Ⓒ Ⓓ Ⓔ
8. Ⓐ Ⓑ Ⓒ Ⓓ Ⓔ
9. Ⓐ Ⓑ Ⓒ Ⓓ Ⓔ
10. Ⓐ Ⓑ Ⓒ Ⓓ Ⓔ
11. Ⓐ Ⓑ Ⓒ Ⓓ Ⓔ
12. Ⓐ Ⓑ Ⓒ Ⓓ Ⓔ

13. Ⓐ Ⓑ Ⓒ Ⓓ Ⓔ
14. Ⓐ Ⓑ Ⓒ Ⓓ Ⓔ
15. Ⓐ Ⓑ Ⓒ Ⓓ Ⓔ
16. Ⓐ Ⓑ Ⓒ Ⓓ Ⓔ
17. Ⓐ Ⓑ Ⓒ Ⓓ Ⓔ
18. Ⓐ Ⓑ Ⓒ Ⓓ Ⓔ
19. Ⓐ Ⓑ Ⓒ Ⓓ Ⓔ
20. Ⓐ Ⓑ Ⓒ Ⓓ Ⓔ
21. Ⓐ Ⓑ Ⓒ Ⓓ Ⓔ
22. Ⓐ Ⓑ Ⓒ Ⓓ Ⓔ
23. Ⓐ Ⓑ Ⓒ Ⓓ Ⓔ
24. Ⓐ Ⓑ Ⓒ Ⓓ Ⓔ

25. Ⓐ Ⓑ Ⓒ Ⓓ Ⓔ
26. Ⓐ Ⓑ Ⓒ Ⓓ Ⓔ
27. Ⓐ Ⓑ Ⓒ Ⓓ Ⓔ
28. Ⓐ Ⓑ Ⓒ Ⓓ Ⓔ
29. Ⓐ Ⓑ Ⓒ Ⓓ Ⓔ
30. Ⓐ Ⓑ Ⓒ Ⓓ Ⓔ
31. Ⓐ Ⓑ Ⓒ Ⓓ Ⓔ
32. Ⓐ Ⓑ Ⓒ Ⓓ Ⓔ
33. Ⓐ Ⓑ Ⓒ Ⓓ Ⓔ
34. Ⓐ Ⓑ Ⓒ Ⓓ Ⓔ
35. Ⓐ Ⓑ Ⓒ Ⓓ Ⓔ

PRACTICE TEST 2
SECTION 1

30 Questions—30 Minutes

Select the best answer to the following questions, then fill in the appropriate space on your Answer Sheet.

Each of the following sentences contains one or two blanks; these blanks indicate that a word or set of words has been left out. Below the sentence are five words or phrases, lettered A through E. Select the word or set of words that best completes the sentence.

Example:
   Fame is -------- ; today's rising star is all too soon tomorrow's washed-up has-been.

(A) rewarding   (B) gradual
   (C) essential   (D) spontaneous
      (E) transitory

---

1. Critics of the welfare system argue that, rather than aiding people's efforts to govern their own lives, it ---- their independence.

(A) supports   (B) saps   (C) hastens
   (D) renews   (E) abets

2. The audience failed to warm to the candidate, whose speech contained nothing but empty promises, ----, and clichés.

(A) candor
(B) platitudes
(C) nuances
(D) ingenuity
(E) threats

3. By dint of much practice in the laboratory, the anatomy student became ---- and was able to manipulate her dissecting tools with either hand.

(A) practical
(B) tricky
(C) ambiguous
(D) ambidextrous
(E) ambivalent

4. Like many other pioneers, Dr. Elizabeth Blackwell, founder of the New York Infirmary, the first American hospital staffed entirely by women, faced ridicule from her contemporaries but has received great honor ----.

(A) posthumously
(B) anonymously
(C) privately
(D) prematurely
(E) previously

5. While a great deal of change and modernization has taken place in India since 1947, the basic economic arrangements, values, and family roles have been generally ----.

(A) overturned
(B) stable
(C) modified
(D) complicated
(E) appropriate

6. The hypocrite ---- feelings which he does not possess but which he feels he should display.

(A) conceals
(B) decries
(C) betrays
(D) simulates
(E) condones

7. Deloria has his detractors, but his critics have had amazingly ---- success at shaking his self-confidence or ---- his reputation.

(A) great...repairing
(B) widespread...bolstering
(C) little...denting
(D) small...enhancing
(E) poor...restoring

8. The linguistic ---- of refugee children is ---- their readiness to adopt the language of their new homeland.

(A) conservatism...indicated by
(B) inadequacy...demonstrated by
(C) adaptability...reflected in
(D) philosophy...contradicted by
(E) structure...equivalent to

9. She kept her late parents' furniture, not for any ---- value it had, but for purely ---- reasons.

(A) potential...monetary
(B) ornamental...aesthetic
(C) financial...pecuniary
(D) intrinsic...sentimental
(E) personal...accidental

Each of the following examples introduces a capitalized pair of words or phrases linked by a colon (:); this colon indicates that these words are related in some way. Following the capitalized pair are five pairs of words or phrases lettered A through E. Select the pair whose relationship is most similar to the relationship illustrated by the capitalized pair.

Example:

CLOCK:TIME::   (A) watch:wrist
(B) pedometer:speed   (C) thermometer:temperature
(D) hourglass:sand   (E) radio:sound

10. WORDS:WRITER::

    (A) honor:thief
    (B) mortar:bricklayer
    (C) child:teacher
    (D) batter:baker
    (E) laws:policeman

11. SNOW:DRIFT::

    (A) mountain:boulder
    (B) sand:dune
    (C) pane:glass
    (D) desert:oasis
    (E) mud:rain

12. GRAIN:SILO::

    (A) tree:acorn
    (B) seed:plant
    (C) water:bucket
    (D) druggist:doctor
    (E) furlong:mile

13. SHRUG:INDIFFERENCE::

    (A) grin:deference
    (B) wave:fatigue
    (C) nod:assent
    (D) blink:scorn
    (E) scowl:desire

14. ANGER:CHOLERIC::

    (A) wrath:ironic
    (B) love:bucolic
    (C) island:volcanic
    (D) greed:avaricious
    (E) pride:malicious

15. BLANDISHMENT:ALLURE::

    (A) admonition:warn
    (B) punishment:reward
    (C) scruple:disregard
    (D) invitation:issue
    (E) entertainment:perform

Read each of the passages below, and then answer the questions that follow each passage. The correct response may be stated outright or merely suggested in the passage.

Questions 16–21 are based on the following passage.

The following passage discusses so-called "hot spots," regions of unusual volcanic activity that record the passage of plates over the face of Earth. According to one theory, these hot spots may also contribute to the fracturing of continents and the opening of new oceans.

Although by far the majority of the world's active volcanoes are located along the boundaries of the great shifting plates that make up Earth's surface, more than 100 isolated

Line areas of volcanic activity occur far from the nearest plate
(5) boundary. Geologists call these volcanic areas hot spots or mantle plumes. Many of these sources of magma (the red-hot, molten material within Earth's crust, out of which igneous rock is formed) lie deep in the interior of a plate. These so-called intra-plate volcanoes often form roughly
(10) linear volcanic chains, trails of extinct volcanoes. The Hawaiian Islands, perhaps the best known example of an intra-plate volcanic chain, came into being when the northwest-moving Pacific plate passed over a relatively stationary hot spot and in doing so initiated this magma-generation and volcano-
(15) formation process. Such a volcanic chain serves as a landmark signaling the slow but inexorable passage of the plates.
   No theorist today would deny that the plates do move. Satellites anchored in space record the minute movement of fixed sites on Earth, thereby confirming the motions of the
(20) plates. They show Africa and South America drawing away from each other, as new lithospheric material wells up in the sea floor between them in the phenomenon known as sea-

floor spreading. That the two coastlines complement one another is beyond dispute; a cursory glance at the map
(25) reveals the common geological features that link these separate shores, reminders of an age eons past when the two continents were joined. In 1963 the Canadian geophysicist J. Tuzo Wilson asserted that while Earth scientists have constructed the relative motion of the plates carrying the
(30) continents in detail, "the motion of one plate with respect to another cannot readily be translated into motion with respect to the Earth's interior." For this reason, scientists were unable to determine whether both continents were moving (diverging in separate directions) or whether one continent
(35) was motionless while the other was drifting away from it. Wilson hypothesized that hot spots, fixed in Earth's depths, could provide the necessary information to settle the question. Using hot spots as a fixed frame of reference, Wilson concluded that the African plate was motionless and that it
(40) had exhibited no movement for 30 million years.

Wilson's hot-spot hypothesis goes well beyond this somewhat limited role. He conceives the hot spots as playing a major part in influencing the movements of the continental plates. As he wrote in his seminal essay in *Scientific*
(45) *American*, "When a continental plate comes to rest over a hot spot, the material welling up from deeper layers creates a broad dome. As the dome grows it develops deep fissures; in at least a few cases the continent may rupture entirely along some of these fissures, so that the hot spot initiates the for-
(50) mation of a new ocean." The hot spot, flaring up from Earth's deepest core, may someday cast new light on the continents' mutability.

16. The term "hot spot" is being used in the passage

   (A) rhetorically
   (B) colloquially
   (C) technically
   (D) ambiguously
   (E) ironically

17. The author regards the theory that the plates making up the earth's surface move as

(A) tentative
(B) irrefutable
(C) discredited
(D) unanimous
(E) relative

18. According to the passage, which of the following statements indicates that Africa and South America once adjoined one another?

   I. They share certain common topographic traits.
  II. Their shorelines are physical counterparts.
 III. The African plate has been stationary for 30 million years.

(A) I only
(B) II only
(C) I and II only
(D) II and III only
(E) I, II, and III

19. The word "constructed" in line 29 most nearly means

(A) interpreted   (B) built   (C) impeded
(D) restricted   (E) refuted

20. According to Wilson, the hot spot hypothesis eventually may prove useful in interpreting

(A) the boundaries of the plates
(B) the depth of the ocean floor
(C) the relative motion of the plates
(D) current satellite technology
(E) major changes in continental shape

21. In maintaining that fissures in an upwelled dome can result in the formation of a new ocean (lines 45–50), Wilson has assumed which of the following points?

(A) The fissures are located directly above a hot spot.
(B) The dome is broader than the continent upon which it rests.
(C) The oceanic depths are immutable.
(D) The fissures cut across the continent, splitting it.
(E) No such fissures exist upon the ocean floor.

Questions 22–30 are based on the following passage.

The following passage is taken from an essay on South-western Native American art.

Among the Plains Indians, two separate strains of decorative art evolved: the figurative, representational art created by
the men of the tribe, and the geometric, abstract art crafted
Line by the women. According to Dunn and Highwater, the artist's
(5) sex governed both the kind of article to be decorated and the
style to be followed in its ornamentation. Thus, the decorative works created by tribesmen consistently depict living
creatures (men, horses, buffalo) or magical beings (ghosts
and other supernatural life-forms). Those created by women,
(10) however, are clearly nonrepresentational: no figures of men
or animals appear in this classically geometric art.

Art historians theorize that this abstract, geometric art, tra-
ditionally the prerogative of the women, predates the figurative art of the men. Descending from those aspects of
(15) Woodland culture that gave rise to weaving, quillwork, and
beadwork, it is a utilitarian art, intended for the embellish-
ment of ordinary, serviceable objects such as parfleche boxes
(cases made of rawhide), saddlebags, and hide robes. The
abstract designs combine classical geometric figures into
(20) formal patterns: a ring of narrow isosceles triangles arranged
on the background of a large central circle creates the well-
known "feather and circle" pattern. Created in bold primary
colors (red, yellow, blue), sometimes black or green, and
often outlined in dark paint or glue size, these non-
(25) representational designs are nonetheless intricately detailed.

Although the abstract decorations crafted by the women
are visually striking, they pale in significance when compared
to the narrative compositions created by the men. Created to
tell a story, these works were generally heroic in nature, and
(30) were intended to commemorate a bold and courageous
exploit or a spiritual awakening. Unlike realistic portraits, the

artworks emphasized action, not physical likeness. Highwater
describes their making as follows: "These representational
works were generally drafted by a group of men—often the
(35) individuals who had performed the deeds being recorded—
who drew on untailored hide robes and tepee liners made of
skins. The paintings usually filled the entire field; often they
were conceived at different times as separate pictorial
vignettes documenting specific actions. In relationship to
(40) each other, these vignettes suggest a narrative."

The tribesmen's narrative artwork depicted not only war-
like deeds but also mystic dreams and vision quests. Part of
the young male's rite of passage into tribal adulthood
involved his discovering his own personal totem or symbolic
(45) guardian. By fasting or by consuming hallucinatory substances, the youth opened himself to the revelation of his
"mystery object," a symbol that could protect him from both
natural and supernatural dangers.

What had been in the early 1700s a highly individualistic,
(50) personal iconography changed into something very different
by the early nineteenth century. As Anglos came West in ever
greater numbers, they brought with them new materials and
new ideas. Just as European glass beads came to replace
native porcupine quills in the women's applied designs, cloth
(55) eventually became used as a substitute for animal hides. The
emphasis of Plains artwork shifted as well: tribespeople came
to create works that celebrated the solidarity of Indians as a
group rather than their prowess as individuals.

22. Which of the following titles best summarizes the content of the
passage?

(A) The Ongoing Influence of Plains Indian Art
(B) Male and Female in Tribal Life
(C) Indian Art as Narrative and Dream
(D) Design Specialization In Plains Art
(E) The History of Indian Representational Art

23. The author cites examples of the work of Plains artists primarily to

(A) show the differences between male and female decorative styles
(B) emphasize the functional role of art in Indian life
(C) describe the techniques employed in the creation of particular works
(D) illustrate the changes made by Anglo influence on Plains art
(E) explore the spiritual significance of representational design

24. The word "strains" in line 1 means

(A) tunes
(B) pressures
(C) varieties
(D) injuries
(E) pressures

25. In lines 15–16, weaving, quillwork, and beadwork are presented as examples of

(A) male-dominated decorative arts
(B) uninspired products of artisans
(C) geometrically based crafts
(D) unusual applications of artistic theories
(E) precursors of representational design

26. With which of the following statements regarding male Plains artists prior to 1800 would the author most likely agree?

   I. They tended to work collaboratively on projects.
  II. They believed art had power to ward off danger.
 III. They derived their designs from classical forms.

(A) I only
(B) III only
(C) I and II only
(D) II and III only
(E) I, II, and III

27. As used in line 34, "drafted" most nearly means

(A) selected
(B) recruited
(C) endorsed
(D) sketched
(E) ventilated

28. According to the passage, dream visions were important to the Plains artist because they

    (A) enabled him to foresee influences on his style
    (B) suggested the techniques and methods of his art
    (C) determined his individual aesthetic philosophy
    (D) expressed his sense of tribal solidarity
    (E) revealed the true form of his spiritual guardian

29. In its narrative aspect, Plains art resembles LEAST

    (A) a cartoon strip made up of several panels
    (B) a portrait bust of a chieftain in full headdress
    (C) an epic recounting the adventures of a legendary hero
    (D) a chapter from the autobiography of a prominent leader
    (E) a mural portraying scenes from the life of Martin Luther King

30. According to lines 51–58, the impact of the Anglo presence on Plains art can be seen in the

    (A) growth of importance of geometric patterning
    (B) dearth of hides available to Plains Indian artists
    (C) shift from depicting individuals to depicting the community
    (D) emphasis on dream visions as appropriate subject matter for narrative art
    (E) growing lack of belief that images could protect one from natural enemies

YOU MAY GO BACK AND REVIEW THIS
SECTION IN THE REMAINING TIME, BUT **S T O P**
DO NOT WORK IN ANY OTHER SECTION
UNTIL TOLD TO DO SO.

SECTION 2

25 Questions—30 Minutes

For each problem in this section determine which of the five choices is correct and blacken in that choice on your answer sheet. You may use any blank space on the page for your work.

Notes:

- You may use a calculator whenever you feel it will be helpful.
- Use the diagrams provided to help you solve the problems. Unless you see the words "Note: Figure not drawn to scale" under a diagram, it has been drawn as accurately as possible. Unless it is stated that a figure is three-dimensional, you may assume it lies in a plane.

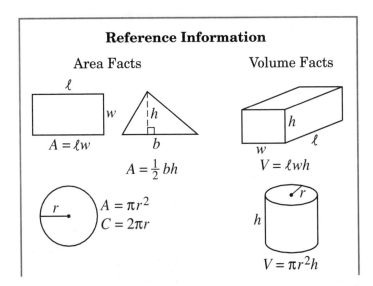

Reference Information

Area Facts

$A = \ell w$

$A = \frac{1}{2} bh$

$A = \pi r^2$
$C = 2\pi r$

Volume Facts

$V = \ell wh$

$V = \pi r^2 h$

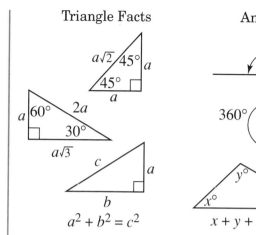

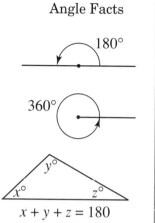

Triangle Facts

$$a^2 + b^2 = c^2$$

Angle Facts

$$x + y + z = 180$$

1. If $5c + 3 = 3c + 5$, what is the value of c?

(A) −1 (B) 0 (C) 1 (D) 3 (E) 5

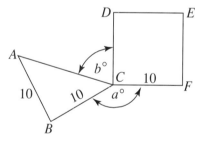

2. In the figure above, C is the only point that right triangle ABC and square $CDEF$ have in common. What is the value of $a + b$?

(A) 135 (B) 180 (C) 210 (D) 225 (E) 270

3. A lacrosse team raised some money. They used 74% of the money to buy uniforms, 18% for equipment, and the remaining $216 for a team party. How much money did they raise?

(A) $2400 (B) $2450 (C) $2500 (D) $2600
(E) $2700

4. If $\frac{3}{4}$ of a number is 7 more than $\frac{1}{6}$ of the number, what is $\frac{5}{3}$ of the number?

(A) 12   (B) 15   (C) 18   (D) 20   (E) 24

---

5. For all positive numbers a and b, let $a \,\square\, b = \sqrt{ab}$.
If $n > 1$, what does $n \,\square\, \frac{1}{n}$ equal?

(A) $\sqrt{n}$ (B) $\sqrt{n^2}$ (C) $\frac{1}{\sqrt{n}}$ (D) $\frac{1}{\sqrt{n^2}}$ 20   (E) 1

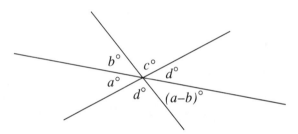

Note: Figure not drawn to scale

6. In the figure above, what is the value of b?

(A) 30   (B) 36   (C) 45   (D) 60   (E) 72

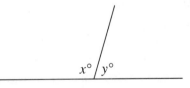

Note: Figure not drawn to scale

7. In the figure above, if x is 150 more than y, what is the value of y?

(A) 10   (B) 15   (C) 20   (D) 25   (E) 30

8. Heidi wrote the number 1 on 1 slip of paper, the number 2 on 2 slips of paper, the number 3 on 3 slips of paper, the number 4 on 4 slips of paper, the number 5 on 5 slips of paper, and the number 6 on 6 slips of paper. All the slips of paper were placed in a bag, and Sally drew 1 slip at random. What is the probability that the number on the slip Sally drew was odd?

(A) $\frac{1}{9}$ (B) $\frac{1}{7}$ (C) $\frac{3}{7}$ (D) $\frac{1}{2}$ (E) $\frac{4}{7}$

9. Sandrine is now 5 times as old as Nicholas, but 7 years from now she will be 3 times as old as he will be then. How old is Sandrine now?

(A) 15   (B) 20   (C) 21   (D) 25   (E) 35

10. For how many positive numbers a is it true that $a \times a \times a = a + a + a$?

(A) 0   (B) 1   (C) 2   (D) 3   (E) more than 3

11. Last year Jose sold a painting for $2000. If he made a 25% profit on the sale, how much had he paid for the painting?

(A) $1200   (B) $1500   (C) $1600   (D) $2400   (E) $2500

12. For any positive integer $n > 1$, $n!$ represents the product of the first n positive integers. For example, $3! = 1 \times 2 \times 3 = 6$. Which of the following is (are) equal to $\frac{10!}{8!}$?

$$\text{I. } 5! - 4! - 3!$$
$$\text{II. } \frac{5!}{4!}$$
$$\text{III. } 15(3!)$$

(A) I only   (B) II only   (C) III only
(D) I and III only   (E) I, II, and III

13. Let the lengths of the sides of a triangle be represented by $x + 3$, $2x - 3$, and $3x - 5$. If the perimeter of the triangle is 25, what is the length of the shortest side?

(A) 5   (B) 7   (C) 8   (D) 10   (E) It cannot be determined from the information given.

---

14. A rectangle is twice as long as it is wide. If the width is a, what is the length of a diagonal?

(A) $a\sqrt{2}$ (B) $a\sqrt{3}$ (C) $a\sqrt{5}$ (D) $3a$ (E) $5a$

---

15. If $abc = 1$, which of the following could be the number of integers among a, b, and c?

I. 1
II. 2
III. 3

(A) none   (B) I only   (C) I and II only
(D) I and III only   (E) I, II, and III

---

16. At Essex High School 100 students are taking chemistry and 80 students are taking biology. If 20 students are taking both chemistry and biology, what is the ratio of the number of students taking only chemistry to the number taking only biology?

(A) $\dfrac{3}{4}$ (B) $\dfrac{1}{1}$ (C) $\dfrac{5}{4}$ (D) $\dfrac{4}{3}$

(E) It cannot be determined from the information given.

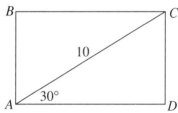

17. In the figure above, a small square is drawn inside a large square. If the shaded area and the white area are equal, what is the ratio of the side of the large square to the side of the small square?

(A) $\frac{\sqrt{2}}{1}$ (B) $\frac{2}{1}$ (C) $\frac{2\sqrt{2}}{1}$ (D) $\frac{2}{\sqrt{2}-1}$

(E) It cannot be determined from the information given.

---

18. In rectangle *ABCD* above, diagonal *AC* makes a 30° angle with side *AD*. If *AC* = 10, what is the area of the rectangle?

(A) $25\sqrt{2}$ (B) $25\sqrt{3}$ (C) 48 (D) 50 (E) 100

---

19. The value of 10 pounds of gold is *d* dollars, and a pound of gold has the same value as *p* pounds of silver. What is the value, in dollars, of one pound of silver?

(A) $\frac{d}{10p}$ (B) $\frac{10p}{d}$ (C) $\frac{dp}{10}$ (D) $\frac{p}{10d}$ (E) $\frac{10d}{p}$

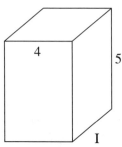
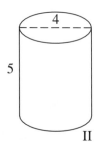

20. Of the figures above, container I is a rectangular solid whose base is a square 4 inches on a side, and container II is a cylinder whose base is a circle of diameter 4 inches. The height of each container is 5 inches. How much more water, in cubic inches, will container I hold than container II?

    (A) 4(4 − π)   (B) 20(4 − π)   (C) 80(π − 1)   (D) 80(1 − π)
    (E) It cannot be determined from the information given.

___

21. A bag contains 3 red, 4 white, and 5 blue marbles. Jason begins removing marbles from the bag at random, one at a time. What is the least number of marbles he must remove to be sure that he has at least 1 marble of each color?

    (A) 3   (B) 6   (C) 8   (D) 10   (E) 12

___

22. The distance between Ali's house and college is exactly 135 miles. If she drove $\frac{2}{3}$ of the distance in 135 minutes, what was her average speed, in miles per hour?

    (A) 40   (B) 45   (C) 60   (D) 67.5
    (E) It cannot be determined from the information given.

___

23. If $x + 2y = a$ and $x - 2y = b$, which of the following is an expression for xy?

(A) ab (B) $\dfrac{a + b}{2}$ (C) $\dfrac{a - b}{2}$ (D) $\dfrac{a^2 - b^2}{4}$

(E) $\dfrac{a^2 - b^2}{8}$

---

24. What is the maximum number of points of intersection between a square and a circle?

(A) fewer than 4   (B) 4   (C) 6   (D) 8   (E) more than 8

---

25. The average (arithmetic mean) weight of five students is 150.4 pounds. If no student weighs less than 130 pounds and if no two students' weights are within 5 pounds of each other, what is the most, in pounds, that any one of the students can weigh?

(A) 172   (B) 192   (C) 202   (D) 232
 (E) It cannot be determined from the information given.

YOU MAY GO BACK AND REVIEW THIS
SECTION IN THE REMAINING TIME, BUT   **S T O P**
DO NOT WORK IN ANY OTHER SECTION
UNTIL TOLD TO DO SO.

SECTION 3

35 Questions—30 Minutes

Select the best answer to the following questions, then fill in the appropriate space on your Answer Sheet.

Each of the following sentences contains one or two blanks; these blanks indicate that a word or set of words has been left out. Below the sentence are five words or phrases, lettered A through E. Select the word or set of words that best completes the sentence.

Example:

Fame is -------- ; today's rising star is all too soon tomorrow's washed-up has-been.

(A) rewarding   (B) gradual
  (C) essential   (D) spontaneous
    (E) transitory

---

1. Like foolish people who continue to live near an active volcano, many of us are ---- about the ---- of atomic warfare and its attendant destruction.

    (A) worried...possibility
    (B) unconcerned...threat
    (C) excited...power
    (D) cheered...possession
    (E) irritated...news

2. By communicating through pointing and making gestures, Charles was able to overcome any ---- difficulties that arose during his recent trip to Japan.

    (A) peripatetic   (B) linguistic   (C) plausible
     (D) monetary   (E) territorial

3. It is the task of the International Wildlife Preservation Commission to prevent endangered species from becoming ---- in order that future generations may ---- the great diversity of animal life.

   (A) tamed...recollect
   (B) evolved...value
   (C) extinct...enjoy
   (D) specialized...anticipate
   (E) widespread...appreciate

4. We find it difficult to translate a foreign text literally because we cannot capture the ---- of the original passage exactly.

   (A) novelty
   (B) succinctness
   (C) connotations
   (D) ambivalence
   (E) alienation

5. It is remarkable that a man so in the public eye, so highly praised and imitated, can retain his ----.

   (A) magniloquence   (B) dogmas   (C) bravado
    (D) idiosyncracies   (E) humility

6. For all the ---- involved in the study of seals, we Arctic researchers have occasional moments of pure ---- over some new idea or discovery.

   (A) tribulations...despair
   (B) hardships...exhilaration
   (C) confusions...bewilderment
   (D) inconvenience...panic
   (E) thrills...delight

7. Despite the growing ---- of Hispanic actors in the American theater, many Hispanic experts feel that the Spanish-speaking population is ---- on the stage.

   (A) decrease...inappropriate
   (B) emergence...visible
   (C) prominence...underrepresented
   (D) skill...alienated
   (E) number...misdirected

8. As a sportscaster, Cosell was apparently never ----; he made ----
comments about every boxing match he covered.

(A) excited...hysterical
(B) relevant...pertinent
(C) satisfied...disparaging
(D) amazed...awe-struck
(E) impressed...laudatory

9. Even critics who do not ---- Robin Williams' interpretation of the part
---- him as an inventive comic actor who has made a serious attempt
to come to terms with one of the most challenging roles of our time.

(A) dissent from...dismiss
(B) cavil at...welcome
(C) agree with...denounce
(D) recoil from...deride
(E) concur with...acknowledge

10. This latest biography of Malcolm X is a nuanced and sensitive picture
of a very complex man, ---- analysis of his personality.

(A) an ineffectual   (B) a telling   (C) a ponderous
 (D) a simplistic   (E) an overblown

Each of the following examples introduces a capitalized pair of
words or phrases linked by a colon (:); this colon indicates that
these words are related in some way. Following the capitalized
pair are five pairs of words or phrases lettered A through E.
Select the pair whose relationship is most similar to the relationship illustrated by the capitalized pair.

Example:

CLOCK:TIME::   (A) watch:wrist
 (B) pedometer:speed   (C) thermometer:temperature
  (D) hourglass:sand   (E) radio:sound

11. HEART:PUMP::

    (A) lungs:collapse
    (B) appendix:burst
    (C) stomach:digest
    (D) intestine:twist
    (E) teeth:ache

12. MASTER:SERVANT::

    (A) judge:jury
    (B) monarch:subject
    (C) serf:peasant
    (D) capital:labor
    (E) landlord:tenant

13. STANZA:POEM::

    (A) flag:anthem
    (B) story:building
    (C) mural:painting
    (D) program:recital
    (E) rhyme:prose

14. MONGREL:COLLIE::

    (A) goose:gosling
    (B) gem:ruby
    (C) alloy:iron
    (D) pony:bridle
    (E) bleat:sheep

15. MASON:TROWEL::

    (A) potter:clay
    (B) doctor:degree
    (C) carpenter:adze
    (D) preacher:sermon
    (E) sculptor:museum

16. AMASS:WEALTH::

    (A) lavish:bribes
    (B) garner:grain
    (C) disperse:enemy
    (D) refund:deposit
    (E) weigh:value

17. WINCE:PAIN:

   (A) pardon:tolerance
   (B) blush:embarrassment
   (C) cry:anger
   (D) sing:gaiety
   (E) march:patriotism

18. CONNOISSEUR:PAINTING::

   (A) egotist:self
   (B) gourmet:viands
   (C) miser:gold
   (D) jury:criminal
   (E) artist:critic

19. HECKLER:JEER:

   (A) snob:flatter
   (B) grumbler:complain
   (C) mentor:repent
   (D) laughingstock:mock
   (E) miser:weep

20. INIQUITOUS:MALEFACTOR::

   (A) conspicuous:leader
   (B) egregious:philanthropist
   (C) reprehensible:altruist
   (D) renowned:benefactor
   (E) mischievous:prankster

21. SLINK:STEALTH::

   (A) whine:querulousness
   (B) snarl:mockery
   (C) disguise:alias
   (D) praise:friendship
   (E) invest:capital

22. AMUSING:UPROARIOUS::

   (A) puzzling:dumbfounding
   (B) quiet:noisy
   (C) intractable:stubborn
   (D) petty:narrow-minded
   (E) exhausted:weary

23. STANCH:BLEEDING::

(A) dam:flood
(B) divert:traffic
(C) squander:money
(D) induce:nausea
(E) color:facts

Read the passage below, and then answer the questions that follow the passage. The correct response may be stated outright or merely suggested in the passage.

Questions 24–35 are based on the following passage.

In this excerpt from a novel, Catherine's Aunt Lavinia comes to make her home with Catherine and her father and becomes involved in Catherine's upbringing.

When the child was about ten years old, he invited his
sister, Mrs. Penniman, to come and stay with him. His sister
Lavinia had married a poor clergyman, of a sickly constitu-
Line tion and a flowery style of eloquence, and then, at the age of
(5) thirty-three, had been left a widow—without children, without
fortune—with nothing but the memory of Mr. Penniman's
flowers of speech, a certain vague aroma of which hovered
about her own conversation. Nevertheless, he had offered her
a home under his own roof, which Lavinia accepted with the
(10) alacrity of a woman who had spent the ten years of her
married life in the town of Poughkeepsie. The Doctor had not
proposed to Mrs. Penniman to come and live with him indefi-
nitely; he had suggested that she should make an asylum of
his house while she looked about for unfurnished lodgings. It
(15) is uncertain whether Mrs. Penniman ever instituted a search
for unfurnished lodgings, but it is beyond dispute that she
never found them. She settled herself with her brother and
never went away, and, when Catherine was twenty years old,
her Aunt Lavinia was still one of the most striking features of

(20) her immediate entourage. Mrs. Penniman's own account of
the matter was that she had remained to take charge of her
niece's education. She had given this account, at least, to
everyone but the Doctor, who never asked for explanations
which he could entertain himself any day with inventing. Mrs.
(25) Penniman, moreover, though she had a good deal of a certain sort of artificial assurance, shrunk, for indefinable reasons, from presenting herself to her brother as a fountain of
instruction. She had not a high sense of humor, but she had
enough to prevent her from making this mistake; and her
(30) brother, on his side, had enough to excuse her, in her situation, for laying him under contribution during a considerable
part of a lifetime. He therefore assented tacitly to the proposi-
tion which Mrs. Penniman had tacitly laid down, that it was
of importance that the poor motherless girl should have a
(35) brilliant woman near her. His assent could only be tacit, for
he had never been dazzled by his sister's intellectual lustre.
Save when he fell in love with Catherine Harrington, he had
never been dazzled, indeed, by any feminine characteristics
whatever; and though he was to a certain extent what is
(40) called a ladies' doctor, his private opinion of the more complicated sex was not exalted. He nevertheless, at the end of
six months, accepted his sister's permanent presence as an
accomplished fact, and as Catherine grew older, perceived
that there were in effect good reasons why she should have a
(45) companion of her own imperfect sex. He was extremely
polite to Lavinia, scrupulously, formally polite; and she had
never seen him in anger but once in her life, when he lost his
temper in a theological discussion with her late husband.
With her he never discussed theology, nor, indeed, discussed
(50) anything; he contented himself with making known, very dis-
tinctly in the form of a lucid ultimatum, his wishes with
regard to Catherine.

Once, when the girl was about twelve years old, he had
said to her—
(55)   "Try and make a clever woman of her,

Lavinia; I should like her to be a clever woman."

Mrs. Penniman, at this, looked thoughtful a moment. "My dear Austin," she then inquired, "do you think it is better to be clever than to be good?"

(60)   From this assertion Mrs. Penniman saw no reason to dissent; she possibly reflected that her own great use in the world was owing to her aptitude for many things.

"Of course I wish Catherine to be good," the Doctor said next day; "but she won't be any the less virtuous for not

(65) being a fool. I am not afraid of her being wicked; she will never have the salt of malice in her character. She is 'as good as good bread,' as the French say; but six years hence I don't want to have to compare her to good bread-and-butter."

"Are you afraid she will be insipid? My dear brother, it is I

(70) who supply the butter; so you need not fear!" said Mrs. Penniman, who had taken in hand the child's "accomplishments," overlooking her at the piano, where Catherine displayed a certain talent, and going with her to the dancing-class, where it must be confessed that she made

(75) but a modest figure.

24. The word "constitution" in lines 4–5 means

(A) establishment   (B) charter   (C) ambience
(D) physique   (E) wit

25. From the description of how Mrs. Penniman came to live in her brother's home (lines 1–11), we may infer all of the following EXCEPT that

(A) she readily became dependent on her brother
(B) she was married at the age of twenty-three
(C) she was physically delicate and in ill health
(D) she had not found living in Poughkeepsie particularly gratifying
(E) she occasionally echoed an ornate manner of speech

26. The word "asylum" in line 13 means

(A) institution   (B) sanitarium   (C) refuge
(D) sanction   (E) shambles

27. In the passage the doctor is portrayed most specifically as

   (A) benevolent and retiring
   (B) casual and easy-going
   (C) sadly ineffectual
   (D) civil but imperious
   (E) habitually irate

28. Lines 25–28 introduce which aspect of the Doctor and Mrs. Penniman's relationship?

   (A) Their mutual admiration
   (B) The guilt Mrs. Penniman feels about imposing on him
   (C) The Doctor's burdensome sense of responsibility
   (D) His inability to excuse her shortcomings
   (E) Her relative lack of confidence in dealing with him

29. The reason the Doctor gives only tacit assent to Mrs. Penniman's excuse for living with him is that he

   (A) actually regrets ever having allowed her to move in
   (B) does not believe in his sister's purported brilliance
   (C) objects to her taking part in his daughter's education
   (D) is unable to reveal the depth of his respect for her
   (E) does not wish to embarrass his sister with his praise

30. It can be inferred that the Doctor views children primarily as

   (A) a source of joy and comfort in old age
   (B) innocent sufferers for the sins of their fathers
   (C) clay to be molded into an acceptable image
   (D) the chief objective of the married state
   (E) their parents' sole chance for immortality

31. The word "reflected" in line 61 means

   (A) mirrored   (B) glittered   (C) considered
    (D) indicated   (E) reproduced

32. In line 68, the analogy to "good bread-and-butter" that the Doctor makes is used to emphasize

(A) the wholesomeness of Catherine's character
(B) his fear that his daughter may prove virtuous but uninteresting
(C) the discrepancy between Catherine's nature and her education
(D) his hostility toward his sister's notions of proper diet
(E) his appreciation of the simple things in life

33. The word "overlooking" in line 72 means

(A) ignoring
(B) slighting
(C) forgiving
(D) watching over
(E) towering above

34. Mrs. Penniman's opinion of her ability to mold Catherine successfully (lines 69–70) can best be described as

(A) characteristically modest
(B) moderately ambivalent
(C) atypically judicious
(D) unrealistically optimistic
(E) cynically dispassionate

35. The remarks about Catherine in the last paragraph reveal her

(A) limited skill as a dancer
(B) virtuosity as a pianist
(C) shyness with her dancing partners
(D) indifference to cleverness
(E) reluctance to practice

YOU MAY GO BACK AND REVIEW THIS SECTION IN THE REMAINING TIME, BUT DO NOT WORK IN ANY OTHER SECTION UNTIL TOLD TO DO SO.

S T O P

SECTION 4

25 Questions—30 Minutes

You have 30 minutes to answer the 15 Quantitative Comparison questions and 10 Student-Produced Response questions in this section. You may use any blank space on the page for your work.

Notes:

- You may use a calculator whenever you feel it will be helpful.

- Use the diagrams provided to help you solve the problems. Unless you see the words "<u>Note</u>: Figure not drawn to scale" under a diagram, it has been drawn as accurately as possible. Unless it is stated that a figure is three-dimensional, you may assume it lies in a plane.

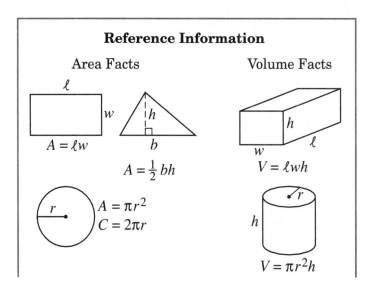

Reference Information

Area Facts

$A = \ell w$

$A = \frac{1}{2}bh$

$A = \pi r^2$
$C = 2\pi r$

Volume Facts

$V = \ell wh$

$V = \pi r^2 h$

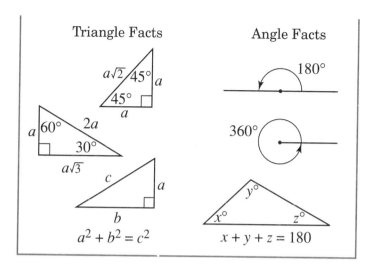

Triangle Facts

Angle Facts

$$a^2 + b^2 = c^2$$

$$x + y + z = 180$$

Directions for the Quantitative Comparison Questions

In each of questions 1–15, two quantities appear in boxes: one in Column A and one in Column B. You must compare them. The correct answer to a question is

A if the quantity in Column A is greater;
B if the quantity in Column B is greater;
C if the two quantities are equal;
D if it is impossible to determine which quantity is greater.

<u>Notes:</u>

- *The correct answer is <u>never</u> E.*
- Sometimes information about one or both of the quantities is centered above the two boxes.
- If the same symbol appears in both columns, it represents the same thing each time.
- All variables represent real numbers.

SAMPLE QUESTIONS		ANSWERS
Column A	Column B	

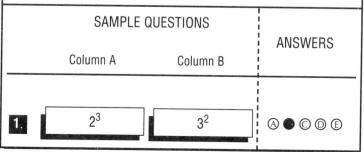

1. | 2^3 | 3^2 | Ⓐ ● Ⓒ Ⓓ Ⓔ

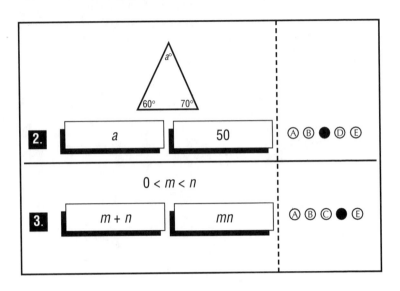

2.

| a | 50 | Ⓐ Ⓑ ● Ⓓ Ⓔ |

$0 < m < n$

3.

| $m + n$ | mn | Ⓐ Ⓑ Ⓒ ● Ⓔ |

SUMMARY DIRECTIONS FOR QUANTITATIVE COMPARISON QUESTIONS

<u>Answer:</u> A if the quantity in Column A is greater;
B if the quantity in Column B is greater;
C if the two quantities are equal;
D if it is impossible to determine which quantity is greater.

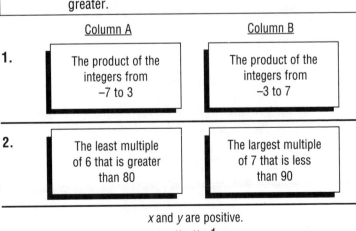

Column A	Column B

1.

| The product of the integers from −7 to 3 | The product of the integers from −3 to 7 |

2.

| The least multiple of 6 that is greater than 80 | The largest multiple of 7 that is less than 90 |

x and y are positive.
$x + y = 1$

3.

| xy | 1 |

SUMMARY DIRECTIONS FOR QUANTITATIVE
COMPARISON QUESTIONS

<u>Answer:</u> A if the quantity in Column A is greater;
B if the quantity in Column B is greater;
C if the two quantities are equal;
D if it is impossible to determine which quantity is
greater.

<u>Column A</u>   <u>Column B</u>

$$a > 0, b > 0$$
$$a \neq b$$

4.

$\dfrac{a}{b}$	$\left(\dfrac{a}{b}\right)^3$

c°

10

$135°$ d°

11

5.

c	d

6.

The largest prime factor of 51	The largest prime factor of 78

The length of rectangle II is 10% more than
the length of rectangle I.

The width of rectangle II is 10% less than
the width of rectangle I.

7.

The area of rectangle I	The area of rectangle II

SUMMARY DIRECTIONS FOR QUANTITATIVE COMPARISON QUESTIONS

<u>Answer:</u> A if the quantity in Column A is greater;
B if the quantity in Column B is greater;
C if the two quantities are equal;
D if it is impossible to determine which quantity is greater.

<u>Column A</u>   <u>Column B</u>

1 dollar is worth 4.9 francs.
5 shekels are worth 8.4 francs.

8.

| The value of 1 dollar | The value of 3 shekels |

$$0 < a < b < 1$$

9.

| $\sqrt{a+b}$ | $\sqrt{a} + \sqrt{b}$ |

$$x < y$$

10.

| The average (arithmetic mean) of x and y | The average (arithmetic mean) of x, y, and y |

$$1 < a < b < 2$$

11.

| ab | $a + b$ |

The measures of the angles in $\triangle$I are in the ratio of 1:2:3.

The measures of the angles in $\triangle$II are in the ratio of 2:7:9.

12.

| The measure of the largest angle of $\triangle$I | The measure of the largest angle of $\triangle$II |

SUMMARY DIRECTIONS FOR QUANTITATIVE COMPARISON QUESTIONS

<u>Answer:</u> A if the quantity in Column A is greater;
B if the quantity in Column B is greater;
C if the two quantities are equal;
D if it is impossible to determine which quantity is greater.

Column A   Column B

500 children were asked, "What is your favorite green vegetable?" The table below shows how many children chose each vegetable. The vegetables are listed in order from most popular to least. There were no ties.

Vegetable	Number of Children
Broccoli	189
String beans	a
Peas	b
Spinach	95
Asparagus	c

13.

| c | 30 |

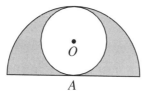

The circle with center O is inscribed in the semicircle with center A.

14.

| The area of the shaded region | The area of the white region |

The average (arithmetic mean) of n numbers is 17.
The average of those n numbers and 25 is 21.

15.

| n | 2 |

Directions for Student-Produced Response Questions (Grid-ins)

In questions 16–25, first solve the problem, and then enter your answer on the grid provided on the answer sheet. The instructions for entering your answers are as follows:

- First, write your answer in the boxes at the top of the grid.
- Second, grid your answer in the columns below the boxes.
- Use the fraction bar in the first row or the decimal point in the second row to enter fractions and decimal answers.

Answer: $\frac{8}{15}$ Answer: 1.75

Write your answer in the boxes

Grid in your answer

Answer: 100

Either position is acceptable

- Grid only one space in each column.
- Entering the answer in the boxes is recommended as an aid in gridding, but is not required.
- The machine scoring your exam can read only what you grid, so you **must grid in your answers correctly to get credit.**
- If a question has more than one correct answer, grid in only one of them.

- The grid does not have a minus sign, so no answer can be negative.
- A mixed number *must* be converted to an improper fraction or a decimal before it is gridded. Enter $1\frac{1}{4}$ as 5/4 or 1.25; the machine will interpret 1 1/4 as $\frac{11}{4}$ and mark it wrong.
- **All decimals must be entered as accurately as possible.** Here are the three acceptable ways of gridding

$$\frac{3}{11} = 0.272727...$$

3/11   .272   .273

- Note that rounding to .273 is acceptable, because you are using the full grid, but you would receive **no credit** for .3 or .27, because they are less accurate.

16. If $7a = (91)(13)$, what is the value of $\sqrt{a}$?

17. If a, b, and c are positive numbers with $a = \frac{b}{c^2}$, what is the value of c when $a = 44$ and $b = 275$?

18. What is the area of a right triangle whose hypotenuse is 25 and one of whose legs is 15?

---

19. In 1980, Elaine was 8 times as old as Adam, and Judy was 3 times as old as Adam. Elaine is 20 years older than Judy. How old was Adam in 1988?

---

20. If $x + y = 10$ and $x - y = 11$, what is the value of $x^2 - y^2$?

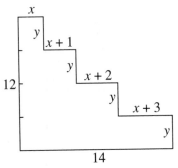

21. In the figure above, all of the line segments meet to form right angles. What is the perimeter of the figure?

---

22. If $a = 2b$, $3b = 4c$, and $5c = 6d$, what is the ratio of a to d?

---

23. If the average (arithmetic mean) of a, b, c, d, and e is 95, and the average of a, b, and e is 100, what is the average of c and d?

---

24. The average (arithmetic mean) of a set of 9 numbers is 99. After one of the numbers is deleted from the set, the average of the remaining numbers is 89. What number was deleted?

---

25. Two circular tables have diameters of 35 inches and 25 inches, respectively. The area of the larger table is what percent <u>more</u> than the area of the smaller table? (Grid in your answer without a percent sign.)

YOU MAY GO BACK AND REVIEW THIS
SECTION IN THE REMAINING TIME, BUT
DO NOT WORK IN ANY OTHER SECTION
UNTIL TOLD TO DO SO.

S T O P

SECTION 5

13 Questions—15 Minutes

Select the best answer to the following questions, then fill in the appropriate space on your Answer Sheet.

The questions that follow the two passages in this section relate to the content of both, and to their relationship. The correct response may be stated outright in the passages or merely suggested.

Questions 1–13 are based on the following passages.

The following passages are excerpted from recent works that discuss the survival of the city in our time. Passage 1 was written by a literary critic and scholar; Passage 2, by an urban planner and sociologist.

Passage 1

When musing on cities over time and in our time, from the first (whenever it was) to today, we must always remember that cities are artifacts. Forests, jungles, deserts, plains,
Line oceans—the organic environment is born and dies and is
(5) reborn endlessly, beautifully, and completely without moral constraint or ethical control. But cities—despite the metaphors that we apply to them from biology or nature ("The city dies when industry flees"; "The neighborhoods are the vital cells of the urban organism"), despite the sentimen-
(10) tal or anthropomorphic devices we use to describe cities— are artificial. Nature has never made a city, and what Nature makes that may seem like a city—an anthill, for instance— only *seems* like one. It is not a city.

Human beings made and make cities, and only human
(15) beings kill cities, or let them die. And human beings do
both—make cities and unmake them—by the same means:
by acts of choice. We enjoy deluding ourselves in this as in
other things. We enjoy believing that there are forces out
there completely determining our fate, natural forces—or
(20) forces so strong and overwhelming as to be like natural
forces—that send cities through organic or biological phases
of birth, growth, and decay. We avoid the knowledge that
cities are at best works of art, and at worst ungainly artifacts—but never flowers or even weeds—and that we, not
(25) some mysterious force or cosmic biological system, control
the creation and life of a city.

We control the creation and life of a city by the choices
and agreements we make—the basic choice being, for
instance, not to live alone, the basic agreement being to live
(30) together. When people choose to settle, like the stars, not
wander like the moon, they create cities as sites and symbols
of their choice to stop and their agreement not to separate.
Now stasis and proximity, not movement and distance,
define human relationships. Mutual defense, control of a river
(35) or harbor, shelter from natural forces—all these and other
reasons may lead people to aggregate, but once congregated,
they then live differently and become different.

A city is not an extended family. That is a tribe or clan. A
city is a collection of disparate families who agree to a fic-
(40) tion: They agree to live as if they were as close in blood or
ties of kinship as in fact they are in physical proximity.
Choosing life in an artifact, people agree to live in a state of
similitude. A city is a place where ties of proximity, activity,
and self-interest assume the role of family ties. It is a con-
(45) siderable pact, a city. If a family is an expression of continuity through biology, a city is an expression of continuity
through will and imagination—through mental choices
making artifice, not through physical reproduction.

Passage 2

It is because of this centrality [of the city] that the financial
(50) markets have stayed put. It had been widely forecast that they
would move out en masse, financial work being among the
most quantitative and computerized of functions. A lot of the
back-office work has been relocated. The main business, however, is not record keeping and support services; it is people
(55) sizing up other people, and the center is the place for that.

The problems, of course, are immense. To be an optimist
about the city, one must believe that it will lurch from crisis
to crisis but somehow survive. Utopia is nowhere in sight
and probably never will be. The city is too mixed up for that.
(60) Its strengths and its ills are inextricably bound together. The
same concentration that makes the center efficient is the
cause of its crowding and the destruction of its sun and its
light and its scale. Many of the city's problems, furthermore,
are external in origin—for example, the cruel demographics
(65) of peripheral growth, which are difficult enough to forecast,
let alone do anything about.

What has been taking place is a brutal simplification. The
city has been losing those functions for which it is no longer
competitive. Manufacturing has moved toward the periphery;
(70) the back offices are on the way. The computers are already
there. But as the city has been losing functions it has been
reasserting its most ancient one: a place where people come
together, face-to-face.

More than ever, the center is the place for news and gos-
(75) sip, for the creation of ideas, for marketing them and swiping
them, for hatching deals, for starting parades. This is the
stuff of the public life of the city—by no means wholly
admirable, often abrasive, noisy, contentious, without
apparent purpose.

(80) But this human congress is the genius of the place, its reason for being, its great marginal edge. This is the engine, the
city's true export. Whatever makes this congress easier,
more spontaneous, more enjoyable is not at all a frill. It is the
heart of the center of the city.

1. The author's purpose in Passage 1 is primarily to

   (A) identify the sources of popular discontent with cities
   (B) define the city as growing out of a social contract
   (C) illustrate the difference between cities and villages
   (D) compare cities with blood families
   (E) persuade the reader to change his behavior

2. The author cites the sentence "The neighborhoods are the vital cells of the urban organism" (lines 8–9) as

   (A) an instance of prevarication
   (B) a simple statement of scientific fact
   (C) a momentary digression from his central thesis
   (D) an example of one type of figurative language
   (E) a paradox with ironic implications

3. The author's attitude toward the statements quoted in lines 8–9 is

   (A) respectful
   (B) ambivalent
   (C) pragmatic
   (D) skeptical
   (E) approving

4. According to the author of Passage 1, why is an anthill by definition unlike a city?

   (A) It can be casually destroyed by human beings.
   (B) Its inhabitants outnumber the inhabitants of even the largest city.
   (C) It is the figurative equivalent of a municipality.
   (D) It is a work of instinct rather than of imagination.
   (E) It exists on a far smaller scale than any city does.

5. Mutual defense, control of waterways, and shelter from the forces of nature (lines 34–35) are presented primarily as examples of motives for people to

   (A) move away from their enemies
   (B) build up their supplies of armament
   (C) gather together in settlements
   (D) welcome help from their kinfolk
   (E) redefine their family relationships

6. We can infer from lines 30–31 that roving tribes differ from city dwellers in that these nomads

   (A) have not chosen to settle in one spot
   (B) lack ties of activity and self-interest
   (C) are willing to let the cities die
   (D) have no need for mutual defense
   (E) define their relationships by proximity

7. By saying a city "is a considerable pact" (lines 44–45), the author primarily stresses

   (A) its essential significance
   (B) its speculative nature
   (C) the inevitable agreement
   (D) the moral constraints
   (E) its surprising growth

8. To the author of Passage 1, to live in a city is

   (A) an unexpected outcome
   (B) an opportunity for profit
   (C) an act of volition
   (D) a pragmatic solution
   (E) an inevitable fate

9. Underlying the forecast mentioned in lines 50–51 is the assumption that

   (A) the financial markets are similar to the city in their need for quantitative data
   (B) computerized tasks such as record keeping can easily be performed at remote sites
   (C) computerized functions are not the main activity of these firms
   (D) the urban environment is inappropriate for the proper performance of financial calculations
   (E) either the markets would all move or none of them would relocate

10. The word "scale" in line 63 means

   (A) series of musical tones
   (B) measuring instrument
   (C) relative dimensions
   (D) thin outer layer
   (E) means of ascent

11. The "congress" referred to in line 80 is

  (A) a city council
  (B) the supreme legislative body
  (C) a gathering of individuals
  (D) an enjoyable luxury
  (E) an intellectual giant

12. The author of Passage 2 differs from the author of Passage 1 in that he

  (A) argues in favor of choosing to live alone
  (B) disapproves of relocating support services to the outskirts of the city
  (C) has no patience with the harshness inherent in public life
  (D) believes that in the long run the city as we know it will not survive
  (E) is more outspoken about the city's difficulties

13. Compared to Passage 1, Passage 2 is

  (A) more lyrical and less pragmatic
  (B) more impersonal and less colloquial
  (C) more sentimental and less definitive
  (D) more practical and less detached
  (E) more objective and less philosophical

YOU MAY GO BACK AND REVIEW THIS
SECTION IN THE REMAINING TIME, BUT **S T O P**
DO NOT WORK IN ANY OTHER SECTION
UNTIL TOLD TO DO SO.

SECTION 6

10 Questions—15 Minutes

For each problem in this section determine which of the five choices is correct and blacken in that choice on your answer sheet. You may use any blank space on the page for your work.

Notes:

- You may use a calculator whenever you feel it will be helpful.
- Use the diagrams provided to help you solve the problems. Unless you see the words "Note: Figure not drawn to scale" under a diagram, it has been drawn as accurately as possible. Unless it is stated that a figure is three-dimensional, you may assume it lies in a plane.

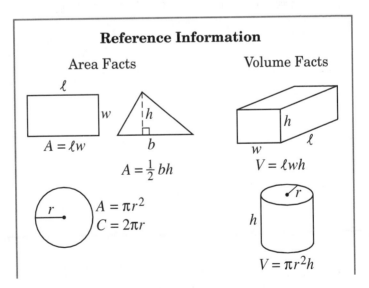

Reference Information

Area Facts

$A = \ell w$

$A = \frac{1}{2} bh$

$A = \pi r^2$

$C = 2\pi r$

Volume Facts

$V = \ell w h$

$V = \pi r^2 h$

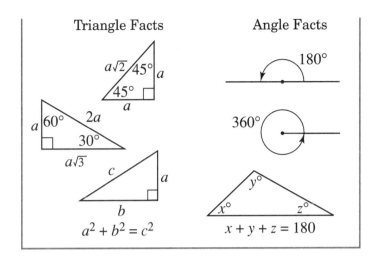

Triangle Facts

Angle Facts

$$a^2 + b^2 = c^2$$

$$x + y + z = 180$$

1. If $2x - 1 = 9$, what is $10x - 5$?

(A) 35   (B) 45   (C) 55   (D) 75   (E) 95

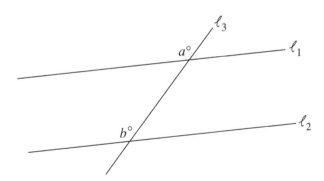

Note: Figure not drawn to scale

2. If in the figure above, $\ell_1 \parallel \ell_2$, which of the following statements about $a + b$ is true?

(A) $a + b < 180$ (B) $a + b = 180$
(C) $180 < a + b \leq 270$ (D) $270 < a + b \leq 360$
(E) It cannot be determined from the information given.

3. Which of the following expressions has the greatest value?

(A) $4 \times 4 \div 4 + 4$ (B) $4 \div 4 \times 4 + 4$
  (C) $4 \times 4 - 4 \times 4$ (D) $4 \div 4 + 4 \times 4$
   (E) $4 + 4 \times 4 - 4$

---

4. Hoover High School has 840 students, and the ratio of the number of students taking Spanish to the number not taking Spanish is 4:3. How many of the students take Spanish?

(A) 280 (B) 360 (C) 480 (D) 560 (E) 630

---

5. Of the 200 seniors at Monroe High School, exactly 40 are in the band, 60 are in the orchestra, and 10 are in both. How many students are in neither the band nor the orchestra?

(A) 80   (B) 90   (C) 100   (D) 110   (E) 120

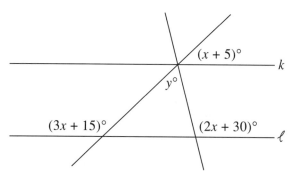

6. In the figure above, if $k \parallel \ell$, what is the value of y?

(A) 40   (B) 45   (C) 50   (D) 60   (E) 65

7. If, for any numbers a and b, $a \odot b$ represents the average of a and b, which of the following MUST be true?

     I. $a \odot (a \odot a) = a$
     II. $a \odot b = b \odot a$
     III. $a \odot (b \odot c) = (a \odot b) \odot c$

(A) I only   (B) II only   (C) I and II only
  (D) II and III only   (E) I, II, and III

Model	Number Sold (1000's)
A	⊕⊕⊕⊕⊕⊕⊕⊕
B	⊕⊕⊕⊕⊕⊕⊕⊕⊕

8. If the selling price of model B is 60% more than the selling price of model A, what percent of the total sales do the sales of model A represent?

(A) 25%   (B) 36%   (C) 40%   (D) 50%   (E) 60%

---

9. If $x = \dfrac{2}{3}(x + y)$, which of the following is an expression for x in terms of y ?

(A) $\dfrac{2}{3}y$ (B) y (C) $\dfrac{3}{2}y$ (D) $2y$ (E) $3y$

---

10. Let P and Q be points 2 inches apart, and let A be the area, in square inches, of a circle that passes through P and Q. Which of the following is the set of all possible values of A?

(A) $0 < A$ (B) $0 < A \leq \pi$ (C) $A = \pi$
  (D) $A > \pi$ (E) $A \geq \pi$

YOU MAY GO BACK AND REVIEW THIS
SECTION IN THE REMAINING TIME, BUT **S T O P**
DO NOT WORK IN ANY OTHER SECTION
UNTIL TOLD TO DO SO.

Answer Key

Section 1   Verbal Reasoning

1. B	7. C	13. C	19. A	25. C
2. B	8. C	14. D	20. E	26. C
3. D	9. D	15. A	21. D	27. D
4. A	10. D	16. C	22. D	28. E
5. B	11. B	17. B	23. A	29. B
6. D	12. C	18. C	24. C	30. C

Section 2   Mathematical Reasoning

1. C	6. B	11. C	16. D	21. D
2. D	7. B	12. D	17. A	22. A
3. E	8. C	13. B	18. B	23. E
4. D	9. E	14. C	19. A	24. D
5. E	10. B	15. E	20. B	25. C

Section 3   Verbal Reasoning

1. B	8. C	15. C	22. A	29. B
2. B	9. E	16. B	23. A	30. C
3. C	10. B	17. B	24. D	31. C
4. C	11. C	18. B	25. C	32. B
5. E	12. B	19. B	26. C	33. D
6. B	13. B	20. E	27. D	34. D
7. C	14. C	21. A	28. E	35. A

Section 4   Mathematical Reasoning

1. C	4. D	7. A	10. B	13. B
2. C	5. A	8. B	11. B	14. C
3. B	6. A	9. B	12. C	15. B

Grid-in Questions

16.

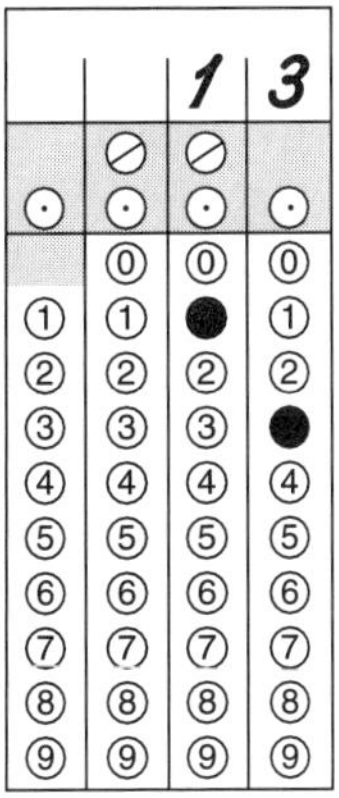

17.

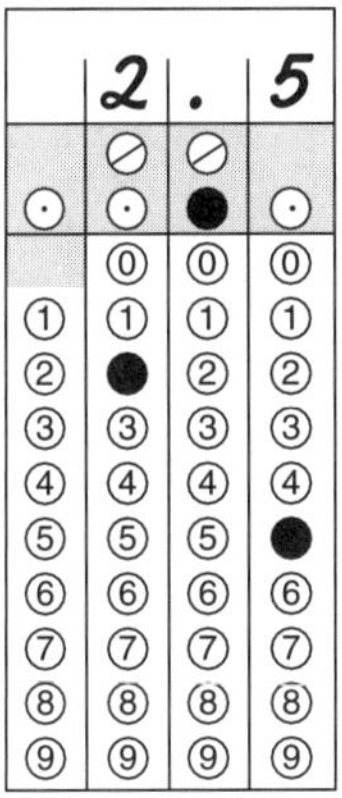

or 5/2

18.

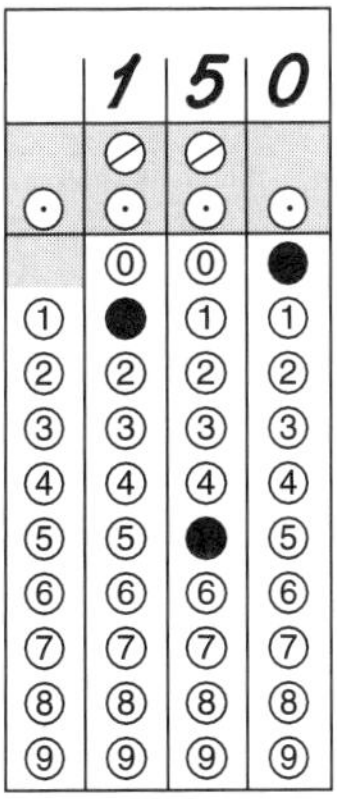

19.

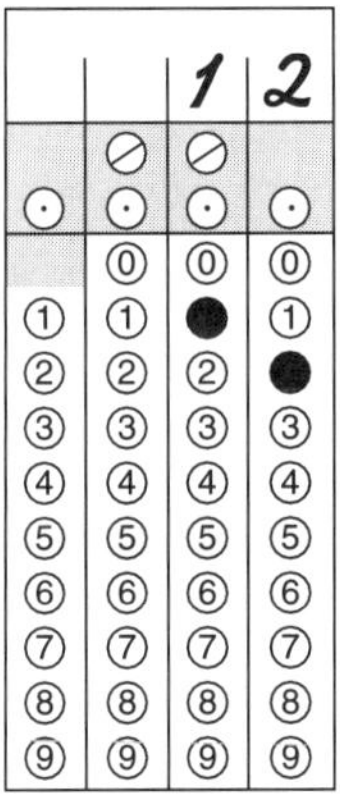

20.

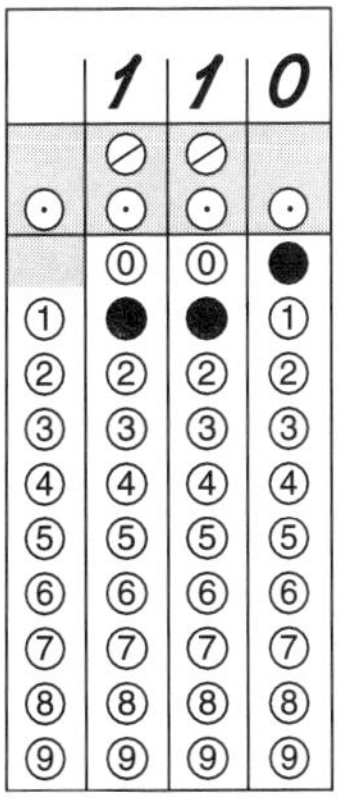

21.

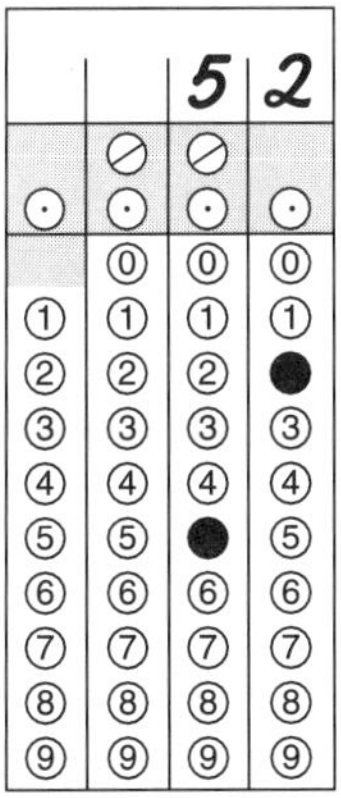

22.

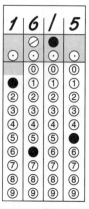

or 3.2

23.

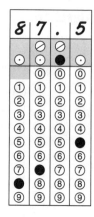

24.

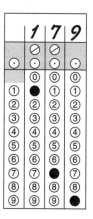

25.

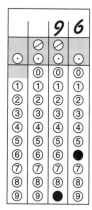

Section 5   Verbal Reasoning

1. **B**	4. **D**	7. **A**	10. **C**	13. **E**
2. **D**	5. **C**	8. **C**	11. **C**	
3. **D**	6. **A**	9. **B**	12. **E**	

Section 6   Mathematical Reasoning

1. **B**	3. **D**	5. **D**	7. **C**	9. **D**
2. **E**	4. **C**	6. **E**	8. **B**	10. **E**

Answer Explanations

Section 1   Verbal Reasoning

1. **(B)** To *sap* or weaken the recipient's self-sufficiency would be contrary to the recipient's true welfare.

    The phrase "argument *against*" is your clue to look for a "negative" verb. Therefore, you can eliminate any answer choices with positive verbs.

    Choices A, C, and D all have positive associations. If the welfare system supported, hastened, or renewed independence in people, that would be an argument for the system, not against it. Choice E makes no sense in the sentence. That leaves you with Choice B.
    (Examples)

2. **(B)** The word *platitudes* (trite, commonplace remarks) complements *empty promises* and *clichés* (overworked phrases). The three linked phrases support the same thought.

    Remember to watch for signal words that link one part of the sentence to another. The presence of *and* linking items in a series indicates that the missing word may be a synonym or near-synonym for the linked words.   (Support Signal)

3. **(D)** Someone able to manipulate things with both hands is *ambidextrous*, capable of using both hands with equal ease.

    The presence of *and* indicates that the missing word supports or explains the other linked words.   (Definition Pattern)

4. **(A)** *Posthumously* means after one's death. Someone who faced ridicule during her lifetime ("from her contemporaries") could only gain honor *after* death. Word Parts Clue: *Post* means *after*.

    Watch for signals that link one part of the sentence to another. *But* signals a contrast. This indicates that the missing word must be an antonym or near-antonym for *from her contemporaries*.
    (Contrast Signal)

5. **(B)** Despite the changes produced by modernization, certain aspects of Indian life have remained *stable* (firmly established; resistant to change).

    Again, watch for signals that link one part of the sentence to another. *While* in the opening clause signals a contrast. This indicates that the missing word must be an antonym or near-antonym for *change*.   (Contrast Signal)

6. **(D)** A *hypocrite* (someone who pretends to be virtuous) would fake feelings he thinks he should show. *Simulates* means pretends or feigns.
Choice A is incorrect. It would not be logical for a hypocrite to *conceal* or hide something he thinks he should display.
Choice B is incorrect. It would not be logical for a hypocrite to *decry* or criticize a feeling he thinks he should show.
Choice C is incorrect. If a hypocrite does not possess certain feelings, he cannot *betray* them or reveal them unintentionally.
Choice E is incorrect. It would not be logical for a hypocrite to merely *condone* or excuse a feeling he thinks he should show.
(Definition)

7. **(C)** The fact that Deloria has detractors or critics leads one to expect his confidence might be shaken. However, the opposite has occurred. The critics have had *little* success at shaking his self-confidence or *denting* or damaging his reputation.
Note the use of *but* signaling the contrast. (Contrast Signal)

8. **(C)** A readiness to adopt or adjust to new things is *adaptability*.
Remember, before you look at the answer choices, to read the sentence and think of a word that makes sense. Likely Words: "versatility," "ability." (Definition Patterns)

9. **(D)** *Intrinsic* value is inherent value, value that essentially belongs to an object, not merely *sentimental* value. She did not keep the furniture because it was worth money or was beautiful (inherent, "real" value). She kept it for emotional reasons (sentimental value).
The words *not for...but for* signal a contrast, telling you that the missing words must be antonyms or near-antonyms. You can immediately eliminate Choices B and C as synonym or near-synonym pairs. (Contrast Signal)

10. **(D)** A *writer* creates a book out of *words*. A *baker* creates a cake out of *batter*. (Worker and Material)

11. **(B)** A ridge of *snow* is a *drift*. A ridge of *sand* is a *dune*. (Definition)

12. **(C)** *Grain* is kept in a *silo*; *water* is kept in a *bucket*. (Function)

13. **(C)** A *shrug* indicates *indifference* or lack of concern; a *nod* indicates *assent* or agreement. (Action and Its Significance)

14. (D) A person characterized by *anger* is defined as *choleric*; a person characterized by *greed* is defined as *avaricious*.
Beware Eye-Catchers: Choice A is incorrect. Don't be fooled because *anger* is a synonym for *wrath*.   (Synonym Variant)

15. (A) A *blandishment* (something tending to flatter or entice) by definition *allures* (entices); an *admonition* (warning; caution) by definition *warns*.   (Degree of Intensity)

16. (C) The author uses the term "hot spot" to indicate a geological phenomenon; she uses the term *technically*, as it is used in the scientific discipline.
Choice B is incorrect. In its informal or colloquial sense, a hot spot is a nightclub.

17. (B) The author states that no theorist today would deny the movement of the plates. Thus, she clearly regards the theory that the plates move as *irrefutable*, unable to be contradicted or disproved.

18. (C) Choice C is correct. You can arrive at it by the process of elimination.
Statement I is correct. There are "common geographical features that link these separate shores" (lines 25–26). These indicate the continents were once joined. Therefore, you can eliminate Choices B and D.
Statement II is correct. The "coastlines complement one another" (lines 23–24); they are *physical counterparts*. This indicates the continents were once joined. Therefore, you can eliminate Choice A.
Statement III is not correct. Though it is true that the African plate has been motionless for ages, this fact is not stated as proof that Africa and South America once were joined. Therefore, you can eliminate Choice E.
Only Choice C is left. It is the correct answer.

19. (A) In constructing the relative motion of the plate in detail, geologists have worked out or *interpreted* the movements involved.

20. (E) Choice E is correct. The concluding sentence of the passage states that hot spots "may someday cast new light on the continents' mutability," helping to explain their tendency to change in shape, even break apart and form a new ocean.

Choice A is incorrect. Lines 34–35 indicates that hot spots are seldom located near the boundaries of plates. Thus, they would be unlikely to provide useful information about plate boundaries.
Choice B is incorrect. It is unsupported by the passage.
Choice C is incorrect. Hot spots have proved useful in studying the *respective* motion of the plates, not their relative motion (lines 29–32).
Choice D is incorrect. According to the passage, satellite technology has proved useful in recording the movement of fixed sites on Earth. The hot spot hypothesis, however, is not mentioned as interpreting current satellite technology.

21. **(D)** Wilson states that "the continent may rupture *entirely* along some of these fissures, *so that* the hot spot initiates the formation of a new ocean" (lines 48–50). Note the use of "so that" to indicate cause and effect. *If* the fissures split the continent, then water from the surrounding oceans may pour into the rift, in process starting off the formation of a new ocean.

22. **(D)** The opening sentence introduces the subject of "specialization by the artist's sex and role in the group" and its impact on the style. These artists specialize or limit themselves to certain designs. The subsequent paragraphs discuss the men's and women's traditional designs. The title that best summarizes this content is *Design Specialization in Plains Arts*.
Choice A is incorrect. The passage does not discuss the continuing or ongoing effect of Plains art.
Choice B is too broad to be correct. The passage deals specifically with male and female *artistic roles* in the tribe, not with male and female roles in general.
Choice C is too narrow to be correct. While the passage discusses male Indian art in terms of narrative and dream, it also discusses several other topics.
Choice E is too narrow to be correct. The passage deals with Indian abstract or geometrical art as well as Indian representational art.
Remember, when asked to choose a title, watch out for choices that are too specific or too broad.

23. **(A)** Throughout the passage the author is supporting his thesis that male and female Indian artists specialized in different sorts of designs. Thus, when he describes specific examples of their work, he is doing so to point out these differences in decorative styles.

Choice B is incorrect. The passage mentions that women's art, for example, appears on functional objects (lines 16–18); however, it stresses these objects' designs, not their usefulness.

Choice C is incorrect. The passage mentions artistic materials and patterns in some detail; it barely touches on technique (*how* the artists worked).

Choices D and E are incorrect. By the time the author mentions Anglo influence (lines 51–53) and the spiritual significance of emblems (lines 45–48), he no longer is discussing specific works of art.

24. **(C)** The two separate strains of decorative art discussed are two separate *varieties* or kinds of decorative art. Remember, when answering a vocabulary-in-context question, test each answer choice by substituting it in the sentence for the word in quotes.

25. **(C)** The crafts of weaving, quillwork, and beadwork are presented as descending from the same aspect of Woodland culture that the women's geometric art does. Thus, they are presented as examples of *geometrically based crafts*.

26. **(C)** You can arrive at the correct answer through the process of elimination.

   The author would agree with statement I. He states in line 34 that Indian men worked in groups (*corporately*) on projects. Therefore, you can eliminate Choices B and D.

   The author also would agree with Statement II. He states in lines 45–48 that the dream images or emblems could "protect him from dangers" and thus could *ward off danger*. Therefore, you can eliminate Choice A.

   The author would *not* agree with Statement III. In lines 12–14 he assigns the use of classical or abstract forms not to the men, but to the women. Therefore, you can eliminate Choice E.

   Only Choice C remains. It is the correct answer.

27. **(D)** In drafting a representational piece of art, the men were *sketching* it, drawing a preliminary version of it on the hide.

   Again, in vocabulary-in-context questions, substitute the answer choices in the original sentence.

28. **(E)** Lines 41–48 talk of the discovery of personal omens or emblems through dream quests and tell of their protective nature. These emblems can thus be described as *spiritual guardians*.

Choices A and C are incorrect. They are not mentioned in the passage.

Choice B is incorrect. The dream vision suggests the artist's subject matter (his omen or emblem), not his methods or technique.

Choice D is also incorrect. Group solidarity is mentioned in the passage, but *not* in connection with the dreams.

29. **(B)** Choice B, the portrait bust, lacks a narrative aspect: it tells no heroic story. Therefore, it does *not* resemble Plains art in its narrative aspect. Choice B is correct.

Choice A, the cartoon strip, has a narrative aspect: it tells a story in panels or "pictorial vignettes."

Choice C, the epic, has a narrative aspect: it tells a heroic story.

Choice D, the autobiography, tells a personal story.

Choice E, the mural showing scenes from the life of George Washington, an American hero, clearly resembles Plains art.

30. **(C)** The concluding sentences of the passage stress the growing emphasis on depicting the group or *community* in Plains art.

Choice A is incorrect. Nothing is said to indicate that geometric patterning increased in importance in the 1800s.

Choice B is incorrect. Though during this period cloth came into use as a substitute for animal hides, this does not necessarily mean that the Plains Indians had fewer hides available to them. Instead, they may simply have had greater access to cloth through the Anglo settlers and traders.

Choices D and E are incorrect. Nothing in passage suggests either possibility.

Section 2   Mathematical Reasoning

In each mathematics section, for some problems, an alternative solution, indicated by two asterisks (**), follows the first solution. When this occurs, one of the solutions is the direct mathematical one and the other is based on one of the tactics discussed in Chapter 5.

1. **(C)** Just solve directly:

$$5c + 3 = 3c + 5 \Rightarrow 2c + 3 = 5 \Rightarrow$$
$$2c = 2 \Rightarrow c = 1.$$

**Use TACTIC 10. Backsolve, starting with C.

2. **(D)** Since $\triangle ABC$ is an isosceles right triangle, $x = 45$; also, $y = 90$, since it is a corner of square $CDEF$. Therefore, $a + b = 360 - (45 + 90) = 360 - 135 = \mathbf{225}$.

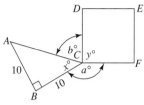

**Use TACTIC 2: trust the diagram. Clearly, 135 and 180 are too small, and 270 is too large. Guess between 210 and 225.

3. **(E)** Since 74% + 18% = 92%, the $216 spent on the party represents the other 8% of the money raised. Then
$0.08m = 216 \Rightarrow m = 216 \div 0.08 = \mathbf{2700}$.

4. **(D)** Let the number be x, and write the equation:

$$\frac{3}{4}x = 7 + \frac{1}{6}x.$$

Multiply both sides by 12: $9x = 84 + 2x$
Subtract $2x$ from each
side and divide by 7: $7x = 84$
  $x = 12$

Be careful: 12 is *not* the answer. You were asked for $\frac{5}{3}$ of the number: $\frac{5}{\cancel{3}}(\cancel{12})^4 = \mathbf{20}$.

5. **(E)** Here, $n \,\square\, \frac{1}{n} = \sqrt{n\left(\frac{1}{n}\right)} = \sqrt{1} = \mathbf{1}$.

**Use TACTIC 12. Pick an easy-to-use number, say 2. (Note that 1 would not be a good choice because then each of the five choices would be 1.)

Then, $2 \,\square\, \frac{1}{2} = \sqrt{2\left(\frac{1}{2}\right)} = \sqrt{1} = \mathbf{1}$. Only **1** equals 1 when $n = 2$.

6. **(B)** Since vertical angles have the same measure, $c = d$, $d = a$, and $b = a - b \Rightarrow a = 2b$. Therefore, $c = d = a = 2b$. Also, the sum of the measures of all six angles is 360°: $a + b + c + d + a - b + d = 2a + c + 2d = 360$. Replacing c, d, and a by $2b$ yields $10b = 360 \Rightarrow b = \mathbf{36}$.

7. **(B)** Since the two angles, x and y, form a straight line, $x + y = 180$. Also, it is given that $x = y + 150$. Therefore, $(y + 150) + y = 180 \Rightarrow 2y + 150 = 180 \Rightarrow 2y = 30 \Rightarrow y = \mathbf{15}$.

   **Use TACTIC 10: backsolve. Start with 20, choice C. If $y = 20$, then $x = 170$, but $20 + 170 = 190$, which is too large. Eliminate C, D, and E, and try A or B. B works.

8. **(C)** There is a total of $1 + 2 + 3 + 4 + 5 + 6 = 21$ slips of paper. Since odd numbers are written on $1 + 3 + 5 = 9$ of them, the probability of drawing an odd number is $\dfrac{9}{21} = \dfrac{3}{7}$.

9. **(E)** Set up a table.

Time	Nicholas	Sandrine
Now	x	$5x$
In 7 years	$x + 7$	$5x + 7$

   Then
   $5x + 7 = 3(x + 7) \Rightarrow 5x + 7 = 3x + 21 \Rightarrow$
   $2x = 14 \Rightarrow x = 7$.
   Sandrine, therefore, is **35**.

   **Use TACTIC 10, but since Sandrine is 5 times as old as Nicholas, avoid C, the only answer that is not a multiple of 5. Try B, 20. Then Nicholas is 4. In 7 years, he'll be 11 and Sandrine will be 27, which is less than 3 times as old. Try a larger number: 25 or 35.

10. **(B)** The given equation can be written as $a^3 = 3a$. Since a is positive, we can divide each side by a: $a^2 = 3$. There is only **1** positive number that satisfies this equation: $\sqrt{3}$. (Note that 0 and $-\sqrt{3}$ also satisfy the original equation, but neither of these is positive.)

11. **(C)** Jose made a 25% profit, so if he bought it for x, he sold it for

$$x + 0.25x = 1.25x = 2000 \Rightarrow$$
$$x = 2000 \div 1.25 = \mathbf{1600}.$$

12. (D) The fraction $\dfrac{10!}{8!}$ reduces to $10 \times 9 = 90$.

Now, evaluate the three choices.

I. $5! - 4! - 3! = 120 - 24 - 6 = 90$ (true).

II. $\dfrac{5!}{4!} = 5$ (false).

III. $15(3!) = 15(6) = 90$ (true).

I and III only are true.

13. (B) Write the equation and solve it:

Set up the equation:	$(x + 3) + (2x - 3) + (3x - 5) = 25$
Collect like terms:	$6x - 5 = 25$
Add 5 to each side:	$6x = 30$
Divide each side by 6:	$x = 5$

Plugging in 5 for x, we get the lengths of the sides: 8, **7**, and 10.

14. (C) Use TACTIC 1: draw a diagram and label it. Use the Pythagorean theorem to find d, the length of the diagonal:

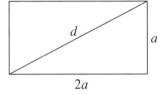

$a^2 + (2a)^2 = d^2 \Longrightarrow$
$a^2 + 4a^2 = d^2 \Longrightarrow$
$5a^2 = d^2 \Longrightarrow d = \mathbf{a}\sqrt{\mathbf{5}}$.

**Use TACTIC 11. Let $a = 1$. Then use TACTIC 1, and draw the rectangle (to scale); that is, let the width be 1 and the length be 2. Now use TACTIC 2: trust your eyes. Clearly, the diagonal is longer than 2 and shorter than 3

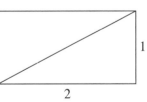

(the width plus the length is 3). The answer *must* be $\mathbf{a}\sqrt{\mathbf{5}}$, the *only* choice between 2 and 3, when $a = 1$.

15. (E) Could exactly one of a, b, and c be an integer?

Sure; $(4)\left(\dfrac{1}{2}\right)\left(\dfrac{1}{2}\right) = 1$. Could exactly two of a, b, and c be

integers? Yes; $(1)(2)\left(\dfrac{1}{2}\right) = 1$.

Could all three be integers? Yes again: $(1)(1)(1) = 1$. *Be careful:* the question does *not* require a, b, and c to be different numbers. Statements **I, II, and III** are all true.

16. **(D)** Draw a Venn diagram. Of the 100 students taking chemistry, 20 take biology, and 80 don't; they take *only* chemistry. Similarly, of the 80 students taking biology, 20 also take chemistry, and 60 take *only* biology. The desired ratio is $80:60 = 4:3 = \dfrac{4}{3}$.

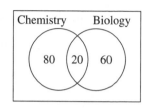

17. **(A)** Let S be a side of the large square, and s a side of the small square. The area of the white region is just s^2, whereas the area of the shaded region is $S^2 - s^2$. Therefore,

$$S^2 - s^2 = s^2 \Rightarrow S^2 = 2s^2 \Rightarrow \frac{S^2}{s^2} = 2 \Rightarrow \frac{S}{s} = \sqrt{2}.$$

The ratio of the side of the large square to the side of the small square is $\dfrac{\sqrt{2}}{1}$.

**Redraw the diagram with the small square in the corner of the large one. If the ratio were 2:1, the white area would be much smaller than the shaded area, so the small square must be larger and the ratio is less than 2:1. Only $\dfrac{\sqrt{2}}{1}$ is less than 2:1.

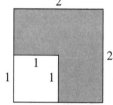

18. **(B)** Since AC is the hypotenuse of a 30-60-90 right triangle, CD, the leg opposite the 30° angle, is 5 (half the hypotenuse), and AD is $5\sqrt{3}$. Then the area of the rectangle is $5 \times 5\sqrt{3} = \mathbf{25\sqrt{3}}$.

19. **(A)** Set up a proportion: $\dfrac{\text{dollars}}{\text{pounds}}$

$$\frac{d \text{ dollars}}{10 \text{ pounds of gold}} = \frac{d \text{ dollars}}{10p \text{ pounds of silver}} = \frac{x \text{ dollars}}{1 \text{ pound of silver}}$$

So, $\dfrac{d}{10p} = \dfrac{x}{1} \Rightarrow x = \dfrac{d}{10p}$.

20. **(B)** The formulas for the volumes of a rectangular solid and a cylinder are $V = \ell wh$ and $V = \pi r^2 h$, respectively. (Remember that these formulas are given to you on the first page of every SAT I math section.) The volume of container I is $(4)(4)(5) = 80$ cubic inches. Since the diameter of container II is 4, its

radius is 2, and so its volume is $\pi(2^2)(5) = 20\pi$. The difference in volumes is $80 - 20\pi = \mathbf{20(4 - \pi)}$.

21. (D) If Jason were really unlucky, what could go wrong in his attempt to get 1 marble of each color? Well, his first nine picks *might* yield 5 blue marbles and 4 white ones. But then the tenth marble would be red, and he would have at least 1 of each color. The answer is **10**.

22. (A) To find the average speed, in miles per hour, divide the distance, in miles, by the time, in hours. Ali drove 90 miles $\left(\dfrac{2}{3} \text{ of } 135\right)$ in 2.25 hours (135 minutes = 2 hours and 15 minutes = $2\dfrac{1}{4}$ hours). Then $90 \div 2.25 = \mathbf{40}$.

23. (E) The easiest way to solve this is to use TACTIC 11. Let $x = 2$ and $y = 1$. Then $xy = 2$, $a = 4$, and $b = 0$. Now, plug in 4 for a and 0 for b, and see which of the five choices is equal to 2. Only E works:

$$\frac{a^2 - b^2}{8} = \frac{4^2 - 0^2}{8} = \frac{16}{8} = 2.$$

24. (D) A circle can cross each side of a square at most twice. The answer is $2 \times 4 = \mathbf{8}$.

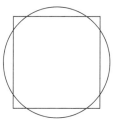

25. (C) Since the average of the five students' weights is 150.4 pounds, their total weight is $5 \times 150.4 = 752$ pounds. No student weighs less than 130 and none is within 5 pounds of another, so the least that the four lightest students can weigh is 130, 135, 140, and 145 pounds, for a total of 550 pounds. The heaviest student, therefore, cannot exceed $752 - 550 = \mathbf{202}$ pounds.

Section 3   Verbal Reasoning

1. (B) Many writers have compared people who seem *unconcerned* about the *threat* of atomic warfare to people who live in areas of danger and lack the sense to move away.

Remember, in double-blank sentences, go through the answer choices, testing the *first* words in each choice and eliminating those that don't fit.

Choice A does not fit. *Foolish* people would be *unworried* rather than worried about living near an active volcano.

Choice C also seems unlikely. Even extremely foolish people would not be *cheered* about atomic warfare.   (Examples)

2. **(B)** Gestures are useful when words are unavailable or when a person has *linguistic* difficulties, as in dealing with a foreign language.

Remember, before you look at the choices, read the sentence and think of a word that makes sense.

Likely Words: translation, language, vocabulary.   (Examples)

3. **(C)** Preservationists would not want a species to die out or become *extinct*, but instead want it to survive for the enjoyment of generations to come.   (Definition)

4. **(C)** *Connotations* (the implications or overtones a word carries in addition to its primary meaning) are most difficult to translate.

Remember, before you look at the choices, read the sentence and think of a word that makes sense.

Likely Words: subtleties, nuances, meaning.

(Cause and Effect Signal)

5. **(E)** It is difficult for a celebrity to keep his *humility*, or sense of his own *unimportance*, while the world is telling him how important he is.

Remember, before you look at the choices, read the sentence and think of a word that makes sense.

Likely Words: modesty, humbleness, humility.

(Implicit Contrast Signal)

6. **(B)** In spite of the difficulties or *hardships* involved in their research, the researchers have some moments of *exhilaration* or cheer.

Remember to watch for signal words that link one part of the sentence to another. The use of "for all the" in the opening clause sets up a contrast. The missing words must be antonyms or near-antonyms. You can immediately eliminate Choices A, C, and E as synonym or near-synonym pairs.   (Contrast Signal)

7. **(C)** Although some Hispanic actors are *prominent* (widely and popularly known), the group as a whole is felt to be *underrepresented* (not represented adequately).

Remember to watch for signal words that link one part of the sentence to another. The use of "despite" sets up a contrast. The

missing words must be antonyms or near-antonyms. Only Choice
C is such a pair. (Contrast Signal)

8. **(C)** Someone *never satisfied* would be likely to make *disparaging* (belittling or carping) comments.
Remember to watch for signal words that link one part of the sentence to another. The use of "never" in the opening clause sets up a contrast. The missing words must be antonyms or near-antonyms. You can immediately eliminate Choices A, B, and D as synonym or near-synonym pairs. (Contrast Signal)

9. **(E)** Even those who do not agree or *concur* with the way Williams plays his part *acknowledge* or grant that he is a serious, inventive actor.
Note that the second missing word must be a positive term. This allows you to eliminate Choices A, C, and D: you would not be likely to *dismiss* (ignore), *denounce* (condemn), or *deride* (treat scornfully) someone you regarded as both a serious and an imaginative actor. (Argument Pattern)

10. **(B)** The biography is described positively as "nuanced" (subtle) and "sensitive." To complete the thought, we need another positive term. A *telling* analysis is effective; it reveals much that would otherwise go unnoticed.
Note that you are looking for a word with positive associations. Therefore, you can eliminate any word with negative ones. Choices A, C, D, and E all have negative associations. Only Choice B can be correct. (Support Pattern)

11. **(C)** The function of the *heart* is to *pump*; the function of the *stomach* is to *digest*. (Function)

12. **(B)** By definition, a *servant* is bound to do the bidding of his or her *master*; a *subject* is bound to do the bidding of his or her *monarch*.
Beware Eye-Catchers: Choice E is incorrect. Although a *landlord* and a *tenant* have a "working relationship," the tenant is not bound to do the bidding of the landlord. (Function)

13. **(B)** A *stanza* is a subdivision of a *poem*; a *story* is a subdivision of a *building*. (Part to Whole)

14. (C) A *mongrel* is a mixed breed while a *collie* is a pure breed. An *alloy* is a mixture of metals. *Iron* is a single metal.
Choice A is incorrect. A gosling is a young goose.
Choice B is incorrect. A ruby is a kind of gem.
Choice C is incorrect. A bridle is a piece of restraining harness for a horse or pony.
Choice E is incorrect. A bleat is the cry of a sheep.
(Part to Whole)

15. (C) A *trowel* is a tool used by a *mason*; an *adze* is a tool used by a *carpenter*.
Remember, if more than one answer appears to fit the relationship in your sentence, look for a narrower approach. "A mason uses a trowel" is too broad a test sentence; it could fit both Choices A and C. While a *potter* uses *clay* in his work, it is his material, not his tool.
(Worker and Tool)

16. (B) One seeks to *amass* (gather) *wealth* to preserve it; one seeks to *garner* (collect) *grain* to store it.
(Purpose)

17. (B) Those who *wince* indicate *pain*; those who *blush* indicate *embarrassment*.
(Action and Its Significance)

18. (B) A *connoisseur* is an expert in the field of art or *paintings*. A *gourmet* is an expert in the field of food or *viands*.
Remember, if more than one answer appears to fit the relationship in your sentence, look for a narrower approach. "A connoisseur enjoys paintings" is too broad a framework; it could fit Choices B and C. A miser enjoys gold, but he is not necessarily a discerning judge of its artistic or aesthetic qualities.
(Function)

19. (B) A *heckler* is someone who *jeers* or mocks; a *grumbler* is someone who *complains*.
Beware Eye-Catchers: Choice D is incorrect. A *heckler* does the jeering; a laughingstock, however, is the one who gets mocked.
(Definition)

20. (E) A *malefactor* (evildoer) is by definition *iniquitous* (wicked); a *prankster* (person who plays tricks on others) is by definition *mischievous*.
(Defining Characteristics)

21. (A) To *slink* is to show *stealth*, to move sneakily; to *whine* is to show *querulousness*, to speak petulantly.
(Defining Characteristic)

22. **(A)** Something *uproarious* is extremely *amusing*; something *dumb-founding* is extremely *puzzling*.
Note that Choices C, D, and E are all pairs of synonyms. Eliminate them: the correct answer must belong to a different analogy type.
(Degree of Intensity)

23. **(A)** One must *stanch bleeding* to stop the flow of blood; one must *dam* a *flood* to prevent an overflow of water. (Function)

24. **(D)** In describing Mr. Penniman's constitution as sickly, James is referring to the clergyman's delicate physical condition or *physique*.

25. **(C)** The author portrays Mrs. Penniman's late husband as sickly. Nothing in the passage, however, allows us to infer that *she* is sickly. Therefore, Choice C is correct.
You can arrive at the correct answer by using the process of elimination.
The passage cites Mrs. Penniman's "alacrity" or willingness to accept her brother's offer. Thus, she readily becomes dependent on him. Choice A is supported by the passage. Therefore, it is incorrect.
The passage states that Mrs. Penniman was widowed at the age of thirty-three and that she had been married for ten years. This suggests that she was married at twenty-three. Choice B is supported by the passage. Therefore, it is incorrect.
The passage describes Mrs. Penniman's willingness to move as "the alacrity of a woman who had spent the ten years of her married life in Poughkeepsie." This suggests she did not think much of Poughkeepsie. Choice D is supported by the passage. Therefore, it is incorrect.
The memory of Mr. Penniman's "flowers of speech" hovered about Mrs. Penniman's conversation (lines 6–8). This suggests she at times echoed her late husband's ornate conversational style. Choice E is supported by the passage. Therefore, it is incorrect.
Only Choice C is left. It is the correct answer.

26. **(C)** As the widow of a poor clergyman, Mrs. Penniman has been left essentially penniless. She cannot afford to stay in whatever housing she shared with her late husband. Thus, her brother offers to let her take temporary *refuge* in his home.

Choices A and B are incorrect. Though an asylum can be an institution, such as a sanitarium or orphanage, the word is used here in its more general sense of *place of refuge*.

27. **(D)** Choice D is correct. The Doctor is *civil*: "polite . . . , scrupulously, formally polite" (line 46); he is also domineering or *imperious*, never discussing anything, but issuing ultimatums instead (lines 50–52).
    Choice A is incorrect. While the Doctor provides his widowed sister with a home, he does not do so in a particularly kindly or benevolent manner.
    Choice B is incorrect. The Doctor is formal, not casual.
    Choice C is incorrect. The Doctor is neither powerless nor ineffectual. He is the center of authority in his home.
    Choice E is incorrect. The Doctor is not habitually angry or irate; his sister has seen him in a temper only once in her life (lines 46–47).

28. **(E)** Mrs. Penniman tells all her friends that she has kept on living with her brother in order to supervise his daughter's education. She never says this to him. Why not? She "shrunk . . . from presenting herself to her brother as a fountain of instruction." Her self-assurance is largely artificial; she *lacks the confidence* or presumption to try to pass herself off as a brilliant woman to him.

29. **(B)** If the Doctor were to back up Mrs. Penniman's story and say he needed his sister to take charge of Catherine's education, he would be lying. Line 36 states he "had never been dazzled by his sister's intellect." The Doctor *does not believe in his sister's brilliance.* Unwilling to lie overtly, he keeps silent, giving only tacit (unspoken) assent to her excuse.

30. **(C)** The Doctor asks his sister to try and make a clever woman of his daughter (lines 55–56). This implies that he views children as *clay to be molded*.
    Choices A, B, D, and E are all unsupported by the passage.

31. **(C)** In reflecting about herself, Mrs. Penniman is contemplating or *considering* her status.
    Note that in line 57 Mrs. Penniman looks *thoughtful. Reflection* is a synonym for *thought*.

32. **(B)** Choice B is correct. The Doctor knows that Catherine is good. Goodness alone, however, does not satisfy him: he finds good-

ness ("good bread-and-butter") bland and dull. He wants his daughter, like his dinner, to have spice. But Catherine will never have the salt of malice or mischievousness in her to make her lively and interesting. ("Salt" here means an element that gives liveliness, piquancy, or zest.) Thus, he fears that, lacking cleverness, she will turn out *virtuous but uninteresting*.

33. **(D)** In overlooking Catherine at the piano, Mrs. Penniman is *watching over* or keeping an eye on Catherine's performance. This is another example of Mrs. Penniman's supervision of her niece's education in womanly accomplishments.

34. **(D)** Mrs. Penniman tells her brother he needn't fear about Catherine's growing up to be insipid or uninteresting; after all, Catherine is being raised by her "clever" aunt. The reader knows, however, that Mrs. Penniman is not particularly clever. She is unlikely to mold Catherine into the sort of young woman the Doctor would admire. Thus, in her assurances to her brother, Mrs. Penniman is *unrealistically optimistic*.

35. **(A)** In stating that Catherine "made but a modest figure" on the dance floor, the passage indicates her moderate or *limited skill as a dancer*. "But" here means only. Her skill was *only* modest or limited.
    Choice B is incorrect. *Virtuosity* means expertise, extreme skill or talent. Catherine had only "a certain talent" at the piano, not the talent of an expert.
    Choice C is incorrect. *Modest* here means moderate or limited. It does not indicate shyness on her part.
    Choice D is incorrect. Nothing in the passage suggests Catherine is indifferent to cleverness.
    Choice E is incorrect. It is unsupported by the passage.

Section 4   Mathematical Reasoning

Quantitative Comparison Questions

1. **(C)** Each column is the product of 11 integers, one of which is 0. Since 0 times any number is 0, each column is 0. The columns are equal (C).

2. **(C)** Column A: the multiples of 6 are 0, 6, 12, ..., 72, 78, 84... . The smallest one greater than 80 is 84. Column B: the multiples of 7 are 0, 7, 14, ... , 77, 84, 91... . The largest one less than 90 is 84. The columns are equal (C).

3. **(B)** Since x and y are positive, $x + y = 1 \Rightarrow x < 1$ and $y < 1 \Rightarrow xy < 1$. Column B is greater.

4. **(D)** Use TACTIC 15. Replace the variables with numbers. If $a = 1$ and $b = 2$, then Column A is $\frac{1}{2}$ and Column B is $\left(\frac{1}{2}\right)^3 = \frac{1}{8}$.
   This time A is larger; eliminate B and C. If $a = 2$ and $b = 1$, Column A is 2 and Column B is $2^3 = 8$.
   This time B is larger; eliminate A. Neither column is *always* greater, and the two columns are not *always* equal (D).

5. **(A)** In any triangle, if one side is longer than a second side, the angle opposite the longer side is greater than the angle opposite the shorter side, so $c > d$. Column A is greater. (It is irrelevant that the third angle is 135°)

6. **(A)** Column A: $51 = 1 \times 51 = 3 \times 17$.
   The largest *prime* factor is 17.
   Column B: $78 = 1 \times 78 = 2 \times 39 = 3 \times 26 = 6 \times 13$.
   The largest *prime* factor is 13. Column A is greater.

7. **(A)** Let ℓ = length and w = width of rectangle I. Then 1.1ℓ = length and $0.9w$ = width of rectangle II. Column A is ℓw, but Column B is $(1.1\ell)(.9w) = 0.99\ell w$. Column A is greater.
   **Use TACTIC 16. Choose easy-to-use numbers. Since percents are involved, use 100. Assume that rectangle I is a 100×100 square; then its area is 10,000. Then rectangle II is 110×90, and its area is 9900. In this case, Column A is larger, so eliminate B and C. With a calculator you can try other values. Column A is always greater.

8. **(B)** Column B: 3 shekels = $\frac{3}{5}$ (5 shekels) = $\frac{3}{5}$ (8.4 francs) = 5.04 francs. Column A: 1 dollar = 4.9 francs. Column B is greater.

9. **(B)**

	Column A	Column B
	$\sqrt{a+b}$	$\sqrt{a}+\sqrt{b}$

Since the quantities in each column are positive, square them (TACTIC 17):

	$a+b$	$a+2\sqrt{ab}+b$

Subtract $a+b$ from each column:

	0	$2\sqrt{ab}$

Since a and b are positive, $2\sqrt{ab}$ is positive and Column B is greater.

10. **(B)** The average of x and y is less than y, so having another y raises the average. Column B is greater.

   **Use TACTIC 15. Plug in numbers. Column A: the average of 2 and 4 is 3. Column B: the average of 2, 4, and 4 is surely more than 3, because the extra 4 raises the average (it's 3.333). The answer is B.

11. **(B)** Column A: since $b < 2$, $ab < 2a$.
   Column B: since $b > a$, $b + a > a + a = 2a$.
   Column B is greater.

   **Use TACTIC 15. Plug in numbers that satisfy the condition.
   Column A: $(1.1)(1.8) = 1.98$.
   Column B: $1.1 + 1.8 = 2.9$.
   Column B is greater. Eliminate A and C, and try other numbers. Choose B.

12. **(C)** In each triangle the largest angle is the sum of the two smaller ones ($3 = 1 + 2$ and $9 = 2 + 7$), so each is a 90° angle. The columns are equal (C).

   **In ratio problems, write x after each number and solve.
   Column A: $x + 2x + 3x = 180 \Rightarrow 6x = 180 \Rightarrow x = 30 \Rightarrow 3x = 90$.
   Column B: $2x + 7x + 9x = 180 \Rightarrow 18x = 180 \Rightarrow x = 10 \Rightarrow 9x = 90$.

13. **(B)** The *least* that a and b can be are 97 and 96. Therefore, the top four choices were selected by at least $189 + 97 + 96 + 95 = 477$ of the 500 children. Then, c is *at most* 23 (less if a and b are larger), and surely less than 30. Column B is greater.

14. (C) If r is the radius of the white circle, $2r$ is the radius of the shaded semicircle. The area of the white circle is πr^2. The area of the semicircle is $\frac{1}{2}\pi(2r)^2 = \frac{1}{2}\pi(4r^2) = 2\pi r^2$, so the area of the shaded region is $2\pi r^2 - \pi r^2 = \pi r^2$. The columns are equal (C).

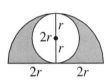

**The solution is even easier if you use TACTIC 15. Let the radius of the circle be 1 instead of r, and proceed as above. The area of each region is π.

15. (B) If the average of n numbers is 17, their sum is $17n$. To find the average of those n numbers and 25, divide $17n + 25$ by $n + 1$:

$$\frac{17n + 25}{n + 1} = 21 \implies 17n + 25 = 21n + 21 \implies$$

$$4n = 4 \implies n = 1$$

Column B is greater.

Grid-in Questions

16. (13) Use your calculator:

$$a = \frac{(91)(13)}{7} = 169 \implies \sqrt{a} = \sqrt{169} = \textbf{13}.$$

17. $\left(\textbf{2.5 or } \dfrac{\textbf{5}}{\textbf{2}}\right)$ Replace a by 44 and b by 275:

$$44 = \frac{275}{c^2} \implies 44c^2 = 275 \implies$$

$$c^2 = \frac{275}{44} = 6.25.$$

Then, $c = \sqrt{6.25} = \textbf{2.5}.$

18. **(150)** Draw and label the right triangle. By the Pythagorean theorem:
$$15^2 + b^2 = 25^2 \Rightarrow$$
$$225 + b^2 = 625 \Rightarrow$$
$$b^2 = 400 \Rightarrow b = 20.$$
The area of the triangle
is $\frac{1}{2}(15)(20) = \mathbf{150}$.

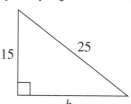

[You can save some work if you recognize this as a 3-4-5 triangle in which each side has been multiplied by 5 (15-20-25).]

19. **(12)** Let x = Adam's age in 1980. Then, in 1980, Judy's age was $3x$ and Elaine's age was $8x$. Since Elaine is 20 years older than Judy, $8x = 3x + 20 \Rightarrow 5x = 20 \Rightarrow x = 4$. Therefore, in 1988, Adam was $4 + 8 = \mathbf{12}$.

**Use TACTIC 20. Test numbers and zoom in.

Adam	Judy	Elaine	Difference between Elaine and Judy
10	30	80	50, much too big
5	15	40	25, slightly too big
4	12	32	20, that's it

20. **(110)** Here, $x^2 - y^2 = (x + y)(x - y) = 10 \times 11 = \mathbf{110}$.

21. **(52)** Ignore the x's and the y's. In any "staircase" the perimeter is just twice the sum of the height and the length, so the perimeter is
$$2(12 + 14) = 2(26) = \mathbf{52}.$$

22. $\left(\frac{\mathbf{16}}{\mathbf{5}} \text{ or } \mathbf{3.2}\right)$ Since $a = 2b$, $b = \frac{4}{3}c$, and $c = \frac{6}{5}d$:
$$a = 2\left(\frac{4}{3}c\right) = \frac{8}{3}\left(\frac{6}{5}d\right) = \frac{16}{5}d \Rightarrow$$
$$\frac{a}{d} = \frac{\mathbf{16}}{\mathbf{5}} \text{ or } \mathbf{3.2}.$$

**Use TACTIC 21. If we let $d = 1$, $c = \frac{6}{5}$.

That's OK, but it's easier if we avoid fractions. We'll let $d = 5$.
Then, $c = 6$, $b = \frac{4}{3}(6) = 8$, and $a = 2(8) = 16$, so $\frac{a}{d} = \frac{\mathbf{16}}{\mathbf{5}}$.

23. **(87.5)** If the average of 5 numbers (*a, b, c, d, e*) is 95, the sum of these numbers is 5 × 95 = 475. Similarly, the sum of the 3 numbers (*a, b, e*) whose average is 100 is 300, leaving 175 (475 − 300) as the sum of the 2 remaining numbers, *c* and *d*. The average of these 2 numbers is their sum divided by 2: average of *c* and *d* = 175 ÷ 2 = **87.5**.

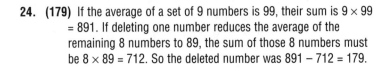

24. **(179)** If the average of a set of 9 numbers is 99, their sum is 9 × 99 = 891. If deleting one number reduces the average of the remaining 8 numbers to 89, the sum of those 8 numbers must be 8 × 89 = 712. So the deleted number was 891 − 712 = 179.

25. **(96)** Since the diameters of the tables are in the ratio of 35:25, or 7:5, the ratio of their areas is $7^2:5^2$ = 49:25. Convert the ratio to a percent:

$49:25 = \dfrac{49}{25} = \dfrac{196}{100} = 196\%$. The area of the larger table is 196% of the area of the small one, or is **96%** *more* than the area of the small one.

Section 5   Verbal Reasoning

1. **(B)** Throughout Passage 1 the author reiterates that human beings make cities, that the creation of a city is an act of choice, that a city is the result of an agreement or pact. In all these ways, he *defines the city as growing out of a social contract* by which human beings choose to bind themselves.

2. **(D)** The sentences quoted within the parentheses are illustrations of the sort of metaphors we use in describing cities. Thus, they are examples *of one type of figurative language*.

3. **(D)** Insisting that cities are not natural but artificial, the author rejects these metaphors as inaccurate. His attitude toward the statements he quotes is clearly *skeptical*.

4. **(D)** An anthill is the work of insects rather than of human beings. *It is a work of instinct rather than of imagination*, human intelligence, and choice; therefore, by the author's definition, it is not like a city.

5. **(C)** The author cites these factors as "reasons (that) may lead people to aggregate" or *gather together in settlements.*

6. **(A)** The nomads have chosen to wander like the moon. The logical corollary of that is that they *have not chosen to settle in one spot.*

7. **(A)** The author clearly is impressed by the magnitude of the choice people make when they agree to live as if mere geographical links, "ties of proximity," can be as strong as blood relationships. In proclaiming a city "a considerable pact," he stresses the *essential significance* or weightiness of this agreement.

8. **(C)** To the author, "a city is an expression of continuity through will and imagination." Thus, to live in a city is *an act of volition* (will).

9. **(B)** One would predict such a mass exodus of financial firms only if one assumed that the firms could do their work just as well at distant locations as they could in the city. Thus, the basic assumption underlying the forecast is that *computerized tasks such as record keeping* (the major task of most financial institutions) *can easily be performed at remote sites.*

10. **(C)** The city's concentration of people necessitates the enormous size of its buildings. These out-sized buildings destroy the scale or *relative dimensions* of the city as it was originally envisioned by its planners.

11. **(C)** The human congress is described in the next-to-last paragraph. It is the *gathering of individuals*, bringing about the vital exchange of ideas and opinions, that the city makes possible.

12. **(E)** While the author of Passage 1 talks in terms of abstractions that keep people dwelling together in cities (the city as pact, the city as an expression of will and imagination), the author of Passage 2 openly mentions the concrete ills that threaten the city: overcrowding, overbuilding of outsize skyscrapers that block the sun, loss of businesses to the suburbs (with the attendant loss of tax revenues). Given his perspective as an urban planner and sociologist, he is inevitably moved to talk about the city's difficulties.

13. **(E)** The author of Passage 1 muses about the nature of the city, defining it and dwelling on its significance. He is *philosophical.* Without romanticizing the city, the author of Passage 2 discusses both its strengths and weaknesses. Though he emphasizes the importance of the city, he tries to be impartial or *objective.* Compared to Passage 1, Passage 2 is *more objective and less philosophical.*

Section 6   Mathematical Reasoning

1. **(B)** Multiplying both sides of $2x - 1 = 9$ by 5 yields $10x - 5 = $ **45**.
   **Just solve:
   $2x - 1 = 9 \Rightarrow 2x = 10 \Rightarrow x = 5 \Rightarrow$
   $10x = 50 \Rightarrow 10x - 5 = $ **45**.

2. **(E)** Since the measures of all of the obtuse angles are equal, $a = b$. Since the figure is not drawn to scale, the angles could just as well be acute as obtuse, as shown in the second figure. The sum **$a + b$** **cannot be determined from the information given.**

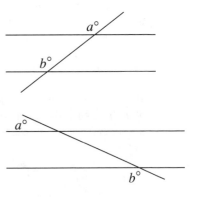

3. **(D)** Since there are no parentheses, you must be careful to follow the proper order of operations (PEMDAS). Do multiplications and divisions left to right *before* any additions and subtractions.
   A: $4 \times 4 \div 4 + 4 = 16 \div 4 + 4 = 4 + 4 = 8$
   B: $4 \div 4 \times 4 + 4 = 1 \times 4 + 4 = 4 + 4 = 8$
   C: $4 \times 4 - 4 \times 4 = 16 - 16 = 0$
   D: $\mathbf{4 \div 4 + 4 \times 4} = 1 + 16 = 17$, the greatest value
   E: $4 + 4 \times 4 - 4 = 4 + 16 - 4 = 20 - 4 = 16$

4. **(C)** Let $4x$ and $3x$ be the numbers of students taking and not taking Spanish, respectively. Then $4x + 3x = 840 \Rightarrow 7x = 840 \Rightarrow x = 120$. The number taking Spanish is $4(120) = $ **480**.

   **Use TACTIC 10. Try choice C. If 480 students take Spanish, $840 - 480 = 360$ do not. Is $\frac{480}{360} = \frac{4}{3}$ a true proportion?
   Yes. Cross-multiply: $480 \times 3 = 360 \times 4$.

5. (D) Draw a Venn diagram. Since 10 seniors are in *both* band and orchestra, 30 are in band only and 50 are in orchestra only. Therefore, $10 + 30 + 50 = 90$ seniors are in at least one group, and the remaining **110** are in neither.

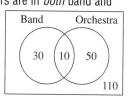

6. (E) Since $k \| \ell$, two interior angles on the same side of the transversal are supplementary, so $z + (3x + 15) = 180$. But $z = x + 5$; (vertical angles are equal). Then,

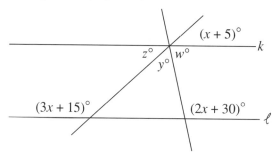

$(3x + 15) + (x + 5) = 180 \Rightarrow 4x + 20 = 180 \Rightarrow 4x = 160 \Rightarrow$ $x = 40$, so $z = x + 5 = 45$. Also, $w + (2x + 30) = 180$; but $2x + 30 = 80 + 30 = 110$, so $w = 70$. Finally, $w + y + z = 180 \Rightarrow$ $70 + y + 45 = 180 \Rightarrow 115 + y = 180 \Rightarrow y = \mathbf{65}$.

7. (C) Check each of the three statements. Since the average of a and a is a, I is true. Clearly, the average of a and b is the same as the average of b and a, so II is also true. Note that $a \circledcirc (b \circledcirc c)$ is *not* the average of the three numbers a, b, and c. To calculate this average, you first take the average of b and c and then take the average of that result and a. Then,
$a \circledcirc (b \circledcirc c) =$

$$\frac{a + \left(\dfrac{b + c}{2} \right)}{2} = \frac{2a + b + c}{4},$$

whereas

$$(a \circledcirc b) \circledcirc c = \frac{\left(\dfrac{a + b}{2} \right) + c}{2} = \frac{a + b + 2c}{4},$$

and these are equal only if $a = c$. Therefore, III is false and **I and II only** are true.

**Use TACTIC 11: plug in some easy numbers. You probably don't need to do this for I and II, but for III it may be a lot easier than the analysis above:

2 ◎ (4 ◎ 6) =

2 ◎ 5 = 3.5, whereas

(2 ◎ 4) ◎ 6 =

3 ◎ 6 = 4.5. III is false.

8. **(B)** As always, with a percent problem use a simple number such as 10 or 100. Assume that model A sells for $10; then, since 60% of 10 is 6, model B sells for $16. The chart tells you that 9000 model A's and 10,000 model B's were sold, for a total of $10(9000) + $16(10,000) = $90,000 + $160,000 = $250,000. The sales of model A ($90,000) represent **36%** of the total sales ($250,000).

9. **(D)** The best approach is to solve directly.
To get rid of the fractions, multiply
both sides of the equation by 3: $3x = 2(x + y)$
Use the distributive law to
get rid of the parentheses: $3x = 2x + 2y$
Subtract $2x$ from each side: $x = 2y$

10. **(E)** If PQ is a diameter of the circle, then the radius is 1 and A, the area, is π. This is the smallest possible value of A, but A can actually be any number larger than π if the radius is made arbitrarily large, as shown by the figures below.

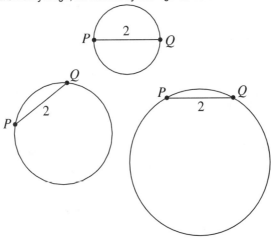

The answer is **A ≥ π**.

ANSWER SHEETS—TEST 3

If a section has fewer than 35 questions, leave the extra spaces blank.

Section 1

1. Ⓐ Ⓑ Ⓒ Ⓓ Ⓔ
2. Ⓐ Ⓑ Ⓒ Ⓓ Ⓔ
3. Ⓐ Ⓑ Ⓒ Ⓓ Ⓔ
4. Ⓐ Ⓑ Ⓒ Ⓓ Ⓔ
5. Ⓐ Ⓑ Ⓒ Ⓓ Ⓔ
6. Ⓐ Ⓑ Ⓒ Ⓓ Ⓔ
7. Ⓐ Ⓑ Ⓒ Ⓓ Ⓔ
8. Ⓐ Ⓑ Ⓒ Ⓓ Ⓔ
9. Ⓐ Ⓑ Ⓒ Ⓓ Ⓔ
10. Ⓐ Ⓑ Ⓒ Ⓓ Ⓔ
11. Ⓐ Ⓑ Ⓒ Ⓓ Ⓔ
12. Ⓐ Ⓑ Ⓒ Ⓓ Ⓔ

13. Ⓐ Ⓑ Ⓒ Ⓓ Ⓔ
14. Ⓐ Ⓑ Ⓒ Ⓓ Ⓔ
15. Ⓐ Ⓑ Ⓒ Ⓓ Ⓔ
16. Ⓐ Ⓑ Ⓒ Ⓓ Ⓔ
17. Ⓐ Ⓑ Ⓒ Ⓓ Ⓔ
18. Ⓐ Ⓑ Ⓒ Ⓓ Ⓔ
19. Ⓐ Ⓑ Ⓒ Ⓓ Ⓔ
20. Ⓐ Ⓑ Ⓒ Ⓓ Ⓔ
21. Ⓐ Ⓑ Ⓒ Ⓓ Ⓔ
22. Ⓐ Ⓑ Ⓒ Ⓓ Ⓔ
23. Ⓐ Ⓑ Ⓒ Ⓓ Ⓔ
24. Ⓐ Ⓑ Ⓒ Ⓓ Ⓔ

25. Ⓐ Ⓑ Ⓒ Ⓓ Ⓔ
26. Ⓐ Ⓑ Ⓒ Ⓓ Ⓔ
27. Ⓐ Ⓑ Ⓒ Ⓓ Ⓔ
28. Ⓐ Ⓑ Ⓒ Ⓓ Ⓔ
29. Ⓐ Ⓑ Ⓒ Ⓓ Ⓔ
30. Ⓐ Ⓑ Ⓒ Ⓓ Ⓔ
31. Ⓐ Ⓑ Ⓒ Ⓓ Ⓔ
32. Ⓐ Ⓑ Ⓒ Ⓓ Ⓔ
33. Ⓐ Ⓑ Ⓒ Ⓓ Ⓔ
34. Ⓐ Ⓑ Ⓒ Ⓓ Ⓔ
35. Ⓐ Ⓑ Ⓒ Ⓓ Ⓔ

Section 2

1. Ⓐ Ⓑ Ⓒ Ⓓ Ⓔ
2. Ⓐ Ⓑ Ⓒ Ⓓ Ⓔ
3. Ⓐ Ⓑ Ⓒ Ⓓ Ⓔ
4. Ⓐ Ⓑ Ⓒ Ⓓ Ⓔ
5. Ⓐ Ⓑ Ⓒ Ⓓ Ⓔ
6. Ⓐ Ⓑ Ⓒ Ⓓ Ⓔ
7. Ⓐ Ⓑ Ⓒ Ⓓ Ⓔ
8. Ⓐ Ⓑ Ⓒ Ⓓ Ⓔ
9. Ⓐ Ⓑ Ⓒ Ⓓ Ⓔ
10. Ⓐ Ⓑ Ⓒ Ⓓ Ⓔ
11. Ⓐ Ⓑ Ⓒ Ⓓ Ⓔ
12. Ⓐ Ⓑ Ⓒ Ⓓ Ⓔ

13. Ⓐ Ⓑ Ⓒ Ⓓ Ⓔ
14. Ⓐ Ⓑ Ⓒ Ⓓ Ⓔ
15. Ⓐ Ⓑ Ⓒ Ⓓ Ⓔ
16. Ⓐ Ⓑ Ⓒ Ⓓ Ⓔ
17. Ⓐ Ⓑ Ⓒ Ⓓ Ⓔ
18. Ⓐ Ⓑ Ⓒ Ⓓ Ⓔ
19. Ⓐ Ⓑ Ⓒ Ⓓ Ⓔ
20. Ⓐ Ⓑ Ⓒ Ⓓ Ⓔ
21. Ⓐ Ⓑ Ⓒ Ⓓ Ⓔ
22. Ⓐ Ⓑ Ⓒ Ⓓ Ⓔ
23. Ⓐ Ⓑ Ⓒ Ⓓ Ⓔ
24. Ⓐ Ⓑ Ⓒ Ⓓ Ⓔ

25. Ⓐ Ⓑ Ⓒ Ⓓ Ⓔ
26. Ⓐ Ⓑ Ⓒ Ⓓ Ⓔ
27. Ⓐ Ⓑ Ⓒ Ⓓ Ⓔ
28. Ⓐ Ⓑ Ⓒ Ⓓ Ⓔ
29. Ⓐ Ⓑ Ⓒ Ⓓ Ⓔ
30. Ⓐ Ⓑ Ⓒ Ⓓ Ⓔ
31. Ⓐ Ⓑ Ⓒ Ⓓ Ⓔ
32. Ⓐ Ⓑ Ⓒ Ⓓ Ⓔ
33. Ⓐ Ⓑ Ⓒ Ⓓ Ⓔ
34. Ⓐ Ⓑ Ⓒ Ⓓ Ⓔ
35. Ⓐ Ⓑ Ⓒ Ⓓ Ⓔ

ANSWER SHEETS—TEST 3

Section 3

1. Ⓐ Ⓑ Ⓒ Ⓓ Ⓔ
2. Ⓐ Ⓑ Ⓒ Ⓓ Ⓔ
3. Ⓐ Ⓑ Ⓒ Ⓓ Ⓔ
4. Ⓐ Ⓑ Ⓒ Ⓓ Ⓔ
5. Ⓐ Ⓑ Ⓒ Ⓓ Ⓔ
6. Ⓐ Ⓑ Ⓒ Ⓓ Ⓔ
7. Ⓐ Ⓑ Ⓒ Ⓓ Ⓔ
8. Ⓐ Ⓑ Ⓒ Ⓓ Ⓔ
9. Ⓐ Ⓑ Ⓒ Ⓓ Ⓔ
10. Ⓐ Ⓑ Ⓒ Ⓓ Ⓔ
11. Ⓐ Ⓑ Ⓒ Ⓓ Ⓔ
12. Ⓐ Ⓑ Ⓒ Ⓓ Ⓔ
13. Ⓐ Ⓑ Ⓒ Ⓓ Ⓔ
14. Ⓐ Ⓑ Ⓒ Ⓓ Ⓔ
15. Ⓐ Ⓑ Ⓒ Ⓓ Ⓔ
16. Ⓐ Ⓑ Ⓒ Ⓓ Ⓔ
17. Ⓐ Ⓑ Ⓒ Ⓓ Ⓔ
18. Ⓐ Ⓑ Ⓒ Ⓓ Ⓔ
19. Ⓐ Ⓑ Ⓒ Ⓓ Ⓔ
20. Ⓐ Ⓑ Ⓒ Ⓓ Ⓔ
21. Ⓐ Ⓑ Ⓒ Ⓓ Ⓔ
22. Ⓐ Ⓑ Ⓒ Ⓓ Ⓔ
23. Ⓐ Ⓑ Ⓒ Ⓓ Ⓔ
24. Ⓐ Ⓑ Ⓒ Ⓓ Ⓔ
25. Ⓐ Ⓑ Ⓒ Ⓓ Ⓔ
26. Ⓐ Ⓑ Ⓒ Ⓓ Ⓔ
27. Ⓐ Ⓑ Ⓒ Ⓓ Ⓔ
28. Ⓐ Ⓑ Ⓒ Ⓓ Ⓔ
29. Ⓐ Ⓑ Ⓒ Ⓓ Ⓔ
30. Ⓐ Ⓑ Ⓒ Ⓓ Ⓔ
31. Ⓐ Ⓑ Ⓒ Ⓓ Ⓔ
32. Ⓐ Ⓑ Ⓒ Ⓓ Ⓔ
33. Ⓐ Ⓑ Ⓒ Ⓓ Ⓔ
34. Ⓐ Ⓑ Ⓒ Ⓓ Ⓔ
35. Ⓐ Ⓑ Ⓒ Ⓓ Ⓔ

Section 4

1. Ⓐ Ⓑ Ⓒ Ⓓ Ⓔ
2. Ⓐ Ⓑ Ⓒ Ⓓ Ⓔ
3. Ⓐ Ⓑ Ⓒ Ⓓ Ⓔ
4. Ⓐ Ⓑ Ⓒ Ⓓ Ⓔ
5. Ⓐ Ⓑ Ⓒ Ⓓ Ⓔ
6. Ⓐ Ⓑ Ⓒ Ⓓ Ⓔ
7. Ⓐ Ⓑ Ⓒ Ⓓ Ⓔ
8. Ⓐ Ⓑ Ⓒ Ⓓ Ⓔ
9. Ⓐ Ⓑ Ⓒ Ⓓ Ⓔ
10. Ⓐ Ⓑ Ⓒ Ⓓ Ⓔ
11. Ⓐ Ⓑ Ⓒ Ⓓ Ⓔ
12. Ⓐ Ⓑ Ⓒ Ⓓ Ⓔ
13. Ⓐ Ⓑ Ⓒ Ⓓ Ⓔ
14. Ⓐ Ⓑ Ⓒ Ⓓ Ⓔ
15. Ⓐ Ⓑ Ⓒ Ⓓ Ⓔ

16. [grid-in response box]

17. [grid-in response box]

ANSWER SHEETS—TEST 3

Section 4 (continued)

18.

19.

20.

21.

22.

23.

24.

25.

ANSWER SHEETS—TEST 3

Section 5

1. Ⓐ Ⓑ Ⓒ Ⓓ Ⓔ   13. Ⓐ Ⓑ Ⓒ Ⓓ Ⓔ   25. Ⓐ Ⓑ Ⓒ Ⓓ Ⓔ
2. Ⓐ Ⓑ Ⓒ Ⓓ Ⓔ   14. Ⓐ Ⓑ Ⓒ Ⓓ Ⓔ   26. Ⓐ Ⓑ Ⓒ Ⓓ Ⓔ
3. Ⓐ Ⓑ Ⓒ Ⓓ Ⓔ   15. Ⓐ Ⓑ Ⓒ Ⓓ Ⓔ   27. Ⓐ Ⓑ Ⓒ Ⓓ Ⓔ
4. Ⓐ Ⓑ Ⓒ Ⓓ Ⓔ   16. Ⓐ Ⓑ Ⓒ Ⓓ Ⓔ   28. Ⓐ Ⓑ Ⓒ Ⓓ Ⓔ
5. Ⓐ Ⓑ Ⓒ Ⓓ Ⓔ   17. Ⓐ Ⓑ Ⓒ Ⓓ Ⓔ   29. Ⓐ Ⓑ Ⓒ Ⓓ Ⓔ
6. Ⓐ Ⓑ Ⓒ Ⓓ Ⓔ   18. Ⓐ Ⓑ Ⓒ Ⓓ Ⓔ   30. Ⓐ Ⓑ Ⓒ Ⓓ Ⓔ
7. Ⓐ Ⓑ Ⓒ Ⓓ Ⓔ   19. Ⓐ Ⓑ Ⓒ Ⓓ Ⓔ   31. Ⓐ Ⓑ Ⓒ Ⓓ Ⓔ
8. Ⓐ Ⓑ Ⓒ Ⓓ Ⓔ   20. Ⓐ Ⓑ Ⓒ Ⓓ Ⓔ   32. Ⓐ Ⓑ Ⓒ Ⓓ Ⓔ
9. Ⓐ Ⓑ Ⓒ Ⓓ Ⓔ   21. Ⓐ Ⓑ Ⓒ Ⓓ Ⓔ   33. Ⓐ Ⓑ Ⓒ Ⓓ Ⓔ
10. Ⓐ Ⓑ Ⓒ Ⓓ Ⓔ   22. Ⓐ Ⓑ Ⓒ Ⓓ Ⓔ   34. Ⓐ Ⓑ Ⓒ Ⓓ Ⓔ
11. Ⓐ Ⓑ Ⓒ Ⓓ Ⓔ   23. Ⓐ Ⓑ Ⓒ Ⓓ Ⓔ   35. Ⓐ Ⓑ Ⓒ Ⓓ Ⓔ
12. Ⓐ Ⓑ Ⓒ Ⓓ Ⓔ   24. Ⓐ Ⓑ Ⓒ Ⓓ Ⓔ

Section 6

1. Ⓐ Ⓑ Ⓒ Ⓓ Ⓔ   13. Ⓐ Ⓑ Ⓒ Ⓓ Ⓔ   25. Ⓐ Ⓑ Ⓒ Ⓓ Ⓔ
2. Ⓐ Ⓑ Ⓒ Ⓓ Ⓔ   14. Ⓐ Ⓑ Ⓒ Ⓓ Ⓔ   26. Ⓐ Ⓑ Ⓒ Ⓓ Ⓔ
3. Ⓐ Ⓑ Ⓒ Ⓓ Ⓔ   15. Ⓐ Ⓑ Ⓒ Ⓓ Ⓔ   27. Ⓐ Ⓑ Ⓒ Ⓓ Ⓔ
4. Ⓐ Ⓑ Ⓒ Ⓓ Ⓔ   16. Ⓐ Ⓑ Ⓒ Ⓓ Ⓔ   28. Ⓐ Ⓑ Ⓒ Ⓓ Ⓔ
5. Ⓐ Ⓑ Ⓒ Ⓓ Ⓔ   17. Ⓐ Ⓑ Ⓒ Ⓓ Ⓔ   29. Ⓐ Ⓑ Ⓒ Ⓓ Ⓔ
6. Ⓐ Ⓑ Ⓒ Ⓓ Ⓔ   18. Ⓐ Ⓑ Ⓒ Ⓓ Ⓔ   30. Ⓐ Ⓑ Ⓒ Ⓓ Ⓔ
7. Ⓐ Ⓑ Ⓒ Ⓓ Ⓔ   19. Ⓐ Ⓑ Ⓒ Ⓓ Ⓔ   31. Ⓐ Ⓑ Ⓒ Ⓓ Ⓔ
8. Ⓐ Ⓑ Ⓒ Ⓓ Ⓔ   20. Ⓐ Ⓑ Ⓒ Ⓓ Ⓔ   32. Ⓐ Ⓑ Ⓒ Ⓓ Ⓔ
9. Ⓐ Ⓑ Ⓒ Ⓓ Ⓔ   21. Ⓐ Ⓑ Ⓒ Ⓓ Ⓔ   33. Ⓐ Ⓑ Ⓒ Ⓓ Ⓔ
10. Ⓐ Ⓑ Ⓒ Ⓓ Ⓔ   22. Ⓐ Ⓑ Ⓒ Ⓓ Ⓔ   34. Ⓐ Ⓑ Ⓒ Ⓓ Ⓔ
11. Ⓐ Ⓑ Ⓒ Ⓓ Ⓔ   23. Ⓐ Ⓑ Ⓒ Ⓓ Ⓔ   35. Ⓐ Ⓑ Ⓒ Ⓓ Ⓔ
12. Ⓐ Ⓑ Ⓒ Ⓓ Ⓔ   24. Ⓐ Ⓑ Ⓒ Ⓓ Ⓔ

PRACTICE TEST 3
SECTION 1

30 Questions—30 Minutes

Select the best answer to the following questions, then fill in
the appropriate space on your Answer Sheet.

Each of the following sentences contains one or two blanks;
these blanks indicate that a word or set of words has been left
out. Below the sentence are five words or phrases, lettered A
through E. Select the word or set of words that best completes
the sentence.

Example:
  Fame is -------- ; today's rising star is all too soon tomorrow's
  washed-up has-been.

  (A) rewarding   (B) gradual
   (C) essential   (D) spontaneous
    (E) transitory

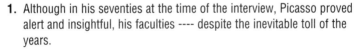

1. Although in his seventies at the time of the interview, Picasso proved
   alert and insightful, his faculties ---- despite the inevitable toll of the
   years.

   (A) atrophied   (B) diminished   (C) intact
    (D) useless   (E) impaired

2. While the 1940s are most noted for the development of black modern
   dance, they are also ---- because they were the last gasp for tap
   dancing.

   (A) irrelevant
   (B) unfounded
   (C) significant
   (D) speculative
   (E) contemporary

3. People who take megadoses of vitamins and minerals should take care: though beneficial in small quantities, in large amounts these substances may have ---- effects.

(A) admirable
(B) redundant
(C) intangible
(D) toxic
(E) minor

4. The number of black hawks has ---- because the encroachments of humans on their territory have caused them to ---- their customary breeding places.

(A) multiplied...endure
(B) extrapolated...alter
(C) increased...locate
(D) diminished...accept
(E) dwindled...shun

5. Although Britain's film makers often produce fine films, they are studiously ---- and rarely aim at a mass market.

(A) commercial
(B) viable
(C) derivative
(D) elitist
(E) collaborative

6. MacDougall's former editors remember him as a ---- man whose ---- and exhaustive reporting was worth the trouble.

(A) domineering...wearisome
(B) congenial...pretentious
(C) popular...supercilious
(D) fastidious...garbled
(E) cantankerous...meticulous

7. The opossum is ---- the venom of snakes in the rattlesnake subfamily and thus views the reptiles not as ---- enemies but as a food source.

(A) vulnerable to...natural
(B) conscious of...mortal
(C) impervious to...lethal
(D) sensitive to...deadly
(E) defenseless against...potential

8. Breaking with established musical conventions, Stravinsky was ----
composer whose heterodox works infuriated the traditionalists of his
day.

(A) a derivative
(B) an iconoclastic
(C) an uncontroversial
(D) a venerated
(E) a trite

9. A code of ethics governing the behavior of physicians during epi-
demics did not exist until 1846 when it was ---- by the American
Medical Association.

(A) rescinded
(B) promulgated
(C) presupposed
(D) depreciated
(E) implied

Each of the following examples introduces a capitalized pair of
words or phrases linked by a colon (:); this colon indicates that
these words are related in some way. Following the capitalized
pair are five pairs of words or phrases lettered A through E.
Select the pair whose relationship is most similar to the relationship illustrated by the capitalized pair.

Example:

CLOCK:TIME::   (A) watch:wrist
(B) pedometer:speed   (C) thermometer:temperature
(D) hourglass:sand   (E) radio:sound

10. DOG:MAMMAL::

    (A) wolf:pack
    (B) tree:forest
    (C) insect:antenna
    (D) snake:reptile
    (E) kennel:house

11. TELLER:BANK::

    (A) guest:motel
    (B) architect:blueprint
    (C) actor:rehearsal
    (D) patient:hospital
    (E) teacher:school

12. VISIONARY:PRACTICAL::

    (A) dilettante:amateurish
    (B) braggart:modest
    (C) rebel:revolutionary
    (D) connoisseur:cultivated
    (E) retainer:loyal

13. INSUBORDINATION:SOLDIER::

    (A) enrollment:student
    (B) indignation:heckler
    (C) autonomy:government
    (D) disobedience:child
    (E) diligence:worker

14. TUMBLER:BEVERAGE::

    (A) quiver:arrows
    (B) juggler:orange
    (C) quibbler:revenge
    (D) glutton:food
    (E) gambler:lottery

15. EPHEMERAL:MAYFLY::

    (A) ravenous:cobra
    (B) graceful:gazelle
    (C) succulent:mosquito
    (D) amorphous:butterfly
    (E) hasty:spider

Read each of the passages below, and then answer the questions that follow each passage. The correct response may be stated outright or merely suggested in the passage.

Questions 16–21 are based on the following passage.

Are Americans today overworked? The following passage is excerpted from a book published in 1991 on the unexpected decline of leisure in American life.

Faith in progress is deep within our culture. We have been taught to believe that our lives are better than the lives of those who came before us. The ideology of modern eco-
Line nomics suggests that material progress has yielded
 (5) enhanced satisfaction and well-being. But much of our confidence about our own well-being comes from the assumption that our lives are easier than those of earlier generations. I have already disputed the notion that we work less than medieval European peasants, however poor they may have
(10) been. The field research of anthropologists gives another view of the conventional wisdom.

The lives of so-called primitive peoples are commonly thought to be harsh—their existence dominated by the "incessant quest for food." In fact, primitives do little work.
(15) By contemporary standards, we'd have to judge them very lazy. If the Kapauku of Papua work one day, they do no labor on the next. !Kung Bushmen put in only two and a half days per week and six hours per day. In the Sandwich Islands of Hawaii, men work only four hours per day. And Australian
(20) aborigines have similar schedules. The key to understanding why these "stone age peoples" fail to act like us—increasing their work effort to get more things—is that they have limited desires. In the race between wanting and having, they have kept their wanting low—and, in this way, ensure their own
(25) kind of satisfaction. They are materially poor by contempo-

rary standards, but in at least one dimension—time—we
have to count them richer.

I do not raise these issues to imply that we would be
better off as Polynesian natives or medieval peasants. Nor
(30) am I arguing that "progress" has made us worse off. I am,
instead, making a much simpler point. We have paid a price
for prosperity. Capitalism has brought a dramatically
increased standard of living, but at the cost of a much more
demanding worklife. We are eating more, but we are burning
(35) up those calories at work. We have color televisions and
compact disc players, but we need them to unwind after a
stressful day at the office. We take vacations, but we work so
hard throughout the year that they become indispensable to
our sanity. The conventional wisdom that economic progress
(40) has given us more things *as well as* more leisure is difficult
to sustain.

16. According to the author, we base our belief that American people
today are well off on the assumption that

(A) America has always been the land of opportunity
(B) Americans particularly deserve to be prosperous
(C) people elsewhere have an inferior standard of living
(D) people elsewhere envy the American way of life
(E) our faith in progress will protect us as a nation

17. The author regards "the conventional wisdom" (line 11) with

(A) resentment
(B) skepticism
(C) complacency
(D) apprehension
(E) bewilderment

18. In lines 17–18, the Kapauku tribesmen and the !Kung Bushmen are
presented as examples of

(A) malingerers who turn down opportunities to work
(B) noble savages with little sense of time
(C) people who implicitly believe in progress
(D) people unmotivated by a desire for consumer goods
(E) people obsessed by their constant search for food

19. The word "raise" in line 28 means

    (A) elevate
    (B) increase
    (C) nurture
    (D) bring up
    (E) set upright

20. The primary purpose of the passage is to

    (A) dispute an assumption
    (B) highlight a problem
    (C) ridicule a theory
    (D) answer a criticism
    (E) counter propaganda

21. The last four sentences of the passage (lines 34–41) provide

    (A) a recapitulation of a previously made argument
    (B) an example of the argument that has been proposed earlier
    (C) a series of assertions and qualifications with a conclusion
    (D) a reconciliation of two opposing viewpoints
    (E) a reversal of the author's original position

Questions 22–30 are based on the following passage.

The following passage, written in the twentieth century, is taken from a discussion of John Webster's 17th-century drama "The Duchess of Malfi."

    The curtain rises; the Cardinal and Daniel de Bosola enter from the right. In appearance, the Cardinal is something between an El Greco cardinal and a Van Dyke noble lord. He
Line has the tall, spare form—the elongated hands and features—
(5) of the former; the trim pointed beard, the imperial repose, the commanding authority of the latter. But the El Greco features are not really those of asceticism or inner mystic spirituality. They are the index to a cold, refined but ruthless cruelty in a highly civilized controlled form. Neither is the imperial repose

(10) an aloof mood of proud detachment. It is a refined expression of satanic pride of place and talent.

To a degree, the Cardinal's coldness is artificially cultivated. He has defined himself against his younger brother Duke Ferdinand and is the opposite to the overwrought emo-
(15) tionality of the latter. But the Cardinal's aloof mood is not one of bland detachment. It is the deliberate detachment of a methodical man who collects his thoughts and emotions into the most compact and formidable shape—that when he strikes, he may strike with the more efficient and devastating
(20) force. His easy movements are those of the slowly circling eagle just before the swift descent with the exposed talons. Above all else, he is a man who never for a moment doubts his destined authority as a governor. He derisively and sharply rebukes his brother the Duke as easily and readily as
(25) he mocks his mistress Julia. If he has betrayed his hireling Bosola, he uses his brother as the tool to win back his "familiar." His court dress is a long brilliant scarlet cardinal's gown with white cuffs and a white collar turned back over the red, both collar and cuffs being elaborately scalloped and
(30) embroidered. He wears a small cape, reaching only to the elbows. His cassock is buttoned to the ground, giving a heightened effect to his already tall presence. Richelieu would have adored his neatly trimmed beard. A richly jeweled and ornamented cross lies on his breast, suspended from his
(35) neck by a gold chain.

Bosola, for his part, is the Renaissance "familiar" dressed conventionally in somber black with a white collar. He wears a chain about his neck, a suspended ornament, and a sword. Although a "bravo," he must not be thought of as a leather-
(40) jacketed, heavy-booted tough, squat and swarthy. Still less is he a sneering, leering, melodramatic villain of the Victorian gaslight tradition. Like his black-and-white clothes, he is a colorful contradiction, a scholar-assassin, a humanist-hang-man; introverted and introspective, yet ruthless in action;

(45) moody and reluctant, yet violent. He is a man of scholarly
taste and subtle intellectual discrimination doing the work of
a hired ruffian. In general effect, his impersonator must
achieve suppleness and subtlety of nature, a highly complex,
compressed, yet well restrained intensity of temperament.

(50) Like Duke Ferdinand, he is inwardly tormented, but not by
undiluted passion. His dominant emotion is an intellectual-
ized one: that of disgust at a world filled with knavery and
folly, but in which he must play a part and that a lowly,
despicable one. He is the kind of rarity that Browning loved

(55) to depict in his Renaissance monologues.

22. The primary purpose of the passage appears to be to

(A) provide historical background on the Renaissance church
(B) describe ecclesiastical costuming and pageantry
(C) analyze the appearances and moral natures of two dramatic
figures
(D) explain why modern audiences enjoy *The Duchess of Malfi*
(E) compare two interpretations of a challenging role

23. The word "spare" in line 4 means

(A) excessive
(B) superfluous
(C) pardonable
(D) lean
(E) inadequate

24. In lines 20–21, the author most likely compares the movements of the
Cardinal to those of a circling eagle in order to emphasize his

(A) flightiness
(B) love of freedom
(C) eminence
(D) spirituality
(E) mercilessness

25. The Cardinal's "satanic pride of place" (line 11) refers to his glorying in his

(A) faith
(B) rank
(C) residence
(D) immobility
(E) wickedness

26. As used in the third paragraph, the word "bravo" most nearly means

(A) a courageous man
(B) a national hero
(C) a clergyman
(D) a humanist
(E) a mercenary killer

27. In describing Bosola (lines 36–55), the author chiefly uses which of the following literary techniques?

(A) Rhetorical questions
(B) Unqualified assertions
(C) Comparison and contrast
(D) Dramatic irony
(E) Literary allusion

28. The word "discrimination" in line 46 means

(A) prejudice
(B) villainy
(C) discretion
(D) favoritism
(E) discernment

29. According to lines 50–54, why does Bosola suffer torments?

(A) His master the Cardinal berates him for performing his duties inadequately.
(B) He feels intense compassion for the pains endured by the Cardinal's victims.
(C) He is frustrated by his inability to attain a higher rank in the church.
(D) He feels superior to the villainy around him, yet must act the villain himself.
(E) He lacks the intellectual powers for scholarly success, but cannot endure common fools.

30. The author of the passage assumes that the reader is

(A) familiar with the paintings of El Greco and Van Dyke
(B) disgusted with a world filled with cruelty and folly
(C) ignorant of the history of the Roman Catholic Church
(D) uninterested in psychological distinctions
(E) unacquainted with the writing of Browning

YOU MAY GO BACK AND REVIEW THIS
SECTION IN THE REMAINING TIME, BUT   **S T O P**
DO NOT WORK IN ANY OTHER SECTION
UNTIL TOLD TO DO SO.

SECTION 2

25 Questions—30 Minutes

For each problem in this section determine which of the five choices is correct and blacken in that choice on your answer sheet. You may use any blank space on the page for your work.

Notes:

- You may use a calculator whenever you feel it will be helpful.
- Use the diagrams provided to help you solve the problems. Unless you see the words "<u>Note</u>: Figure not drawn to scale" under a diagram, it has been drawn as accurately as possible. Unless it is stated that a figure is three-dimensional, you may assume it lies in a plane.

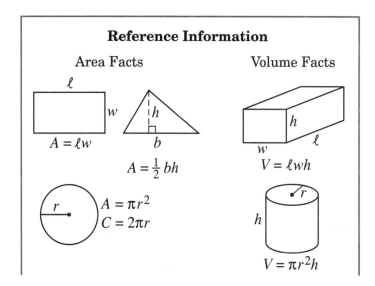

Reference Information

Area Facts

$A = \ell w$

$A = \frac{1}{2} bh$

$A = \pi r^2$
$C = 2\pi r$

Volume Facts

$V = \ell w h$

$V = \pi r^2 h$

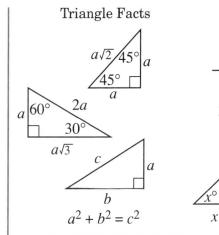

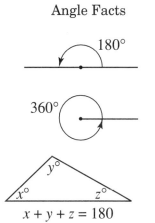

Triangle Facts

$a^2 + b^2 = c^2$

Angle Facts

$x + y + z = 180$

---

1. If $2x + 4x + 6x = -12$, then $x =$

(A) −1 (B) $-\dfrac{1}{2}$ (C) 0 (D) $\dfrac{1}{2}$ (E) 1

---

2. If $(w + 12) - 12 = 12$, then $w =$

(A) 0 (B) 1 (C) 12 (D) 24 (E) 36

<u>Questions 3–4</u> refer to the information in the following table, which shows the number of students in each of the five fifth-grade classes at Taft Elementary School and, for each class, the number of students in the school band.

Class	Number of Students	Number in Band
A	20	5
B	30	7
C	23	5
D	27	6
E	25	6

3. What is the average number of students per class?

   (A) 23   (B) 24   (C) 24.5   (D) 25   (E) 26

---

4. Which class has the highest percent of students in the band?

   (A) A   (B) B   (C) C   (D) D   (E) E

---

5. What is the product of 1.1 and 1.9 rounded to the <u>nearest tenth</u>?

   (A) 1.5   (B) 1.7   (C) 2.0   (D) 2.1   (E) 3.0

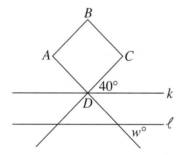

6. In the figure above, lines k and ℓ are parallel, and line k passes through D, one of the corners of square $ABCD$. What is the value of w?

   (A) 30   (B) 40   (C) 45   (D) 50   (E) 60

---

7. If 24 of the 40 students in a club are girls, what is the ratio of boys to girls in the club?

   (A) 2:5   (B) 3:5   (C) 2:3   (D) 3:2   (E) 5:2

8. Steve took a bike trip in which he covered half the total distance on Monday. After going 100 kilometers on Tuesday, he determined that he still had 10% of the trip to complete. What was the total length, in kilometers, of the trip?

(A) 200   (B) 250   (C) 400   (D) 500   (E) 600

---

9. A number, x, is chosen at random from the set of positive integers less than 10. What is the probability that $\frac{9}{x} > x$?

(A) $\frac{1}{5}$ (B) $\frac{2}{9}$ (C) $\frac{1}{3}$ (D) $\frac{2}{3}$ (E) $\frac{7}{9}$

---

10. The members of the French Club conducted a fund-raising drive. The average (arithmetic mean) amount of money raised per member was $85. Then Jean joined the club and raised $50. This lowered the average to $80. How many members were there before Jean joined?

(A) 4   (B) 5   (C) 6   (D) 7   (E) 8

---

11. R, S, and T are points with $RT = 2RS$. Which of the following could be true?

   I. R, S, and T are the vertices of a right triangle.
   II. R, S, and T are three of the vertices of a square.
   III. R, S, and T all lie on the circumference of a circle.

(A) I only   (B) III only   (C) I and II only
 (D) I and III only   (E) I, II, and III

---

12. At Music Outlet the regular price for a CD is d dollars. How many CDs can be purchased for m dollars when the CDs are on sale at 50% off the regular price?

(A) $\frac{m}{50d}$ (B) $\frac{md}{50}$ (C) $\frac{md}{2}$ (D) $\frac{m}{2d}$ (E) $\frac{2m}{d}$

13. There are 12 men on a basketball team, and in a game 5 of them play at any one time. If the game is 1 hour long, and if each man plays exactly the same amount of time, how many minutes does each man play?

(A) 10   (B) 12   (C) 24   (D) 25   (E) 30

---

14. The volume of pitcher I is A ounces, and the volume of pitcher II is B ounces, with $B > A$. If pitcher II is full of water and pitcher I is empty, and if just enough water is poured from pitcher II to fill pitcher I, what fraction of pitcher II is now full?

(A) $\dfrac{1}{2}$ (B) $\dfrac{1}{B}$ (C) $\dfrac{A}{B}$ (D) $\dfrac{A-B}{B}$ (E) $\dfrac{B-A}{B}$

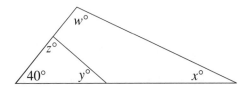

15. In the figure above, $w + x + y + z =$

(A) 140   (B) 280   (C) 300   (D) 320   (E) 360

$$
\begin{array}{r}
AB \\
+\ CD \\
\hline
AAA
\end{array}
$$

16. In the addition problem above, A, B, C, and D are positive integers. What is the value of C?

(A) 1   (B) 3   (C) 5   (D) 7   (E) 9

$$x + y = 10 \qquad y + z = 15 \qquad x + z = 17$$

17. What is the average (arithmetic mean) of x, y, and z?

(A) 7   (B) 14   (C) 15   (D) 21
(E) It cannot be determined from the information given.

---

18. A number of people boarded a bus at the terminal. At the first stop,

half of the passengers got off and 1 got on. At the second stop, $\frac{1}{3}$

of the passengers on the bus got off and 1 got on. If the bus then
had 15 passengers, how many were there when the bus left the
terminal?

(A) 40   (B) 48   (C) 58   (D) 60   (E) 62

---

19. The route from Peter's house to Wendy's house is exactly 10 miles.
At the same time, Peter and Wendy each left home and walked
toward the other's house. If Peter walked at a rate of 4 miles per
hour, and they met 4 miles from Wendy's house, how fast, in miles
per hour, did Wendy walk?

(A) 2   (B) $2\frac{2}{3}$ (C) $3\frac{1}{2}$ (D) 4   (E) 6

---

20. $A = \{2, 3\}$ $B = \{4, 5\}$ $C = \{6, 7\}$

In how many ways is it possible to pick 1 number from each set, so
that the 3 numbers could be the lengths of the three sides of a
triangle?

(A) 0   (B) 2   (C) 4   (D) 6   (E) 8

---

21. If a, b, and c are positive numbers such that $3a = 4b = 5c$, and if
$a + b = kc$, what is the value of k?

(A) $\frac{12}{35}$ (B) $\frac{5}{7}$ (C) $\frac{10}{7}$ (D) $\frac{7}{5}$ (E) $\frac{35}{12}$

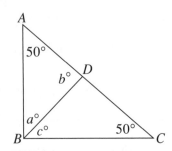

22. Which of the following statements concerning the triangle in the figure above must be true?

   I. $c = 80 - a$
   II. $c = b - 50$
   III. $a + b = c + d$

(A) I only   (B) II only   (C) I and II only
   (D) I and III only   (E) I, II, and III

---

23. If c carpenters can build a garage in d days, how many days will it take e carpenters, working at the same rate, to build 2 garages?

(A) $\dfrac{2cd}{e}$ (B) $\dfrac{2d}{ce}$ (C) $\dfrac{2e}{ce}$ (D) $\dfrac{cd}{2e}$ (E) $\dfrac{ce}{2d}$

---

24. If $a^2 \neq b^2$, then $\dfrac{a^2 - b^2}{b^2 - a^2} + \dfrac{a - b}{b - a} =$

(A) −2   (B) 0   (C) 2   (D) $\dfrac{a + b}{a - b}$ (E) $\dfrac{a - b}{b - a}$

25. Let A = total area of five circles of radius r, and let B = total area of three circles of radius s. If $A = B$,

then $\dfrac{r}{s}$ =

(A) $\dfrac{3}{5}$ (B) $\dfrac{\sqrt{3}}{\sqrt{5}}$ (C) $\dfrac{3\pi}{5}$ (D) $\dfrac{\sqrt{3\pi}}{\sqrt{5}}$ (E) $\dfrac{\sqrt{3}}{\sqrt{5}}\pi$

YOU MAY GO BACK AND REVIEW THIS
SECTION IN THE REMAINING TIME, BUT
DO NOT WORK IN ANY OTHER SECTION
UNTIL TOLD TO DO SO.

S T O P

SECTION 3

35 Questions—30 Minutes

Select the best answer to the following questions, then fill in the appropriate space on your Answer Sheet.

Each of the following sentences contains one or two blanks; these blanks indicate that a word or set of words has been left out. Below the sentence are five words or phrases, lettered A through E. Select the word or set of words that best completes the sentence.

Example:

Fame is -------- ; today's rising star is all too soon tomorrow's washed-up has-been.

(A) rewarding   (B) gradual
  (C) essential   (D) spontaneous
    (E) transitory

---

1. The critics were distressed that an essayist of such glowing ---- could descend to writing such dull, uninteresting prose.

   (A) obscurity   (B) ill-repute   (C) shallowness
    (D) promise   (E) amiability

2. Famous in her time and then forgotten, the 17th-century Dutch painter Judith Leyster was ---- obscurity when, in 1993, the Worcester Art Museum organized the first retrospective exhibition of her work.

   (A) resigned to
   (B) rewarded with
   (C) rescued from
   (D) indifferent to
   (E) worthy of

3. The testimony of eyewitnesses is notoriously ----; emotion and excitement all too often cause our minds to distort what we see.

(A) judicious
(B) interdependent
(C) credible
(D) unreliable
(E) gratifying

4. Although Henry was not in general a sentimental man, occasionally he would feel a touch of ---- for the old days and would contemplate making a brief excursion to Boston to revisit his childhood friends.

(A) exasperation   (B) chagrin   (C) nostalgia
(D) lethargy   (E) anxiety

5. We had not realized how much people ---- the library's old borrowing policy until we received complaints once it had been ----.

(A) enjoyed...continued
(B) disliked...administered
(C) respected...imitated
(D) ignored...lauded
(E) appreciated...superseded

6. During the Dark Ages, hermits and other religious ---- fled the world to devote themselves to silent contemplation.

(A) renegades   (B) skeptics   (C) altruists
(D) recluses   (E) convictions

7. No real life hero of ancient or modern days can surpass James Bond with his nonchalant ---- of death and the ---- with which he bears torture.

(A) contempt...distress
(B) disregard...fortitude
(C) veneration...guile
(D) concept...terror
(E) ignorance...fickleness

8. Even though the basic organization of the brain does not change after birth, details of its structure and function remain ---- for some time, particularly in the cerebral cortex.

(A) plastic   (B) immutable   (C) essential
(D) unavoidable   (E) static

9. Lavish in visual beauty, the film *Lawrence of Arabia* also boasts ---- of style: it knows how much can be shown in a shot, how much can be said in a few words.

(A) extravagance   (B) economy   (C) autonomy
(D) frivolity   (E) arrogance

10. Unlike the highly ---- Romantic poets of the previous century, Arnold and his fellow Victorian poets were ---- and interested in moralizing.

(A) rhapsodic...lyrical
(B) frenetic...distraught
(C) emotional...didactic
(D) sensitive...strange
(E) dramatic...warped

Each of the following examples introduces a capitalized pair of words or phrases linked by a colon (:); this colon indicates that these words are related in some way. Following the capitalized pair are five pairs of words or phrases lettered A through E. Select the pair whose relationship is most similar to the relationship illustrated by the capitalized pair.

Example:

CLOCK:TIME::   (A) watch:wrist
(B) pedometer:speed   (C) thermometer:temperature
(D) hourglass:sand   (E) radio:sound

11. JOURNALIST:TYPEWRITER::

    (A) surgeon:bones
    (B) carpenter:lumber
    (C) poet:beauty
    (D) floorwalker:flower
    (E) electrician:pliers

12. MUTTON:SHEEP::

    (A) bleat:lamb
    (B) sow:pig
    (C) hide:buffalo
    (D) beef:steer
    (E) calf:cow

13. ENTRY:DIARY::

    (A) sonnet:ballad
    (B) paragraph:prose
    (C) missive:epistle
    (D) episode:serial
    (E) book:leaf

14. MURAL:WALL::

    (A) statue:courtyard
    (B) painting:portrait
    (C) quarry:stone
    (D) etching:paper
    (E) water color:tempera

15. LIBRETTO:AUTHOR::

    (A) aria:tenor
    (B) score:composer
    (C) drama:reviewer
    (D) chisel:sculptor
    (E) portfolio:architect

16. TETHER:HORSE::

    (A) safari:tiger
    (B) specimen:animal
    (C) brand:calf
    (D) muzzle:dog
    (E) fetters:prisoner

17. BLIND:SIGHT::

(A) diabetic:sugar
(B) indigent:tact
(C) amnesiac:memory
(D) benevolent:charity
(E) misanthropic:hate

18. PECKISH:STARVING::

(A) proper:seemly
(B) rural:urban
(C) plain:hideous
(D) drunken:sober
(E) sterile:contaminated

19. POET:ODE::

(A) philosopher:nature
(B) dramatist:scenery
(C) sculptor:marble
(D) seamstress:gown
(E) astronomer:planet

20. TIME:SCYTHE::

(A) liberty:sickle
(B) justice:scales
(C) honesty:badge
(D) ignorance:chains
(E) freedom:mountaintop

21. VIRTUOSO:EXPERIENCED::

(A) rogue:knavish
(B) democrat:dictatorial
(C) saint:naive
(D) leader:deferential
(E) evildoer:repentant

22. CAUSTIC:CORRODE::

(A) aesthetic:judge
(B) chaotic:erupt
(C) hypnotic:mesmerize
(D) defunct:revive
(E) durable:harden

23. CARAPACE:TURTLE::

(A) speed:hare
(B) chameleon:lizard
(C) amphibian:frog
(D) shell:snail
(E) kennel:dog

Read the passage below, and then answer the questions that follow the passage. The correct response may be stated outright or merely suggested in the passage.

Questions 24–35 are based on the following passage.

In this adaptation of an excerpt from a short story set in Civil War times, a man is about to be hanged. The first two paragraphs set the scene; the remainder of the passage presents a flashback to an earlier, critical encounter.

A man stood upon a railroad bridge in Northern Alabama, looking down into the swift waters twenty feet below. The man's hands were behind his back, the wrists bound with a
Line cord. A rope loosely encircled his neck. It was attached to a
 (5) stout cross-timber above his head, and the slack fell to the level of his knees. Some loose boards laid upon the sleepers supporting the metals of the railway supplied a footing for him and his executioners—two private soldiers of the Federal army, directed by a sergeant, who in civil life may have been
(10) a deputy sheriff. At a short remove upon the same temporary platform was an officer in the uniform of his rank, armed. He was a captain. A sentinel at each end of the bridge stood with his rifle in the position known as 'support'—a formal and unnatural position, enforcing an erect carriage of the body. It
(15) did not appear to be the duty of these two men to know what was occurring at the center of the bridge; they merely blockaded the two ends of the foot plank which traversed it.
 The man who was engaged in being hanged was appar-

ently about thirty-five years of age. He was a civilian, if one
(20) might judge from his dress, which was that of a planter. His
features were good—a straight nose, firm mouth, broad fore-
head, from which his long, dark hair was combed straight
back, falling behind his ears to the collar of his well-fitting
frock coat. He wore a moustache and pointed beard, but no
(25) whiskers; his eyes were large and dark grey and had a kindly
expression that one would hardly have expected in one
whose neck was in the hemp. Evidently this was no vulgar
assassin. The liberal military code makes provision for hanging many kinds of people, and gentlemen are not excluded.
(30)   Peyton Farquhar was a well-to-do planter, of an old and
highly respected Alabama family. Being a slave-owner, and,
like other slave-owners, a politician, he was naturally an
original secessionist and ardently devoted to the Southern
cause. Circumstances had prevented him from taking service
(35) with the gallant army that had fought the disastrous campaigns ending with the fall of Corinth, and he chafed under
the inglorious restraint, longing for the release of his energies, the larger life of the soldier, the opportunity for distinction. That opportunity, he felt, would come, as it comes to all
(40) in war time. Meanwhile, he did what he could. No service
was too humble for him to perform in aid of the South, no
adventure too perilous for him to undertake if consistent with
the character of a civilian who was at heart a soldier, and
who in good faith and without too much qualification
(45) assented to at least a part of the frankly villainous dictum
that all is fair in love and war.
     One evening while Farquhar and his wife were sitting near
the entrance to his grounds, a grey-clad soldier rode up to
the gate and asked for a drink of water. Mrs. Farquhar was
(50) only too happy to serve him with her own white hands. While
she was gone to fetch the water, her husband approached
the dusty horseman and inquired eagerly for news from the
front.
     "The Yanks are repairing the railroads," said the man, "and
(55) are getting ready for another advance. They have reached the

Owl Creek bridge, put it in order, and built a stockade on the other bank. The commandant has issued an order, which is posted everywhere, declaring that any civilian caught interfering with the railroad, its bridges, tunnels, or trains, will be
(60) summarily hanged. I saw the order."

"How far is it to the Owl Creek bridge?" Farquhar asked.

"About thirty miles."

"Is there no force on this side of the creek?"

"Only a picket post half a mile out, on the railroad, and a
(65) single sentinel at this end of the bridge."

"Suppose a man—a civilian and a student of hanging—should elude the picket post and perhaps get the better of the sentinel," said Farquhar, smiling, "what could he accomplish?"

(70)   The soldier reflected. "I was there a month ago," he replied. "I observed that the flood of last winter had lodged a great quantity of driftwood against the wooden pier at the end of the bridge. It is now dry and would burn like tow."

The lady had now brought the water, which the soldier
(75) drank. He thanked her ceremoniously, bowed to her husband, and rode away. An hour later, after nightfall, he repassed the plantation, going northward in the direction from which he had come. He was a Yankee scout.

24. The word "civil" in line 9 means

(A) polite
(B) individual
(C) legal
(D) collective
(E) nonmilitary

25. In cinematic terms, the first two paragraphs most nearly resemble

(A) a wide-angle shot followed by a close-up
(B) a sequence of cameo appearances
(C) a trailer advertising a feature film
(D) two episodes of an ongoing serial
(E) an animated cartoon

26. In lines 25–27, by commenting on the planter's amiable physical appearance, the author suggests that

(A) he was innocent of any criminal intent
(B) he seemed an unlikely candidate for execution
(C) the sentinels had no need to fear an attempted escape
(D) the planter tried to assume a harmless demeanor
(E) the eyes are the windows of the soul

27. The author's tone in discussing "the liberal military code" (line 28) can best be described as

(A) approving
(B) ironic
(C) irked
(D) regretful
(E) reverent

28. Peyton Farquhar would most likely consider which of the following a good example of how a citizen should behave in wartime?

(A) He should use even underhanded methods to support his cause.
(B) He should enlist in the army without delay.
(C) He should turn to politics as a means of enforcing his will.
(D) He should avoid involving himself in disastrous campaigns.
(E) He should concentrate on his duties as a planter.

29. The word "consistent" in line 42 means

(A) unfailing
(B) agreeable
(C) dependable
(D) constant
(E) compatible

30. In line 44, the word "qualification" most nearly means

(A) competence
(B) eligibility
(C) restriction
(D) reason
(E) liability

31. It can be inferred from lines 49–50 that Mrs. Farquhar is

(A) sympathetic to the Confederate cause
(B) uninterested in news of the war
(C) too proud to perform menial tasks
(D) reluctant to ask her slaves to fetch water
(E) inhospitable by nature

32. Farquhar's inquiry about what a man could accomplish (lines 66–69) illustrates which aspect of his character?

(A) Morbid longing for death
(B) Weighty sense of personal responsibility
(C) Apprehension about his family's future
(D) Keenly inquisitive intellect
(E) Romantic vision of himself as a hero

33. From Farquhar's exchange with the soldier (lines 61–73), we can infer that Farquhar most likely is going to

(A) sneak across the bridge to join the Confederate forces
(B) attempt to burn down the bridge to halt the Yankee advance
(C) remove the driftwood blocking the Confederates' access to the bridge
(D) attack the stockade that overlooks the Owl Creek bridge
(E) undermine the pillars that support the railroad bridge

34. As used in the next-to-last paragraph, "tow" is

(A) an act of hauling something
(B) a tugboat
(C) a railroad bridge
(D) a highly combustible substance
(E) a picket post

35. We may infer from lines 76–78 that

(A) the soldier has deserted from the Southern army
(B) the soldier has lost his sense of direction
(C) the scout has been tempting Farquhar into an unwise action
(D) Farquhar knew the soldier was a Yankee scout
(E) the soldier returned to the plantation unwillingly

YOU MAY GO BACK AND REVIEW THIS
SECTION IN THE REMAINING TIME, BUT   **S T O P**
DO NOT WORK IN ANY OTHER SECTION
UNTIL TOLD TO DO SO.

SECTION 4

25 Questions—30 Minutes

You have 30 minutes to answer the 15 Quantitative Comparison questions and 10 Student-Produced Response questions in this section. You may use any blank space on the page for your work.

Notes:

- You may use a calculator whenever you feel it will be helpful.
- Use the diagrams provided to help you solve the problems. Unless you see the words "<u>Note</u>: Figure not drawn to scale" under a diagram, it has been drawn as accurately as possible. Unless it is stated that a figure is three-dimensional, you may assume it lies in a plane.

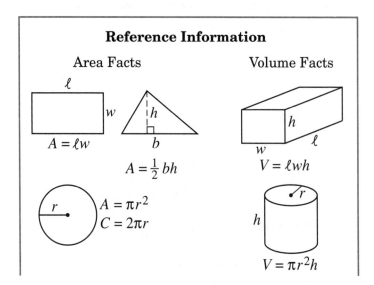

Reference Information

Area Facts

$A = \ell w$

$A = \frac{1}{2} bh$

$A = \pi r^2$
$C = 2\pi r$

Volume Facts

$V = \ell wh$

$V = \pi r^2 h$

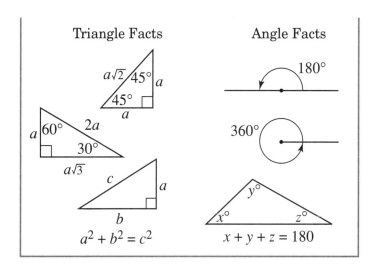

Triangle Facts

Angle Facts

$a^2 + b^2 = c^2$

$x + y + z = 180$

In each of questions 1–15, two quantities appear in boxes: one in Column A and one in Column B. You must compare them. The correct answer to a question is

A   if the quantity in Column A is greater;
B   if the quantity in Column B is greater;
C   if the two quantities are equal;
D   if it is impossible to determine which quantity is greater.

Notes:
- *The correct answer is <u>never</u> E.*
- Sometimes information about one or both of the quantities is centered above the two boxes.
- If the same symbol appears in both columns, it represents the same thing each time.
- All variables represent real numbers.

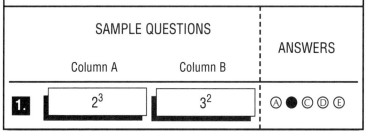

SAMPLE QUESTIONS

ANSWERS

Column A

Column B

1. 2^3 3^2 Ⓐ ● Ⓒ Ⓓ Ⓔ

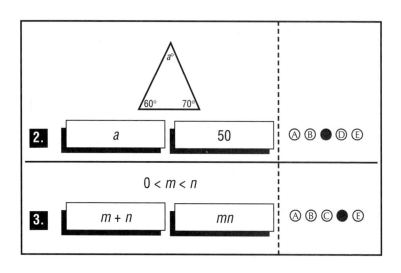

2. | a | 50 | Ⓐ Ⓑ ● Ⓓ Ⓔ

$0 < m < n$

3. | $m + n$ | mn | Ⓐ Ⓑ Ⓒ ● Ⓔ

SUMMARY DIRECTIONS FOR QUANTITATIVE COMPARISON QUESTIONS

<u>Answer:</u> A if the quantity in Column A is greater;
B if the quantity in Column B is greater;
C if the two quantities are equal;
D if it is impossible to determine which quantity is greater.

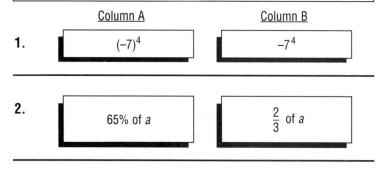

	Column A	Column B
1.	$(-7)^4$	-7^4
2.	65% of a	$\frac{2}{3}$ of a

$A = \{1, 2, 3\}$
$B = \{3, 4, 5\}$

| **3.** | A number picked at random from A | A number picked at random from B |

SUMMARY DIRECTIONS FOR QUANTITATIVE COMPARISON QUESTIONS

<u>Answer:</u> A if the quantity in Column A is greater;
B if the quantity in Column B is greater;
C if the two quantities are equal;
D if it is impossible to determine which quantity is greater.

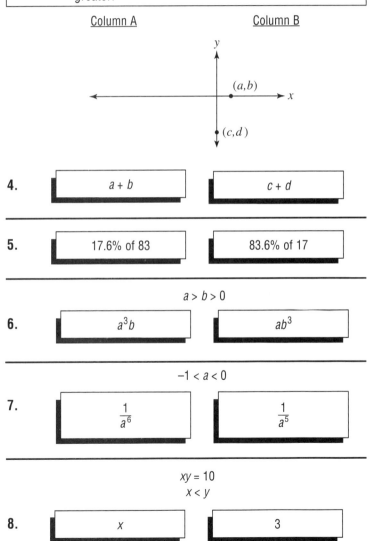

	Column A	Column B

4. $a + b$ | $c + d$

5. 17.6% of 83 | 83.6% of 17

$a > b > 0$

6. $a^3 b$ | ab^3

$-1 < a < 0$

7. $\dfrac{1}{a^6}$ | $\dfrac{1}{a^5}$

$xy = 10$
$x < y$

8. x | 3

SUMMARY DIRECTIONS FOR QUANTITATIVE COMPARISON QUESTIONS

<u>Answer:</u> A if the quantity in Column A is greater;
B if the quantity in Column B is greater;
C if the two quantities are equal;
D if it is impossible to determine which quantity is greater.

Column A   Column B

3 beeps = 2 clicks
4 beeps = 2 tweets

9.   1 click   2 tweets

$ab = 0$

10. $(a + b)^2$ $(a - b)^2$

$a > 0$

11.   The average (arithmetic mean) of 1, 2, and $-a$ The average (arithmetic mean) of -1, -2, and a

---

Note: Figure not drawn to scale

12. $r + t$ s

Column A   Column B

$0 < a < 1$

13.

| The area of a square whose side is a | The area of a circle whose diameter is a |

A wooden cube whose edges are
4 inches is painted red.
The cube is then cut into 64 small cubes
whose edges are 1 inch.

14.

| The number of small cubes that have exactly three red faces | The number of small cubes that have no red faces |

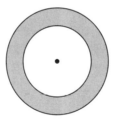

The radius of the large circle is R.
The radius of the small circle is r.
The areas of the shaded region and
the white region are equal.

15.

| $\dfrac{R}{r}$ | 1.5 |

Directions for Student-Produced Response Questions (Grid-ins)

In questions 16–25, first solve the problem, and then enter your answer on the grid provided on the answer sheet. The instructions for entering your answers are as follows:

- First, write your answer in the boxes at the top of the grid.
- Second, grid your answer in the columns below the boxes.
- Use the fraction bar in the first row or the decimal point in the second row to enter fractions and decimal answers.

Answer: $\frac{8}{15}$ Answer: 1.75

Write your answer in the boxes

Grid in your answer

Answer: 100

Either position is acceptable

- Grid only one space in each column.
- Entering the answer in the boxes is recommended as an aid in gridding, but is not required.
- The machine scoring your exam can read only what you grid, so you **must grid in your answers correctly to get credit.**
- If a question has more than one correct answer, grid in only one of them.
- The grid does not have a minus sign, so no answer can be negative.
- A mixed number *must* be converted to an improper fraction or a decimal before it is gridded. Enter $1\frac{1}{4}$ as 5/4 or 1.25; the machine will interpret 1 1/4 as $\frac{11}{4}$ and mark it wrong.
- **All decimals must be entered as accurately as possible.** Here are the three acceptable ways of gridding

$$\frac{3}{11} = 0.272727...$$

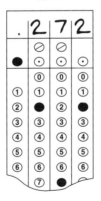

- Note that rounding to .273 is acceptable, because you are using the full grid, but you would receive **no credit** for .3 or .27, because they are less accurate.

16. If $a \otimes b = (a^2 + b^2) - (a^2 - b^2)$, what is the value of $6 \otimes 7$?

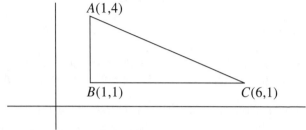

17. In the figure above, what is the area of △*ABC*?

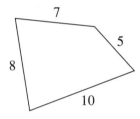

18. A square, not shown, has the same perimeter as the quadrilateral above. What is the length of a side of the square?

19. A factory can produce 1 gizmo every 333 seconds. How many <u>hours</u> will it take to produce 40 gizmos?

20. If the average of *a*, *b*, and 10 is 100, what is the average of *a* and *b*?

21. If the rent on an apartment goes up 10% every year, next year's rent will be how many times last year's rent?

22. Boris was 26 years old in 1970, when his daughter, Olga, was born. In what year was Boris exactly 3 times as old as Olga.

---

23. When 25 students took a quiz, the grades they earned ranged from 2 to 10. If exactly 22 of them passed, by earning a grade of 7 or higher, what is the highest possible average the class could have earned on the quiz?

---

24. Jason has twice as many red marbles as blue marbles. He puts them in two jars so that the ratio of the number of red marbles to blue marbles in jar I is 2:7 and there are only red marbles in jar II. The number of red marbles in jar II is how many times the number of red marbles in jar I?

---

25. If a and b are positive integers and their product is 3 times their sum, what is the value of $\dfrac{1}{a} + \dfrac{1}{b}$?

YOU MAY GO BACK AND REVIEW THIS SECTION IN THE REMAINING TIME, BUT **S T O P** DO NOT WORK IN ANY OTHER SECTION UNTIL TOLD TO DO SO.

SECTION 5

13 Questions—15 Minutes

Select the best answer to the following questions, then fill in the appropriate space on your Answer Sheet.

The questions that follow the two passages in this section relate to the content of both, and to their relationship. The correct response may be stated outright in the passages or merely suggested.

Questions 1–13 are based on the following passages.

The following passages deal with the exotic world of sub-atomic physics. Passage 1, written by a popularizer of contemporary physics, was published in 1985. Passage 2 was written nearly 15 years later.

Passage 1

The classical idea of matter was something with solidity and mass, like wet stone dust pressed in a fist. If matter was composed of atoms, then the atoms too must have solidity
Line and mass. At the beginning of the twentieth century the atom
(5) was imagined as a tiny billiard ball or a granite pebble writ small. Then, in the physics of Niels Bohr, the miniature billiard ball became something akin to a musical instrument, a finely tuned Stradivarius 10 billion times smaller than the real thing. With the advent of quantum mechanics, the musical
(10) instrument gave way to pure music. On the atomic scale, the solidity and mass of matter dissolved into something light and airy. Suddenly physicists were describing atoms in the

vocabulary of the composer—"resonance," "frequency,"
"harmony," "scale." Atomic electrons sang in choirs like
(15) seraphim, cherubim, thrones, and dominions. Classical distinctions between matter and light became muddled. In the
new physics, light bounced about like particles, and matter
undulated in waves like light.

    In recent decades, physicists have uncovered elegant sub-
(20) atomic structures in the music of matter. They use a strange
new language to describe the subatomic world: *quark,*
squark, gluon, gauge, technicolor, flavor, strangeness,
charm. There are *up* quarks and *down* quarks, *top* quarks
and *bottom* quarks. There are particles with *truth* and
(25) *antitruth,* and there are particles with *naked beauty.* The simplest of the constituents of ordinary matter—the proton, for
instance—has taken on the character of a Bach fugue, a four-
part counterpoint of matter, energy, space, and time. At
matter's heart there are arpeggios, chromatics, syncopation.
(30) On the lowest rung of the chain of being, Creation dances.

    Already, the astronomers and the particle physicists are
engaged in a vigorous dialogue. The astronomers are prepared to recognize that the large-scale structure of the uni-
verse may have been determined by subtle interactions of
(35) particles in the first moments of the Big Bang. And the
particle physicists are hoping to find confirmation of their
theories of subatomic structure in the astronomers' observations of deep space and time. The snake has bitten its tail
and won't let go.

Passage 2

(40)   Consider a dew drop, poised at the tip of a grass blade.
Only one millimeter in diameter, this tiny dew drop is composed of a billion trillion molecules of water, each consisting
of two hydrogen atoms and one oxygen atom (H_2O). At the
onset of the twentieth century, this was the accepted view of
(45) the nature of matter. Atoms were seen as matter's basic
building blocks, elementary or fundamental particles that
could not be divided into anything smaller.

This relatively simple picture, however, changed drastically as physicists came to explore the secrets of the subatomic
(50) world. The once-indivisible atom, split, was revealed to consist of a nucleus made up of protons and neutrons around which electrons orbited. Protons and neutrons, in turn, were composed of even smaller subatomic particles whimsically dubbed quarks. At first, theorists claimed that all matter was
(55) made of three fundamental particles: electrons and paired up and down quarks. Later, however, experiments with powerful accelerators and colliding particle beams suggested the existence of other pairs of quarks, three generations in all, whose mass increased with each generation. Lightest of all were the
(60) first generation quarks, up and down, which combined to create the basic protons and neutrons; somewhat heavier were the second generation quarks, strange and charm, the building blocks of the more esoteric particles produced in the physicists' labs. Then in 1977 a team headed by Fermilab
(65) physicist Leon Lederman uncovered the possibility of a third generation of quarks. Using new accelerators with higher energies, they produced a short-lived heavy particle, the upsilon, whose properties suggested it could not be made of the four quarks then known. They concluded it must be made
(70) of a fifth quark, which they named bottom, whereupon scientists throughout the world set off in hot pursuit of bottom's hypothetical partner, top.

The hunt for the top quark consumed the world's particle physicists for nearly twenty years. It was their Grail, and they
(75) were as determined as any knight of King Arthur's court to succeed in their holy quest. To Harvard theorist Sheldon Glashow in 1994, it was "not just another quark. It's the last blessed one, and the sooner we find it, the better everyone will feel." Indeed, they had to find it, for the Standard Model
(80) of particle physics, the theoretical synthesis that reduced the once-maddening hordes of particles (the so-called "particle zoo") to just a few primary components, hinged upon its existence. Physicists likened the missing quark to the key-

stone of an arch: the Standard Model, like an arch, was sup-
(85) ported by all its constituents, but it was the keystone, the last
piece to go in, that ensured the structure's stability.

In 1995 the physicists found the keystone to their arch,
and with it, new questions to answer. Surprisingly the top
quark was far heavier than theorists had predicted, nearly
(90) twice as heavy in fact. Fermilab physicist Alvin Tollestrup
originally had estimated top to weigh at least as much as a
silver atom. At the hunt's end, top was determined to have a
mass similar to that of an atom of gold. (With an atomic
weight of 197, a gold atom is made up of hundreds of up and
(95) down quarks.) The question thus remains, why is top so
massive? Why does any fundamental particle have mass?
With its astonishing heft, the top quark should help clarify
the hidden mechanisms that make some particles massive
while others have no mass at all.

1. Which of the following would be the most appropriate title for
Passage 1?

(A) Linguistic Implications of Particle Physics
(B) The Influence of Music on Particle Interactions
(C) Matter's Transformation: The Music of Subatomic Physics
(D) Trends in Physics Research: Eliminating the Quark
(E) The Impossible Dream: Obstacles to Proving the Existence of
Matter

2. The author of Passage 1 refers to quarks, squarks, and charms (paragraph 2) primarily in order to

(A) demonstrate the similarity between these particles and earlier
images of the atom
(B) make a distinction between appropriate and inappropriate terms
(C) object to suggestions of similar frivolous names
(D) provide examples of idiosyncratic nomenclature in contemporary
physics
(E) cite preliminary experimental evidence supporting the existence of
subatomic matter

3. The author's tone in the second paragraph of Passage 1 can best be described as one of

   (A) scientific detachment
   (B) moderate indignation
   (C) marked derision
   (D) admiring wonder
   (E) qualified skepticism

4. "Matter's heart" mentioned in lines 28–29 is

   (A) outer space
   (B) the subatomic world
   (C) the language of particle physics
   (D) harmonic theory
   (E) flesh and blood

5. In line 38, the image of the snake biting its tail is used to emphasize

   (A) the dangers of circular reasoning
   (B) the vigor inherent in modern scientific dialogue
   (C) the eventual triumph of the classical idea of matter
   (D) the unity underlying the astronomers' and particle physicists' theories
   (E) the ability of contemporary scientific doctrine to swallow earlier theories

6. The word "properties" in line 68 most nearly means

   (A) lands   (B) titles   (C) investments
    (D) civilities   (E) characteristics

7. Glashow's comment in lines 77–79 reflects his

   (A) apprehension
   (B) impatience
   (C) imagination
   (D) jubilation
   (E) spirituality

8. The references to the "keystone" of the arch (lines 83–84) serve to

   (A) diminish the top quark's status to that of a commodity
   (B) provide an accurate physical description of the elusive particle
   (C) highlight the contrast between appearance and reality
   (D) give an approximation of the top quark's actual mass
   (E) illustrate the importance of the top quark to subatomic theory

9. The word "hinged" (line 82) most nearly means

   (A) folded   (B) vanished   (C) remarked
    (D) depended   (E) weighed

10. The author of Passage 2 does all of the following EXCEPT

    (A) cite an authority
    (B) use a simile
    (C) define a term
    (D) pose a question
    (E) deny a possibility

11. The author of Passage 2 mentions the gold atom (lines 93–95) primarily to

    (A) clarify the monetary value of the top quark
    (B) explain what is meant by atomic weight
    (C) illustrate how hefty a top quark is compared to other particles
    (D) suggest the sorts of elements studied in high-energy accelerators
    (E) demonstrate the malleability of gold as an element

12. As Passage 2 suggests, since the time Passage 1 was written, the Standard Model has

    (A) determined even more whimsical names for the subatomic particles under discussion
    (B) taken into account the confusion of the particle physicists
    (C) found theoretical validation through recent experiments
    (D) refuted significant aspects of the Big Bang theory of the formation of the universe
    (E) collapsed for lack of proof of the existence of top quarks

13. The author of Passage 2 would most likely react to the characterization of the constituents of matter in lines 25–30 by pointing out that

    (A) this characterization has been refuted by prominent physicists
    (B) the characterization is too fanciful to be worthwhile
    (C) the most recent data on subatomic particles support this characterization
    (D) this characterization supersedes the so-called Standard Model
    (E) the current theoretical synthesis is founded on this characterization

---

YOU MAY GO BACK AND REVIEW THIS
SECTION IN THE REMAINING TIME, BUT   **S T O P**
DO NOT WORK IN ANY OTHER SECTION
UNTIL TOLD TO DO SO.

SECTION 6

10 Questions—15 Minutes

For each problem in this section determine which of the five choices is correct and blacken in that choice on your answer sheet. You may use any blank space on the page for your work.

Notes:

- You may use a calculator whenever you feel it will be helpful.
- Use the diagrams provided to help you solve the problems. Unless you see the words "<u>Note</u>: Figure not drawn to scale" under a diagram, it has been drawn as accurately as possible. Unless it is stated that a figure is three-dimensional, you may assume it lies in a plane.

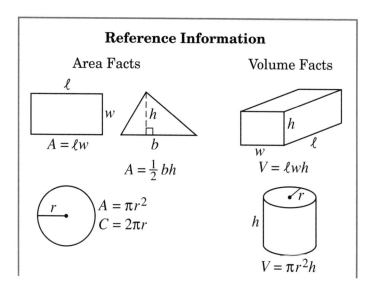

Reference Information

Area Facts

$A = \ell w$

$A = \frac{1}{2} bh$

$A = \pi r^2$
$C = 2\pi r$

Volume Facts

$V = \ell wh$

$V = \pi r^2 h$

Triangle Facts	Angle Facts
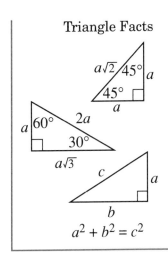	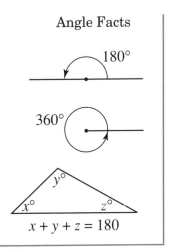
$a^2 + b^2 = c^2$	$x + y + z = 180$

1. If $\dfrac{1}{a} + \dfrac{1}{a} + \dfrac{1}{a} = 12$, then $a =$

(A) $\dfrac{1}{12}$ (B) $\dfrac{1}{4}$ (C) $\dfrac{1}{3}$ (D) 3   (E) 4

---

2. What is the value of $2x^2 - 3x - 7$ when $x = -5$?

(A) 28   (B) 42   (C) 58   (D) 78   (E) 108

<u>Questions 3–4</u> refer to the information in the following bar graph, which shows the number of books read in January 1995 by the five members of a book club.

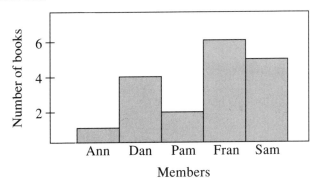

3. What was the total number of books read in January 1995 by the members of the club?

(A) 14   (B) 15   (C) 16   (D) 17   (E) 18

---

4. What percent of the members read more books than the average (arithmetic mean) number of books read?

(A) 20%   (B) 40%   (C) 50%   (D) 60%   (E) 80%

---

5. What is the diameter of a circle whose area is A?

(A) $2\sqrt{\dfrac{A}{\pi}}$ (B) $\sqrt{\dfrac{A}{\pi}}$ (C) $\dfrac{A}{2\pi}$ (D) $\dfrac{A}{\pi}$

(E) $\dfrac{2\sqrt{A}}{\pi}$

---

6. Laurie inherited 40% of her father's estate. After paying a tax equal to 30% of her inheritance, what percent of her father's estate did she own?

(A) 10%   (B) 12%   (C) 25%   (D) 28%   (E) 30%

---

7. What is the value of a if a is positive and $a \times a \times a = a + a + a$?

(A) $\dfrac{1}{3}$ (B) $\sqrt{3}$ (C) 3   (D) $3\sqrt{3}$ (E) 9

---

8. What is the volume of a cube whose surface area is 60?

(A) $10\sqrt{10}$ (B) $15\sqrt{15}$ (C) $60\sqrt{60}$

(D) 1000   (E) 3375

9. If the circumference of circle I is equal to the diameter of circle II, what is the ratio of the area of circle II to the area of circle I?

(A) $\dfrac{1}{\pi^2}$ (B) $\sqrt{\pi}$ (C) π (D) π^2 (E) $4\pi^2$

---

10. If A is 25 kilometers east of B, which is 12 kilometers south of C, which is 9 kilometers west of D, how far, in kilometers, is A from D?

(A) 20   (B) $5\sqrt{34}$ (C) $5\sqrt{41}$ (D) $10\sqrt{13}$ (E) 71

YOU MAY GO BACK AND REVIEW THIS
SECTION IN THE REMAINING TIME, BUT   **S T O P**
DO NOT WORK IN ANY OTHER SECTION
UNTIL TOLD TO DO SO.

Answer Key

Section 1   Verbal Reasoning

1. C	7. C	13. D	19. D	25. B
2. C	8. B	14. A	20. A	26. E
3. D	9. B	15. B	21. C	27. C
4. E	10. D	16. C	22. C	28. E
5. D	11. E	17. B	23. D	29. D
6. E	12. B	18. D	24. E	30. A

Section 2   Mathematical Reasoning

1. A	6. D	11. D	16. E	21. E
2. C	7. C	12. E	17. A	22. E
3. D	8. B	13. D	18. A	23. A
4. A	9. B	14. E	19. B	24. A
5. D	10. C	15. B	20. C	25. B

Section 3   Verbal Reasoning

1. D	8. A	15. B	22. C	29. E
2. C	9. B	16. E	23. D	30. C
3. D	10. C	17. C	24. E	31. A
4. C	11. E	18. C	25. A	32. E
5. E	12. D	19. D	26. B	33. B
6. D	13. D	20. B	27. B	34. D
7. B	14. D	21. A	28. A	35. C

Section 4   Mathematical Reasoning

1. A	4. A	7. A	10. C	13. A
2. D	5. A	8. D	11. D	14. C
3. D	6. A	9. B	12. C	15. B

Grid-in Questions

16.

```
      9 | 8
```

17.

```
    7 . 5
```

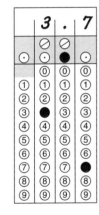

18.

```
  7 . 5
```

19.

```
  3 . 7
```

20.

```
  1 4 5
```

21.

```
  1 . 2 1
```

22.

23.

24.

25.

or .333

Section 5   Verbal Reasoning

1. **C**	4. **B**	7. **B**	10. **E**	13. **B**
2. **D**	5. **D**	8. **E**	11. **C**	
3. **D**	6. **E**	9. **D**	12. **C**	

Section 6   Mathematical Reasoning

1. **B**	3. **E**	5. **A**	7. **B**	9. **D**
2. **C**	4. **D**	6. **D**	8. **A**	10. **A**

Answer Explanations

Section 1   Verbal Reasoning

1. **(C)** If one is alert and insightful, one's faculties (mental powers) are *intact* (sound or whole).
   Note how the phrase set off by the comma restates and clarifies the idea that Picasso has continued to be perceptive and alert.
   (Contrast Signal)

2. **(C)** *While* suggests a contrast between the fates of the two dance forms during the 1940s. The decade was *most* noted for the growth of Black modern dance. However, it was also noteworthy or *significant* for the decline of tap dancing.   (Contrast Signal)

3. **(D)** Something beneficial or helpful in small amounts may be *toxic* (poisonous) in large amounts.
   Remember to watch for signal words that link one part of the sentence to another. The use of "though" in the second clause sets up a contrast. The missing word must be an antonym or near-antonym for beneficial.   (Argument Pattern)

4. **(E)** The encroachments or trespassing of human beings on the hawk's territory would frighten the birds, leading them to *shun* or avoid their usual locations for breeding. Frightened away from their nests, disturbed in their breeding routines, the hawks would have fewer offspring. Thus, their numbers would diminish or *dwindle*.
   You can immediately eliminate Choices A, B, and C. Choices A and C you can rule out on the basis of general knowledge: when humans come close, wild birds abandon their nests (and their eggs): they have fewer offspring. Choice B you can rule out on the basis of usage. People may *extrapolate* or make projections on the basis of known data about the number of hawks. The "number of black hawks," however, doesn't extrapolate anything.
   (Argument Pattern)

5. **(D)** To aim at a mass market is to try to appeal to the lowest common denominator. British films rarely do this. Instead of trying to appeal to the masses, they try to appeal to the elite. They are thus *elitist*.   (Contrast Signal)

6. **(E)** The key phrase here is "worth the trouble." What sort of person creates trouble for his employers? Not a *congenial* (agreeable) or *popular* one. You can immediately eliminate Choices B and C. A *cantankerous* (bad-tempered) employee creates problems. However, if he turns in *meticulous* (very careful and exact) work, his employers may think he's worth the trouble he makes.

    Note that, after eliminating the answer choices whose first word does not work in the sentence, you must check the second words of the remaining answer choices. A *domineering* (bossy) or *fastidious* (fussy) employee might create problems around the newspaper office. However, he would not get on his employers' good side by turning in *wearisome* (boring) or *garbled* (confused) stories.   (Argument)

7. **(C)** Because the opossum is *impervious* to (unharmed by) the poison, it can treat the rattlesnake as a potential source of food and not as a *lethal* or deadly enemy.

    Note the cause and effect signal "thus." The nature of the opossum's response to the venom explains *why* it can look on a dangerous snake as an easy prey.   (Cause and Effect Signal)

8. **(B)** By definition, someone who breaks with established convention is *iconoclastic* or nonconformist. Go through the answer choices, eliminating anything you can.

    Choices A and E are incorrect. Someone who departs from tradition is unlikely to be *derivative* (lacking originality) or *trite* (commonplace; timeworn).

    Choices C and D are incorrect. Someone who infuriates (enrages) the traditionalists is controversial, not *uncontroversial*, and is unlikely to be *venerated* (deeply respected) by them. This is one of the last sentence completion questions, so its answer is an extremely difficult word.   (Definition Pattern)

9. **(B)** If the code did not exist until 1846, it could not have been *rescinded* (canceled), *presupposed* (required as an already existing condition), or *depreciated* (disparaged) at that time. It makes most sense that the code was *promulgated* or made known to the public by the A.M.A. at that time.   (Definition)

10. **(D)** A *dog* is a *mammal*; a *snake*, a *reptile*.   (Member and Class)

11. **(E)** A *teller's* working place is a *bank*; a *teacher's*, a *school*.
                                    (Worker and Workplace)

12. (B) A *visionary* (dreamer) is not *practical*; a *braggart* (boaster) is not *modest*.   (Antonym Variant)

13. (D) What is *disobedience* in a *child* is *insubordination* in a *soldier*.
                                          (Defining Characteristic)

14. (A) A *tumbler* is a container for *beverages*; a *quiver* is a container for *arrows*.
Consider secondary meanings of the capitalized words as well as their primary meanings. Here a *tumbler* is a stemless drinking glass, not an acrobat.   (Definition)

15. (B) A *mayfly* is known to be *ephemeral* (short-lived); a *gazelle* is known to be *graceful*.   (Defining Characteristic)

16. (C) According to the author, "We have been taught to believe that our lives are better than the lives of those who came before us" and the lives of those today who live in similarly "primitive" circumstances. We base our belief that we Americans are well off today on the assumption that people in earlier generations and people living in "primitive" circumstances have an *inferior standard of living*.

17. (B) The conventional wisdom is that the lives of primitive peoples are filled with toil. The author, however, states that primitives do little work. Thus, she regards the conventional wisdom with *skepticism* or doubt.

18. (D) According to the author, these "stone age peoples" have limited desires. They are not motivated by any particular *desire for consumer goods* or other material comforts.

19. (D) To raise an issue is to bring it up for discussion.

20. (A) Throughout the passage the author *disputes the assumption* made by the conventional wisdom that our economic progress has been an unmitigated blessing. She argues instead that we "have paid a price for prosperity."

21. (C) The author makes an assertion: "We are eating more." She then qualifies or limits her assertion: "but we are burning up those calories at work." She repeats this pattern of assertion followed by qualification. She then draws her conclusion: it is hard to support the conventional wisdom that economic progress has been an unmixed blessing for us.

22. **(C)** The author provides the reader both with physical details of dress and bearing and with comments about the motives and emotions of the Cardinal and Bosola.
Choice A is incorrect. The passage scarcely mentions the church. Choice B is incorrect. The description of ecclesiastical costumes is only one item in the description of the Cardinal. Choice D is incorrect. While audiences today might well enjoy seeing the characters acted as described here, the author does not cite specific reasons why the play might appeal to modern audiences. Choice E is incorrect. The author's purpose is to describe two separate roles, not to compare two interpretations of a single role.

23. **(D)** "Spare" is being used to describe the Cardinal's physical appearance. He is tall and *lean*.

24. **(E)** The eagle is poised to strike "with exposed talons." It, like the Cardinal, gathers itself together to strike with greater force. The imagery suggests the Cardinal's *mercilessness*.
Choice A is incorrect. The Cardinal is not *flighty* (light-headed and irresponsible); he is cold and calculating. Choice B is incorrect. He loves power, not freedom. Choice C is incorrect. An eagle poised to strike with bare claws suggests violence, not *eminence* (fame and high position). Choice D is incorrect. Nothing in the passage suggests he is spiritual.
Beware of eye-catchers. "Eminence" is a title of honor applied to cardinals in the Roman Catholic Church. Choice C may attract you for this reason.

25. **(B)** The Cardinal glories in his place in the hierarchy of the Church: his *rank* or status as an ecclesiastical lord.

26. **(E)** Although Bosola is not a "leather-jacketed" hoodlum, he is a hired "assassin," a "hangman" (despite his scholarly taste and humanist disposition).

27. **(C)** Answer this question by using the process of elimination.
Choice A is incorrect. In describing Bosola the author makes no use of *rhetorical questions* (questions asked solely to produce an effect).
Choice B is incorrect. Though the author makes many assertions about Bosola, he limits or *qualifies* many of them. For example,

the author asserts that Bosola "is inwardly tormented." He then immediately qualifies his assertion, adding "but not by undiluted passion." Thus, the author does not chiefly use *unqualified assertions* in describing Bosola.

Choice D is incorrect. *Dramatic irony* is irony built in to a speech or a situation, which the audience understands, but which the characters onstage have yet to grasp. The author does not use this literary technique in describing Bosola.

Choice E is incorrect. The author makes one brief literary allusion (to Browning's verse monologues). He does not chiefly use *literary allusions* in describing Bosola.

Only Choice C is left. It is the correct answer. Throughout the passage's final paragraph, the author describes Bosola through *comparisons* ("Like his black-and-white clothes," "Like Duke Ferdinand") and *contrasts* ("not . . . a leather-jacketed, heavy-booted tough," "Still less . . . a sneering, leering melodramatic villain").

28. (E) The author is contrasting the two sides of Bosola, the scholar and the assassin. As a scholar, he is a man of perceptive intellect, noted for discrimination or *discernment.*

29. (D) Lines 50–54 state that Bosola "is inwardly tormented ... (by) disgust at a world filled with knavery and folly, ... in which he must play a part and that a lowly, despicable one." The villainy and foolishness around him disgust him. He feels intellectually superior to the evil around him, *yet must act the villain himself.*

30. (A) The casual references to the elongated hands and features of El Greco's work and to the trim beards and commanding stances in the work of Van Dyke imply that the author assumes the reader has seen examples of both painters' art.

Section 2   Mathematical Reasoning

In each mathematics section, for some problems, an alternative solution, indicated by two asterisks (**), follows the first solution. When this occurs, one of the solutions is the direct mathematical one and the other is based on one of the tactics discussed in Chapter 5.

1. (A) If $2x + 4x + 6x = -12$, then $12x = -12$ and $x = -1$.
   **Note that x *must* be negative, so only A and B are possible. Test these choices.

2. **(C)** The left-hand side of $(w + 12) - 12 = 12$ is just w, so $w = $ **12**. **Of course, you can use TACTIC 10: backsolve, starting (and ending) with C.

3. **(D)** The average is just the sum of the number of students in the five classes (125) divided by 5: $125 \div 5 = $ **25**.

4. **(A)** In class **A**, one-fourth, or 25% (5 of 20), of the students are in the band. In each of the other classes, the number in the band is *less than* one-fourth of the class.

5. **(D)** Use your calculator: $1.1 \times 1.9 = 2.09$, which, to the nearest tenth, is **2.1**.

6. **(D)** Since *ABCD* is a square, $y = 90$.
Then $x + 90 + 40 = 180 \Rightarrow x = 50$.
But $x = z$ (vertical angles have equal measures) and $z = w$ [when parallel lines are cut by a transversal, the four acute angles have the same measure.] Therefore $w = $ **50**.
**Use TACTIC 2: trust the diagram; *w* appears to be slightly more than a 45° angle.

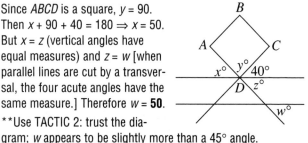

7. **(C)** If 24 of the students are girls, then $40 - 24 = 16$ are boys. The ratio of boys to girls is 16:24 which reduces to **2:3**.

8. **(B)** Since 50% of the trip was completed on Monday and 10% of the trip is left, the 100 kilometers traveled on Tuesday represents the other 40% of the total distance, d, so
$$0.40d = 100 \Rightarrow d = 100 \div 0.40 = \textbf{250}.$$
Estimate. Since half of the trip was completed Monday, the 100 kilometers traveled on Tuesday plus the 10% still to go constitutes the other half. The 100 kilometers by itself is slightly less than half, and 200 kilometers would be slightly less than the whole distance. Of the choices, only **250 is possible.

9. **(B)** There are nine positive integers less than 10:

1, 2, ... , 9. For which of them is $\frac{9}{x} > x$? Only 1 and 2: $\frac{9}{1} > 1$

and $\frac{9}{2} > 2$. When $x = 3$, $\frac{9}{x} = x$, and for all the others

$\frac{9}{x} < x$. The probability is $\frac{2}{9}$.

10. **(C)** Let n represent the number of members of the club before Jean joined. These members raised a total of $85n$ dollars. After Jean was in the club, the total raised was $85n + 50$, the average was 80, and the number of members was $n + 1$:

$$\frac{85n + 50}{n + 1} = 80$$

Cross-multiply: $85n + 50 = 80(n + 1)$
Distribute: $85n + 50 = 80n + 80$
Subtract $80n$ and 50
from each side $5n = 30$
Divide by 5: $n = \mathbf{6}$

**Use TACTIC 10: backsolve. Try 6, choice C. If there were 6 members, the total raised would be $6 \times 85 = 510$. Now add Jean's 50 and the total goes to 560 for 7 members; and $560 \div 7 = 80$. It works!

11. **(D)** Draw pictures. R, S, T *could be* the vertices of a right triangle (I is true.) R, S, T *could not be* the vertices of a square: $RT = \sqrt{2}\ RS$.

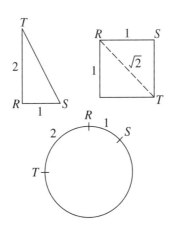

(II is false.) *R, S, T could* all lie on a circle. In fact, the only way they couldn't would be if they all were on the same line. (III is true.) Statements **I and II only** are true.

12. **(E)** Use TACTIC 12: plug in easy-to-use numbers. If a CD regularly costs $10, then on sale at 50% off, they cost $5 each. How many can be purchased on sale for $20? The answer is 4. Which of the choices equals 4 when $d = 10$ and $m = 20$?

Only $\dfrac{2m}{d}$

13. **(D)** Since the game takes 1 hour, or 60 minutes, and there are always 5 men playing, there is a total of $5 \times 60 = 300$ man-minutes of playing time. If that amount of time is evenly divided among the 12 players, each one plays $300 \div 12 =$ **25** minutes.

14. **(E)** When A ounces of water are removed from pitcher II, that pitcher will contain $B - A$ ounces. Since its capacity is B,

pitcher II will be $\dfrac{B-A}{B}$ full.

**Use TACTIC 12: plug in easy-to-use numbers. Suppose pitcher II holds 10 ounces and pitcher I holds 3. Then, if 3 ounces are poured from pitcher II into pitcher I, pitcher II will

have 7 ounces and be $\dfrac{7}{10}$ full. Which of the choices equals

$\dfrac{7}{10}$ when $B = 10$ and $A = 3$? Only $\dfrac{B-A}{B}$.

15. **(B)** In $\triangle ABC$, $w + x + 40 = 180 \Rightarrow w + x = 140$. Similarly, in $\triangle ADE$, $y + z + 40 = 180 \Rightarrow y + z = 140$.
Then $w + x + y + z = 140 + 140 =$ **280**.

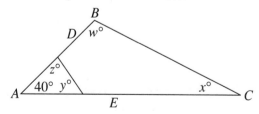

16. (E) The sum of 2 two-digit numbers must be less than 200, so $A = 1$ and the sum is 111. Since B and D are positive, $B + D$ cannot be 1, and so must be 11, which means that a 1 is carried into the tens column. In the tens column we must add 1 (for A), the 1 we carried, and C, and the sum is 11. Then $1 + 1 + C = 11$, and $C = \mathbf{9}$.

$$\begin{array}{r} 1\,B \\ +\ CD \\ \hline 1\,1\,1 \end{array}$$

B, D can be any digits whose sum is 11.

$C = 9$

17. (A) Use TACTIC 13: when you have more than two equations, add them.

$$\begin{array}{r} x + y = 10 \\ y + z = 15 \\ +\ x + z = 17 \\ \hline 2x + 2y + 2z = 42 \end{array}$$

Divide by 2: $x + y + z = 21$

To get the average, divide the sum by 3:

$$\frac{x+y+z}{3} = \frac{21}{3} = \mathbf{7}$$

18. (A) Let x = the number of passengers originally on the bus, and keep track of the comings and goings. At the first stop half the people got off, leaving $\frac{1}{2}x$ on the bus, and 1 more got on: $\frac{1}{2}x + 1$. At the second stop $\frac{1}{3}$ of the passengers got off, leaving two-thirds on the bus, and 1 person got on: $\frac{2}{3}\left(\frac{1}{2}x + 1\right) + 1$. This simplifies to $\frac{1}{3}x + \frac{2}{3} + 1$, which equals 15, so $\frac{1}{3}x + \frac{2}{3} = 14 \Rightarrow x + 2 = 42 \Rightarrow x = \mathbf{40}$.

**Use TACTIC 9: backsolve. Start with C, 58: 29 got off and 1 got on; then there were 30; 10 got off and 1 got on; then there were 21, but we should have only 15. Since 58 is too big, eliminate C, D, and E. Try A or B; A works.

19. (B) Since Peter walked 6 miles at a rate of 4 miles per hour, it took him $1\frac{1}{2}$ or $\frac{3}{2}$ hours. Since Wendy walked 4 miles in the same time, she was walking at a rate of

$$4 \div \frac{3}{2} = 4 \times \frac{2}{3} = \frac{8}{3} = 2\frac{2}{3} \text{ miles per hour.}$$

20. (C) According to the triangle inequality, the sum of the lengths of two sides of a triangle must be greater than the length of the third side. There is only one way to pick a number, a, from A and a number, b, from B so that their sum is greater than 7: $a = 3$ and $b = 5$. There are three ways to choose a and b so that their sum is greater than 6: $a = 2$ and $b = 5$; $a = 3$ and $b = 4$; and $a = 3$ and $b = 5$. So in all there are **4** ways to pick the lengths of the three sides.

21. (E) If $3a = 4b = 5c$, then $a = \frac{5}{3}c$ and $b = \frac{5}{4}c$, so

$$a + b = \left(\frac{5}{3} + \frac{5}{4}\right)c = \frac{35}{12}c. \text{ Then } k = \frac{35}{12}.$$

**Use TACTIC 11: plug in easy-to-use numbers. The factors 3, 4, 5 suggest the number 60. Let $a = 20$, $b = 15$, $c = 12$.

Then $a + b = 35$, so $35 = 12k \Rightarrow k = \dfrac{35}{12}$.

22. (E) In $\triangle ABC$, $\angle B$ measures 80°, so $a + c = 80$ and $c = 80 - a$. (I is true.) Since the measure of an exterior angle of a triangle equals the sum of the measures of the two opposite interior angles, $b = c + 50 \Rightarrow c = b - 50$. (II is true.) Since $a + b = 130$ and $c + d = 130$, then $a + b = c + d$. (III is true.) Statements **I, II, and III** are true.

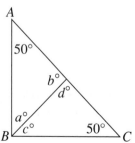

23. (A) Use TACTIC 11: plug in easy-to-use numbers. If 2 carpenters can build a garage in 10 days, they will take 20 days to build 2 garages. It will take 4 carpenters half as long: 10 days. Which choice is equal to 10 when $c = 2$, $d = 10$, and $e = 4$? Only $\dfrac{2cd}{e}$. Remember: test each choice with your calculator, and eliminate a choice as soon as you can see that it is not equal to 10.

24. (A) This question is easier than it seems at first. In each fraction, the numerator is the negative of the denominator, so each fraction equals –1 and the sum of the fractions is **–2**.

**Of course, you can use TACTIC 11: plug in numbers. If $a = 1$ and $b = 2$, then each fraction is equal to –1.

25. (B) Here $A = 5\pi r^2$ and $B = 3\pi s^2$, so

$$5\pi r^2 = 3\pi s^2$$

Divide both sides by π:

$$5\ r^2 = 3s^2$$

Divide both sides by $5s^2$:

$$\frac{r^2}{s^2} = \frac{3}{5}$$

Take the square root of each side:

$$\frac{r}{s} = \frac{\sqrt{3}}{\sqrt{5}}.$$

Section 3   Verbal Reasoning

1. (D) The critics would regret any lapse on the part of a *promising* writer.

The adjective *glowing* is your clue that you are looking for a word with positive associations. Therefore, you can eliminate any word with negative ones. Choices A, B, and C have negative associations. Only Choices D or E can be correct.

(Cause and Effect Pattern)

2. (C) To be the subject of a major exhibition would surely *rescue* a forgotten artist from obscurity (the state of being unknown).

(Cause and Effect Pattern)

3. (D) If we see things in a distorted or altered fashion, our testimony is *unreliable*.

Note how the second clause serves to clarify or define the meaning of the missing word.

Remember, before you look at the choices, read the sentence and think of a word that makes sense.

Likely Words: undependable, misleading.   (Definition)

4. (C) A longing for old friends and familiar scenes is *nostalgia* or home-sickness.
Remember, before you look at the choices, read the sentence and think of a word that makes sense.
Likely Words: homesickness, nostalgia, yearning.   (Definition)

5. (E) Borrowers would complain that an old, *appreciated* borrowing policy had been set aside or *superseded*.
Remember, in double-blank sentences, go through the answer choices, testing the *first* words in each choice and eliminating those that don't fit. The fact that the new policy has received complaints indicates that the old policy was viewed positively. You can immediately eliminate Choice B, *disliked*, and Choice D, *ignored*. Both are negative terms.   (Contrast Pattern)

6. (D) People who shut themselves away from society are, by definition, hermits or *recluses*.   (Definition)

7. (B) Heroic virtues include *disregard* or ignoring of death and *fortitude* or courage in the face of torture. Through it all, Bond remains nonchalant or cool.   (Examples)

8. (A) *Even though* signals a contrast. The brain's fundamental organization does not change. However, the details of the brain's organization do change: they remain *plastic*, pliable, capable of being molded or shaped.   (Contrast Signal)

9. (B) The key phrase here is "in a few words." Although the movie is lavish in its beauty, it is not lavish in its use of words or film. Instead, it demonstrates *economy* of style.   (Definition)

10. (C) The Romantic poets can be described as *emotional*; Arnold and the later "moralizing" Victorian era poets can be described as *didactic* (interested in teaching).
Remember to watch for signal words that link one part of the sentence to another. The use of "unlike" in the opening clause sets up a contrast. The missing words must be antonyms or near-antonyms. You can immediately eliminate Choices A and B as synonyms or near-synonym pairs.   (Contrast Signal)

11. (E) A *typewriter* is a tool used by a *journalist*; a pair of *pliers* is a tool used by an *electrician*.   (Worker and Tool)

12. (D) The meat of a *sheep* is called *mutton*; the meat of a *steer* is called *beef*.   (Definition)

13. (D) An *entry* is one day's record that is part of a *diary*; an *episode* is one separate performance that is part of a *serial*.
                                                                                (Part to Whole)

14. (D) A *mural* (wall painting) is painted on a *wall*; an *etching* is imprinted on *paper*.   (Defining Characteristic)

15. (B) A *libretto* (the words of an opera or musical play) is written by an *author*; the *score* (musical arrangement), by a *composer*.
                                                                                (Worker and Creation)

16. (E) To restrict the movements of a *horse*, a *tether* is used. To restrict those of a *prisoner*, *shackles* are used.   (Function)

17. (C) A *blind* person suffers from a loss of *sight*. Similarly, an *amnesiac* suffers from a loss of *memory*.   (Antonym Variant)

18. (C) *Peckish* (slightly hungry) is less extreme a condition than *starving*. *Plain* (homely, unattractive) is less extreme a condition than *hideous* (extremely ugly).   (Degree of Intensity)

19. (D) A *poet* writes or creates an *ode* (lyric poem); a *seamstress* sews or creates a *gown*.   (Worker and Creation)

20. (B) The symbol of *time* is a bearded man carrying a *scythe*; the symbol of *justice* is a blindfolded woman carrying a *scale*.
                                                            (Symbol and the Abstraction It Represents)

21. (A) A *virtuoso* (expert performer) is by definition *experienced*; a *rogue* (scoundrel) is by definition *knavish*.   (Synonym Variant)

22. (C) Something *caustic* (biting; corrosive) by definition *corrodes* (eats away); something *hypnotic* (tending to induce a sleep-like trance) by definition *mesmerizes* (hypnotizes).   (Definition)

23. (D) A *carapace* (hard case) protects a *turtle*; a *shell* protects a *snail*.   (Function)

24. (E) Substitute the answer choices in the original sentence. The sergeant is a person who might have been a deputy sheriff before he joined the army—that is, in his civil or *nonmilitary* life.

25. (A) Paragraph 1 presents a general picture of the man on the bridge, the executioners and the officer standing nearby, the sentinels at the far ends of the bridge. Cinematically, it is like *a wide-angle shot* of the whole panorama. Paragraph 2 takes a closer look at the man, examining his clothes, his face, his expression. It is as if the camera has moved in for a *close-up* shot.

26. (B) The author's comment that the man "had a kindly expression that one would hardly have expected in one whose neck was in the hemp" suggests that he is an *unlikely candidate for execution* and that some unusual circumstances must have brought him to this fate.

27. (B) In calling the military code "liberal" because it doesn't exclude members of the upper classes from being executed, the author is being highly *ironic.* Generally, people would like regulations to be interpreted liberally to permit them to do the things they want. Here, the liberal military code is permitting the man to be hanged. Clearly, the gentleman facing execution would have preferred the code to be less liberal in this case.

28. (A) Farquhar agrees readily with the saying that all is fair in love and war. This implies he is willing to use underhanded or unfair methods to support the Southern cause.

29. (E) Farquhar has no objection to performing humble errands or undertaking dangerous tasks as long as these tasks are appropriate to someone who sees himself as a sort of "undercover soldier," a secret agent of the Confederacy. Anything he does must be consistent or *compatible* with his image of himself in this role.

30. (C) At heart a soldier, Farquhar fundamentally agrees that all's fair in war. He doesn't particularly qualify or restrict his commitment to this viewpoint: he's ready to go out and do something underhanded for his cause without much *restriction* as to what he's willing to do.

31. (A) Mrs. Farquhar's readiness to fetch water for the gray-clad Confederate soldier suggests some degree of sympathy on her part for the Confederate cause.
Choices B and D are incorrect. There is nothing in the passage to suggest either of them. Choices C and E are incorrect. Mrs. Farquhar's action, in hospitably fetching water "with her own white hands," contradicts them.

32. **(E)** Earlier in the passage, Farquhar is described as frustrated by "the inglorious restraint" preventing his serving the Southern cause. He sees the life of the soldier as larger than that of the civilian, a life filled with opportunities for distinction, for renown. Thus, when he speaks about someone managing to sneak past the guards and accomplishing something for the cause, he is *envisioning himself as a hero*.

33. **(B)** Farquhar wishes to prevent the Yankee advance. To do so, he must somehow damage the railroad, its bridges, its tunnels, or its trains. The soldier tells him that some highly flammable driftwood is piled up at the base of the wooden railroad bridge. Clearly, it would make sense for Farquhar to try to set fire to the driftwood in order to destroy the bridge.

34. **(D)** The phrase "burn like tow" and the reference to dry driftwood suggest that tow will catch fire readily. Remember, when asked to give the meaning of an unfamiliar word, to look for nearby context clues.

35. **(C)** The scout is a Yankee soldier disguised as a member of the enemy. By coming to the Farquhars' plantation in Confederate disguise, he is able to learn they are sympathetic to the enemy. By telling Farquhar of the work on the bridge, stressing both the lack of guards and the abundance of fuel, he is tempting Farquhar into an attack on the bridge (and into an ambush). The scout's job is to locate potential enemies and draw them out from cover.

Section 4 Mathematical Reasoning

Quantitative Comparison Questions

1. **(A)** Column A is positive, and Column B is negative. Remember PEMDAS: $(-7)^4 = (-7)(-7)(-7)(-7)$, whereas $-7^4 = -(7)(7)(7)(7)$. Column A is greater.

2. **(D)** Since $\frac{2}{3} = 66\frac{2}{3}$ %, which is clearly more than 65%, it *appears* that Column B is greater. *Be careful*! That would be true if *a* were positive, but no restrictions are placed on *a*. If $a = 0$, the columns are equal; if *a* is negative, Column A is greater. Neither column is *always* greater, and the columns are not *always* equal (D).

   **Use TACTIC 15. Just let $a = 0$, and then let $a = 1$.

3. (D) If the number picked from B is 4 or 5, it will be greater than any number picked from A. If, however, the numbers picked from A and B are both 3, the columns are equal. Neither column is *always* greater, and the columns are not *always* equal. (D).

4. (A) Since (a,b) is on the positive portion of the x-axis, a is positive and $b = 0$, so $a + b$ is positive. Also, since (c,d) is on the negative portion of the y-axis, c is negative and $d = 0$, so $c + d$ is negative. Column A is greater.

5. (A) It looks as though the columns *may* be equal (without the .6 in each percent they would be), but don't chance it. Use your calculator and multiply. Column A: $.176 \times 83 = 14.608$. Column B: $.836 \times 17 = 14.212$. Column A is greater.

6. (A) Use TACTIC 17.

Column A	Column B
a^3b	ab^3

Since a and b are positive, divide each column by ab:

$$\frac{a^3b}{ab} = a^2 \qquad \frac{ab^3}{ab} = b^2$$

Take the square root of each side: a b

Since it is given that $a > b$, Column A is greater.

**Use TACTIC 15: plug in numbers. If $a = 2$ and $b = 1$, Column A is 8 and Column B is 2, so eliminate B and C. Try some other numbers. A is always greater.

7. (A) Since a is negative, a^5 is negative, whereas a^6 is positive. Column A is greater.

8. (D) *Be careful!* It is *not* given that x and y are integers; $x = 1$, $y = 10$ and $x = 2$, $y = 5$ are not the only values of x and y satisfying the conditions. In these cases, x is less than 3, so Column B is greater. But $x = 3$, $y = \frac{10}{3}$ also satisfies the conditions, and in this case the columns are equal. Neither column is *always* greater, and the columns are not *always* equal (D).

**Use TACTIC 18. Could $x = 3$? Yes. Must $x = 3$? No. (See above.)

9. (B) Use b, c, and t for "beeps," "clicks," and "tweets," respectively. Then the given equations are: $3b = 2c$ and $4b = 5t$

Multiply the first equation by 4 and the second by 3: $12b = 8c$ and $12b = 15t$

Then $8c = 15t \Rightarrow c = \dfrac{15}{8}t < 2t$, so 1 click is less than 2 tweets.

Column B is greater.

10. (C) Since $ab = 0$, either a or b is 0. If $a = 0$, each column is b^2, whereas if $b = 0$, each column is a^2. Either way, the columns are equal (C).

11. (D) Use TACTIC 15: replace the variable with a number. Let $a = 1$. Then Column A is the average of 1, 2, and –1:

$\dfrac{1+2+(-1)}{3} = \dfrac{2}{3}$, and Column B is the average of –1, –2,

and 1: $\dfrac{(-1)+(-2)+1}{3} = -\dfrac{2}{3}$. In this case Column A is

greater, so eliminate B and C. Let $a = 10$. Now Column A is

$\dfrac{1+2+(-10)}{3} = -\dfrac{7}{3}$, whereas Column B is

$\dfrac{(-1)+(-2)+10}{3} = \dfrac{7}{3}$. This time B is greater. Neither

column is *always* greater, and the columns are not *always* equal (D).

12. (C) Since $6^2 + 8^2 = 10^2$ (36 + 64 = 100), the triangle, despite its appearance, is a right triangle and $s = 90$. Also, in a right triangle the sum of the measures of the two acute angles is 90°, so $r + t = 90$. The columns are equal (C).

13. (A) Column A: the area of a square of side a is a^2. Column B:

since the diameter of the circle is a, the radius is $\dfrac{1}{2}a$. Then,

the area of the circle is $\pi\left(\dfrac{1}{2}a\right)^2 = \dfrac{\pi}{4}a^2$, which is less than

a^2, since $\dfrac{\pi}{4} < 1$. Column A is greater.

14. (C) Draw a diagram, and on each small cube write the number of red faces it has. The cubes with three red faces are the eight corners. The cubes with no red faces are the "inside" ones that can't be seen. If you cut off the top and bottom

3	2	2	3
2	1	1	2
2	1	1	2
3	2	2	3

rows, the front and back rows, and the left and right rows, you are left with a small 2-inch cube none of whose faces is red. That 2-inch cube is made up of eight 1-inch cubes. The columns are equal (C).

15. (B) The area of the large circle is πR^2, and the area of the small circle is πr^2, so the area of the shaded region is $\pi R^2 - \pi r^2 = \pi(R^2 - r^2)$. Since the shaded region and the white region have the same area,

$$\pi(R^2 - r^2) = \pi r^2 \Rightarrow R^2 - r^2 = r^2 \Rightarrow$$

$$R^2 = 2r^2 \Rightarrow \frac{R^2}{r^2} = 2 \Rightarrow \frac{R}{r} = \sqrt{2},$$

which is *less* than 1.5. Column B is greater.

Grid-in Questions

16. (98) The easiest way is to simplify first:
$(a^2 + b^2) - (a^2 - b^2) = 2b^2$. Then
$6 \otimes 7 = 2(7^2) = 2(49) = \textbf{98}$.

**If you don't think to simplify (or you can't), just do the arithmetic:

$$(6^2 + 7^2) - (6^2 - 7^2) = (36 + 49) - (36 - 49) =$$
$$85 - (-13) = 85 + 13 = \textbf{98}.$$

17. (7.5) Here, $\triangle ABC$ is a right triangle and its area is given by $\frac{1}{2}(AB)(BC)$. Since AB is vertical, find its length by subtracting the y-coordinates: $AB = 4 - 1 = 3$. Similarly, since BC is horizontal, find its length by subtracting the x-coordinates: $BC = 6 - 1 = 5$. Then

$$\text{area of } \triangle ABC = \frac{1}{2}(3)(5) = \frac{15}{2} = \textbf{7.5}.$$

18. **(7.5)** The perimeter of the quadrilateral in the figure is 30 ($5 + 7 + 8 + 10$). Then $4s = 30$, where s is a side of the square, and $s =$ **7.5**.

19. **(3.7)** To produce 40 gizmos takes $40 \times 333 = 13{,}320$ seconds. Since there are 60 seconds in a minute and 60 minutes in an hour, there are $60 \times 60 = 3600$ seconds in an hour; $13{,}320 \div 3600 =$ **3.7** hours.

$13{,}320$ seconds $\div 60 = 222$ minutes, and 222 minutes $\div 60 =$ **3.7 hours.

20. **(145)** Since the average of a, b, and 10 is 100, their sum is 300. Then

$$a + b + 10 = 300 \Rightarrow a + b = 290 \Rightarrow$$
$$\frac{a+b}{2} = \frac{290}{2} = \textbf{145}.$$

21. **(1.21)** Use TACTIC 21. Since this is a percent problem, assume the rent *last year* was $100. Since 10% of 100 is 10, this year the rent went up $10 to $110. Now, 10% of 110 is 11, so next year the rent will go up $11 to $121. Finally, 121 is **1.21** $\times$ 100.

22. **(1983)**

Year	Boris's Age	Olga's Age
1970	26	0
$1970 + x$	$26 + x$	x

The equation is $26 + x = 3x \Rightarrow 26 = 2x \Rightarrow x = 13$. Boris was 3 times as old as Olga 13 years after 1970, in **1983** (when they were 39 and 13, respectively).

23. **(9.36)** The class average will be highest when all the grades are as high as possible. Assume that all 22 students who passed earned 10's. Of the 3 who failed, 1 received a grade of 2; but assume that the other 2 students had 6's, the highest failing grade. Then the total is $22 \times 10 + 2 + 2 \times 6 = 220 + 2 + 12 = 234$, so the highest possible class average is $234 \div 25 =$ **9.36**.

24. **(6)** Let $2x$ and $7x$ represent the number of red and blue marbles, respectively, in jar I. Then in total there are $7x$ blue marbles and $14x$ red ones. Since there are $2x$ red marbles in jar I, there are $12x$ red marbles in jar II. So there are **6** times as many red marbles in jar II as there are in jar I.

**Do the same analysis, except let $x = 1$. Then jar I contains 2 red and 7 blue marbles, whereas jar II contains 12 red ones.

25. ($\frac{1}{3}$) Adding the fractions, we get $\frac{1}{a} + \frac{1}{b} = \frac{a+b}{ab}$. But it is given

that ab is 3 times $(a + b)$. Therefore, $\frac{a+b}{ab} = \frac{1}{3}$.

Section 5   Verbal Reasoning

1. (C) The opening paragraph discusses changes in the idea of matter, emphasizing the use of musical terminology to describe the concepts of physics. The second paragraph then goes on to develop the theme of the music of matter.

Choice B is incorrect. Music does not directly influence the interactions of particles; physicists merely use musical terms to describe these interactions.

2. (D) The author mentions these terms as examples of what he means by the strange new language or *idiosyncratic nomenclature* of modern particle physics.

3. (D) In his references to the elegance of the newly discovered subatomic structures and to the dance of Creation, the author conveys his *admiration* and *wonder.*

4. (B) "Matter's heart," where the physicist can observe the dance of Creation, is *the subatomic world*, the world of quarks and charms.

5. (D) The image of the snake swallowing its tail suggests that the astronomers' and physicists' theories are, at bottom, one and the same. In other words, there is an *underlying unity* connecting them.

6. (E) The properties of the upsilon particle that implied it could not be made of up, down, strange, or charm quarks were its *characteristics* or attributes.

7. (B) Glashow is eager for the end of the hunt. His words ("last blessed one," "the sooner...the better") reflect his *impatience.*

8. **(E)** The keystone of the arch (the wedge-shaped block that is inserted last into the arch and locks the other pieces in place) completes the arch. By comparing the top quark to the keystone, the author of Passage 2 *illustrates the importance of the top quark to subatomic theory.*

9. **(D)** The physicists had to find the top quark because their theory *depended* on the top's existence.

10. **(E)** The author of Passage 2 cites authorities (Glashow, Tollestrup) and uses similes ("like an arch"). She defines the Standard Model as the theoretical synthesis that reduced the zoo of subatomic particles to a manageable number. She poses a question about what makes certain particles more massive than others. However, she *never denies a possibility.*

11. **(C)** Physicists are familiar with the weight of a gold atom. In stating that the top was determined to weigh about as much as a gold atom, the author is illustrating just *how hefty* or massive a top quark is.

12. **(C)** The 1995 experiments succeeded: The physicists found the keystone to their arch. From this we can infer that the Standard Model was not disproved but instead received its *validation.*

13. **(B)** In lines 35–36, the author of Passage 1 develops a fanciful metaphor for the nature of matter. To him, subatomic matter is like a Bach fugue, filled with arpeggios. While the author of Passage 2 resorts to some figurative language ("Grail," "keystone") in attempting to describe the top quark, she is more factual than figurative: she never uses any metaphor as extended as the metaphor "the music of matter." Thus, her most likely reaction to lines 36–37 would be to point out that this metaphor *is too fanciful to be worthwhile.*

Section 6   Mathematical Reasoning

1. **(B)** Solve the given equation:

$$\frac{1}{a} + \frac{1}{a} + \frac{1}{a} = 12$$

Add the fractions:

$$= \frac{3}{a} \quad 12$$

Multiply both sides by a:

$$3 = 12a$$

Divide both sides by 12:

$$a = \frac{3}{12} = \frac{1}{4}.$$

2. (C) If $x = -5$, then

$$2x^2 - 3x - 7 = 2(-5)^2 - 3(-5) - 7 =$$
$$2(25) + 15 - 7 = \mathbf{58}.$$

3. (E) Carefully read the values from the chart. Ann, Dan, Pam, Fran, and Sam read 1, 4, 2, 6, and 5 books, respectively. The sum is **18**.

4. (D) The average number of books read by the five members is the sum, 18 (calculated in the solution to question 3), divided by 5: 3.6. Three of the five members, or **60%**, read more than 3.6 books.

5. (A) The formula for the area of a circle is:

$$A = \pi r^2$$

Divide both sides by π:

$$r^2 = \frac{A}{\pi}$$

Take the square root of each side:

$$r = \sqrt{\frac{A}{\pi}}$$

The diameter is twice the radius:

$$d = 2r = \mathbf{2} \sqrt{\frac{A}{\pi}}$$

**Let the radius of the circle be 1. Then the area is π, and the diameter is 2. Which of the five choices is equal to 2 when $A = \pi$? Only $\mathbf{2} \sqrt{\dfrac{A}{\pi}}$.

6. (D) If Laurie had to pay 30% of the value of her inheritance in taxes, she still owned 70% of her inheritance: 70% of 40% is **28%** $(0.70 \times 0.40 = 0.28)$.

Assume the estate was worth $100. Laurie received 40%, or $40. Her tax was 30% of $40, or $12. She still had $28, or **28%, of the $100 estate.

7. (B) Write the given equation as: $\qquad\qquad\qquad a^3 = 3a$
Since a is positive, divide both
sides by a: $\qquad\qquad\qquad\qquad\qquad\qquad a^2 = 3$
Take the square root of each side: $\qquad\qquad a = \sqrt{3}$

8. (A) If e is the edge of the cube, the surface area, A, is $6e^2$ and the volume, V, is e^3. Then

$$A = 6e^2 = 60 \Rightarrow e^2 = 10 \Rightarrow e = \sqrt{10} \Rightarrow$$
$$V = (\sqrt{10})^3 = (\sqrt{10})(\sqrt{10})(\sqrt{10}) = \mathbf{10\sqrt{10}}.$$

9. (D) Let r = radius of circle I, and let R = radius of circle II. Then $2R$ is the diameter of circle II, and $2\pi r$ is the circumference of circle I.

It is given that: $\qquad\qquad\qquad 2\pi r = 2R$
Divide both sides by 2: $\qquad\qquad\quad R = \pi r$

Then $\dfrac{\text{area of circle II}}{\text{area of circle I}} = \qquad \dfrac{\pi R^2}{\pi r^2} = \dfrac{\pi(\pi r)^2}{\pi r^2}$

$$= \dfrac{\pi^3 r^2}{\pi r^2} = \boldsymbol{\pi}^2$$

**Use TACTIC 11. Pick some easy-to-use number, such as 1, for the radius of circle I. Then the circumference of circle I is 2π, which is the diameter of circle II, and the radius of circle II is π (one-half its diameter). The area of a circle is given by $A = \pi r^2$, so the area of circle I is $\pi(1) = \pi$, and the area of circle II is $\pi(\pi^2) = \pi^3$. Finally, the ratio of their areas is $\dfrac{\pi^3}{\pi} = \boldsymbol{\pi}^2$.

10. (A) Use TACTIC 1: draw a diagram. In the figure below, form rectangle $BCDE$ by drawing $DE \perp AB$. Then, $BE = 9$, $AE = 16$, and $DE = 12$. Finally, $DA = \mathbf{20}$, because right triangle AED is a 3-4-5 triangle in which each side is multiplied by 4. If you don't realize that, use the Pythagorean theorem to get DA:

$$(DA)^2 = (AE)^2 + (DE)^2 = 256 + 144 = 400 \Rightarrow DA = \mathbf{20}.$$

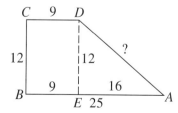